3000 JOKES
2997 LAUGHS

COMPILED AND EDITED BY
MIKE HASKINS & STEPHEN ARNOTT

PORTICO

"I CAN ALWAYS TELL STRAIGHT AWAY IF AN AUDIENCE IS GOING TO BE GOOD OR BAD ... GOODNIGHT!"

TOMMY COOPER

Thanks to Nicola, Cheryl and everyone at Portico. And belated thanks to Ian Carter for all the floppy disks of jokes. That's how belated that thanks is!

First published in the United Kingdom in 2017 by
Portico
43 Great Ormond Street
London
WC1N 3HZ

An imprint of Pavilion Books Company Ltd

Copyright © Pavilion Books Company Ltd 2017

Text copyright © Mike Haskins and Stephen Arnott 2017

All rights reserved. No part of this publication may be copied, displayed, extracted, reproduced, utilised, stored in a retrieval system or transmitted in any form or by any means, electronic, mechanical or otherwise including but not limited to photocopying, recording, or scanning without the prior written permission of the publishers.

ISBN 978-1-91104-201-3

A CIP catalogue record for this book
is available from the British Library.

10 9 8 7 6 5 4 3 2 1

Reproduction by Mission Productions Ltd, Hong Kong

Printed and bound by Bookwell Oy, Finland

This book can be ordered direct from
the publisher at www.pavilionbooks.com

CONTENTS

A page 4

B page 36

C page 61

D page 121

E page 162

F page 179

G page 204

H page 218

I page 242

J page 258

K page 263

L page 266

M page 290

N page 329

O page 337

P page 345

Q page 374

R page 375

S page 392

T page 433

U page 451

V page 455

W page 461

X page 474

Y page 475

Z page 476

Index of Joke Categories 478

ABSTINENCE

Sammy is soon to be 100 years old. He has never touched alcohol, he doesn't smoke or eat rich food and he has been celibate for his whole adult life. The local newspaper send a reporter to ask how he is going to celebrate his birthday. 'I have absolutely no idea,' says Sammy.

ACCIDENTS

Apparently these days the great majority of accidents occur in the home. So a bit of good news for homeless people for once.

Dwayne tells Josh, 'I've had terrible news. My girlfriend was in a car crash and she's lost both her legs.' 'How terrible,' says Josh. 'Yes it is,' says Dwayne. 'I bought her a pair of jeans for her birthday and it's too late to get a refund.'

A man sends a text to his wife: 'Darling, I've been in a terrible car accident. Anna got me to the hospital but the doctors say that I've got a fractured skull, a wound that will require 19 stitches, three broken ribs and it's possible I will never walk again.' The wife texts back, 'Who the **** is Anna!?'

A midair collision occurred this afternoon involving two pedestrians when a skydiver collided with a man doing the high jump.

The police knock on Bill's front door and show him a photograph of his wife. 'Is this your wife, sir?' they ask. 'Yes,' says Bill. 'What's the matter?' 'I'm afraid it looks like she's been hit by a lorry,' says the policeman. 'That's not a very nice thing to say,' says Bill. 'And anyway she's got a lovely personality.'

Dick goes to visit Harry in the hospital and finds him wrapped from head to foot in bandages. 'What happened?' asks Dick. 'I fell through a plate-glass window,' says Harry. 'That sounds bad,' says Dick, 'but there again, look on the bright side. If you hadn't been wrapped in all those bandages, you'd probably have been cut to ribbons.'

Last night Barry fell asleep at the wheel. It was terrible. Clay and bits of pot all over the place.

There was a bit of a disaster at our local air show last weekend. It started raining so in the end the Red Arrows had to attempt their display in the church hall.

Ted tells Norman, 'Did you hear that Frank is dead? He was driving over to my house and when he arrived he braked too suddenly, the car turned over, he was thrown out of the sunroof and crashed through my bedroom window.' 'So was that what killed him?' asks Norman. 'No,' says Ted, 'he landed on my bed covered in broken glass, reached to pull himself up but instead pulled the wardrobe down, crushing himself under it.' 'OK. So he was killed when the wardrobe crushed him?' says Norman. 'No,' says Ted. 'He crawled out from underneath, made it to the staircase, crashed through the banisters, dragged himself into the kitchen, knocked a pan of boiling water over himself, reached up to get the phone but grabbed the light switch instead and caused an electric shock to shoot through him which set fire to the kitchen.' 'Right,' says Norman, 'so that must have been what killed him.' 'No,' says Ted, 'he survived all that but then I came home, saw what was going on and shot him.' 'Why did you shoot him?' asks Norman. 'I had no choice,' says Ted. 'He was destroying my house.'

Oliver ended up in hospital after a visit to a local furniture store ended up in him being buried under an avalanche of 50 pillows and 100 cushions. The hospital has described his condition as being 'very comfortable'.

A drunk falls from a high window into the street. A crowd gathers and a policeman pushes through the crowd to reach the man. 'What happened here?' asks the policeman. 'How should I know?' says the drunk. 'I only just got here myself.'

Beryl is driving her car when she sees a truck shedding its load all over the highway. Being a good Samaritan she pulls ahead of the vehicle and forces it to stop. 'What are you doing?' calls the driver. 'I had to stop you!' says Beryl. 'You're dropping stuff all over the road!' 'Of course I am!' says the driver. 'This is a gritting truck.'

This morning I saw a poor old lady fall over in the street. Well, I say she was poor. She only had 50p in her purse at the time.

A biker gets into a bar fight and when he's finished pounding the other guy, he finds all the buttons have been pulled off his jacket. Not wishing to get cold on the way home he puts the jacket on backwards to stop it flapping in the wind. Unfortunately, he's had a little too much to drink and winds up crashing into a tree. An hour later the coroner and ambulance driver are staring at the biker's corpse lying on a slab in the morgue. 'It's a damn shame,' says the ambulance driver. 'He wasn't looking too bad when we found him. He only passed away after I twisted his head back round the right way.'

Cecil has invented an infallible method for surviving plane crashes: you just wait by the door and step out when it's a couple of feet off the ground.

Sammy is blind and is being interviewed by the police about the death of a man who jumped out of a nearby office building. 'He must have jumped off the tenth floor at least,' says Sammy. 'How could you tell that?' asks the policeman. 'Another witness said he jumped off the second floor.' 'No,' says Sammy. 'If he'd jumped from the second floor, I'd have heard him go, "Thump – Aargh!" What I heard was "Arrrrrgh – Thump!"'

ACROBATICS

Lenny walks into a bar, does a triple somersault, two back flips and a cartwheel and lands himself slap-bang on one of the barstools. 'Wow,' says the barman. 'I'm impressed. I didn't know the circus was in town. Are you some kind of acrobat?' 'No,' says Larry. 'I'm a bookkeeper. I just tripped on my shoelace.'

ACTORS AND ACTING

Algernon was an ageing actor. Each night when he went into the kitchen and opened his fridge door, he took a bow when the little light came on.

> "
> GIVE ME A COUPLE OF YEARS AND I'LL MAKE THAT ACTRESS AN OVERNIGHT SUCCESS.
> "
> SAMUEL GOLDWYN

Jasper is an elderly stage actor who gets a small role in a romantic melodrama. He doesn't have much to do – at the beginning of the second act he comes on stage with a rose blossom held in his fingertips and says, 'Ah, the divine smell of my dear wife.' The rehearsals go well, but on the first night Jasper is baffled by the audience's reaction. He says the line, smells the flower in his fingers and the audience bursts into laughter. He comes off-stage and says to the producer, 'What happened? Did I say the line wrong?' 'No,' says the producer. 'You forgot the rose.'

> "
> THE SCENE IS DULL. TELL HIM TO PUT MORE LIFE INTO HIS DYING.
> "
> SAMUEL GOLDWYN

Larry the actor goes on his first solo skydive. The instructor reminds him to count to three then pull his rip-cord. Larry jumps, but plummets to the ground. Luckily he lands in a haystack and only breaks both his legs. The instructor comes to visit him in hospital. 'What happened?' he asks. 'Did you count like I told you to?' 'Sorry, love,' says Larry. 'I forgot my line.'

ADAM AND EVE

The only perfect marriage was between Adam and Eve – she never had to hear about the quality of her mother-in-law's cooking and he never had to hear about all the men Eve could have married.

ADDICTION

Barry's son was caught sniffing Tippex. He's been sent away to a correction centre.

I've spent years struggling with an addiction to alcohol gel but now I'm finally clean.

For years I struggled to overcome my addiction to doing the hokey cokey. Recently though I've managed to turn myself around, and that's what it's all about.

Nancy's doctor doesn't know what to do with her. It seems she's become addicted to counselling.

I went to the doctor because of my addiction to glue. He said he was giving me some special strips like Nicorette patches that would help get me off the glue. Actually, I think he just gave me some Sellotape. But it's been quite good because I've been able to use it to wax my bikini line at the same time.

ADOPTION

A couple who work in a travelling circus apply to adopt a child. The adoption agency are unsure that their lifestyle will be appropriate for adopting a child but the couple produce pictures of their luxury motor-home and show how they have equipped it with a beautiful nursery. They also show that they have arranged for a full-time tutor to travel with the circus to provide the child with an education and that they have employed a nanny who is an expert in children's welfare and diet. The social workers are very impressed and ask, 'OK. So what age and sex of child are you hoping to adopt?' 'We don't really mind,' say the couple, 'just as long as he fits in the cannon.'

ADVERTISING

Bill is at the funeral service for his wife. Her gravestone is unveiled and the vicar is shocked to see the inscription: 'Here lies Hannah Smith. Loving wife of Bill. Local handyman. No job too small.' The vicar notices Bill is shedding a tear. 'I expect you're feeling guilty now at this attempt to use your wife's grave as a cheap advertisement,' says the vicar. 'No,' says Bill, 'It's just I forgot to put the phone number on.'

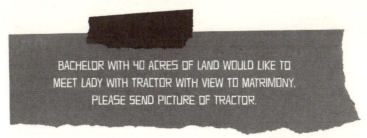

ADVERT IN US NEWSPAPER

Last night I saw an advert for a new film. It said it was 'Coming to a cinema near you'. I'm worried about this. How the hell do these people know where I live?

Glenda used to say her husband was like a TV commercial – you couldn't trust a word he said and when you turned him on he was finished in less than a minute.

ADVICE

When I went away to university, my mum said, 'Don't forget to write.' It was good advice but a bit unlikely as it's quite a basic skill.

If old people attempt to give you good advice, remember that they're only compensating for their inability to set a bad example.

AFFAIRS AND ADULTERY

Brian finds out that his wife is having an affair. 'What does he have, that I don't?' he asks. 'Sex,' says his wife.

A man gets home early from work and hears strange noises from the bedroom. He rushes upstairs and finds his wife naked and gasping for air. 'What's happened?' he asks. 'I'm having a heart attack,' she says. The man runs to get the phone but just then his little son comes and says, 'Daddy! Uncle Ted's hiding in your wardrobe and he's got nothing on!' The man slams the phone down, storms back up into the bedroom and throws open the wardrobe door to reveal Uncle Ted stark naked. 'How could you do this?' asks the husband. 'My wife is having a heart attack and all you can do is run around the house naked scaring the kids!'

Gary is talking to his friend Steve. 'I emailed my wife to say I'd be home a day early and when I walked into our bedroom I found she was having sex with our postman. How could she be so callous and unfeeling?' 'Now be fair,' says Steve. 'Maybe she didn't get your email . . .'

A man gets off work early and comes home only to catch his wife in flagrante with his best friend, Marvin. 'Oh no,' says the man devastated by the sight, 'I have to. But *you*, Marvin?!'

John comes home late after an afternoon of passion with his secretary. Before he opens the door, he walks on the lawn and stains his shoes with mud and grass, then he goes inside where his wife is waiting for him. 'Where have you been?' she asks. John says, 'Having sex with my secretary.' Looking at his dirty shoes, his wife says, 'Don't lie to me. You've been playing golf again, haven't you?'

A boss is in a hotel bar with his secretary. 'Did you call my wife like I asked?' he said. 'And did you tell her I won't be home till late because I've been held up in the office?' 'Yes I did,' says the secretary. 'Did she mind?' asks the boss. 'No,' says the secretary, 'she just asked, "Can I depend on that?"'

Ted visits Ken in hospital. 'I couldn't believe you were in here,' says Ted, 'I only saw you a couple of nights ago out dancing with a gorgeous blonde.' 'Yes,' says Ken, 'unfortunately my wife saw us as well.'

Larry takes his secretary for a dirty weekend. As he's driving her home, he says, 'Well, that's two days you'll never forget.' His secretary says, 'I might. What's it worth to you?'

Harry is in the supermarket when he sees a woman staring at him. 'I recognise you,' says the woman, 'you're the father of one of my children.' Harry has a flashback to the only time he was unfaithful to his wife. 'Oh my God!' he says. 'I recognise you now. You're that stripper I woke up in bed with on my stag do.' 'No,' says the woman, 'I'm your son's primary school teacher.'

A glamorous secretary joins Bill's firm and he starts having an affair with her. Everything is fine until Bill notices the secretary has begun slacking. 'You're having two-hour lunch breaks, you arrive at ten and leave at four,' he says. 'Who said you could behave like that just because you're sleeping with me?' 'My lawyer,' says the secretary.

Doctor Klein is seeing one of his psychiatric patients. 'My wife is driving me nuts,' says the patient. 'She used to be a showgirl and she's developed an insatiable appetite for men. All a man has to do is compliment her shoes and she'll do anything for them. Absolutely anything.' 'I see,' says Doctor Klein. 'And where does she find these men?' 'At our local bar,' says the patient. 'I see,' says Doctor Klein. 'And she likes her shoes complimented?' 'That's right,' says the patient. 'I see,' says Doctor Klein. 'And where exactly is this bar?'

A judge is overseeing a divorce case. He asks a woman, 'Do you admit that you stayed in a hotel with Mr Smith?' 'I do,' says the woman, 'but I couldn't help it because he deceived me.' 'How did he deceive you?' asks the judge. 'He told the reception clerk that I was his wife,' says the woman.

A man confronts his wife with evidence that she's been having an affair. He knows she's been seeing someone, but he's not sure who. 'Was it Bob?' he asks. His wife says no. 'Was it Larry?' he asks. His wife says no. 'Surely it wasn't Pete?' he says. Again, his wife says no. 'How about Nigel?' he asks. Once more, the answer is no. 'So you decide to have an affair,' says the man. 'And to cap it all, it seems none of my friends are good enough for you!'

A small boy is sitting at the dinner table with his parents when his mother asks him what he did that day. 'I was playing in the wood behind the house,' says the boy. 'And there I saw Daddy take the housekeeper behind a tree and take her clothes off . . .' 'That's enough of that, son,' says the father. 'I'm sure Mummy isn't interested in any of that.' 'Oh, but I am,' says the mother. 'So tell me, what happened next?' The boy says, 'Then they started doing what you and the postman do once Daddy's gone to work.'

A lion and a zebra are having an illicit affair on the African savannah. They're having sex behind a bush when the zebra gives a gasp. 'Oh no. My husband just walked over the horizon. Quick. Pretend you're trying to bite my head off.'

Ted tells Brendan, 'Your missus likes a practical joke, doesn't she?' 'What do you mean?' asks Brendan. 'Well,' says Ted, 'when you were away last week, I called round and she was pretending to be in bed with your next-door neighbour. He was playing along with it all too because neither of them had any clothes on!' Brendan immediately senses something isn't right. 'Hang on a minute,' says Brendan, 'what exactly were you doing going round to see my wife while I was away?'

AFTERLIFE

AT THE EVENING SERVICE TONIGHT, THE SERMON TOPIC WILL BE 'WHAT IS HELL?' COME EARLY AND LISTEN TO OUR CHOIR PRACTICE.

PARISH NOTICES

If you die wearing a particularly horrible outfit does that mean you have to spend all eternity wearing the same clothes?

A teacher asks the class, 'Now who can tell me what sort of people go to heaven?' A little boy puts his hand up and says, 'Dead ones, miss.'

I'm not sure what happens after you die, but I bet the first thing is that you get charged some sort of fee.

If I died and got sent straight to hell, I think it would be several weeks before I realised I wasn't at work any more.

A girl at a Catholic school asks one of the nuns how Charles Darwin came up with the theory of evolution. 'I don't know,' says the nun. 'And you shouldn't ask questions like that.' 'OK,' says the girl. 'I guess I'll have to wait till I get to heaven and ask him myself.' 'And what if he went to hell?' asks the nun. The girl says, 'Then you can ask him.'

A group of Women's Institute fundraisers are killed in a car crash, but due to a clerical error they are sent to hell rather than heaven. A few months later, St Peter is doing the books when he realises he's a few souls short. He gets to the bottom of the problem and phones the Devil to organise a transfer. 'Can't they stay a bit longer?' asks the Devil. 'Why?' says St Peter. 'I would have thought you needed the room.' 'We do,' says the Devil. 'But in the time they've been down here they've raised enough cash to install an air-conditioning system, a drinks cooler and an ice rink.'

During the religion lesson at school, the teacher asks the class, 'Who knows where girls and boys go to if they indulge in sinful behaviour?' A boy puts his hand up and says, 'Usually it's behind the bike sheds.'

Sandra was married four times: First to a banker; then a magician; then a vicar; and, lastly, to an undertaker. As she put it: 'One for the money, two for the show, three to get ready and four to go.'

Liam dies and goes to heaven. He meets many old friends in the afterlife, but is surprised to find his old parish priest sitting in a heavenly pub with an attractive blonde on his lap. 'I knew you liked a drink, Father,' says Liam, 'but I'm surprised to see you with a woman. I'd always thought you were particularly moral in that respect and, frankly, I'm amazed that you'd choose a floozy like that to be a reward for your many years of service on earth.' 'Oh, don't be like that, Liam,' says the priest. 'It's not what it looks like. The truth is, she's not my reward; I'm her punishment.'

Jesus is taking his turn minding the gates of heaven when an old man comes up asking for admission. Jesus starts asking questions for the heavenly entry form. 'What was your occupation?' he asks. 'I was a humble carpenter,' says the man. 'Really?' says Jesus, 'so was my dad. Do you have any children?' 'A son,' says the old man. 'But he was taken away from me.' 'I see,' says Jesus. 'And what can you tell me about him?' 'Well, he wasn't really my son,' says the old man. 'But he was given to me and I raised him like my own. He had holes in his hands and feet and he wasn't alive for a while, but somehow he was brought to life. He became very famous and people still talk about him all over the world.' Jesus puts down the form and wipes away a tear. 'At last. I've found you.' He grabs the old man in a hug and shouts, 'Daddy!' The old man shouts back, 'Pinocchio!'

In heaven, the chefs are French, the police are English, the engineers are German, the lovers are Italians and the bankers are Swiss. In hell, the chefs are English, the police are Germans, the engineers are French, the lovers are Swiss and the bankers are Italians.

> "I'M CONFUSED ABOUT THE DIRECTION OF HEAVEN. IT'S NOT UP THERE, BECAUSE THE EARTH REVOLVES AND SOMETIMES YOU CAN GO TO HELL AT 8.30 AND HEAVEN AT 12.06."
>
> LENNY BRUCE

AGEING

A small girl is introduced to her great-grandmother, but doesn't say a word. The girl's mother says, 'Come now, you must have something to say to such a fine old lady.' The girl stares at her great-grandmother and says, 'OK. How come your skin doesn't fit your face?'

For years Vera has been saying that 40 is the new 30. And that is the reason she is now banned from driving.

Ron thinks he must be getting old. He says there are times when, try as he might, he just cannot prevent clean thoughts entering his mind.

Ernest is getting on a bit. He's so old that when he receives advertising material from the local old people's home, the envelope is marked 'Urgent'.

I can understand why people's earlobes and noses get bigger as they get older, but why does the same thing seem to happen to their glasses?

A reporter goes to interview a man celebrating his 100th birthday. 'To what do you attribute your great age?' asks the reporter. 'Mainly,' says the old man, 'it's down to the fact I was born a long time ago.'

Through my life I've learned one thing. Trying to please everyone is impossible. Annoying the hell out of everyone, on the other hand, is a piece of cake.

I'm beginning to think I won't live to see the day when I'm old enough to know better.

Tom's eyesight is getting very bad. He's had to get a special new pair of glasses to help him find where he left his old glasses.

Three old men are at the doctor's for a check-up. The first old man is 80. He comes out from the surgery and says, 'The doctor thinks I'm very healthy for an 80-year-old. He says I could live for another 20 years.' The next old man is 90. He comes out of the surgery and says, 'The doctor thinks I'm very healthy for a 90-year-old. He says I could live for another ten years.' The third old man is 100. He comes out of the surgery and says, 'The doctor told me to have a nice day.'

Elsie is getting very old. They lit the candles on her birthday cake last year and a group of boy scouts formed a circle round it and started singing 'Kumbaya'.

Old Joe announced that he'd be celebrating his 100th birthday party by making love to his housekeeper. The Queen sent him a congratulatory telegram and the Duke of Edinburgh sent him a diagram.

Albert reaches his 100th birthday and a doctor asks him what he attributes his good health to. 'No red meat or alcohol,' says Albert, 'but plenty of fresh fruit and vegetables.' 'I see,' says the doctor. 'From your records I notice that your twin brother died at the age of 40. Did he follow the same diet?' 'Yes,' says Albert, 'but he didn't do it long enough.'

A small girl goes up to her grandma and says, 'How come your skin is so dry and wrinkly, while mine is so smooth and soft?' 'Well,' answers Grandma. 'The reason is that God made me a long time ago, but you were made only a few years back.' 'I see,' says the girl. 'So you're saying that he's getting better with practice.'

As Jerry got older, he found his mind used to wander. Luckily it was too feeble to get very far.

Beryl has to provide some ID to get a loan. 'On your form you said you're 50,' says the clerk, 'but your driving licence says you're 60.' 'That's right,' says Beryl. 'I don't count the ten years I spent married.' 'Why not?' asks the clerk. 'We need to know how long you've lived, not some made-up number.' Beryl says, 'If you knew my ex-husband, you wouldn't call that living . . .'

The definition of senility; you kind of remember faces, but you forget your name.

AGREEMENT

Part of me would like to agree with you, but unfortunately then we'd both be wrong.

Definition of the majority – a load of idiots devoid of independent thought who therefore ended up agreeing with each other.

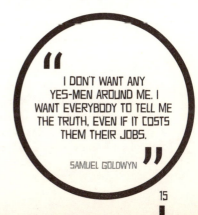

" I DON'T WANT ANY YES-MEN AROUND ME. I WANT EVERYBODY TO TELL ME THE TRUTH, EVEN IF IT COSTS THEM THEIR JOBS.

SAMUEL GOLDWYN "

AIR GUITAR

Nobby thinks someone has stolen his air guitar. He was playing it last night and put it down and now he can't find it anywhere.

AIR TRAVEL

Hattie is taking her first trip in a plane. 'You will bring me down again safely, won't you?' she tells the pilot before they take off. 'Don't worry,' says the pilot, 'I've never left anyone up there yet.'

> I KNEW I'D CHOSEN THE WRONG AIRLINE WHEN THE FLIGHT ATTENDANT WARNED US TO KEEP OUR HANDS AND ARMS INSIDE THE AIRCRAFT WHILE IT WAS IN MOTION. THE AIRSICK BAG WAS PRINTED WITH THE LORD'S PRAYER.
>
> LES DAWSON

A plane has been sitting on the runway waiting to take off for over an hour. One of the passengers asks the stewardess what the reason is for the delay. 'Sorry about this, sir,' she says, 'but the pilot heard a funny noise coming from the engine.' 'So,' says the man, 'are you waiting for an engineer to come and fix it?' 'No,' says the stewardess, 'we're trying to find another pilot who can't hear it.'

Cecil is the pilot of a passenger jet that is redirected to an unfamiliar airport. He curses when he sees how short the runway is, but he sticks on the brakes, throws the engines into full reverse and manages to bring down the plane safely in a cloud of burning tyre rubber. 'Jesus,' he says, mopping his brow. 'That was close. It's criminal to build a runway as short as that.' 'You're right there,' says his co-pilot, looking out of the window. 'Whoever designed it was a maniac. And look at all that wasted space. It must be a mile wide at least.'

A nervous-looking man is getting on a plane ready for a flight. As he takes his seat, he asks the stewardess, 'Do these planes crash very often?' 'No!' says the stewardess. 'Just the once.'

> IF AIRLINE TRAVEL IS SO SAFE, HOW COME THE STEWARDESSES SIT RIGHT NEXT TO THE EMERGENCY EXITS?
>
> JOHNNY CARSON

I overheard two men talking the other day saying that they wouldn't feel safe on an aircraft if the pilot was a woman. That was very sexist of them. It wouldn't make any difference. They don't ever have to reverse the things, do they?

A passenger jet is crossing the Atlantic when the pilot announces they they've lost power to one of the engines. It will add one hour to the crossing time. A little while later, the pilot announces they've lost power to a second engine and that this will add two hours to the crossing time. A few moments pass, then the pilot informs the passengers that due to a third engine failing, the crossing time will be extended by three hours. One of the passengers shakes his head, 'Typical. If we lose another one, we'll be stuck up here all night.'

> "WHEN I'M ON A PLANE, I CAN NEVER GET MY SEAT TO RECLINE MORE THAN A COUPLE OF CENTIMETRES, BUT THE GUY IN FRONT OF ME – HIS SEAT COMES BACK FAR ENOUGH FOR ME TO DO DENTAL WORK ON HIM."
>
> ELLEN DEGENERES

ALCOHOL

Harry picks up a can of beer. On the side of the can is printed: 'Best drunk before 2016.' Harry immediately calls up Tom and Dick to go out celebrating because he thinks he's just won an award.

A man walks into a bar and sees a sign saying, 'All you can drink for £10.' 'I'll have £20 worth,' says the man.

I walked into a bar the other day and asked the barman for a double. So he went round the back and brought out another bloke who looked exactly the same as me.

A man goes into a bar and asks how much the beer is. 'Two pounds a pint,' says the barman, 'and seven pounds a pitcher.' 'I'll just have a pint,' says the man, 'I can't be bothered with the photo.'

A missionary, a cowgirl and a doggy walk into a bar. 'I'm sorry, but I'm not in a position to serve you,' says the barman.

Nobby and Tom are in the pub. 'Alcohol doesn't agree with me,' says Nobby. 'Really?' says Tom. 'Yeah,' says Nobby, 'it keeps telling me my wife is attractive.'

I am a very accomplished bartender. The only problem is I don't get paid, I work from home and I'm my only customer.

Nobby's doctor tells him he's spending too much time drinking and he should do something that will get him out of the pub. So he's taken up smoking.

A doctor regularly calls in for a hazelnut daiquiri at a bar on his way home. Unfortunately, one night the barman has run out of hazelnut flavouring so he uses hickory nuts instead. It doesn't fool the doctor, who takes one sip and says, 'Hang on! This isn't my usual hazelnut daiquiri!' 'No,' says the barman, 'it's a hickory daiquiri, doc.'

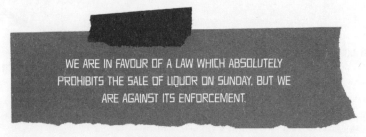

WE ARE IN FAVOUR OF A LAW WHICH ABSOLUTELY PROHIBITS THE SALE OF LIQUOR ON SUNDAY, BUT WE ARE AGAINST ITS ENFORCEMENT.

US DEMOCRATIC PARTY POLICY IN SYRACUSE DURING THE 1920s

A judge turns to the accused in the dock and tells him, 'It is entirely due to alcohol that you are here today.' 'That's very nice of you to say,' says the defendant, 'everyone else keeps telling me it's all my fault.'

Did you hear about the guy who got stuck on the pub roof? He'd heard that the drinks were on the house.

What do you find on the bottom of an idiot's beer bottle? 'Open other end' written in big letters.

A man goes into a bar and asks the barman for three pints of beer. He takes the beers, sits on his own and drinks one pint after another. The next week he comes back in and again orders three pints and goes to sit on his own. 'You don't have to order them all at once, you know,' says the barman. 'I know,' says the man, 'but I have two brothers. One has emigrated to Canada. The other has emigrated to Australia. Although we can't see each other each week, we vowed we would still have a drink together every week. Right now each of my brothers is also sitting somewhere with three beers so we can all share a drink together.' The barman thinks this is a wonderful tradition and each week the man keeps coming back to have his three pints. Then one day, the man comes in and orders only two pints. 'I'm terribly sorry,' says the barman as the man starts sipping his pints, 'I presume this must mean that one of your brothers has passed away.' 'No,' says the man, 'they're both fine. It's just me. I've given up drinking.'

Harry is sitting finishing a drink in the pub. Tom walks in, notices Harry's drink and says, 'I see your glass is empty. Do you want another?' 'Don't be stupid,' says Harry, 'why would I want two empty glasses?'

I went into our local pub and ordered a pint of beer. 'That's six pounds,' said the landlord. 'That's a bit much,' I said. 'I came in here last week and a pint was three pounds.' 'We have a new policy, sir. To save on breakages we now charge three pounds for a pint and three pounds to rent the glass it's served in.' That seemed reasonable so I handed over six pounds. The landlord gave me an empty glass and three pounds change. He said, 'We're out of beer.'

Sammy goes to a bar and orders a martini. Then he has a second, then a third and a fourth. When he orders his fifth martini, the barman says, 'I notice you keep taking out the olives and putting them in your handkerchief. If you don't like them, I don't have to put them in.' 'You're right,' says Sammy. 'I don't like olives. But my wife loves them. That's why I'm here. She sent me out to buy a jar but the grocery store had run out.'

A woman is talking to a man in a bar. 'How much beer do you drink?' she asks. 'Maybe three pints a day,' says the man. 'OK,' says the woman, 'so that's £10 every day. That means you spend £3,650 a year just on beer. Over ten years that's £36,500. Over 30 years that's £109,500. Do you realise if you had saved all that money you could have bought a Porsche?' 'So,' says the man, 'do you drink beer?' 'No,' says the woman. 'Right,' says the man, 'can I have a lift home in your Porsche then?'

ALLERGIES

You can't say there haven't been advances in medicine recently. If you used to have an itch, you don't have an itch any more. These days it's an allergy.

Mavis decided she had to get her husband to move out. She had no choice. She'd just found out her cat was allergic to him.

Phil buys a can of Alphabet Spaghetti. On the label it says, 'Warning: may contain N, U, T and S.'

When old Stan went into the care home they put a rubber bracelet on his wrist that listed all the foods he's allergic to. At least, that's what they told him. It just had the word 'Bananas' written on it.

ALLIGATORS

A man walks into a bar with an alligator. 'Roll up! Roll up!' he says. 'Now watch this!' He then commands the alligator to open its jaws, drops his pants and stuffs his tackle into the creature's gaping mouth. The crowd gasps as he then tops the performance by producing a stick and walloping the alligator on the head. The man whips out his willy without having suffered so much as a scratch. The crowd erupt into a huge round of applause. 'Now,' says the man, 'who else here would like to have a go at doing that?' 'OK!' says a little old lady in the crowd. 'But you have to promise me, you won't hit me so hard with the stick.'

AMPUTATION

A labourer on a building site gets his ear sliced off in an accident. He is rushed to hospital and the severed ear is recovered and prepared for re-attachment. Just as the doctor is preparing for surgery, the labourer notices his ear lying on a plate. 'That's not mine,' says the labourer. 'Mine had a cigarette behind it.'

ANCESTRY

The Smiths are an American family with a heritage going back to the *Mayflower*. They employ an author to write the family history but there is just one problem. The black sheep of the family, Uncle George, was executed in the electric chair. The author says he will mention George but find a way to do it tactfully. When the book comes out it says, 'Uncle George occupied a chair of applied electronics at an important government institution. He was attached to his position by the strongest of ties and his death was an enormous shock.'

ANCIENT ROME

Knackerus the slave has a heart attack while rowing a Roman galley. The overseer chucks him overboard then gives all the other slaves a good thrashing. 'Why?' asks one of the slaves. 'It wasn't our fault he died.' 'It's tradition,' says the overseer. 'When someone leaves, we always have a whip-round.'

Two Christian slaves are about to be thrown to the lions in the Roman Coliseum. They're hurled down onto the sand and a ferocious lion bounds up and prepares to sink its teeth into them. Suddenly, one of the slaves leans forwards and whispers into the lion's ear. The lion immediately yelps and runs away. 'What on earth did you say to it?' asks the other slave. 'I told him to eat us if he wanted, but afterwards he'd have to give an after-dinner speech to 10,000 people.'

Ancient Rome provided us with many technological innovations, one of which was the world's first laundry business. Cleaning the vast number of togas of the Roman citizens was a significant issue and Julius Caesar himself decreed the establishment of a huge laundry on the coast to deal with the problem. Here togas would be washed en masse. In order to do this a large amount of detergent was deposited into a tidal pool and the togas stirred in afterwards. It was believed that the natural action of the waves ebbing and flowing would assist in the washing process, after which the togas would be heavily starched. Unfortunately, as the starch was being applied a tidal wave washed over the laundry workers and froze them solid like statues. It was on hearing of this terrible tragedy that Caesar finally understood the words of a soothsayer uttered to him many weeks before: 'Beware, the tides of starch.'

ANGER MANAGEMENT

I don't need anger management therapy. What I need is for all of you lot to stop winding me up all the time!

ANIMAL HUSBANDRY

The farmer's son is out playing in the farmyard when his mum calls him in for breakfast. She watches as he comes over to the house and sees him kick a cow, a pig and a chicken along the way. When he gets to the table, he finds no breakfast set out for him. 'Where's my breakfast?' he asks. 'Sorry,' says his mum, 'but you kicked the cow so no milk for you, you kicked the pig so no bacon for you, and you kicked the chicken so no eggs for you.' Just then his father walks in and kicks the cat. The boy turns to his mum and says, 'Do you want to tell him or shall I?'

Glenda is reading a book on chicken breeding. She turns to her husband and says, 'It says here that a cockerel can have sex three times a day, every day of the year. It seems like you've got some catching up to do.' Her husband replies, 'Does it say that the cockerel does it every day with the same chicken?'

Q: Which is heavier, 200 pounds of bricks or 200 pounds of feathers?
A: The feathers. Bricks are just bricks, but 200 pounds of feathers come with the weight of what you did to all those poor birds.

Farmer Giles has started giving his hens boiling water to drink. He says he's trying to get them to lay hard-boiled eggs.

ANIMAL RIGHTS

A gang of blonde animal rights protestors broke into a seafood restaurant to liberate the live lobsters. They were later charged with animal cruelty when they let them free in the local wood.

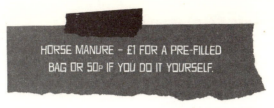

SIGN SEEN ON A FARM GATE

ANIMAL TESTING

Barry works in an animal testing laboratory. They're quite successful. They have a guinea pig with eight GCSEs, a goat with an A level in business studies and a chicken with a City and Guilds Diploma in hairdressing.

A cat goes to the doctor's and is stunned to hear the doctor tell him, 'We've got your test results back and, I'm very sorry to tell you, it's curiosity.'

ANNIVERSARIES

Brenda tells Tom, 'It's our wedding anniversary. What should we do?' 'How about we both stand in silence for two minutes?' says Tom.

Bert and Glenda celebrate their 60th wedding anniversary by booking a room in their old honeymoon hotel. However, once they get there, they're shown to the bridal suite. 'I think there's been a mistake,' says Bert. 'We're hardly young enough to make use of the bridal suite.' 'Don't worry,' says the bell-boy. 'If we put you in the ballroom, we wouldn't expect you to spend all night dancing.'

Dave's wife is furious that he keeps forgetting their anniversary. Finally, one year, his friend Terry thinks he'd better remind him and says, 'It's eight weeks until your anniversary. But you need to plan ahead and get your wife's present ready now.' 'Don't worry,' says Dave, 'I've got it sorted. She's going to love the flowers I've bought her.'

ANTIQUES

Gary takes some examples of his taxidermy collection to the *Antiques Roadshow*. 'This is a very fine pair of preserved German shepherds,' says the antiques expert, 'made by one of the most famous taxidermists in London. If these were in good condition, do you know what they would fetch?' 'Yes,' says Gary, 'sticks!'

A man comes into a recording of the *Antiques Roadshow* hauling a huge metal box behind him. An antiques expert examines it and is intrigued. 'Where did you find this?' he asks. 'I found it while I was rooting around in the attic,' says the man. 'It's been in the family for over 40 years. Should I get insurance?' 'I think you should,' says the expert. 'This is your water tank.'

APATHY

At today's International Apathy Awards, nobody won anything at all for the 18th successive year.

APHRODISIACS

Two women are talking about their husbands. The first says her husband seems to have lost interest in sex. Her friend tells her she had that problem as well but she started giving her husband powdered rhino horn as an aphrodisiac and his performance subsequently improved. The first woman tries this and starts giving her husband a substantial dose each morning. A few weeks later she meets her friend again who asks her if the rhino horn has had any effect. 'Yes,' says the woman, 'he is now an insatiable lover. The only trouble is if we're out anywhere and he sees a Land Rover he tries to charge it!'

Rhino horn is prized as a great aphrodisiac. If that's true, how come there's hardly any rhinos left anywhere?

APOLOGIES

I MAKE NO APOLOGIES FOR THEIR ABSENCE; I'M SORRY THEY'RE NOT HERE.

MURRAY WALKER

I'M SORRY AND 'I APOLOGISE' ALWAYS MEAN THE EXACT SAME THING . . . UNLESS YOU'RE AT A FUNERAL.

DEMETRI MARTIN

APPLAUSE

I wonder who first invented applause. It must have looked really weird to the rest of the audience the first time he did it.

APPLE ELECTRONICS

Norma was a large lady. In fact, she was the one who invented the iPad after accidentally sitting on an iPhone.

Steve Jobs died in 2011. But every year since he has been dug up and reburied in a slightly improved coffin.

I witnessed a hold-up at the Apple shop in town. Now I've got to go and speak to the police because apparently I'm an iWitness.

The invention of the iPod is said to have been inspired by the film *2001: A Space Odyssey*. Presumably it was that bit at the beginning when a bunch of monkeys go mad after they see a weird rectangular object.

APPLES

QUESTION MASTER: WHAT SMALL VEGETABLE IS AN ANAGRAM OF 'APE'?
CONTESTANT: APPLE.

THE WEAKEST LINK

Is it true that an apple a day keeps the doctor away? Or is that just one of Granny's myths?

They say that an apple a day keeps the doctor away and an onion a day makes sure you don't get bothered by anyone else either.

ARCHAEOLOGY

Archaeologists working in Egypt have unearthed a mummy covered all over in chocolate and chopped nuts. They believe they may at long last have discovered the original Pharaoh Rocher.

ARCHITECTURE

One day Big Ben notices the Leaning Tower of Pisa and says, 'I've got the time, if you've got the inclination.'

Why do people pay to go up the top of tall buildings and then pay more money to look through binoculars to see things down on the ground?

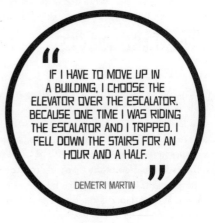

" IF I HAVE TO MOVE UP IN A BUILDING, I CHOOSE THE ELEVATOR OVER THE ESCALATOR. BECAUSE ONE TIME I WAS RIDING THE ESCALATOR AND I TRIPPED. I FELL DOWN THE STAIRS FOR AN HOUR AND A HALF. "

DEMETRI MARTIN

ARGUMENTS

It can be awkward when you're with a couple and they start having a really fierce argument right in front of you. You'd think they could have at least waited for me to put my clothes back on and get out of the bedroom.

Fred tells George he had an argument with his wife last night. 'In the end she came crawling to me on her hands and knees.' 'What did she say?' asks George. 'Get out from under the bed, you coward,' says Fred.

Harry and Barry get into an argument. 'That's the most stupid thing you ever said,' says Barry. 'In fact, you might be the most stupid person I know.' 'How dare you?' says Harry. 'I demand an apology.' 'All right,' says Barry. 'I'm sorry you're so stupid.'

A couple are driving through the country in solemn silence after a fierce argument. They pass a farmyard full of donkeys, goats and pigs. 'Relatives of yours?' asks the husband. 'Yes,' says his wife. 'In-laws!'

Betty and Fred made a pact when they got married. They're both hot-tempered, but they agreed that if they ever started to argue, they'd both take time out to cool down: Betty would go into the kitchen and Fred would go into the garden. Which worked out well for a time, although for the last 20 years Fred has been virtually homeless.

A little boy and a little girl are squabbling at the dinner table and their mum shouts at them. 'You two are always quarrelling,' says Mum. 'Why can't you agree once in a while?' 'We do agree!' says the boy. 'She wants the biggest piece of cake and so do I.'

ARMED FORCES

Barry tells Gary that his grandfather was given a medal in the First World War for single-handedly destroying the German lines of communication. 'What did he do?' asks Gary. 'He ate their pigeon,' says Barry.

Josh was in the military and survived assault by mustard gas and pepper spray. He is now known as a seasoned veteran.

A woman goes to the post office and says she wants to send her son three socks. 'Why are you sending him three socks rather than an even number?' asks the assistant. 'I got a letter from him,' says the woman, 'and he said that since he's been in the army, he's grown another foot.'

A soldier is on sentry duty when a car drives up and he sees a general in the back. The sentry demands to see the driver and passenger's ID. 'Don't be a damn fool, man!' says the general. 'Can't you see who I am.' 'Sorry, sir,' says the sentry, 'but my orders are to check everyone's ID.' 'I haven't got time for this,' says the general. 'Drive on!' 'OK, sir,' says the sentry, 'but could I just ask – am I now supposed to shoot you or your driver?'

Back in the 1950s a man is called up for National Service but has to have a medical examination first. He decides to try and get himself deemed unfit for service because of his poor eyesight. The examiner tries checking his sight by holding up a bin lid. 'Can you see what this is?' asks the examiner. 'Is it a penny,' asks the man, 'or is it a half-crown?' The examiner notes that he is not fit to be in the army and on the way home the man goes to the cinema to celebrate. Just as the film is about to start, the man sees the examiner come into the cinema and sit down next to him. The examiner turns to look at him suspiciously but the man, quick as a flash, says, 'I'm sorry. I am on the right bus for Guildford, aren't I?'

Three men go for a medical before joining the army. The doctor checks the first man by putting a stethoscope to his chest. He says, 'Rihanna!' and then he hears the man's heart go: 'Bdm bdm bdm.' Then he says, 'Scarlett Johansson!' The man's heartbeat speeds up even more: 'Bdm bdm bdm bdm bdm.' 'Ann Widdecombe!' says the doctor. And the man's heartbeat slows down again. 'B-dmmm. B-dmmm.' 'That's fine,' says the doctor. 'Go into the next room and take your clothes off.' The next recruit steps up. 'Rihanna!' says the doctor. 'Bdm bdm bdm.' ' Scarlett Johansson!' 'Bdm bdm bdm bdm.' ' Ann Widdecombe!' ' B-dmmm. B-dmmm.' 'That's fine. Go into the next room and take your clothes off.' The final recruit steps up. 'Rihanna!' says the doctor. 'B-dmmm. B-dmmm.' 'That's odd,' says the doctor and tries again: 'Scarlett Johansson!' ' B-dmmm. B-dmmm.' 'OK,' says the doctor. 'Ann Widdecombe!' 'B-dmmm. B-dmmm.' 'OK. Never mind,' says the doctor. 'Go into the next room with the other men and take your clothes off. 'Bdm bdm bdm bdm bdm.'

A soldier tells his commanding officer that he has lost his rifle. The officer says the cost of the rifle is £5,000 and it will be taken out of his wages. 'What if I'd lost an armoured car?' asks the soldier. 'That would be £50,000 and that would also be taken out of your wages,' says the officer. 'Wow!' says the soldier. 'No wonder naval officers always go down with their ships.'

> "AS SOON AS I ARRIVED IN CAMP THEY GAVE ME A 10-GUN SALUTE. OR SO THEY TOLD ME ON THE OPERATING TABLE."
>
> BOB HOPE

A squad are on the parade ground when the sergeant major marches up and barks, 'Are there any men here who are keen on music?' A couple of the more cultured-looking squaddies indicate their interest. 'Excellent!' says the sergeant major. 'Fall out and report to the canteen. The piano needs shifting.'

A fearsome sergeant major one day asks one of his soldiers, 'I suppose when I die you'll want to come and dance on my grave.' 'Certainly not,' says the soldier, 'once I get out of here I've sworn never to stand in another queue again!'

A British pilot is shot down and captured by the Germans during the war. He wakes up in hospital with terrible injuries. A German doctor comes to his bedside, tells him how bad his injuries are and that they have had to amputate his right arm. The doctor takes pity on the pilot and asks if there is anything that can be done to help him. 'Yes,' says the pilot, 'I would like you to give my arm to the Luftwaffe and get them to take it on their next mission and drop it somewhere in England so it can go back home.' The doctor arranges for the arm to be dropped over England but a few days later the doctor has to amputate the pilot's left leg. Again the pilot asks for it to be dropped over England and the doctor agrees. A few days later, the doctor has to amputate the pilot's left arm and his right leg. Again the pilot wants them dropped over England. The next day a Luftwaffe officer turns up to interrogate him. 'You asked us to drop your right arm over England. Then you wanted us to do the same with your left leg.' 'Yes,' says the pilot. 'Now you want us to take your left arm and your right leg and drop them over England as well,' says the Luftwaffe officer. 'Yes. What of it?' asks the pilot. 'Tell me honestly,' says the Luftwaffe officer, 'are you trying to escape?'

An officer calls to a soldier, 'Private, do you have change for a pound?' 'Yes, mate,' says the soldier. 'How dare you,' says the officer, 'that is no way to address an officer! I will ask again and this time you will answer properly. Private, do you have change for a pound?' 'No I don't, sir,' says the soldier.

A man is called up to join the army. He goes for his medical but tells the doctor he's sure he can't be certified fit to serve as one of his legs is three inches shorter than the other. 'Don't worry,' says the doctor, 'we'll make sure you get to fight on a slope.'

General Simkins, Admiral Jones and Air Marshal Smith are all giving speeches at a military conference. Both the general and the admiral have digs at the air marshal by describing the RAF as the 'Cinderella' of the armed forces. When it's Smith's turn to speak he says, 'I don't know as much about fairy tales as my colleagues, but I do know that Cinderella had two really ugly sisters . . .'

An admiral visiting one of the ships in his squadron has a bizarre mishap when a refrigerated container falls off a dock crane and covers him from head to foot in whipped cream at the dockside. Luckily he's uninjured, though later he has to be piped on board.

Nancy has been going out regularly with an entire brigade of soldiers. She says it's not a physical relationship, it's all completely platoonic.

There's an old army adage that says: 'Shoot first; ask questions later.' Which is all well and good, but you never get to hear many answers.

Before they let lads into the army they ought to see if they can aim properly; they don't even have to give them a gun, first just see if they can wee into a toilet.

A young man is caught naked in the corridor of a London hotel chasing his girlfriend back to their room. He is arrested and found to be an army officer so he has to face a court martial for his behaviour. His defence lawyer manages to get him off the hook by invoking a clause of the military code which says: 'An officer shall be properly dressed in the uniform of the day at all times except when appropriately attired for the sport in which he is engaging.'

ART

A famous female artist is worried she is losing her sight so she goes to an eye doctor. The doctor treats her and over the next year successfully restores her sight. The artist is so grateful she paints a massive mural of a human eye on the front wall of the doctor's surgery. 'What do you think of that?' she asks the doctor. 'I think,' says the doctor, 'thank God I'm not a gynaecologist!'

"ERNIE: 'MY AUNTIE'S GOT A WHISTLER.' ERIC: 'NOW THERE'S A NOVELTY.'"

MORECAMBE AND WISE

Q: How many art gallery visitors does it take to change a light bulb?
A: Two. One to change the light bulb and the other to say, 'My four-year-old could have done that.'

Lady Constance hires a portrait painter. When the artist arrives he's impressed to find that her ladyship is wearing huge ruby earrings, a diamond choker and a tiara made of emeralds. 'That's very impressive jewellery,' says the artist. 'It must be worth a small fortune.' 'It's fake,' says her ladyship. 'I bought it yesterday on eBay. In fact, I can't stand the stuff. I intend to throw it away when we're done.' 'But why do you want to be painted wearing it?' asks the artist. 'Because,' says Lady Constance, 'if I die before my husband, I want his new wife to go crazy looking for it.'

"DID YOU KNOW RICHARD NIXON IS THE ONLY PRESIDENT WHOSE FORMAL PORTRAIT WAS PAINTED BY A POLICE SKETCH ARTIST?"

JOHNNY CARSON

When a burglar robbed the apartment of Salvador Dali, the police were fortunate to have an identikit image of the culprit provided by the great artist. They spent three months looking for a multi-coloured tortoise with a bicycle sticking out of its mouth wearing a bowler hat made from a fried egg.

ARTHRITIS

An old man hobbles into the doctor's surgery bent double and walking only with the aid of a stick. Five minutes later he walks out standing straight upright. 'This is a miracle cure,' says another patient in the waiting room. 'What did he do?' 'He gave me a longer stick,' says the old man.

ASPIRATION

It was drummed into me from an early age that you can be anyone you want to be. Unfortunately, this is what we now call identity theft.

> I MENTIONED EARLY ON THAT I RECOGNISE THERE ARE HURDLES AND WE'RE GOING TO ACHIEVE THOSE HURDLES.
>
> GEORGE W. BUSH

ASSERTIVENESS

They are running a course on self-assertiveness at the local college. The notice on the door says, 'Just barge straight in.'

My wife left me because I was too meek and mild and never stood up for myself. Well, I didn't like to argue with her.

ATTENTION

It has been announced that talks between representatives of the National Attention Disorder Federation and the Society for the Terminally Impatient have broken down once again after another eight seconds of dialogue.

If I had a pound for every time somebody has told me I wasn't paying attention, I have no idea whatsoever how much I'd have.

ATTRACTIVENESS

Mum is in the bathroom getting ready for work when her little daughter walks in. 'What are you doing?' asks the little girl. 'Putting on my wrinkle cream,' says Mum. 'Really?' says the little girl. 'I thought they were all natural.'

Barry produces a picture of his new girlfriend to show Gary. 'She's beautiful, isn't she?' says Barry. 'If you think she's beautiful, you should see *my* new girlfriend?' says Gary. 'Why?' asks Barry. 'Is she even more beautiful?' 'No,' says Gary. 'She's an optician.'

> "I HAVE SO LITTLE SEX APPEAL MY GYNAECOLOGIST CALLS ME 'SIR'."
>
> JOAN RIVERS

I believe I am God's gift to women. If, that is, God had to stop at a petrol station at the last minute.

I am considered dark and handsome. When it gets dark, people think I'm handsome.

If you think you might be repulsively ugly, don't worry. You look just like all your ancestors and you are living proof that all of them managed to have sex at least once.

> "WE USED TO PLAY SPIN THE BOTTLE WHEN I WAS A KID. A GIRL WOULD SPIN THE BOTTLE AND IF IT POINTED TO YOU WHEN IT STOPPED, THE GIRL COULD EITHER KISS YOU OR GIVE YOU A DIME. BY THE TIME I WAS 14, I OWNED MY OWN HOME."
>
> GENE PERRET

Flora is speaking to her friend Betty. 'I worry about losing my looks. I think my husband might start to lose interest in me as I get older.' 'Well, that doesn't bother me,' says Betty. 'My Frank often tells me he'll cherish me all the more with the passing years.' 'Well, yes,' says Flora. 'But remember, he is an antiques dealer.'

AUCTIONS

Brian the auctioneer stops a sale to announce that someone has lost a roll of money containing £10,000. 'There's a £100 reward for anyone who finds it,' says Brian. A voice from the room shouts out: '£150!'

AUDITORS

Q: What is an auditor?
A: A person who arrives after the main battle and goes round bayoneting all the wounded.

AUTOBIOGRAPHY

I've just read the third volume of a glamorous celebrity's autobiography. It's very interesting. It tells the story of how she managed to cobble together the material for the second volume of her autobiography.

AUTOCORRECT

Autocorrect is my worst enema.

When the inventor of autocorrect dies he will find there is a special place reserved for him in Hull.

Harry texts his boss to tell him he won't be going in to work because he's in bed with a migraine. Unfortunately, his phone autocorrected it and his boss thinks he's having a day in bed with a migrant.

AWARDS

Fred's grandfather was the man who invented the door knocker. It was very successful. He was awarded the No Bell Prize.

Owing to a slight misprint engraved on his trophy, Geoff Capes has officially been declared Britain's Strangest Man.

The winner of the award for the Person Most Likely To Suddenly Assassinate A Celebrity With No Warning Whatsoever accepted his trophy this afternoon and immediately offered it as a tribute to the late Christopher Biggins, who had just presented it to him.

Norman says he was the winner of this year's Britain's Most Confident Man Award. To be honest, he just invited all his work colleagues into his office and presented a trophy to himself.

This year's awards ceremony for workers in the oil industry had to be called off. Apparently they found the whole thing was rigged.

Terry was going to enter the Repair Man of the Year contest, but then he found it had been fixed.

BABIES

Clive is visiting some friends who have just had a new baby. 'Would you like to wind it?' asks the mum, handing Clive the baby. Clive thinks that sounds a bit extreme so he decides to just give it a dead leg instead.

Did you hear about the husband and wife scientists who had twins? They called one Billy and the other Control.

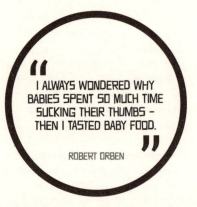

" I ALWAYS WONDERED WHY BABIES SPENT SO MUCH TIME SUCKING THEIR THUMBS – THEN I TASTED BABY FOOD. "

ROBERT ORBEN

Bonnie takes a baby into a clinic to get it checked. The nurse asks Bonnie to hold the baby and step onto a set of scales. 'What for?' asks Bonnie. 'To see how much the baby weighs,' says the nurse. 'First, we take the weight of the mother and baby together, then we weigh the mother by herself. We can then subtract one from the other to see how much the baby weighs.' 'That's not going to work,' says Bonnie. 'I'm not the kid's mother, I'm her aunt.'

BACK PROBLEMS

A man walks into a library and asks for a book on back ache. The librarian says, 'It's the one with the broken spine.'

BACKSIDES

WARNING: DO NOT USE ORALLY AFTER USE RECTALLY.

INSTRUCTIONS ON A THERMOMETER

Do you know why the gap in your buttocks goes up and down and not side to side? It's to stop you mumbling when you go down a slide.

BAD LANGUAGE

When I was growing up, every time my dad swore he would then say, 'Pardon my French.' I'll never forget my first day at school when the teacher asked if any of us knew any French words.

A little boy gets sent home from school for using a four-letter word beginning with 'c'. 'That wasn't clever was it?' says his mum. 'No it wasn't,' says the little boy, 'it was c**p.'

Q: What exactly does 'heck' mean?
A: It's the place where people go if they don't believe in gosh.

Q: What's slippery, black and keeps yelling, 'Arsehole!'? **A:** Crude oil.
Q: What's slippery, black and keeps yelling, 'Anus!'? **A:** Refined oil.

Halfway through a football match between two teams of boys at the park, the coach of one of the teams calls one of his nine-year-old players over and gives him a little talk. 'Look, son,' says the coach, 'we all want to win and we all feel passionately about the game but I've heard a lot of shouting and swearing and terrible language today and that is simply not acceptable. Do you understand?' 'Yes, sir,' says the little boy. 'Good,' says the coach, 'so if you could just go over to the touchline and explain all that to your grandmother we can carry on the game!'

Father O'Leary borrows a petrol lawnmower from his neighbour. Time and again he tries to start it, but the engine won't catch. He goes to the neighbour and says, 'Is there a knack for starting that mower of yours? I'm having terrible trouble.' 'You just have to swear at it, Father,' says the neighbour. 'Swear like the blue blazes and it'll get going eventually.' 'I'm not sure I can,' says Father O'Leary. 'It's been a long while since I uttered any word of profanity.' 'Don't worry, Father,' says the neighbour. 'It'll soon come back to you after you've tried starting that f***ing thing for an hour.'

> "I HAVE A JAR AT HOME AND I PUT PENNIES IN IT WHENEVER I CURSE. THE OTHER DAY I SPILLED THE JAR. I OWE IT ABOUT $25."
>
> DEMETRI MARTIN

Janice has to tell her husband that their unmarried teenage daughter is pregnant. Afterwards, her daughter asks how dad took the news. 'Do you want me to leave out all the swearing?' asks Janice. 'I think you'd better,' says the daughter. 'OK,' replies Janice, 'in which case, your father said absolutely nothing whatsoever.'

BAGPIPES

Q: Why do bagpipe players like to march while they're playing?
A: They're trying to get away from the sound.

Q: What sort of diary does a bagpipe player use to keep track of his engagements? **A:** Year-at-a-glance.

Q: How do you make a chainsaw sound like a set of bagpipes?
A: Don't! Why would you want to make it worse?

Q: How do you tell a considerate Scotsman?
A: He's the one who can play the bagpipes, but doesn't.

Q: What's the difference between a lawnmower and a set of bagpipes?
A: The mower sounds better after it's been tuned.

Bert has a musical octopus. He has a standing bet of £100 that his octopus can play any musical instrument it's given, and so far he's never been beaten. One day a man goes up to Bert and gives him a set of tartan bagpipes. 'I'll double your bet. I'll put down £200 that your octopus can't play these.' Bert hands the bagpipes to the octopus and is appalled when the octopus starts flailing its arms around, not producing a note. 'What are you doing?' says Bert to the octopus. 'I've got £200 riding on this. Don't tell me you can't play it?' 'Who's talking about playing it,' says the octopus. 'Once I figure out how to get its pyjamas off, I'm going to screw it.'

BAKING AND BAKERY PRODUCTS

I hate it when you get those people knocking on your door wanting to convert you to a different sort of loaf. Damn those Hovis witnesses.

Muriel walks into a bakery and asks to see the manager. 'What's up?' says the manager. 'I'll tell you what's up,' says Muriel. 'I came in here yesterday to buy a currant bun and when I bit into it, I found one of the currants was actually a dead fly.' 'Don't worry, madam,' says the manager. 'We pride ourselves on our customer-friendly returns policy.' 'Oh,' says Muriel. 'So will I get a new bun?' 'No,' says the manager. 'Bring in the fly and I'll give you a new currant.'

A man goes into a cake shop and says, 'I'd like to buy a wasp, please.' 'Don't be stupid,' says the assistant, 'we don't sell wasps.' 'Oh?' says the man, 'but you've got one in the window!'

The health inspectors are inspecting a local bakery. One of the inspectors notices the baker take out his false teeth and use them to crimp round the edge of an apple pie. 'Hey,' says the inspector, 'you're not supposed to do that. Don't you have a special tool?' 'Of course I do,' says the baker, 'but I only use it to make the holes in the doughnuts.'

A man goes into a cake shop and asks the price of a couple of cakes in the window. 'The one on the left is £1,' says the cake shop proprietor, 'and the one on the right is £10.' 'Why such a difference in price?' asks the man. 'They both look the same.' 'Yes,' says the proprietor, 'but the one on the right is Madeira cake.'

A great big muscly tattooed man with a shaved head walks into a bakery and says in a gruff angry voice, 'I want that loaf of bread there but I only want half of it.' 'Sorry, says the assistant, 'I can't sell you half a loaf.' 'Just sell me half the loaf!' yells the man, slamming his fist down on the counter. The assistant goes to the office and tells the manager, 'A great big ugly gorilla of a bloke has walked in and asked to buy half a loaf.' At that moment the assistant realises that the man has walked into the office behind him. 'And this gentleman,' says the assistant, 'then came in and asked to buy the other half!'

> UNLEAVENED BREAD IS BREAD MADE WITHOUT ANY INGREDIENTS.
>
> SCHOOLBOY HOMEWORK ANSWER

BALLOONING

Norman has just come back from a ballooning holiday. He managed to put on four stone.

BANKS AND BANKING

A little old lady toddles into the bank and asks the cashier if he could help her check her balance. So he comes round and pushes her over.

If people who work in banks are so good with numbers, how come there's always three times as many windows as cashiers?

A banker, a *Daily Mail* reader and a benefit claimant sit down at a café table. There are 12 biscuits on a plate in front of them. The banker takes 11 of the biscuits then whispers to the *Daily Mail* reader, 'Hey! You'd better watch out for that benefit claimant. I think he's after your biscuit.'

Bert's overdraft is huge. It's so enormous, the bank now officially has all its savings with him.

A hooded robber bursts into a bank and orders the staff to start filling a bag with money. Once he has the cash he makes for the door but a have-a-go hero steps up and whips off his hood. The robber immediately shoots him and looks around the rest of the customers in the bank. 'Did anyone else get a look at my face?' he asks. 'I think my wife did,' says one man.

Gerry should have been a banker: he's the kind of guy who'll lend you an umbrella on a sunny day, then take it back as soon as it starts raining.

Larry complained when his bank charged him for having insufficient funds, he reckons they should have warned him.

BAPTISM

The vicar had an accident during a recent christening which is why Mr and Mrs Harris are now the proud parents of little George Ooops Splosh Come Here You Slippery Little So-and-so Harris.

A mother is watching her two little boys playing outside after a heavy shower of rain. Suddenly the bigger of the two picks up his little brother and drops him into a deep pothole full of water. The mother runs out calling, 'What are you doing?' 'I was playing church,' says the older brother. 'I was just baptising him: In the name of the Father and of the Son and into the hole he goes!'

THIS AFTERNOON THERE WILL BE A MEETING IN THE SOUTH AND NORTH ENDS OF THE CHURCH. CHILDREN WILL BE BAPTISED AT BOTH ENDS.

PARISH NOTICES

BARBECUES

A man walks into a builders' merchants and says he want to build a barbecue and needs 25,000 bricks and a two-foot-square steel mesh. 'You don't need that many bricks for a barbecue,' says the assistant. 'I do,' says the man, 'I live on the top floor of a block of flats.'

BARRIERS

Barriers across roads are all very well but they would prove useless in the event of the country being invaded by an army of limbo dancers.

BATHROOMS AND BATHROOM PRODUCTS

Harry is taking a shower but can't find the shampoo. He calls to his wife who tells him where to find it in the cupboard. 'No, this one's no good,' says Harry. 'What's the matter with it?' asks his wife. 'It says it's for dry hair,' says Harry, 'and I've already wet mine.'

Harry has invented a self-powered, wireless, hand-operated hair drier. He calls it 'a towel'.

INSTRUCTIONS ON A HAIR DRIER

INSTRUCTIONS ON A SET OF CURLING TONGS

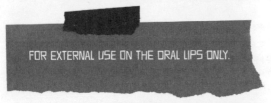

INSTRUCTIONS ON A STICK OF LIP GLOSS

> **QUESTION MASTER: COTTON BUDS CARRY A WARNING NOT TO INSERT THEM INTO WHICH PART OF THE BODY?**
> **CONTESTANT: EYES.**
>
> THE WEAKEST LINK

Geoff takes a bottle of 'No More Tears' shampoo back to Boots. He complains that he fed the baby half a bottle of the stuff but it didn't stop him crying.

I've started using extra-sensitive toothpaste. It gets really upset when I use other toothpastes.

Dick goes to the hardware shop and buys a bath tub. He takes it back the next day because, he says, the water keeps running out of it. 'Did you buy a plug to go with it?' asks the assistant. 'No I didn't!' says Dick. 'No one told me it was an electric one.'

George sues a deodorant manufacturer. He complains about the injuries he suffered as a result of the misleading instructions on the packaging which said: 'Remove from wrapper and push up bottom'.

BATTERIES

A man walks into a shop and says, 'I need a new battery so I can tell the time.' 'I see,' says the shopkeeper, 'is it for a clock?' 'How the hell should I know!' says the man. 'That's why I need a new battery.'

How can you tell a phone battery from a scally who's just been let out of prison? The battery might last a week without a new charge.

BEARS

Q: What do you call a bear that has no ear?
A: A B . . .

> QUESTION MASTER: NAME A KIND OF BEAR.
> CONTESTANT: POPPA BEAR.
>
> FAMILY FEUD

A teddy bear is employed as a navvy on a building site. He goes off to the toilet and when he comes back he finds that the pick he had been using has been stolen. He is furious and goes to the foreman to report what has happened. 'You should have realised,' says the foreman. 'Really? Why?' says the bear. 'Because,' says the foreman, 'today's the day the teddy bears have their picks nicked.'

A huge bear walks into a bar and starts tearing the place up. He culminates by chewing off the end of the bar-top and spitting the splinters into the bartender's face. 'There,' snarls the bear. 'Now I've worked off some steam, give me a drink.' The bartender shakes his head. 'We don't serve drug users.' 'What?' exclaims the bear. 'What makes you think I'm on drugs?' 'I saw you have some just now,' says the bartender. 'That's a lie,' says the bear. 'What drugs are you talking about?' The bartender says, 'I'm talking about that bar bit you ate . . .'

Jim goes on a hunting trip with his boss, Steve. They're after a bear, but Steve is feeling tired after the journey and decides to spend some time in their hunting lodge. Determined to impress his boss, Jim sets out alone. A short time later he sees a huge bear and takes a shot, but only manages to graze it. He runs for his life as the bear chases him and makes it back to the lodge with the animal hot on his heels. He rushes in and the enraged bear follows him inside. 'What the hell is going on? shouts Steve. 'It's a present for you!' shouts Jim, as he dives for the open window. 'You have this one. I'll go get us another.'

A couple are on holiday in the USA and are on a visit to Yellowstone Park. Their guide tells them, 'If you encounter a bear, the best thing to do is act like you're dead.' 'How am I supposed to do that?' the woman asks her husband. 'It will be easy,' says the husband: 'Just act like you do when we're having sex.'

BEAUTY AND BEAUTY TREATMENT

At 21, Myra was chosen to be Miss America. Mind you, back in those days, there weren't quite so many Americans.

Nora spent two hours at the beauty shop last week – they didn't actually do anything, that was just for the estimate.

There is scientific proof that anti-wrinkle cream doesn't work. If it did, women would have no fingerprints.

A couple are in the supermarket. The husband picks up a case of beer but his wife tells him they can't afford it and makes him put it back. In the next aisle, the woman picks up a jar of face cream. 'What's that for?' asks the husband. 'It will make me look beautiful,' says his wife. 'So will the crate of beer,' says the husband, 'and that's half the price.'

BEDS

Harry's wife really hit the roof last night. She had just found out that he'd replaced their bed with a trampoline.

Do you know the perfect cure for a bedwetting toddler? An electric blanket.

> ON WEDNESDAY THE LADIES' LITURGY GROUP WILL MEET. MRS JOHNSON WILL SING 'PUT ME IN MY LITTLE BED' ACCOMPANIED BY THE PASTOR.
>
> PARISH NOTICES

BIG QUESTIONS

▶ If all is not lost, where exactly is it?

▶ Time is said to heal all wounds, so is the bellybutton a notable exception?

▶ How is it that we put a man on the moon before we figured out it would be a good idea to put wheels on luggage?

▶ When a guide dog does its business, who picks it up?

▶ What do you get when you cross a joke with a rhetorical question?

▶ If people get goose bumps, do geese ever get people bumps?

▶ If common sense is supposed to be so common, why do so few people have it?

▶ If the workers in a coffee factory get tea breaks, do the workers in a tea factory get coffee breaks?

▶ If you 'draw a blank' does that mean you show someone some plain paper?

▶ If we were put on earth to help others, what exactly are the 'others' here for?

▶ On the label for cured ham, why does it never tell you what was wrong with it in the first place?

▶ Why do the expressions 'wise man' and 'wise guy' have opposite meanings?

▶ Why is it that tugboats push their barges?

▶ Why do we see no problem leaving cars that are worth thousands of pounds in our driveways but we keep piles of worthless junk in our garages?

▶ Why is it that the sun lightens our hair but darkens our skin?

▶ Woolly jumpers shrink when you put them in the wash so why don't sheep shrink if they're left out in the rain?

BIKES

Q: Why is a bicycle unable to stand up on its own? **A:** It's two-tyred.

Our son is a terror. Last week he accidentally set fire to the garage, smashed three windows with his ball, blew up the septic tank with a firework and blocked the toilet with his underwear. I told my wife I was thinking of buying him a bicycle. 'A bike?' she said. 'What's a bike going to do to control his bad behaviour? That won't help at all.' 'It might not help,' I said. 'But it will spread him over a wider area.'

BILLS

I got a call from the electricity company to tell me my bill was outstanding. I said, 'That's nice of you to say! Thanks very much!' and hung up.

I received an advert from Oxfam that said for a donation of just £2 a month they could supply water to a whole African village. I was furious. The water company here keeps charging me £500 a year.

Grandma's name was Edna, but her nickname was Bernadette – every time she got a bill, she set fire to it.

BINGO

The local bingo hall has just introduced a new hand-held device, which allows people to keep playing bingo even when they're standing outside having a fag. It's a 20-foot-long magic marker pen that reaches all the way back inside the hall to their bingo card.

Two old ladies are having an afternoon's fun in the bingo hall when they see a hearse slowly drive past the glass doors. There's a huge wreath on top that has the name 'Bert' spelled out in flowers. One of the old ladies reaches into her handbag and wipes her eyes with a handkerchief. 'Don't be so soppy,' says her friend. 'I can't help it,' says the old lady. 'We were married more than 40 years.'

BIOLOGY

> Q: WHAT IS AN APPENDIX?
> A: AN APPENDIX IS SOMETHING USUALLY FOUND AT THE END OF A BOOK. BUT SOMETIMES THEY GET INSIDE PEOPLE AND HAVE TO BE SURGICALLY REMOVED.
>
> SCHOOL EXAM ANSWER

> HOST: WHAT 'O' IS THE GENERIC TERM FOR ANY LIVING ANIMAL OR PLANT, INCLUDING BACTERIA AND VIRUSES?
> CONTESTANT: ORGASM?
>
> BLOCKBUSTERS

BIRDS

Q: What is the distinguishing feature of a bald eagle? **A:** You can see that it's tried to use the feathers on one side to do a comb-over.

A man is driving behind a van down a narrow road. He's getting irritated by the fact that, every ten minutes, the van comes to a halt and the driver runs round to bang on the back doors before running back to the cab and driving forward once more. Eventually, the man is able to overtake the van, but instead of going ahead, he puts on the brake and blocks the way. He then gets out to have a stern word with the van driver. 'What do you mean by stopping every ten minutes and banging on the back doors?' he says. 'I'm sorry,' says the driver. 'But the weight limit of the van is one ton and I've got two tons of parakeets in the back. To stay legal, I have to stop every so often and get half of them flying again.'

Why is that birds aren't rolling round laughing all the time because they're being tickled by their own feathers?

> QUESTION MASTER: NAME A BIRD WITH A LONG NECK.
> CONTESTANT: NAOMI CAMPBELL.
>
> FAMILY FORTUNES

BIRTHDAYS AND BIRTHDAY PRESENTS

Nobby's wife tells him, 'You know you've ruined my birthday.' 'Don't talk rubbish,' says Nobby, 'I didn't even know it *was* your birthday.'

Gus is taken into hospital on his wife's birthday. A couple of days later his friend Bob goes to visit him. 'I've just had to have 18 stitches taken out,' says Gus. 'That's terrible,' says Bob. 'By the way, what did you get your wife for her birthday?' 'A sewing kit,' says Gus.

Harry tells Tom he has bought his wife a new bag and a belt for her birthday. 'That sounds a nice present,' says Tom. 'She needed them,' says Harry. 'The vacuum cleaner hasn't been working very well recently.'

My mother-in-law asked me why I hadn't bought her a birthday present this year. I said, 'Because you still haven't used the one I got you last year.' 'I know,' she said, 'but last year you bought me a plot in the cemetery.'

My wife asked me to get her something in silk for her birthday but she wasn't pleased with her present. I think I must have got the wrong colour emulsion.

What did the little boy with no hands get for his birthday? Gloves! No, that's a joke. Nobody knows. He hasn't managed to open the wrapping yet.

Norma is getting ready to go out for her birthday. She asks her husband Nobby if he would like to see her in something long and flowing. 'Yes, love!' he says. 'The Thames!'

Q: What do you get if you cross a birthday cake with a tin of baked beans?
A: A cake capable of blowing out its own candles.

Dick enjoyed his birthday party apart from the fact that he got heartburn from his birthday cake. His wife said it was his own fault. He should have taken the candles off before he ate it.

The newspapers are reporting the latest scientific discovery. Apparently birthdays are good for your health. The more of them you have, the longer you live.

It's Vera's birthday and her husband, Harry, presents her with a gift-wrapped little box. She tears the package open in excitement but then looks disappointed when she finds a pack of cards inside. 'What's the matter?' asks Harry. 'You told me you wanted something with diamonds on it.'

Norman buys his mother-in-law a novelty chair for her birthday. Unfortunately, his wife walks in and catches him just as he's plugging it in.

When I asked my wife what she wanted for her birthday, she said she wanted to be six again. OK. So I bought her a cake with a unicorn on it, got in a bunch of balloons and hired a clown. She was furious. She said, 'You idiot, I meant my dress size.'

Young Roger is born without a body. All he has is a head. Despite this, he manages to have a comfortable life thanks to his doting parents. One day the parents are contacted by a famous surgeon who claims that he can cure Roger by giving him a body transplant. In fact, the donor has already been found, all they have to do is bring Roger to the hospital and within a month he'll be able to walk out by himself. The parents rush home to tell Roger the good news. He's where they left him, sitting on a pillow in the living room. 'Roger,' cries Mum. 'You'll never guess what marvellous news we have. It's the best present you could ever ask for.' 'It's true, son,' says Pa. 'It's the finest gift proud parents could ever give to their boy.' 'Don't tell me,' says Roger, rolling his eyes. 'I've heard it all before. It's another flipping hat isn't it . . .'

It is Norma's birthday and Nobby presents her with what he calls her first gift. She unwraps it and finds a stick with a sparkly star stuck on the end. 'What the hell's this?' she asks. 'It's a magic wand,' says Nobby. 'Rubbish!' says Norma. 'No, really,' says Nobby, 'try shaking it and saying the magic word "Abracadabra" and something magic will happen.' 'OK,' she says, and shakes it and says, 'Abracadabra.' 'Oh no!' says Nobby, looking beneath their bed. 'You're not going to believe this. You've just made all your other presents disappear!'

BISEXUALITY

Bernie says his wife is a bisexual. She only does it twice a year.

Q: What do you call a 25-stone person who is attracted to both sexes?
A: A bisexual built for two.

BLACKSMITHS

A boy walks into a blacksmith's looking for work. The blacksmith asks, 'Do you have any experience shoeing horses?' 'No,' says the boy, 'but I did once tell a donkey to f*** off!'

BLAME

Remember – there is never any problem that is so large or difficult that you won't be able to blame it on somebody else.

Granddad is taking his little grandson out for the day. 'This is nice,' says Granddad. 'But just think, in ten years' time you won't want to go out walking and cycling and swimming with me any more. 'Never mind, Granddad,' says the little boy. 'In ten years' time, you won't be able to do any of those things any more anyway.'

BLINDNESS

A blind man walks into a bar. And then into a table. And then a chair.

Q: Why did the blind lady fall into the well?
A: Because she couldn't see that well.

Tom and Dick are walking in the park when they see a man walking four dogs. 'Wow!' says Dick. 'That guy must be really blind.'

A man walks into a bar with a tiny Chihuahua on a lead. 'I'm sorry, mate,' says the barman, 'but we don't allow dogs in here.' 'What?' says the man. 'Not even guide dogs.' 'Oh yes,' says the barman, 'guide dogs are OK. But usually they are German shepherds or Labradors.' 'Oh no,' says the man, 'so what have they given me this time?'

A blind man walks into a shop and starts swinging his guide dog round and round on the end of its lead. An assistant hurries over and asks, 'Can I help you, sir?' 'No, thanks,' says the blind man. 'I'm just looking round.'

BOATS

A man has to catch the last ferry home but realises he will only just be in time for the boat. As he comes to the landing stage he sees the ferry a few feet out in the water. He makes a huge effort and leaps across into the boat. 'That was good,' says the ferry captain, 'although I'm not sure why you did it when we were just about to come in to dock.'

BOMBS

Two workmen dig up an unexploded bomb on a building site. 'Oh no,' says the one, 'what should we do with this?' 'Stick it on the wheelbarrow,' says the other, 'we'll show it to the foreman at clocking-off time.' Later on they find a second bomb. 'What shall we do with this?' asks the first. 'Stick it on the wheelbarrow with the other one,' says the other, 'we'll take them both to the foreman at clocking-off time.' Eventually clocking-off time comes round and they start pushing the wheelbarrow over to the foreman. The wheelbarrow goes over a bump and one of the bombs starts ticking. 'Oh no!' says the first workmen. 'What will we do if it blows up?' 'Stop worrying,' says the other, 'we'll just tell the foreman we only found one.'

> "GENTLEMEN, DO NOT UNDERESTIMATE THE DANGER OF THE ATOM BOMB. IT'S DYNAMITE!"
>
> SAMUEL GOLDWYN

The security services have uncovered a plot to booby-trap tins of alphabet soup. Apparently if one goes off it could spell disaster.

What did the bomb-disposal technician say to his new assistant? 'If you see me running, try to keep up.'

BONES

Barry is trying a little too hard chatting up a girl in a bar. She tells him, 'I suffer from brittle bone disease.' 'So do I!' says Barry. 'Snap!'

BOOMERANGS

Did you hear about the aborigine who forgot how to throw his boomerang? Eventually it came back to him.

Today is the birthday of the inventor of the boomerang. I think we should all wish him Many Happy Returns.

BORROWING

Tom hears a knock at the front door and knows it will be his next-door neighbour, Barry, come round yet again to borrow his gardening equipment. 'Hello,' says Barry when Tom answers the door, 'I'm sorry to bother you but I wondered if you would be using your shears this afternoon?' 'Yes, I'm afraid I will,' says Tom, 'in fact I will need all my gardening equipment today because I'm planning on working in the garden all afternoon.' 'Oh that's good,' says Barry, 'because I actually came round to see if I could borrow your golf clubs.'

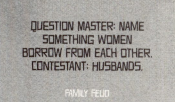

QUESTION MASTER: NAME SOMETHING WOMEN BORROW FROM EACH OTHER.
CONTESTANT: HUSBANDS.

FAMILY FEUD

BOXING

Tommy Cooper told Henry Cooper, 'I was in the ring once with Cassius Clay and I got him worried.' 'Oh really?' says Henry. 'Yes,' says Tommy, 'he thought he'd killed me.'

I was going away so I asked my flatmate to record a boxing match for me on the television. When I got back, I found he'd recorded over it. 'What did you do that for?' I said. 'You knew I wanted to watch it.' 'There was no point,' he says. 'One of them fell over in the fourth round and they had to stop it early.'

BOY SCOUTS

> "A SCOUT TROOP CONSISTS OF 12 LITTLE KIDS DRESSED LIKE SCHMUCKS FOLLOWING A BIG SCHMUCK DRESSED LIKE A KID."
>
> JACK BENNY

BRASS BANDS

I saw one of those traditional northern colliery bands. It's very impressive to think how coalminers used to dig themselves deep underground to play brass arrangements of popular tunes.

BREAK-UPS

After years of continual threats to leave, last night my wife finally broke my heart. She told me she's staying.

When a girl tells you she is finishing with you but she wants you both to stay friends, it's no use. It's a bit like finding that your dog has died but you're still expected to carry on walking it.

An ex-girlfriend texted me to say, 'Will you delete my number off your phone.' I texted straight back asking, 'Who is this?'

Stan lost his wife five years ago. He's never played poker since.

Harry and Vera go to a school reunion where Vera sees a man who is appallingly drunk at the next table, singing and dancing and laughing hysterically. 'Oh my God!' she says. 'I've just realised that's my old boyfriend. Apparently he started drinking just after we split up and has never stopped since.' 'Wow!' says Harry. 'Not many people would carry on celebrating that long.'

Colin's girlfriend tells him she has found someone else to go out with and hands him back his engagement ring. 'Right,' says Colin, 'what's your new feller's name and address?' 'Oh, Colin,' gasps the girlfriend, 'are you going to go round and fight over me?' 'No,' says Colin, 'I'm going to go round and see if he wants to buy a ring.'

Jeremy says to his friend Jeff, 'If you don't mind me asking, why did your marriage to Julia break up?' 'It was due to sickness,' says Jeff. 'I didn't know either of you had been ill,' says Jeremy. 'We hadn't. It was just that Julia got sick of the sight of me.'

A soldier is far from home when he gets a letter from his girlfriend saying she doesn't want to go out with him any more and asking for her photograph back. The soldier is annoyed so he finds as many photographs of other women that he can, stuffs them all in an envelope and writes back to his girlfriend with a note saying, 'Sorry, I can't remember which one you are. Please go through these pictures, keep your photo and send the others back to me!'

Frank's girlfriend walked out on him and left him a note telling him he was stupid and bigoted. Frank found this very unfair because he wasn't stupid, he was dyslexic, and it wasn't his fault he had big toes.

Men, remember that the mother of your children can do something for you that no other woman can – she can sue you for child maintenance.

Bruce's wife goes up to him and says, 'You're going to be sorry, Bruce. I'm leaving you.' Bruce says, 'Come on, love. Make your mind up. Which one?'

Cindy tells her friend, 'Things have been really bad with my boyfriend for over a month now. We're always arguing and it's put a terrible strain on me – in fact, I've been so upset I've lost eight pounds in the last three weeks.' 'Why don't you leave him?' asks the friend. 'I would,' says Cindy, 'but I'm aiming for ten.'

BREAKFAST

I accidentally mistook a box of mini Brillo pads for Shredded Wheat and ate a bowlful before I realised. My doctor told me he expects I'll scrape through.

A child-minder makes breakfast for her latest client, a little boy of six. She pours him out a nice big bowl of frosted flakes. 'Yuck,' says the boy. 'When I'm at home, Mummy makes me toast and jam for breakfast.' So the child-minder makes some toast and jam. The boy looks at it, turns up his nose and pushes away the plate. 'What's the matter?' says the child-minder. 'You said your mummy makes you toast and jam at home.' 'She does,' says the boy. 'But I never eat it.'

BREASTFEEDING

One day a little girl sees her next-door neighbour feeding her baby. 'What are you doing?' asks the little girl, so the neighbour explains all about a woman's breasts and breastfeeding. 'Oh, yes,' says the little girl, 'my mummy has a pair of those as well but I don't think she knows how to work them.'

Nobby tells his wife, 'I was disgusted on the bus today. There was a woman sitting on the next seat with her breasts out feeding her son.' 'You blokes are all the same,' says Norma, 'that was a completely natural, beautiful thing.' 'No it wasn't,' says Nobby. 'She was feeding him a packet of Quavers at the time.'

Barry is on the bus when the woman next to him begins breastfeeding her baby. The baby is reluctant to feed and the mother says, 'Come on, or I'll have to give your dinner to the nice man here.' A few minutes later Barry is sweating and saying, 'Come on, kid! Make up your mind! I was supposed to get off ten miles ago!'

BREASTS

I wouldn't say my enormous breasts have helped me in my career, but they have opened many doors for me.

The woman with the largest breast implants in the world attended a wedding reception in a ski chalet. Sadly, she stood too near the fire and toasted the happy couple.

A range of holy bras are available according to your religion. Apparently, Buddhist bras support the heaving masses. A Catholic bra raises the fallen. A Protestant bra keeps them upright. A Jewish bra makes mountains out of molehills.

Aunt Gladys finally realised she was getting past it when she won third prize in a 'Wet Shawl' contest.

A company has launched a new range of breast implants for women that contain a DAB radio inside them. This is a major breakthrough because women have been complaining for years that men just stare at their breasts and never listen to them.

> "IN THE LAST COUPLE OF WEEKS I'VE SEEN THE ADS FOR THE WONDER BRA. IS THAT REALLY A PROBLEM IN THIS COUNTRY? MEN NOT PAYING ENOUGH ATTENTION TO WOMEN'S BREASTS?"
>
> JAY LENO

BUBBLE-WRAP

Just think how much self-control the people who make bubble-wrap must have.

Barry is tidying up the stationery cupboard and finds a huge roll of bubble-wrap. He goes to his boss and asks, 'What should I do with this?' 'Oh,' says the boss, 'just pop it in the corner.' Four hours later he was still going.

BULLYING

A little boy runs to his mummy and cries, 'The big boys up the road keep making fun of me because they say my head is grotesquely enormous. 'Don't listen to them,' says Mum. 'That's not true at all. Now I want you to go back up the road, straight past those boys and go to the shop and get me five cabbages, ten pounds of potatoes and four pints of milk.' 'Shall I take a shopping bag?' asks the boy. 'No,' says Mum, 'just stick them all in your balaclava.'

BUREAUCRATS

Q: How many local council officials does it take to change a light bulb?
A: Fifty, one to change the light bulb and 49 to go on a fact-finding mission to the South of France to find out how they change light bulbs there.

Q: How many civil servants does it take to screw in a light bulb?
A: Two. One to assure everyone that everything possible is being done and another to try and screw the bulb into a wall socket.

BUSES

Harry sees Nobby waiting at the bus stop so he pulls up in his car and winds the window down. 'Do you want a lift, Nobby?' asks Harry. 'Better not, mate,' says Nobby. 'I might miss my bus.'

Mary is refused entry to the bus. 'Sorry, madam,' says the driver. 'This one's full. You'll have to wait for the next.' 'Oh dear,' says Mary. 'How long will it be?' 'About 15 metres!' says the driver. 'The same as all the others on this route.'

> "LA BUS DRIVERS ARE STRIKING. THEY WANT A BIG RAISE AND THEY WANT IT IN EXACT CHANGE."
>
> JAY LENO

Mike and Steve get drunk one night and are out so late they miss the last bus. They happen to be close to the bus depot so Mike offers to break in and steal them a vehicle. He nips over the fence but takes so long that Steve goes in after him. He finds Mike wandering up and down the rows of buses peering at their numbers. 'What are you doing?' asks Steve. 'Trying to find the number 29,' says Mike. 'That goes right to the bottom of our road.' 'Don't be so stupid,' says Steve. 'There's a number 4 right in front of you. If we get off at the church it's only a two-minute walk.'

A group of bikini models go on a promotional tour in a double-decker coach. As it happens all the brunettes and redheads end up sleeping downstairs, while all the blondes go upstairs. The lower-deck girls have a great time partying, but they gradually realise that the blondes are completely silent. One redhead goes up and finds all the blondes staring out of the front window. They look terrified. 'What's up?' says the redhead. 'We're having a fabulous time downstairs. You lot look scared to death.' 'We are,' says one of the blondes. 'It's OK for you. But we don't have a driver up here.'

BUSINESS

It has been announced that the Xerox and Wurlitzer companies are going to merge. The new company will specialise in making reproductive organs.

Clive was an aged but very successful and wealthy businessman. When he was lying on his deathbed the world's best surgeons worked round the clock to extend his life expectancy so he could fit in a few more appointments.

Always remember – to err is human; but if you can pin the blame on someone else that shows management potential.

In any business the grandeur of the entrance lobby is in inverse proportion to the solvency of the company.

Calvin is a business guru. That means he knows more jargon than everyone else.

A friend of mine talked me into going into business with him. He said we would make the perfect team because he had the experience while I had the money. Unfortunately, I've now got the experience and he's got the money.

Neville is asked to buy some office stationery, but can't make sense of the discount scheme the supply company is running. He goes to ask Beryl in the billing department what to do. Neville says, 'If I gave you £7,890 with a 20 per cent discount, how much would you take off?' Beryl says, 'Everything except my glasses.'

Norman's new restaurant 'The Herb Kitchen' has run into financial trouble. Last week his bank called in the bay leafs.

BUSY

No matter how busy you get, you are never too busy to stop and complain about how busy you are.

BUTCHERS

Did you hear about the butcher who stepped backwards and caught himself on the meat slicer? He managed to get a little behind in his work.

Harry tells Dick, 'A feller down at the market offered me eight legs of venison for £70. Does that sound right to you?' 'No,' says Dick, 'I think that might be two deer.'

BUTTER

Stanley made a fortune out of his new, improved butter-production process. Instead of building a milking and churning facility, he just let his cows play in a bouncy castle.

Did you hear the joke about the butter? I could tell you it but I suspect you'd just spread it around.

CAGE FIGHTING

Barry tells his mate he's going to take part in a cage fight next week. 'Are you sure you're up to this?' asks his mate. 'Of course,' says Barry, 'that budgie won't know what's hit him.'

CALAMITY

Benjamin Disraeli, the 19th-century Conservative leader and long-time adversary of William Gladstone, was once asked to explain the difference between a misfortune and a calamity. 'Well,' Disraeli said, 'if Mr Gladstone fell into the Thames, it would be a misfortune; but if someone pulled him out it would be a calamity.'

CALL CENTRES

A study of people working in call centres has shown they are under intense pressure not to hang up their phones for a moment during the day. If they do there's a danger they will get a call from another call centre.

Today there are over two million people in the UK who work in telephone call centres. And I know this for a fact because last year every single one of them phoned my house.

CAMELS

A small camel walks into his mum and dad's room in the middle of the night and says, 'Could I have a glass of water, please.' 'I don't believe this, son,' says his dad, 'this is the second time this month.'

CAMOUFLAGE

Tom went to the shops to buy a pair of camouflage trousers. But there were none to be seen.

A sergeant major catches a young soldier and shouts at him, 'I didn't see you at camouflage training this morning.' 'Oh didn't you?' says the soldier. 'Thank you very much, sir.'

CANALS

Larry was the world's greatest thief, but he could never figure out how to steal a canal – too many locks.

CANDLES

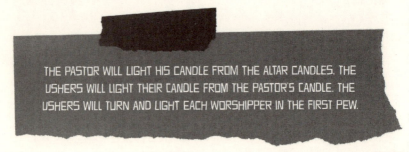

THE PASTOR WILL LIGHT HIS CANDLE FROM THE ALTAR CANDLES. THE USHERS WILL LIGHT THEIR CANDLE FROM THE PASTOR'S CANDLE. THE USHERS WILL TURN AND LIGHT EACH WORSHIPPER IN THE FIRST PEW.

PARISH NOTICES

CANNIBALISM

Tom, Dick and Harry are on a jungle safari when they are caught by a tribe of cannibals. The cannibals take them back to their village and tell them they will skin them alive, cook them, eat them and use their skins to build canoes. The men are however all allowed a final request. Tom asks for a pen and paper so he can write a last letter to his wife. Dick asks for a bottle of whisky so he can drink himself senseless. And Harry asks for an ordinary kitchen fork. The cannibals look confused but nevertheless they provide him with a fork. Harry immediately grabs it off them and starts stabbing himself all over his body with it while yelling, 'You're not making any canoes out of me!'

Did you hear about the comedian who performed a show for an audience that consisted entirely of cannibals? Apparently he went down really well!

Two cannibals sit down to dinner. 'Mmm,' says the first, 'your wife makes lovely soup.' 'I know,' says the second, 'but I'm still going to miss her.'

A lady cannibal says to her friend, 'I just don't know what to make of my husband these days.' 'How about casserole and then, if there's any left over, sausages,' says her friend.

Sven and Kurt are trekking through the jungle when they get caught by cannibals. The cannibals tie them up and put them in a big cauldron with some vegetables and gravy. The cannibals then light a fire beneath the pot to bring them to the boil. Sven notices that Kurt seems to find the situation amusing. 'What's the matter with you?' he asks. 'How can you possibly find this funny?' 'Ah!' says Kurt. 'But what the cannibals don't realise is that I'm peeing in their gravy!'

Did you hear about the frustrated cannibal? In the end he threw up his arms.

A rescue boat finds the survivor of a plane crash who's been stranded on a small island. The survivor is surrounded by the skeletons of his fellow travellers. Their bones been picked clean. 'I did what I had to,' says the man. 'You can't blame me for that. I did what I had to in order to survive. I was starving. You'd have done the same.' 'I'm not so sure about that,' says the boat captain. 'There were 20 of you and you only went down this morning.'

CAPITAL PUNISHMENT

> I'M FOR A STRONGER DEATH PENALTY.
>
> GEORGE W. BUSH

> I BELIEVE THERE WOULD BE PEOPLE ALIVE TODAY IF THERE WERE A DEATH PENALTY.
>
> NANCY REAGAN

I traced my family history back to an ancestor in Roman times who was condemned to be crucified. Luckily his lawyer was able to get the charges reduced so they just stuck him up with Blu-Tack.

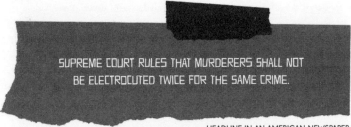

> SUPREME COURT RULES THAT MURDERERS SHALL NOT BE ELECTROCUTED TWICE FOR THE SAME CRIME.
>
> HEADLINE IN AN AMERICAN NEWSPAPER

CAR ACCIDENTS AND BREAKDOWN

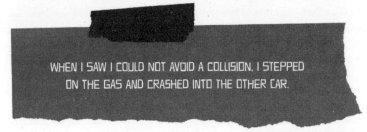

> WHEN I SAW I COULD NOT AVOID A COLLISION, I STEPPED ON THE GAS AND CRASHED INTO THE OTHER CAR.
>
> MOTOR INSURANCE CLAIM

Did you hear about the man who had an ice-cream van drive into the back of his car? He's now suffering from Mr Whippylash.

Two policemen are in a car when they accidentally crash into a tree. They sit for a moment then one says, 'That must be the fastest response time to get to an accident site ever.'

Tom takes his car into the garage. 'There's white smoke coming from under the bonnet,' he tells the mechanic. 'What does it mean?' 'Well,' says the mechanic, 'either your starter's gone or your car has just elected a new Pope.'

> THERE'S NOTHING WRONG WITH THE CAR EXCEPT THAT IT'S ON FIRE.
>
> MURRAY WALKER

> I WAS ON MY WAY TO THE DOCTOR'S WITH REAR-END TROUBLE WHEN MY UNIVERSAL JOINT GAVE WAY, CAUSING ME TO HAVE AN ACCIDENT.
>
> MOTOR INSURANCE CLAIM

Last week Dick got run over by a Smart Car. Apparently the owner is now suing Dick for the damage to his vehicle.

A travelling salesman is driving through the country when his car breaks down. He walks for miles and calls at the first farmhouse he reaches. When the farmer opens the door, the salesman says, 'My car died just up the road. Could I stay here for tonight?' 'OK,' says the farmer, 'but I have a very handsome son and you'll have to promise not to sleep with him.' 'Excuse me,' says the salesman, 'but I think I'm in the wrong joke.'

CARPETS

A woman walks into a shop selling expensive Persian rugs. She sees a beautiful rug and bends over to inspect it. Just as she does so, she lets fly with a reverberant fart. A few moments later, an assistant comes over to ask if she needs any assistance. 'How much does this rug cost?' asks the woman. 'Well, madam,' says the assistant, 'if you farted just looking at it, I dread to think what you'll do when you hear the price!'

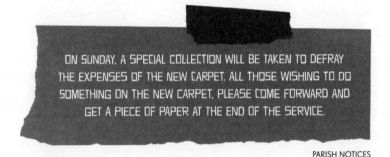

ON SUNDAY, A SPECIAL COLLECTION WILL BE TAKEN TO DEFRAY THE EXPENSES OF THE NEW CARPET. ALL THOSE WISHING TO DO SOMETHING ON THE NEW CARPET, PLEASE COME FORWARD AND GET A PIECE OF PAPER AT THE END OF THE SERVICE.

PARISH NOTICES

CARS

Russell has bought himself a personalised number plate that really sums up his character. His car now has the registration:
'M O R E M O N E Y T H A N S E N SE 1'

Dick converted his car horn. Instead of tooting, it makes a machine-gun noise. Dick says not only is it pretty cool, people get out of his way a lot quicker now.

The only vehicle I ever drove that genuinely proved to be 'all terrain' was the car I borrowed off my dad.

At last a way has been introduced to avoid high British fuel duties. A petrol station has opened in Calais that boasts 20-mile-long petrol hoses which are capable of reaching all the way across the English Channel to cars in Dover. On the downside, it is a bit of a swim to the kiosk to pay.

Phil sells a car to his neighbour, Pete. Only Pete can't pay straight away and asks if he can do it the next week. A week passes. Then another week. And another. Then a whole month. And another month. Then two months. Phil fumes to his wife, 'If I'd have known he was never going to pay up, I'd have charged him three times the price.'

Harry sees a car stop with a couple of men's boots dangling from the back bumper. 'Hello!' says Harry to the driver. 'Have you just been to a wedding?' 'No,' says the driver. 'I'm just going to the hospital to report an accident.'

Barry takes his new sports car out for a spin on the highway. He goes faster and faster and faster, until there's a horrible shrieking sound and the entire engine bursts out of the bonnet in a shower of torn, broken metal. A traffic cop rushes to the scene of the accident and pulls Barry from the wreckage. 'What happened?' he asks. 'I don't know,' groans Barry. 'I was going really fast, but I wanted to go a bit quicker, so I put the gear thingy into "R".' 'What the hell did you do that for?' exclaims the cop. 'Why shouldn't I?' says Barry. 'The "R" stands for 'Race' doesn't it?'

As part of her divorce settlement Martha agreed to sell her husband's sports car and send him the cash. Her gardener now drives to work in a £15 Ferrari.

I was out looking at new cars with my wife, but we couldn't agree. I wanted a sensible, low-mileage runaround, but she wanted something that would go from 0 to 60 in seconds as soon as she put her foot down. In the end I compromised and bought her some new bathroom scales.

Bill often wishes he had enough money to buy a dozen Cadillacs. He can't drive, he just wishes he had that much money.

Larry went to a big car show, but was disappointed to find that the models on display were pretty dowdy and old-fashioned looking. It was only later that he discovered he'd been walking round the show-ground car park.

If a man opens a car door for his wife it means one of two things: either the car is new, or the wife is.

Barry's new car-horn is made in China; it's from a town called 'Hong King'.

A woman is crying by the side of the road. A soldier is passing by and asks her what the problem is. She explains she has locked herself out of her car. The soldier strides over to the vehicle, takes off his trousers and uses them to hold the door handle. A moment later the car unlocks. 'That's amazing,' says the woman, 'how did you do that?' 'No problem,' says the soldier, 'these are my Khakis.'

CARTOON CHARACTERS

Have you noticed how Mickey Mouse and Pluto are more-or-less the same size? Is Mickey a really big mouse, or is Pluto a really small dog?

A TV company has been trying to sell the rights to *The Flintstones* to the Middle East, with limited success. Apparently the people of Dubai don't get it, but those in Abu Dhabi do.

> "ALL CASTLES HAD ONE MAJOR WEAKNESS. THE ENEMY USED TO GET IN THROUGH THE GIFT SHOP."
>
> BILL BAILEY

CASTLES

Q: Why do castles swear so much?
A: They're suffering from turrets.

CATALOGUE SHOPPING

Two idiots are leafing through a mail-order catalogue. 'The ladies in this catalogue are absolutely gorgeous,' says the first idiot. 'Well,' says the other, 'it seems to say underneath that you can send off some money and buy one of them.' The first idiot decides to do just that. A few days later he meets his friend again. 'Did they send you that lovely woman you saw in the catalogue?' asks the friend. 'She hasn't arrived just yet,' says the first idiot, 'but it shouldn't be long now. She sent all her clothes over this morning.'

CATS

George tells Ken that he's just installed a cat flap. 'Does it work OK?' asks Ken. 'Yes,' says George, 'it's made it a whole lot easier to get at my cat's internal organs.'

> QUESTION MASTER: NAME SOMETHING A CAT DOES.
> CONTESTANT: GOES TO THE TOILET.
>
> FAMILY FORTUNES

Both cats and dogs instinctively know the mood of their owner; the difference is, the cats just don't give a damn.

Don't forget – your cat doesn't really love you. In fact, it's even worse than that – if it were bigger it would eat you.

A vicar is walking through the village when he sees a little girl with a cat. 'What a lovely cat,' he says. 'What's his name?' 'Flora Margarine,' says the little girl. 'That's an odd name,' says the vicar. 'Why is he called that?' 'Well,' says the little girl, 'I asked Mummy what cooking fat was and she said Flora Margarine. Then the next day when we got the cat, Daddy said, 'Who brought that cooking fat in here?'

A man is talking to his neighbour. 'My wife hates our cat,' says the man, 'so she told me to put it in a basket and take it miles out into the countryside and lose it.' 'So did you get rid of it?' asks the neighbour. 'Not really,' says the man, 'I had to follow it to find my way back home again.'

A teacher asks the class, 'Who can name four members of the cat family?' 'Please, miss,' says a boy, 'daddy cat, mummy cat and two kittens.'

Brenda has a cat. One day the cat dies so Brenda asks her husband to go out and get another one just like it. Now she's got a pair of matching dead cats.

Q: What's the best way to make a cat go woof?
A: Spray it with petrol and chuck a match at it.

A man knocks on Ted's front door and asks, 'Are you the bloke who's lost a black and white cat?' 'Yes,' says Ted. 'I think I've just seen it,' says the man and leads Ted up the road. 'Whereabouts?' asks Ted. 'Just over here,' says the man as they approach a tree, 'on this poster.'

Nobby's cat used to appear on television in adverts for cat food. But after a couple of years the cat was laid off and never got any work again. So much for them always landing on their feet.

Mavis shows her friend a cat video she's just uploaded to the internet. It shows a cat chasing a ball of wool across the floor. 'My cats are so smart,' says Mavis. 'Just look at her go.' 'Well, I don't see that it's that clever,' says the friend. 'It's only a ball of wool. Anyway, where are the others? I only see one.' 'The others don't perform,' says Mavis. 'Slinky is the camera operator, Jasper does the sound and Mickey is the editor.'

Little Johnny tells his mum about a dead cat he found in the street. 'Are you sure it was dead, Johnny? It might have been asleep.' 'No, it was dead, sure enough,' says Johnny. 'I pushed it and poked it and it wasn't moving. I even pissed in its ear.' 'You what?!' yells mum. 'Johnny, that's disgusting!' 'Why all the hullabaloo?' says Johnny. 'I just got down on my knees, leaned in real close to his head and went – "Pssst, you OK?"'

There are two cats. One is called One Two Three and the other is called Un Deux Trois. They both try to cross a river but only one of them makes it. Which one? One Two Three because Un Deux Trois cat sank.

CATTLE

'Knock, knock!' 'Who's there?' 'Cows go.' 'Cows go who?' 'No, cows go moo!' 'Knock knock.' 'Who's there?' 'Interrupting cow.' 'Interrupting co—' 'MOOOOOO!'

Bert is staying with his friend Farmer Giles. Early one morning Bert finds there is no milk in the kitchen and decides to go and help himself from the farmyard. Half an hour later Giles is having his corn flakes. 'This milk tastes funny,' he says. 'It shouldn't do,' says Bert, 'I got it straight from your cow this morning.' 'We don't have a cow,' says Giles, 'We've only got a bull!'

CAUGHT SHORT

Two Scotsmen are walking home along a dark country lane. 'Oh no!' says one of them all of a sudden. 'I've been taken short!' 'No problem,' says his friend. 'Just go behind this bush and do what's necessary.' A couple of minutes later the first Scotsman calls to his friend, 'Have you got any paper with you?' The friend snaps back, 'Och, don't be so mean. Just leave it there.'

CELEBRITIES

They've just announced the housemates for the next series of *Celebrity Big Brother*. They're going to lock Boris Johnson, Geri Halliwell, George Galloway and Jedward together in a house and raise money for charity by seeing which of them is prepared to pay the most to be let out.

A big Hollywood female film star marries a big male Hollywood film star and moves into his house in Beverly Hills. 'This all looks very familiar,' says the woman on walking into the entrance lobby. 'Are you sure we haven't been married before?'

Big Jim is a Texas billionaire who boasts he knows everyone in the world. His friend, Larry, tries to catch him out, but every time he names a celebrity, he can be sure that Big Jim will always be able to phone them up and get to pay them a visit. It seems there's no one he doesn't know, be it movie stars, world leaders, famous scientists, singers, sports stars . . . He knows them all. 'I got one,' says Larry. 'I bet you don't know the Pope.' 'Sure I do,' says Big Jim. 'I'll prove it. I'll fly us over, visit him on Sunday and come out on the balcony to wave to you.' Sure enough, Big Jim and Larry fly to Rome and Big Jim vanishes inside the Vatican. An hour or two later, the Pope and Big Jim come out on the balcony and wave to the crowd. 'Well, I'll be darned,' says Larry. 'Big Jim really does know everybody.' The man standing in front of him turns round and says, 'Well sure, everyone knows Big Jim. I'm just trying to figure out who the guy in the white dress is.'

> "I HAD A WONDERFUL DREAM LAST NIGHT. I DREAMED THAT BRIGITTE BARDOT CAME UP TO ME AND SAID: 'I WILL GRANT YOU THREE WISHES. NOW WHAT ARE THE OTHER TWO?'"
>
> TOMMY COOPER

CHAIN LETTERS

Despite constant warnings I have yet to see an obituary for anyone where the cause of death is given as 'failing to forward a spam email to ten different people as requested'.

CHALLENGES

A guy at the gym with incredible muscle tone kept telling me to try hitting him as hard as I could in the stomach. I don't think he realised I had my car parked so nearby.

CHARISMA

Many people have commented that Vernon is the sort of person who immediately lights up a room. In the end the police convicted him of arson.

Norman thought everyone was being nice to him when they told him that he could light up a room. It turned out it was because he was so fat and they just wanted him to move away from the window.

CHARITY

A charity collector asks a man, 'Would you like to enter a raffle for the Chelsea Pensioners?' 'No thanks,' says the man, 'I'd have nowhere to put them if I won them.'

A man came to Fred's door asking for donations for the new town swimming pool. Fred gave him a glass of water.

The main charity I give to is to help the desperate plight of all the South American fruit farmers to whom the Man from Del Monte said no.

Fred was really pleased. He'd just discovered a place at the local recycling centre where you could get as many used batteries as you want. All completely free of charge.

Quentin thought he was sponsoring a disadvantaged child. He sent off a cheque every few months which covered the child's food, sanitation, education and basic medical requirements and once a year he received a photo of the child and a report on how he was getting on. But then his wife reminded him that this was their actual son who had been away at boarding school for the last seven years.

I get involved in some crazy stunts to help raise money for my kids' school. Last weekend me and the headmaster and a few of the other parents all dressed up in clown costumes and went and held up a sub post office.

A man knocks on Jock McTavish's door and asks for a donation to the local orphanage. Jock disappears inside and comes back a minute later with a couple of orphans.

Gerald knocks on the door of a homeless charity and asks to see someone about a family in terrible need. 'There's six of them,' says Gerald. 'Four children, their mother and their blind grandfather. They're all in terrible health and if they don't get some money to pay the rent they'll be thrown into the streets. I doubt they'd survive the winter. Can you give them something?' 'Well of course we can,' says the charity worker. 'And it was very kind of you to come here on their behalf. Are you related to them?' 'No,' says Gerald. 'I'm their landlord.'

An old lady writes to God begging him to send her £100 to pay her rent. Since the letter obviously isn't going anywhere, it's opened by one of the workers at the sorting office. The worker is touched by the old lady's plight and he and the other postal workers gather together £95 to help the old lady out and send it to her in an envelope. A few days later, the same old lady writes another letter to God. The postal worker opens it and reads: 'Dear Lord. Many thanks for answering my prayers, but, sadly, your kind donation was short by £5. I don't like to think ill of people, but I can only imagine it was those thieving swines at the post office.'

I'm very unfit, so I laughed off the idea of doing a charity marathon. Then I heard it was for disabled children and I thought, 'Hang on. I could win this . . .'

At the end of last night's shift helping out at the Salvation Army soup kitchen, they asked me not to come any more. Just because I'd told the clientele: 'Eat up, gents! Some of us have got homes to go to!'

Harry hosted a charity night for the Bulimia Society but he made a terrible mistake. He realised afterwards that it would have been better to pass the collection bucket round *before* the buffet was served.

A charity worker gets a meeting with the most successful lawyer in the city and says, 'Your income is over five million a year but our research shows that you have never made any contributions to our charity.' 'Oh yes,' says the lawyer, 'but does your research show that my mother is extremely unwell and requires 24-hour care? Does it show that my brother suffered terrible injuries while he was in the army and is now confined to a wheelchair and unable to support his wife and children? And does it show that my sister's husband was killed in a car crash and left her penniless with a mountain of debts?' 'No,' says the charity worker, 'our research did not show that. I'm so sorry.' 'Exactly,' says the lawyer 'so if I've never paid a penny to any of those grovellers I'm certainly not giving any to you.'

The teacher is talking to a group of little children about charity. She tells the children all about Comic Relief workers helping poor people in Africa and asks them if they would give £1,000,000 to help them. 'Yes!' shout all the children. 'OK,' says the teacher. 'Would you give £1,000?' 'Yes,' shout the children. 'OK. What about £100?' asks the teacher. 'Yes!' shout the children. 'OK,' says the teacher. 'How about one pound?' The children all shout 'Yes!' again apart from one little boy. 'Why didn't you say "yes" this time?' asks the teacher. 'Because,' says the little boy, 'I actually have a pound.'

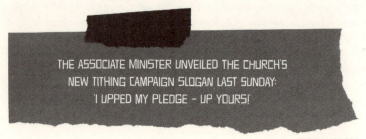

THE ASSOCIATE MINISTER UNVEILED THE CHURCH'S NEW TITHING CAMPAIGN SLOGAN LAST SUNDAY: 'I UPPED MY PLEDGE – UP YOURS!'

PARISH NOTICES

CHASTITY BELTS

A knight is setting off for the crusades. Before he leaves he tells his chief servant, 'You are my oldest, most faithful attendant and I trust you more than anyone else. For this reason I am leaving you the key for my wife's chastity belt. If I do not return, you will have to use it to release her.' 'Thank you, sire,' says the servant. And with that the knight sets off on his quest. A mile from his castle, he hears thundering hooves behind him and sees his trusty old servant racing to catch him. 'Sorry, sire,' says the servant, 'but I think you may have given me the wrong key.'

CHAT-UPS

Gary tells his date, 'It's true you're not the best-looking girl, but don't worry. I can always unscrew the light bulb in the bedroom.'

Gus meets a girl in a bar and asks for her number. 'Do you have a pen?' she asks. 'Yes,' he says. 'Well,' says the girl, 'you'd better get back to it, before the farmer notices you're missing.'

Harry tries to pick up a girl in a bar. 'Where have you been all my life?' he asks. 'Well,' says the woman, 'for most of it, nowhere, because I hadn't been born.'

Brian decides to propose to Marjorie. 'My dear,' says Brian, 'do you think you could be happy with a man like me?' Marjorie looks him up and down. 'I guess,' she says. 'If you weren't around so often.'

A man approaches a woman at a bar. 'Hi, baby,' he says. 'Do you think fate has brought us together?' 'No,' says the woman. 'It was just plain bad luck!'

A man says to a woman, 'Do you know what? I think they should rearrange the alphabet and then I would put U and I together.' 'No,' says the woman. 'I think they got it right the first time with the N and O.'

Gerry the accountant is sitting in a hotel bar when a glamorous young lady comes and sits next to him. 'Hi, feller,' she says, batting her eyelashes. 'Do you fancy a little company?' 'I might,' says Gerry. 'What does it make in a year?'

A man asks a woman, 'Can I buy you a drink?' 'You could,' says the woman. 'But I'd rather have the cash.'

Brian doesn't have much luck with the ladies. The last time he was in a bar and asked a lady what she was having, she said, 'A bilious attack.'

Neville goes up to a woman in a bar and says, 'Hey, beautiful, how did you get so good-looking?' The woman says, 'No idea. Perhaps I got your share too.'

Freddie approaches a gorgeous blonde in a nightclub. He says, 'Hey, I know a way you could burn off a few calories tonight.' The woman says, 'I know one too,' and runs out the door.

Brian goes up to a girl in a bar and asks for a dance. She notices the wedding ring on his finger. 'That's OK,' says Brian. 'Tonight I'm single. I gave the missus the evening off.' 'What was that for?' asks the girl. 'Good behaviour?'

Frank asks the girl at the bar which music station she'd like him to tune into the next morning. She says, 'Hospital radio.'

Nigel, to Belinda: 'Where have you been all my life?' Belinda: 'Where I've always been. In your wildest dreams.'

A man tells a woman, 'You are the reason why men fall in love.' 'Thank you so much,' says the woman. 'And you are the reason why women don't.'

A man tells a woman, 'Your face must turn a few heads!' 'That's a bit like you,' says the woman. 'Except with you, it's stomachs!'

A man sidles up to a woman and says, 'I'm a photographer. I've been looking for a face like yours to work on.' 'That's funny,' says the woman, 'because I'm a plastic surgeon and I've been looking for a face like yours to work on.'

Brenda asks Tom, 'How would you describe me?' 'ABCDEFGHIJK,' says Tom. 'What does that mean?' asks Brenda. 'Adorable, beautiful, cute, delightful, elegant, fashionable, gorgeous, hot,' says Tom. 'Aww!' says Brenda. 'That's lovely. But does the 'IJK' stand for?' 'I'm just kidding,' says Tom.

CHEESE

Q: What sort of cheese is most popular with feminists? **A:** Germaine Gruyere.

Q: What is Mary J. Blige's favourite type of cheese? **A:** R 'n' Brie

Q: What did the cheese say when it saw itself in the mirror? **A:** Halloumi!

Q: Where did the psychopathic Swiss cheese get sent to? **A:** Emmenthal home.

Did you hear about the cheese maker who painted his wife from head to toe in two coats of paint? Apparently he Double Gloucester.

It has been announced that a huge explosion has devastated a cheese factory in France. The whole area is now covered in de Brie.

CHEMISTS

A man walks into a chemist's and asks the assistant, 'Have you got cotton wool balls?' 'What do you think I am?' says the assistant. 'A teddy bear?'

A man walks into a chemist's and says, 'Do you have any shampoo, please?' 'Extra volume?' asks the assistant. 'DO YOU HAVE ANY SHAMPOO, PLEASE?'

Young Josh walks into a chemist's. Two old ladies are serving behind the counter. Josh says, 'I have a problem with my penis. It's ten inches long and six inches round the middle and hardly ever gets soft. I walk around all day with a huge erection. I've got one now. It's kind of embarrassing.' 'So what do you want?' says one of the old ladies. 'I don't know,' says Josh. 'I was hoping you could suggest something.' The two old ladies get in a huddle and discuss what to do. Eventually, one of them turns to Josh and says, 'Our best offer is £1,750 in cash and a half interest in the shop.'

CHEQUES

When Dick got his new cheque book, he went through and signed every slip. 'Why did you do that?' asks Tom. 'Well,' says Dick, 'if it gets lost, I want to make sure no one else can use any of them.'

CHICKENS

A man walks in to the doctor's and says, 'Doctor, please help me. I can't stop thinking I'm a chicken.' 'Oh dear,' says the doctor, 'and how long has this been going on?' 'Ever since I was an egg,' says the man.

A man is speeding along a country lane when he sees a three-legged chicken run past his car. He puts his foot down but can't catch the bird. He follows it as it runs into a farm. 'Can I help you?' says the farmer. 'Yes,' says the man, and explains what he has just seen. 'Ah!' says the farmer. 'That's because we are running a genetic experiment on this farm. Me, my wife and my son all like a drumstick each so that's why we developed the three-legged chicken.' 'Wow!' says the man. 'So what do they taste like?' 'I don't know,' says the farmer. 'So far we've never managed to catch one.'

George and Beryl are shopping in the supermarket when Beryl puts a frozen chicken in their trolley. 'I never thought about it before,' says George. 'But I wonder why chickens are called chickens?' 'Well, they look like chickens,' says Beryl. 'And they sound like chickens and they taste like chickens. So what else are you going to call them?'

Q: Why did the chicken cross the Möbius strip?
A: To get back to the same side.

CHILDBIRTH

Sally books herself into the maternity hospital. 'And will the father be at the birth?' asks the midwife. 'Best not invite him,' says Sally. 'Him and my husband don't get on.'

Jenny's waters break at home and she has to give birth in the front room. Luckily their doctor lives next door and is on hand to help with the delivery. The whole family is gathered round when the baby appears and the doctor lifts him up by his feet and smacks him on the bottom to get him breathing. As the baby starts crying, Jenny's three-year-old daughter shouts, 'Smack him again, he's naughty. He shouldn't have climbed up there in the first place.'

Some authorities have said that it's not a good idea for women to have children after 35. Quite right. You would think 35 children would be enough for anyone.

A woman is in hospital having a baby. The doctor comes and says, 'There is something I must tell you about your baby. It is a hermaphrodite. Your baby has both male and female parts.' 'Oh my God?' says the woman. 'You mean it has both a penis and a brain?'

> "SHE HAD POST-NATAL DEPRESSION. SHE SHOWED ME THE BABY . . . AND THEN I HAD IT AS WELL."
>
> VICTORIA WOOD

A doctor arrives at a remote farm to assist with the birth of the farmer's baby. The farm turns out to have no electricity supply so the doctor has to ask the farmer to hold a lantern while he helps his wife deliver the baby. The farmer stands there with the lantern and a few minutes later the baby is out. The farmer is putting the lantern down when the doctor cries, 'No! Lift the lantern up again! I think there's another one coming!' Sure enough, the farmer's wife gives birth to a second child and the farmer again goes to put down the lantern. 'No! Not yet!' says the doctor. 'I think there's a third one on the way!' A few minutes later the farmer and his wife have triplets and the farmer is just about to put the lantern down when the doctor says, 'Hang on! I think there might be one more . . .' 'Doctor,' says the farmer, looking at his lantern, 'do you think maybe it's the light that's attracting them?'

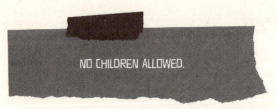

SIGN IN A HOSPITAL MATERNITY WARD IN SOUTH AFRICA

A couple are in hospital after having a baby. The man asks the doctor, 'Do you know how long before we can start having sex again?' 'That depends,' says the doctor. 'Are you on a ward or in a private room?'

A couple are looking at their newborn baby. 'Wow!' says the dad. 'His todger is massive!' 'Yes, but never mind,' says the mum, 'at least he has your ears.'

The reverend greets little Jenny at Sunday school. 'Why, hello. I understand that God is sending you a new brother or sister to play with.' 'Yup,' says Jenny. 'And Daddy says He knows where the damn money is coming to pay for it, too.'

Roger offers to bathe the new baby. His wife agrees and leaves him to fill the bath while she gets some dry towels. When she returns, she's horrified to find that the baby is floating in the bath on its back while Roger pulls it through the water by its nose. 'What are you doing?' she says. 'That's no way to bath a baby.' Roger replies, 'It is when the water's this hot.'

Sammy and Sally are celebrating the birth of their third child. They find an old bottle of champagne in a cupboard and Sammy remembers that it was given to them as a housewarming present when they bought their first house. As Sally pours him a glass of bubbly, Sammy reads the message on the card. 'Look after this one, kiddo. This time it's actually yours.'

My wife's a librarian. When our baby was born two weeks overdue she gave it a 70p fine.

Chantelle is expecting a baby. A nurse says to her, 'Would you like a natural childbirth?' 'What?' says Chantelle. 'You mean with no make-up?'

CHILDREN

A man is walking through the town centre with six children following him. A woman asks him, 'Are those children all yours?' 'No,' says the man, 'I work in a condom factory and these are customer complaints.'

My hope for my kids is that when they grow up they will have all the things I couldn't afford. And then once they have them, I'll move in with them.

Steph thinks it's very stressful having two small children. She was sure she had three when she set out for the shops.

Mum asks her daughter, 'So what do you think you'll do when you're as big as me?' 'Go on a diet,' says the little girl.

A couple have four boys. Three of them are great strapping handsome lads, each with a crop of blond hair. The fourth is short, fat, ginger and awkward. On his deathbed, the dad asks his wife, 'Before I die, tell me the honest truth – is our youngest son really my child?' 'Yes,' says wife, 'I swear he is.' With that her husband gives a sigh of relief and dies with a contented look on his face. 'Thank God he didn't ask about the other three,' says the wife.

A little girl has a toy tea set. One day she pours her daddy a 'cup of tea' out of her toy teapot into one of the teacups. 'Mmm! Lovely!' says Dad, drinking down the cup of tea even though it was only filled with water. 'Don't forget,' says Mum, 'she's too small to reach the tap and get any water.' 'So where is she able to reach?' asks Dad. 'The toilet,' says Mum.

Toby knows where he's not wanted. His mum and dad put a sign on his door that read, 'Checkout time is 18!'

INSTRUCTIONS GIVEN ON A BABY BUGGY

A woman gets on a bus followed by seven children. The conductor asks, 'Are these all yours? Or is it a picnic?' 'They're all mine,' says the woman, 'and I'm telling you, it's definitely no picnic.'

Even when your kids have left home, they will still keep coming back regularly. Once they've bought their own washer and tumble dryer, however, you will never see them again.

A little girl comes home from school and tells her mum that the boys keep wanting to see her do cartwheels in front of them. 'Don't do that,' says Mum, 'those boys only want you to get a look at your knickers.' 'I know,' says the little girl, 'that's why I always hide them in my bag before I do them.'

A boy runs in and tells his mum that his little brother has just broken a pane of glass in the greenhouse. 'How did he manage that?' asks Mum. 'Well,' says the boy, 'I threw my cricket bat at him and he ducked.'

A boy runs to his mum crying, 'Come quick! There's a strange man in the other room kissing the au pair girl.' His mum jumps up, looking frightened. 'Ha! Fooled you!' says the little boy. 'It's not a strange man. It's Daddy!'

Little Tommy comes to his dad in the night and asks if he can have another glass of water. 'I've told you to stop waking me up,' says Dad. 'I've had to go and get ten glasses of water for you already.' 'I know,' says Tommy, 'but my bedroom's still on fire.'

> **"WE SPEND THE FIRST 12 MONTHS OF OUR CHILDREN'S LIVES TEACHING THEM TO WALK AND TALK AND THE NEXT 12 TELLING THEM TO SIT DOWN AND SHUT UP."**
>
> PHYLLIS DILLER

A little girl asks her mum, 'Why have some of your hairs gone white?' 'Well,' says her mum, 'every time you upset me by doing something naughty, one of my brown hairs turns white.' 'Wow!' says the little girl. 'What did you do to Grandma?'

A man sees his son pulling the family dog around the garden on its leash. The dog is obviously suffering so the father goes out to tell him not to be so cruel. Once the boy has been told off, the father says, 'Now then, do you want to tell me how sorry you are?' 'It depends,' says the boy. 'Depends on what?' asks the father. The boy says, 'It depends on how much you saw.'

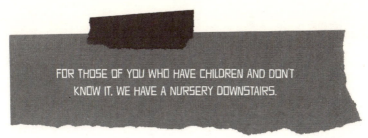

PARISH NOTICES

The parents were concerned by what their teenage offspring knew. And the thing that concerned them even more is how the teenager found out in the first place.

Amy is a cheat,' says little Johnny. 'What's the matter?' asks his friend. 'She said she'd show me hers if I showed her mine, so I did, but when she showed me hers it turned out she doesn't have one at all!'

I spent a fortune on child-proofing our home and they STILL get in.

My mum kept telling me, 'You treat this place like a hotel!' She's going to regret that when she sees the low score I've given her on TripAdvisor for 'rude staff'.

A woman is applying for child benefit. 'How many children do you have?' asks the welfare officer. 'Ten,' says the woman. 'I see,' says the officer. 'And what are their names?' 'Nathan,' says the woman, 'Nathan, Nathan, Nathan, Nathan, Nathan, Nathan, Nathan, Nathan and Nathan.' 'All ten of them have the same name!' says the welfare officer. 'Isn't that confusing?' 'No,' says the woman, 'if I have to call them in for their dinner I just shout "Nathan!" and they all come running.' 'But what if you want to call any of them individually?' asks the officer. 'Then I use their surnames,' says the woman.

CHILDREN'S TELEVISION

Q: How many children's TV presenters does it take to change a light bulb?
A: Six. One to manically stick in the bulb and five to react hysterically to everything the first one does.

CHINESE

Dick is very impressed by the Chinese. In particular he likes the way they have created their entire written language out of tattoo designs.

CHINESE WHISPERS

It has been announced that the man who invented Chinese whispers has died. May he test tin peas.

CHOCOLATE

I've just read a book about how men and women are separated by their interest in different types of chocolate. It's called 'Men Are From Mars, Women Are From Twix'.

A boy is sitting on a bench in the park eating sweets. A man notices him and says, 'You're eating a lot of sweets there. You know they're not good for you. They will make your teeth rotten, they'll make you fat and unhealthy and they'll give you diabetes.' 'Well,' says the boy, 'my granddad lived to be 100.' 'Did he?' says the man. 'So did he reach such a great age by eating bags and bags of sweets every day?' 'No,' says the boy, 'he reached such a great age mostly by minding his own flipping business.'

CHOKING

Jasper and Bernie are having dinner when Jasper goes red in the face and starts coughing and gasping for air. 'My God,' says Bernie. 'Are you choking?' Jasper shakes his head. 'No,' he wheezes. 'I'm serious.'

CHRISTMAS

Barry suffers from the fear of getting stuck in chimneys during December. The medical term for his condition is santaclaustrophobia.

> WE'RE QUITE LUCKY THIS YEAR BECAUSE CHRISTMAS FALLS ON CHRISTMAS DAY.
>
> BOBBY GOULD, FOOTBALL MANAGER

Two men are talking. 'I notice,' says one, 'that this year, Christmas is on a Friday.' 'Oh no,' says the other, 'let's hope it's not going to be on the 13th as well.'

Tom goes to buy an artificial Christmas tree. The man in the shop says, 'Are you planning to put it up yourself.' 'Of course not!' says Tom, 'I'm just going to put in the corner of the living room like normal.'

Q: What weighs eight pounds and isn't going to get plucked this Christmas?
A: Prince's guitar.

It's Christmas Day and Nobby gives his wife a present. She unwraps it and finds a wooden leg. 'What's this meant to be?' she asks. 'Oh,' he says, 'it's just a stocking filler.'

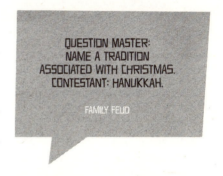

QUESTION MASTER: NAME A TRADITION ASSOCIATED WITH CHRISTMAS. CONTESTANT: HANUKKAH.

FAMILY FEUD

Tom's mother-in-law has come to his house every Christmas for the last seven years. This year his wife is insisting that they have a change and actually let her in.

I got the kids to make all the Christmas presents for the rest of the family this year. I put them in a child labour sweat shop for a few weeks in November.

When Jack was little he told his mother he wanted a puppy for Christmas. His mother said he had to have turkey like everyone else.

A boy climbs on Santa's lap at the grotto and Santa asks him what he wants for Christmas. The boy looks puzzled and asks 'What do you mean – what do I want? Didn't you get my email?'

Edna goes into a post office to buy some stamps for her Christmas cards. The man at the counter says, 'What denomination would you like?' 'I'm not sure,' says Edna. 'But I'd better have 20 Church of England and couple of Catholics.'

CHURCH

A priest has been giving his sermon for over half an hour. A little boy turns and asks his mum, 'If we just give him the money now, will he stop and let us go?'

Several years ago, the Catholic Church required women to wear a head covering in order to enter the sanctuary. One Sunday a lady arrives without her head covering. The priest informs her that she cannot enter without it. A few moments later, the lady reappears, wearing her blouse tied to her head. The shocked priest says, 'Madam, I cannot allow you to enter this holy place without wearing anything on your chest.' 'But, Father,' she says, 'I have a divine right.' 'I know,' says the priest, 'and the left one's not bad either, but you still can't come in this church.'

The vicar is doing his sermon. He turns to the congregation and says, 'Now who can tell me what we must do before we can be forgiven our sins.' 'Sin,' says a voice from the back of the church.

The vicar comes to do the Sunday service in church and finds only a farmer has turned up. 'Do you mind if we cancel the service?' says the vicar. 'Yes, I do,' says the farmer, 'if I go out with my bucket of corn to feed my hens and only one comes out to me, I don't let her go hungry.' The vicar is so inspired by the farmer's words that he performs the full service and even does a 40-minute sermon. Afterwards the vicar tells the farmer how inspired he was by the countryman's words and asks him if he enjoyed the service. 'No, I didn't,' says the farmer. 'It went on for over an hour.' 'But what about your story about going with the bucket of corn and even if only one hen comes out you don't let her go hungry?' 'I know,' says the farmer, 'but if only one hen comes out, I don't give her the whole flipping bucket, do I?'

One day in church a priest makes an impassioned appeal for contributions to the renovation of the crumbling old building. He keeps his eye directly on the richest man in the congregation as he does so and at the end of his appeal, the rich man stands up and says, 'Father, I will contribute £1,000!' As he goes to sit down a lump of plaster falls from the ceiling and hits him on the shoulder. 'Make that £2,000!' says the rich man. Just then another lump of plaster falls on him. 'OK! £5,000!' says the rich man. The priest pauses, looks upwards and says, 'Hit him again, Lord!'

A young vicar, looking for inspiration with his sermons, goes to the local cathedral to see how his bishop tackles the problem. The bishop begins his sermon by saying, 'The best years of my life were spent in the arms of a woman who wasn't my wife!' There is a shocked intake of breath from the congregation but the bishop continues, 'And that woman was my mother!' The congregation bursts into laughter and listens attentively to the rest of the sermon. The next Sunday the young vicar tries the same trick in his own church. 'The best years of my life were spent in the arms of a woman who wasn't my wife!' he tells his congregation, but then realises he can't remember the rest of the joke. 'I can't quite recall who she was now,' he continues, 'but I do know the bishop recommends her very highly.'

Bert is sitting through a very boring church sermon. It's so bad the woman in the pew behind him is snoring her head off. It gets so bad the vicar stops talking and gestures to Bert. 'I say, could you turn round and wake up that lady.' Bert shrugs. 'Why do I have to? You're the one who sent her off.'

A man is coming out of church on Sunday and he tells the priest, 'Do you know what, Father? Your sermon today reminded me of the peace and love of God!' 'That's very kind of you,' says the priest. 'Yes,' says the man, 'it passed all understanding and it endured forever!'

Two builders are working high up on scaffolding, restoring the ceiling of a Catholic church. They look down below and see an old lady in one of the pews mumbling to herself as she goes through her rosary. The builders decide to have a bit of fun with her and call down to her, 'Old woman! This is the voice of Jesus!' The old lady carries on regardless, so they shout down again: 'Old woman! Are you deaf! Can you not hear me! This is Jesus!' At which point the old lady snaps back angrily, 'Will you shut up. I'm trying to talk to your mother!'

DURING THE ABSENCE OF OUR PASTOR, WE ENJOYED THE RARE PRIVILEGE OF HEARING A GOOD SERMON FROM E.J. STUBBS.

PARISH NOTICES

CIGARETTES

My grandmother smoked a pack of cigarettes every day of her adult life and lived till 98. She'd probably still be alive today if she hadn't started mainlining heroin.

Vernon has finally got himself out of the habit of smoking in bed. He bought a waterbed and filled it with petrol.

I'll always remember the day my dad finally quit smoking. We all filed out of the crematorium and agreed it had been a lovely service.

The pro-smoking lobby group is called FOREST. Apparently if you fall over at their annual conference, you don't make a sound.

The pro-smoking group FOREST held their annual conference in my town last year. It was a complete waste of time. They paid for a conference hall and then all had to spend the weekend standing outside the entrance smoking.

A man walks into a corner shop and lights up a cigarette. 'Hoi!' says the shopkeeper. 'Can't you see the sign? It's no smoking in here.' 'Really?' says the man. 'But I notice that you sell cigarettes here. So why aren't I allowed to smoke?' 'We also sell toilet paper,' says the shopkeeper, 'but I don't want you using that in here either.'

An army officer is inspecting the sentries when he sees a smouldering cigarette stub lying at one man's feet. Smoking on duty is not allowed, so the officer picks up the stub and holds it in front of the man's face. 'Is this yours, private?' 'No, sir,' says the private. 'Go on, you have it, you saw it first . . .'

Did you know that smokers have a significantly lower chance of getting Alzheimer's than non-smokers? That's because you die before you get it.

Maurice, trying to give up smoking, discovered that he could control his cravings by nibbling on wooden toothpicks. Three years later, he died of Dutch elm disease.

Frank is a dedicated smoker, so to help him give up the habit, his wife tells him she won't sleep with him till he stops. Now he's gambling that he won't become crippled by RSI before she dies and he can remarry.

Bill and his wife Janice develop a plan to help Bill give up smoking — from now on Bill can only have a cigarette after he and Janice make love. Three weeks later Janice's friend comes to visit and is horrified to find that Janice is now confined to a wheelchair. 'Oh dear,' she says. 'How are you getting on?' 'Not so good,' says Janice. 'He's only down to 20 a day.'

Brian has invented something to help passive smokers — they're nicotine patches you put on other people.

A new law has come in that says you're not allowed to smoke in the car while your kids are in it. I don't agree with this. Yesterday they all got absolutely soaked while I was sitting in the car having a fag.

A survey has revealed that cigarettes are the most significant cause of statistics in the world today.

Scientists have demonstrated that cigarettes can harm your children. That's quite right. You should definitely use an ashtray.

Stan is walking through Liverpool city centre. A little boy comes up to him and asks, 'Will you go in that shop and buy me some ciggies?' 'No!' says Stan. 'But they're not for me. They're for my dad,' says the child. 'Well, why can't he buy his own cigarettes?' asks Stan. 'He would,' says the boy, 'but he's not 18 till May.'

CINEMA

Nineteen young idiots walk into a cinema and go to buy their tickets. 'You've come in a big group,' says the cinema attendant. 'I know,' says one of the idiots. 'But the film says it's only for 18 or over.'

A girl tells her friend she had a terrible time in the cinema the previous night and had to keep changing her seat. 'Oh no,' says her friend, 'did some guy bother you?' 'Eventually, yes,' says the girl.

Two idiots froze to death outside their local cinema. They had been queuing up to see 'Closed for the winter'.

Are orphans allowed to watch PG movies?

In the 1980s the distributors of *Cannibal Holocaust* attempted to publicise their video nasty by writing anonymously to Mary Whitehouse to complain about it. But the stunt backfired horribly because Mary Whitehouse subsequently hunted them down, killed them with a chainsaw and ate their brains in front of their children.

Q: How many young Hollywood actresses does it take to change a light bulb?
A: Only one, but the queue outside the producer's office stretched back half a mile.

Q: How many movie directors does it take to change a light bulb?
A: One, but he'll insist on recording a commentary about how he did it.

> PRESENTER: NAME A FILM STARRING BOB HOSKINS THAT IS ALSO THE NAME OF A FAMOUS PAINTING BY LEONARDO DA VINCI.
> CONTESTANT: WHO FRAMED ROGER RABBIT?
>
> ROCK FM PRESTON

I tried to get into the cinema a dozen times yesterday, but every time I bought a ticket the girl on the door kept tearing it up!

Our cinema usherette had an accident yesterday, she was showing me to my seat when she tripped up, landed on her torch and showed herself up in the circle.

I think there is a new film coming out all about caravans. I saw a trailer last night.

It has been reported that the local cinema was held up and thieves made off with over £500 worth of merchandise – a bucket of popcorn, a bag of pick and mix and an extra-large cola.

CIRCULATION

The teacher asks her class what colour her face would go if she did a handstand. A little boy sticks up his hand. 'Your face would go red,' he says. 'That's right,' says the teacher. 'Because all the blood would run to my head. But why is it that my feet don't go red when I stand here normally?' The boy says, 'Because your feet aren't empty like your head is.'

CIRCUMCISION

When my friend went to the hospital he was treated like a king. The nurses couldn't do enough for him. A few even asked for his autograph. It turned out he was the first man they'd ever had who needed 40 stitches for a circumcision.

I don't have an opinion about circumcision – either way, it's no skin off my nose.

CIRCUS

After a long career working at the circus, the human cannonball decides he is getting a bit old and is going to retire. The circus owner is very upset. 'You can train someone else,' says the cannonball. 'It's not just that,' says the circus owner, 'where are we going to find anyone else of the same calibre?'

The human cannonball at the circus is called in to see his boss. 'I'm sorry,' says the boss, 'but we're going to have to fire you.'

The circus owners had to take their new clown car back to the shop for repairs – one of the doors wasn't falling off.

Q: How many acrobats does it take to change a light bulb?
A: Three. One to change the bulb and two to go, 'Tah-daaaa!'

A circus comes to town and Harry gets a front-row seat. At the start of the show a clown comes to the edge of the ring and points to Harry. 'Sir,' he says. 'Are you the back end of an ass?' 'I certainly am not,' says Harry. 'I see,' says the clown. 'Then are you the front end of an ass?' 'I'm not that either,' says Harry. 'I understand, sir,' says the clown. 'Then it seems, sir, that you are, in fact, no end of an ass!'

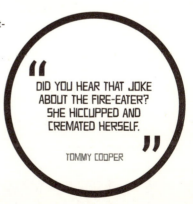

"DID YOU HEAR THAT JOKE ABOUT THE FIRE-EATER? SHE HICCUPPED AND CREMATED HERSELF."

TOMMY COOPER

CLAUSTROPHOBIA

Harry thinks that he suffers from claustrophobia – the fear of closed spaces. For example, if he starts walking to the pub he will develop a terrible fear that it might be closed.

CLEANING LADIES

A group of cleaning ladies have finished their evening's work at a large corporate headquarters and are sitting round the CEO's conference table. One says to the others, 'Do you think the executives here ever pretend they're us?'

CLERGY

A man is driving through the countryside when he sees two priests at the side of the road holding up a sign that says, 'The end is near! Turn back before it's too late!' The man winds down the window and shouts, 'You religious maniacs!' He disappears round the corner and there is a huge crash. One of the priests says to the other, 'Do you think we should have written "Bridge out" on the sign instead?'

In Ireland, a man finds a little boy sitting crying by the side of the road. 'What's happened?' asks the man. 'It's my mother,' says the little boy, 'she died last night.' 'That's terrible,' says the man, 'do you want me to call a priest for you?' 'Not really,' says the boy, 'sex is the last thing on my mind just at the moment.'

A Catholic priest and a rabbi meet up at a charity luncheon. The priest teases the rabbi by holding up a ham sandwich. 'Best ham I ever tasted,' says the priest. 'You really don't know what you're missing.' The rabbi says, 'My wife is a 25-year-old ex-bikini model. You really don't know what *you're* missing.'

A rabbi gets on a train and discovers there are no seats in second class. Seeing some spaces in the first-class coach, he finds a nice window seat and settles down to eat a salt-beef sandwich and read the *Jewish Chronicle*. The conductor comes along and says, 'I'm sorry, but that seat has been reserved for the Archbishop of Canterbury.' The rabbi shrugs, 'So? Who says I'm not him?'

A celebration dinner is held for a priest who has worked in the same parish for 25 years. The local MP is a leading member of the congregation and has agreed to give a speech. Unfortunately, the MP is delayed and the priest has to get up to say a few words until he arrives. 'I thought this was going to be a terrible place when I heard my very first confession here,' says the priest. 'The first young man who entered my confessional told me he had stolen from his parents; he had stolen from his employer; he had broken into his neighbours' homes and taken expensive and precious items; he had an affair with his boss's wife and then with the boss's teenage daughter; and he regularly went round exposing himself to people in the park. However, I soon found out he was the exception and the rest of the congregation were good, decent people.' Just then the MP arrives and begins his speech. 'I'll never forget the day our new priest arrived,' he says, 'in fact, I had the honour of being the first person to go to him for confession . . .'

A clergyman was the victim of an unprovoked attack when a man poured a bottle of toilet cleaner over him. A police spokesman said the assailant has been charged with a bleach of the priest!

A vicar finds a sheet of paper lying on his doormat; it has one word on it – 'Idiot'. The next Sunday, the reverend holds up the paper and says, 'I often get people sending me notes, but this is the first time someone signed it before writing the actual letter.'

Our vicar joined a motorcycle gang. Now they call him 'Rev'.

CLOCKS AND TIMEPIECES

I'm really into clock towers – big time.

Nobby's wife tells him, 'That great big clock in the kitchen nearly killed my mother today. It fell just a few seconds after she'd got up to go to the toilet.' 'Stupid clock,' says Nobby, 'it was always slow.'

A man goes to his doctor and says, 'Doctor, you've got to help me. I was messing around last night and I ended up swallowing my wristwatch. What should I do?' 'Take these pills,' says the doctor, 'they should help you pass the time.'

CLONING

My cousin Brian is working at the forefront of cloning technology. As a young boy he was the first person in the world to clone his imaginary friend.

I can't understand why people are worried about human clones so much. Aren't they the funny people with big red noses you find at circuses?

A world famous scientist has become the first person to successfully clone his own entire genetic structure. He looked very pleased when they showed him on the news. In fact, he was completely beside himself.

I often say to myself, 'Wow! I can't believe I got that cloning machine to work!'

CLOTHES

Tom's wife is furious with him. He keeps pointing out the ladders in her stockings despite the fact she never wears them.

According to a recent survey 90 per cent of women don't like men in pink shirts. But on the other hand, 90 per cent of men in pink shirts aren't that keen on women either.

"
A GENIUS IS A MAN WHO CAN REWRAP A NEW SHIRT AND NOT HAVE ANY PINS LEFT OVER.

DINO LEVI
"

Gary tries for 20 minutes but he just can't manage to get his girlfriend's bra off. In the end he begins to wish he'd never tried it on.

A manufacturer of denim clothing attributed a drop in sales to the fact that an ageing celebrity kept appearing on TV wearing tight jeans. Even worse, the makers of Heinz tinned sausage and meatballs reported a similar fall in profits for the same reason.

Q: What's the best way to make trousers last?
A: Make the jacket first.

A few days ago, Timmy's mum told him he must put a clean pair of socks on each morning. He's beginning to find it difficult to squeeze his shoes on.

Q: What was the name of the first person to wear a shell suit?
A: Humpty Dumpty.

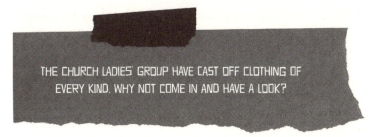

THE CHURCH LADIES' GROUP HAVE CAST OFF CLOTHING OF EVERY KIND. WHY NOT COME IN AND HAVE A LOOK?

SIGN ON THE DOOR OF A CHURCH HALL

A man goes into a tailor's shop and asks to try on a shirt. The tailor tells him that the best shirts they have are made from a unique unshrinkable fabric that's guaranteed to hold its shape, no matter what. The man likes the shirt he's given to try on, but finds it a little too big under the arms. 'Don't worry,' says the tailor, 'it'll shrink.'

Gloria goes into a store to order some underwear with a message written across the front. 'I'd like it to say, "If you can read this, you're too close".' says Gloria. 'And what sort of lettering would you like that in?' asks the store clerk. Gloria says, 'Braille.'

My wife spends a fortune on clothes and always makes up stories about why she needs more. I've started calling her 'Narnia' – the lying witch with a wardrobe.

ORDER YOUR SUMMER SUIT. BECAUSE IS BIG RUSH WE WILL EXECUTE CUSTOMERS IN STRICT ROTATION.

SIGN IN WINDOW OF A TAILOR'S SHOP IN GREECE

Nancy goes to buy a new sweater and finds one she likes that's priced at £400. 'Why is this so expensive?' she asks. The sales assistant says, 'It's made from virgin lamb's wool.' 'Have you got anything cheaper?' Nancy replies. 'I don't really care if the lambs are sluts or not.'

I ordered a leopard-skin coat off the internet. It was spotless, so I had to send it back.

Gladys found that the only way to make her husband pay any attention to her was to dress in a tight black jump-suit covered in white polka dots. It wasn't very flattering, but it did make her look just like a giant TV remote.

Freddie won the store's Salesman of the Month award last week. A widow came into the menswear department to buy a funeral suit for her dead husband and he managed to sell her an extra pair of trousers.

Great-aunt Edna went into a clothes store and asked if she could try a dress on in the window; the manager declined, he said it would be bad for business.

Maurice was a tailor for 30 years. He never really liked it though, he always said it was a so-so occupation.

Two small girls are discussing their new teacher. 'I wonder how old she is?' says one. The other says, 'We ought to try and look in her underwear. It'll say her age on the label.' 'Will it?' says the first girl. 'Yes,' says the other. 'If you look in mine it says, "Seven to Eight Years".'

A man is up in court for repeatedly breaking into a dress shop. 'You realise,' says the judge, 'you might not have been arrested if you hadn't kept going back and breaking into the same shop three nights in a row.' 'Yes, your honour,' says the man, 'but my wife kept making me take the dress back to exchange it.'

Bert is called in by his manager at work. The manager wants to talk to him about the official dress code. 'You can't come into work dressed in your pyjamas,' says the manager. 'What do you mean?' says Bert. 'There's lots of people wandering round in their pyjamas here.' 'That's because it's a hospital,' says the manager, 'and they are the flipping patients!'

Police are searching for a thief who has been stealing people's clothes off their washing lines in order of size. They say the criminal is still at large.

Norma and her husband Nobby are out shopping. Norma tries on a new dress and asks Nobby, 'Does this make my bum look big?' 'No, love,' says Nobby, 'it's all the cake you keep eating does that.'

I read in a survey that 75 per cent of women buy clothes but never wear them. They sound like my kind of women.

COFFEE

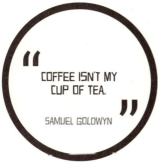

"COFFEE ISN'T MY CUP OF TEA."
SAMUEL GOLDWYN

George has found a way to combine the power of Viagra with the smooth taste of Colombian coffee. He calls it the Viagralatte – one cup and you're up all night.

COLOUR BLINDNESS

I'm colour blind. Last week I got into a fight and got beaten grey and grey.

A man goes to the optician to have his eyes tested. At the end of the sight test the optician tells him, 'It looks very much as though you may have colour blindness.' 'My goodness!' says the man. 'That's come as a bit of a bolt out of the green!'

COLOURFUL YET MYSTERIOUS OBJECTS

▶ **Q:** What's blue and not heavy?
A: Light blue.

▶ **Q:** What's black and white and goes round and round?
A: A penguin in a revolving door.

▶ **Q:** What's black and white and red all over?
A: A penguin with sunburn.

▶ **Q:** What's white, cold and goes upwards?
A: A snowflake with no sense of direction.

▶ **Q:** What's yellow and smells of wee?
A: The 'To Let' sign outside my dyslexic friend's house.

▶ **Q:** What's blue and surrounded by water?
A: Navy blue.

▶ **Q:** What's large, brown, gives off steam and comes out of cows backwards?
A: The Isle of Wight ferry.

▶ **Q:** What's black and white and sticks two fingers up at the Pope?
A: A nun who's just won the lottery.

▶ **Q:** What's blue and smells like red paint?
A: Blue paint.

▶ **Q:** What's green and misty?
A: Kermit the fog.

▶ **Q:** What's green and white and bounces?
A: A spring onion.

▶ **Q:** What's grey and comes in pints?
   A: An elephant.

▶ **Q:** What's orange and sounds like a parrot?
   A: A carrot.

▶ **Q:** What's white and sits by your bed taking the p*ss out of you?
   A: Your dialysis machine.

▶ **Q:** What's big, grey and doesn't matter?
   A: An irrelephant.

▶ **Q:** What's pink and hard first thing every morning?
   A: The *Financial Times* crossword.

COMMON SENSE

> " COMMON SENSE IS THE COLLECTION OF PREJUDICES ACQUIRED BY AGE 18. "
> — ALBERT EINSTEIN

> YOU SEEM TO BE A MAN WHO LIKES TO KEEP HIS FEET ON THE GROUND. YOU SAIL A LOT.
> — ALAN TITCHMARSH

> " HORSE SENSE IS THE GOOD JUDGEMENT THAT PREVENTS HORSES FROM BETTING ON PEOPLE. "
> — W.C. FIELDS

COMMUNICATION

The ability to talk to animals, to communicate with the dead and the ability to speak to alien space creatures from different dimensions – I can't believe the functions on my new iPhone.

COMPETITION

> "YOU WOULDN'T HAVE WON IF WE HAD BEATEN YOU."
> — YOGI BERRA

Gary and Barry challenge each other to a race up a hill. 'If I get up to the top first,' says Gary, 'I'm going to write my name on it!' 'And if I get to the top first,' says Barry, 'I'll rub it out.'

Dick decides to enter a local Iron Man Challenge competition. On the night of the contest he turns up with a basket of wrinkled shirts and an ironing board.

COMPLAINING

God's got a mean streak: the more you complain about life, the longer he seems to make it.

I hate it when people complain about everything. I have a friend who lost his vocal cords and his legs in an accident. But you don't find him making a song and dance about it.

COMPOST

The shops are all selling bags of what they call 'multi-purpose compost'. Besides using it to grow plants in, exactly what are all the other purposes you can use 'multi-purpose' compost for?

COMPUTERS

Last year I got the official Microsoft advent calendar. I wasn't able to open windows 8 or 10.

Jerry rings his computer's technical support line. 'I'm trying to input my password, but all I see is a row of asterisks,' he says. 'That's to preserve your privacy,' says the tech support. 'They keep your password secret in case anyone else is looking.' 'Well, it's not working properly,' says Jerry. 'I'm all by myself and the things still keep coming up.'

CONCISION

I would really like someone to tell me what 'concise' means? Please be short, brief and to the point.

Fred is a man of very few words; when he was asked to describe himself he said, 'Concise.'

CONCRETE

Norman had just laid a new concrete path outside his house. Just then his grandchildren came round the corner and ran straight across it. Norman stood there cursing and shouting at them. 'Don't shout at them like that,' said his wife, 'I thought you liked the grandchildren.' 'I do,' said Norman, 'but I like them more in the abstract. Not in the concrete.'

CONFERENCES

People by themselves can do nothing, but get them in a conference and they'll decide they can do nothing as a group.

CONFESSION

After years of not going to church, a man decides to go to confession. He walks in and finds a fully equipped bar with Guinness on tap and a range of cigars and chocolates to choose from. Just then a priest comes in. 'Father, forgive me,' says the man, 'it's many years since my last confession. But I must say the confessional box is much more inviting than I remember it.' 'You've come in through the wrong door,' says the priest. 'This is my side.'

A boy goes to confession and the priest tells him that for his penance he must say three Hail Marys. 'I don't think I can do that,' says the boy. 'I only know one.'

The new priest at my church has some modern ideas. He's set up two confessionals: one for the normal number of sins and the other as an express lane for those with eight sins or fewer.

A young priest starts in a new parish. After his first few attempts at hearing confession he asks an older fellow priest for advice. 'Well,' says the older priest, 'when you hear confession you need to give the impression that you're listening carefully and seriously. So let them see you cross your arms, stroke your chin and look deep in thought. It's also helpful if you use phrases like "Go on" and "I understand" to encourage the parishioners to speak from the heart. And finally, try to avoid what you were doing in the confessional just now. People really don't like it if you keep slapping your knee, giggling and saying, "Wow! That's cool! So what happened next?"'

Four old ladies meet for coffee. As they are talking, one old lady says, 'There's something I must confess. Although I have never stolen from any of you, I'm a terrible kleptomaniac.' A second old lady says, 'I have to confess as well. Although I have never had relations with any of your husbands, I am a hopeless nymphomaniac and have had sex with almost all the other men in the neighbourhood.' The third old lady says, 'I have to confess that although none of you are my type, I am in fact a rampant lesbian.' The fourth old lady gets up and says, 'I'd better confess as well. I am an incurable gossip. I hope you won't mind if I make a quick few phone calls.'

CONGESTION

I was crawling along on the motorway yesterday. I only went half a mile in two hours. The drivers behind me all looked furious when they managed to overtake.

A lorry carrying a consignment of Vicks Nasal Spray has shed its load on the motorway. Police have warned motorists to expect no congestion for up to eight hours.

CONSCIENCE

I have trained my conscience really well. It never stops me from doing anything but it does at least prevent me from enjoying any of it.

CONSTIPATION

An anthropologist is travelling through South America studying folk remedies. An old man in a village tells him that the leaves of a particular fern are used to cure any sort of constipation. 'I don't believe that,' says the anthropologist. 'It's true,' says the old man, 'with fronds like these, who needs enemas?'

Have you heard about the new Hollywood blockbuster called *Constipation*? No one's sure exactly when it's coming out.

I've got my first meeting with Constipation Anonymous this evening but unfortunately there's no way I can go.

A builder goes to his doctor complaining of terrible constipation. He's bunged-up something terrible. The doctor examines him and says, 'I see you work on a building site.' 'I do,' says the builder, 'how did you know that?' The doctor says, 'Because I've come across this sort of thing before. The next time you use the porta-loo at work, don't wipe yourself with an old concrete sack.'

I told my doctor that I hadn't been to the toilet for over a week. I'd sit on the pan for hours, but nothing ever came out. He asked me if I took anything to help, I said, 'Only a book.'

CONSTRUCTION

Two workmen are hammering the floorboards down in a house. One of the workmen keeps picking up nails and throwing them away. 'What are you doing?' asks the other. 'These nails are no good,' says the first, 'they're all pointing upwards and we need nails that point downwards.' 'Yes, but there's no need to waste them,' says the other, 'put them aside and we'll use them for the ceiling!'

Notice printed in a newspaper: 'A new swimming pool is rapidly taking shape since the contractors have thrown in the bulk of their workers.'

CONSULTANTS

Q: How many management consultants does it take to change a light bulb?
A: Three. One to change the bulb and two to write the documentation about how to change it next time.

Q: How many management consultants does it take to change a light bulb?
A: Ten. One to change the bulb and nine to write a report on how much better they could have done it.

Q: How many management consultants does it take to change a light bulb?
A: Unknown. They still haven't finished analysing the feasibility study and Environmental Impact Report.

A good consultant should have two qualities: silver hair and piles. The hair makes you look wise; the piles make you look concerned.

When they bring consultants into my office, they are revered and paid more than anyone working in the company. Clearly management believe them to have great credibility and wisdom exhibited by the fact that they're not so stupid as to get a job at our company.

CONTRACEPTION

According to a study, these days 56 per cent of women carry condoms. The remaining 44 per cent carry babies.

Percy was wearing a condom when the husband of the woman he was with walked in on them and shot him. So it's not true what they say. Condoms do not guarantee safe sex.

A woman has ten kids and doesn't want any more. She goes to the doctor to ask about contraceptives and the doctor wheels out a massive pill that is about 7 feet across. 'How do you expect me to swallow that?' asks the woman. 'You don't swallow it,' says the doctor, 'you just roll it against the bedroom door to keep your husband out.'

An old grandmother goes to the doctor and asks to go on the pill. 'Why do you want that?' asks the doctor. 'Because,' says the granny, 'I don't want to have any more grandchildren.'

A Scottish soldier wearing his kilt and full uniform marches into a chemist's, opens his sporran and carefully takes out a folded cloth. He unwraps it and inside is a condom with a number of patches on it. 'How much would it be to repair this?' asks the soldier. The chemist examines it and says, 'Sixpence.' 'And how much for a new one?' asks the soldier. 'Ten pence,' says the chemist. The soldier wraps up his condom and marches out again. Half an hour later he is back. 'The regiment has taken a vote,' he says, 'we'll have a new one.'

Freddie is in bed with his married girlfriend when they hear her husband's car pull into the drive. Freddie panics and jumps out of the window stark naked; the husband catches sight of him as he runs down the street. The husband chases him and corners him in an alley. 'What were you doing outside my house?' snarls the husband. 'Nothing,' says Freddie. 'Just out for a run.' 'So you go running stark naked?' asks the husband. Freddie replies, 'Sure. It cools me down.' 'And you go running without any shoes on?' asks the husband. Freddie replies, 'Certainly. It toughens the feet.' 'And tell me,' says the husband. 'Do you always go running wearing a condom?' 'Well, not always,' says Freddie. 'Normally only when it's raining.'

Harold walks into a chemist's and goes up to the counter where a fusty old woman is serving. 'Miss,' he says. 'I'd like six condoms, please.' The woman glares at him. 'Don't you "miss" me.' 'Well, OK,' says George. 'If you insist. Make that seven.'

A teenager walks into a chemist's and asks for a packet of condoms. 'I'd better take the strongest you have,' he says. 'The girl I'm going out with is hot stuff. I'm going to need some rubber with staying power, if you get my drift. Actually give me two packs, she's super-horny.' The chemist has heard it all before. He gives the teenager two packets of extra-durable condoms and the boy pays and leaves. That evening the boy visits his girlfriend's house and gets invited to dinner by the mother of the house. The three of them have just sat down at the table when they hear the father come in from work. The teenager immediately ducks his head and starts saying grace. He goes on and on until the girl eventually bends over and whispers to him. 'Hey, you never let on you were so religious.' 'Yeah,' says the teenager. 'And you never said your dad worked in a chemist's.'

One day Kevin's dad sits him down and tells him, 'Son, I've got something that I want you to look at which will show you why you should always wear a condom.' 'Dad,' says Kevin, 'why are you holding a load of photographs of me.'

CONVERSATION

"IT WAS IMPOSSIBLE TO GET A CONVERSATION GOING; EVERYBODY WAS TALKING TOO MUCH."

YOGI BERRA

After 'Alcoholics Anonymous' and 'Gamblers Anonymous', they've established a new self-help group for people who can't stop talking. It's called 'On and On and On Anonymous'.

COOKING

Q: What is round, yellow and hovers in the air in the kitchen?
A: An unidentified flying omelette.

A man is unimpressed by the dinner his wife has made for him. 'This is like eating horse manure,' he says. 'How dare you!' says his wife, 'that's completely untrue!' 'I suppose so,' says the man. 'Horse manure is usually warm.'

Norma wakes up her husband Nobby in the night and says, 'I've just been downstairs and I saw an intruder in the kitchen eating my leftover shepherd's pie.' Nobby reaches for the phone. 'Are you calling for the police?' she asks. 'No,' says Nobby. 'An ambulance.'

Great-aunt Jemima visits her nephew for a family dinner. She asks her great-niece, Joy, what they're having to eat. 'Goat,' says Joy. 'Really?' says Jemima. 'That's very unusual. Are you sure that's right?' Joy shrugs. 'It's what I heard, Dad said that tonight was as good as any other to have the old goat for a meal.'

> AND I HOPE THAT ALL YOUR DOUGHNUTS TURN OUT LIKE FANNY'S.
>
> FRANK BOUGH (FOLLOWING A COOKERY DEMONSTRATION BY FANNY CRADDOCK)

Q: What's lumpy and yellow and keeps going round in circles?
A: A long-playing omelette.

Definition of 'chef' – another name for a cook who knows how to swear in French.

CORROSION

Quentin has invented a new substance that is so corrosive that it will literally go through anything it comes into contact with. Now he has to invent something to store it in.

CORRUPTION

I would like to see less corruption. And if I can't have that, I'd like a chance to be involved.

COSMETIC SURGERY

Many people that have plastic surgery end up being disappointed by the results. You can't tell though because they always look pleasantly surprised.

It's the annual convention for plastic surgeons. The organiser gets up to make the opening speech and says, 'Nice to see so many new faces this year . . .'

I got my daughter a facelift when she was 10. Currently she's got her eyes and nose balanced on the top of her head. It looks a bit odd at the moment but they say that she'll eventually grow into it.

> " I LENT A FRIEND OF MINE $10,000 FOR PLASTIC SURGERY. AND NOW I DON'T KNOW WHAT HE LOOKS LIKE. "
>
> — EMO PHILIPS

After my recent cosmetic surgical procedure I've been trying to find a firm that could help me recycle my discarded liposuction and re-use it as cavity wall insulation.

A woman comes home with her head completely covered in thick white paint and a smiley face drawn on the face with a marker pen. Her husband looks at her and says, 'Are you sure that cosmetic surgeon is properly qualified?'

Glenys went to have a facelift last week but she wasn't very happy with the results. After an hour on the operating table they found another one exactly like it underneath.

Jane had her face lifted, her tummy tucked and her backside hoisted. Now she floats a foot above the ground.

COUNTRY AND WESTERN SONG TITLES

- Get the Hammer Mama, There's a Fly on Papa's Head

- I Went Back to My Fourth Wife for the Third Time and Gave Her a Second Chance to Make a First-Class Fool Out of Me

- I'd Rather Pass a Kidney Stone than Another Night with You

- If the Phone Don't Ring, Baby, You'll Know It's Me

- If You Leave Me Can I Come Too?

- If You See Me Getting Smaller It's Cos I'm Leaving You

- I've Got Hair Oil on My Ears and My Glasses Are Slipping Down, but Baby I Can See Through You

- When You Wrapped My Lunch in a Roadmap I Knew You Meant Goodbye

- Who's Gonna Take the Garbage Out When I'm Dead and Gone?

- You Changed Your Name from Brown to Jones and Mine from Brown to Blue

- You're the Reason Our Kids Are So Ugly

- I Bought the Shoes that Just Walked Out on Me

- I Gave Her My Heart and a Diamond and She Clubbed Me with a Spade

- I Gave Her the Ring and She Gave Me the Finger

COURT

A woman is up in court and a policeman is giving evidence against her. 'I met her,' he tells the judge, 'when I was in plain clothes and she tried to pass off these fake £50 notes.' 'Counterfeit?' asks the judge. 'Yes I did,' says the policeman, checking his notes, 'and she had two.'

A judge is sentencing an old offender. 'I trust,' says the judge, 'that this is the last time that I will see you up before me.' 'Why?' asks the old offender, 'are you retiring?'

Calvin's appeal against his conviction for homicide was broadcast live on prime-time network television across the USA. His lawyer didn't manage to get him released from prison. But on the plus side he did manage to get him released on DVD.

A man is taken to court and, being shy, asks if he can present his evidence as written testimony. The judge says, 'I'm sorry, sir, but all your responses to the questions put to you by this court must be oral. Do you understand?' The man nods and says, 'Oral.'

The judge says to the defendant in the dock, 'How do you plead? Guilty or not guilty?' 'I'm not telling you that,' says the defendant. 'That's what you're paid to work out.'

Vince is up in court charged with shooting his wife. The judge says to him, 'Do you really expect us to believe that you shot your wife by accident?' 'Yes! She's only got herself to blame,' says Vince, 'she walked straight in front of her mother just as I was pulling the trigger.'

Phil is taken to court for gross indecency. The charge is that on the 2nd April he skateboarded nude down the town high street with a firework up his backside as he juggled a collection of 'adult toys'. 'Do you admit these charges?' asks the judge. 'I'm not sure,' says Phil. 'What was the date again?'

Bert goes to defend himself in court and swears to tell the truth, the whole truth and nothing but the truth. When the judge asks him if he'd like to present his position, he says, 'Given those restrictions, I'd better keep my mouth shut.'

A man goes into the witness box and the judge gives him a warning. 'Are you aware of the consequences of not being absolutely truthful in this courtroom?' 'Yes,' says the man. 'I stand a much better chance of winning.'

The definition of a jury: 12 people randomly assigned to decide which client has been able to afford the better lawyer.

Big Tony is defending himself in court. The jury files in and sits down and the judge asks if he would like to challenge any of its members. Tony looks them over, cracks his knuckles and says, 'Yeah. Let's start with the old lady in the back row.'

COWBOYS

A man goes to the doctor and says, 'Doctor, I can't stop thinking I'm a cowboy.' 'How long has this been going on?' asks the doctor. 'About a yeeee-haaah!' says the man.

Butch rides into a saloon on his horse and orders a whisky. 'You want water with that?' asks the barkeep. 'No,' says Butch. 'It's for the horse and he likes it straight.' 'Straight it is,' says the barkeep. 'Having anything for yourself?' 'Better not,' says Butch. 'I'm driving.'

Jeb walks into a Western outfitters and asks to buy a single spur. 'Single?' says the shopkeeper. 'We normally sell them in pairs.' 'No reason for it,' says Jeb. 'If one half of ma horse gits going the other half follows right along.'

A cowboy gets talking to a gunslinger in a saloon. The cowboy says, 'So, you got any tips on improving my draw?' 'Sure,' says the gunslinger. 'Tie your holster to your leg. That'll let you snap off a shot real easy.' So the cowboy does what he's told, aims a shot at the piano player and blows his hat off. 'That's great,' says the cowboy. 'Got any other tips?' 'Sure,' says the gunslinger. 'File the sight off your gun. That'll make a draw real easy.' The cowboy runs over to the blacksmith to get the job done and when he comes back he draws on the piano player again. This time he shoots off the man's bowtie.' 'Fantastic,' says the cowboy. 'Give me another tip.' 'Well,' says the gunslinger. 'If I were you, I'd cover that gun with as much butter as you can find.' 'Really,' says the cowboy. 'How will that help my draw?' 'It won't,' says the gunslinger. 'But you'll appreciate it when Buffalo Bill stops playing that piano and jams your gun up your ass.'

Jessie is riding shotgun on a stagecoach. A Red Indian starts chasing them and Jessie tells the driver he's about to take a shot at their pursuer. 'How far away is he?' asks the driver. 'He's about the size of my thumb,' says Jessie. The driver says, 'Wait till he gets closer.' They wait a while, then Jessie says, 'He's about the size of my hand. Shall I shoot him now?' The driver says, 'No. Wait till he gets closer.' They wait a while, then Jessie says, 'He's catching up. He's the size of my head. Can I shoot him now?' The driver says, 'Wait till he gets closer.' A little while later, Jessie says, 'He's much closer now. He's the size of my leg.' 'Then shoot him,' says the driver, 'that's close enough.' 'Dang it!' says Jessie. 'How can I shoot him now?' He holds up his thumb. 'I've known him since he was this big . . .'

A Wild West rancher hates Apaches so much that he offers a $200 bounty on any Apache head that's brought to him. A pair of cowboys hear about the rich pickings to be had and go out on a hunt. They soon spy an Apache brave and chase him into a ravine. The ravine quickly comes to a dead-end and the brave is cornered. The two cowboys start to aim their rifles at him, when one taps the other on the shoulder. 'Look at that,' he says. The cowboy points to the canyon rim and the second cowboy realises that they're surrounded by a huge Apache war-party of around 5,000 men. 'This is fantastic!' he squeals. 'We're going to make so much money!'

In the interests of accuracy they ought to rename the Lone Ranger as the 'Lone Apart from Tonto and Silver' Ranger.

CREATION

A soldier, a surgeon and a politician are talking. The surgeon says that his is the world's oldest profession. 'How do you work that out?' ask the others. 'Because,' says the surgeon, 'in the Garden of Eden, Eve was made from one of Adam's ribs. Obviously only a surgeon could have done something like that.' 'No,' says the soldier, 'before Adam and Eve the world existed and when the world was created, order had to be created out of chaos. Obviously only a soldier could have managed that.' 'Ah,' says the politician, 'but who do you think created the chaos that needed sorting out?'

Scientists have revealed that they have traced the universe back to the moment just after the Big Bang and discovered there was still a sale going on at DFS even then.

CREATIVE WRITING

Reggie reads about a study that says the most popular subjects in best-selling fiction are: Religion, Royalty, Sex and Mystery. He starts his next book with the line: 'Jesus, I'm pregnant,' said the Princess. 'I wonder who did it?'

CREMATION

When I'm lying on my deathbed, the last thing I'm going to eat is an enormous bag of popcorn kernels. My cremation will be incredible!

CRICKET

I remember the days when all the boys in our street would go out and play cricket with an old bat and ball. I'd come home black and blue. They used to use me as the wicket.

Harry made the mistake of having a large vindaloo while watching the Test match. Pretty soon the runs were flowing.

> THE BOWLER'S HOLDING, THE BATSMAN'S WILLEY.
>
> BRIAN JOHNSTON (COMMENTING ON A CRICKET MATCH INVOLVING MICHAEL HOLDING OF THE WEST INDIES AND ENGLAND'S PETER WILLEY)

> WELCOME TO WORCESTER, WHERE BARRY RICHARDS HAS JUST HIT ONE OF D'OLIVEIRA'S BALLS CLEAN OUT OF THE GROUND.
>
> BRIAN JOHNSTON

CRIME

Q: Where is the best place to hide a body?
A: On page three of Google's search results.

It has been announced that the police are trying to apprehend the serial killer who has murdered several people using knitting needles. The police believe he is following some kind of pattern.

Police are uncertain exactly how many victims have fallen foul of the serial killer dubbed the Sandpaper Murderer but say he may have killed 20 people roughly.

Bob tells Harry, 'I've spent the past five years trying to find my wife's killer.' 'That's terrible,' says Harry. 'It's no good,' says Bob, 'I can't get anyone to do it.'

Someone climbed into Norman's back garden and stole a pair of his wife's knickers from the washing line. He says he's not bothered about the knickers but he wouldn't mind getting the 15 pegs back.

A police officer is called out to a domestic disturbance. He gets to the house and finds that a wife has shot her husband for walking across her kitchen floor just after she had mopped it. He calls up his sergeant at the police station and reports what has happened. 'OK,' says the sergeant at the station, 'so have you gone in and placed the woman under arrest?' 'No, sir,' says the policeman. 'Why not?' asks the sergeant. 'Firstly, she is still in possession of a loaded weapon,' says the policeman, 'and secondly, the kitchen floor is still wet.'

The police get a call and hear a terrified voice whispering, 'Help! Come quick! A burglar has broken into old Mrs Jones's house and she's managed to trap him in her bedroom.' 'OK,' says the policeman, 'but could I ask, who is this calling?' 'It's the burglar,' says the voice.

Dick is invited to be in an identity parade at the police station after a woman reports that a man exposed himself to her in the park. Dick lines up with the other men and when the women walks in, he shouts out, 'That's the one, officer. I'd recognise her anywhere!'

An old man is going to bed when he remembers he has left the lights on in his garden shed. He goes down and hears the voices of two intruders coming from the shed. He calls the police and tells them that someone has broken into his shed. The police say there are no officers but they will send one when there is. The old man puts the phone down, waits a couple of minutes then phones back again and says, 'Don't worry about sending an officer. I just went in and shot the intruders and now my dog is eating their bodies!' A few seconds later three police cars screech up outside and ten armed policemen go racing round to the shed where they find the intruders and arrest them. 'I thought you said you had shot the intruders and your dog was eating them,' says one of the policemen. 'Yes,' says the old man, 'and I thought you said there weren't any officers available.'

The police discover a dead body. The forensic team examine it and find it is completely covered in mashed chickpeas, oil and garlic. 'This confirms my worst suspicion,' says the police inspector. 'This man has been a victim of hummuside.'

In a dawn raid this morning the police arrested Adobe Acrobat. Apparently they discovered evidence that he was a pdf file.

> "I'VE HAD DEATH THREATS. WELL, OK, A PETITION."
>
> JACK DEE

There have been a lot of burned-out cars dumped in the area where I live. However, there is a simple explanation why this keeps happening. I'm a car thief and my wife is an arsonist.

Nobby is a convict but has been classified as non-violent and not dangerous to the public. As a result he has been put on a trial scheme. He has to return to his detention centre each evening but during the day he gets to go out and do his normal full-time job. Which is being a car thief.

A woman phones up the police and says, 'I've just been molested by an idiot.' 'How do you know he was an idiot?' asks the policeman. 'I had to give him directions,' says the woman.

A sergeant is sitting at the incident desk of a police station when an old lady comes up to him and tells him she's been molested. 'I'm so sorry,' says the sergeant, 'but we'll catch the man who did it, don't you worry. Now, where did it happen?' 'In the woods behind the church,' says the old lady. 'At what time?' says the sergeant. 'At around 4pm on this very date,' says the old lady. 'What?' says the sergeant. 'That can't be right. It's barely past noon.' 'It happened 40 years ago,' explains the old lady. 'So why tell me now?' asks the sergeant. The old lady says, 'Once in a while I like to reminisce.'

Two prison inmates get chatting in the exercise yard. One says, 'Before they locked me up, I lived the life of Riley. I bought fast cars, a fancy house and a yacht. I had scores of women and ate at expensive restaurants every night of the week.' 'So what happened?' asks the second guy. The first guy says, 'Riley found out his credit cards were missing.'

Lady Agatha often goes shoplifting for a thrill, but one day a store manager catches her slipping a diamond bracelet into her handbag. 'Please don't tell the police,' says her Ladyship. I'll make you an offer. I'll buy the bracelet if you promise to leave it at that.' 'Very well,' says the store manager. 'That particular bracelet is £7,000.' 'Good grief,' says her Ladyship. '£7,000 for that thing? Haven't you got anything cheaper?'

Bert has his wallet stolen and reports it at the police station. 'I know who must have done it,' he says. 'There were these two women down at the park. I was sitting on a bench when they said the aftershave I was wearing was driving them wild. They had their hands all over me, fondling and groping. It must have been them that done it.' 'I see,' says the police sergeant. 'And when did this happen exactly?' Bert says, 'Once yesterday afternoon and twice this morning.'

Jarvis is a world-class cat burglar, but don't worry if you find him outside your house staring at your windows, it's the neighbours who should be worried – he's cross-eyed.

Everyone thought that Barry's career as a pickpocket was over when he lost all but one finger in an accident; instead he adapted – now he specialises in stealing Polo mints.

Sammy was not the world's brightest criminal. He once turned himself in to collect the reward money.

What did Gerry say to the man he found stealing his garden gate? Nothing. He didn't want the man take a fence.

A group of thieves broke into the local shop and stole 100 jars of instant coffee. I don't know how these people sleep at night.

Dick and Harry see the police setting up a tent at the scene of a serious crime. 'I don't believe it,' says Dick. 'What a stupid place to go camping.'

CRIMES OF PASSION

A man comes home early. He goes upstairs and finds his best friend in bed with his wife, so he pulls out a gun and shoots him. 'You know what?' says his wife. 'If you carry on behaving like that, pretty soon you won't have any friends left!'

A man is in court for murder. The prosecution lawyer says to him, 'When you came home and found your wife in bed with a strange man, why did you only shoot her and not him.' 'It seemed easier,' says the man, 'otherwise I'd have had to shoot a different man every day.'

CRISPS

Barry has put all his money into a business making a new brand of crisps. He says he's going to make a packet. Surely that won't be enough to make a decent return on his investment.

A man walks into a shop and asks for a pack of helicopter-flavoured crisps. 'Sorry, mate,' says the shopkeeper, 'we've only got plane.'

CROCODILES

Q: What do you get when you cross a railway line with a crocodile?
A: Three slices of crocodile.

CROSSWORDS

Two men are trying to work out a clue in a crossword puzzle. 'Six down,' says one of the men, 'the clue says it's "a female relation" and it's a word ending in "U-N-T".' His friend thinks for a moment and then tells him, 'The answer is aunt.' 'Damn it!' says the first. 'I've already put a different letter in.'

A man is doing a crossword puzzle and asks his friend for help. 'Eight across – the clue is "Old Macdonald had one"' 'I know,' says the other, 'it's "farm"!' 'OK, but how do you spell that?' asks the first. 'E-I-E-I-O!' says the second.

Two men are stuck on a clue in a crossword puzzle. One of them reads it out: '"Someone who has never had sex". The answer is six letters. Something – I – something – G – something – something – something.' 'I know what it is,' says his friend. 'Ginger!'

Two idiots are doing a crossword. The clue for two down is 'a flightless bird from Iceland' and it is two words, one of six letters and the other seven letters. 'That's easy,' says one of the idiots, 'it's "frozen chicken" isn't it?'

Larry goes to the doctor and says, 'You've got to help me, doctor. I am addicted to doing crosswords and finishing them off quickly.' 'My advice to you,' says the doctor, 'is try not to get two down.'

Two men are struggling with a crossword puzzle. 'Two across,' says one of the men, 'the clue is "overworked postman".' 'How many letters?' asks his friend. 'How should I know that?' says the first man. 'Probably thousands.'

CROWDS

> "NOBODY GOES THERE ANY MORE; IT'S TOO CROWDED."
>
> YOGI BERRA

The Queen is visiting the Vatican. She and the Pope stand in front of the crowd in St Peter's Square and the Queen says to the Pope, 'A tenner says I can make all the English people in the crowd go crazy with just a wave of my hand.' 'You're on!' says the Pope. The Queen duly waves her hand and the English people in the crowd go crazy cheering. 'You win,' says the Pope. 'But double or quits – I can make all the Irish people in the crowd go crazy with just a nod of my head.' 'Rubbish!' says the Queen. 'Let's see you then.' So he head-butts her.

Q: What's the best way to break up a crowd of angry Scotsmen?
A: Run straight at them holding a collection box.

CRUISES

Tom and Harry are on a cruise. 'It seems to have gone very quiet up on deck,' says Tom. 'Ah!' says Harry, 'that must be because everyone is watching the band.' 'What band?' asks Tom. 'I don't know,' says Harry, 'but earlier on I definitely heard someone shouting out "a band on ship!"'

CULTURE

Two historians are discussing the contributions of Greece and Italy to Western culture. One says, 'You can't deny the advances in philosophy made by the Greeks.' 'True,' says the other, 'but don't downplay Roman engineering.' 'The Greeks also had their engineers and builders,' says the first. 'Just look at the Acropolis.' 'Yes,' says the other. 'But the Romans built the Coliseum.' 'There's sex, too,' says the first. 'The Greeks practically invented it.' 'I'll grant you that,' says the other. 'But then again, it was the Romans who decided to introduce it to women.'

CURRENCY

> DARYL DENHAM: IN WHICH COUNTRY WOULD YOU SPEND SHEKELS?
> CONTESTANT: HOLLAND?
> DENHAM: TRY THE NEXT LETTER OF THE ALPHABET.
> CONTESTANT: ICELAND? IRELAND?
> DENHAM: IT'S A BAD LINE. DID YOU SAY ISRAEL?
> CONTESTANT: NO.
>
> DARYL DENHAM'S DRIVETIME, VIRGIN RADIO

The pound coin was introduced in Britain in 1983. Thank goodness it was. Up till then it had been impossible to release any of the trolleys at Asda.

They did a survey in Liverpool city centre asking if people wanted to go with the euro or the pound. As it turned out, most people preferred to stay with the giro.

CUSTOMS

A priest is on a flight to Ireland when a young girl sitting next to him says, 'Father, can I ask you a favour. I've bought a brand new, very large, state-of-the-art hair drier which will be well over my customs limits. I'm afraid it will be confiscated. Could you carry it through customs for me under your cassock?' 'I will help,' says the priest, 'but of course I will not be able to tell a lie.' 'Don't worry,' says the girl, 'with your honest face, they probably won't question you.' But when they reach customs, an official stops the priest and asks, 'Father, do you have anything to declare?' 'From the top of my head to my waist,' says the priest, 'I have nothing to declare.' The official thinks this is a strange answer so he asks, 'Do you have anything to declare from your waist to the floor?' 'Yes,' says the priest, 'I have to declare I am carrying a large and extraordinary instrument which was designed to be used on a woman, but which, to date, is unused.' 'God bless you, Father,' says the official, laughing, 'there's no need to declare that sort of thing!'

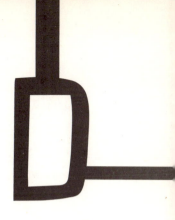

DANCING

I studied ballet dancing at university. I did quite well. I managed to get a 2:2.

I would have been the world's greatest dancer if it were not for two great obstacles — my feet.

DARKNESS

According to the well-known saying, 'The darkest time is just before dawn.' And that makes it the ideal moment to nick people's milk bottles.

DARTS

THERE'S ONLY ONE WORD FOR THAT – MAGIC DARTS!

SID WADDELL

DATING

Barry tells Gary, 'My girlfriend is a very experienced woman. I think she had 61 boyfriends before me.' 'How do you work that out?' asks Gary. 'She likes to call me her sixty-second lover,' says Barry.

George says he could have had any woman he pleased. Unfortunately, he never managed to please any of them.

Two girls are talking. 'Last night my boyfriend told me he loves me for my mind,' says one of them. 'What did you think of that?' asks her friend. 'I've never been so insulted in my life,' says the first.

Gary takes his new girlfriend home after their first date. On the doorstep, she tells him she won't invite him in and he will have to wait at least six months before she will have sex with him. 'OK,' says Gary. 'I'll call you nearer the time.'

My girlfriend has really annoyed me. She thinks I'm nosy and intrusive. At least that's what she wrote in her diary.

Sam is a big comic book fan. He starts going out with a new girlfriend and takes her out to 12 different restaurants before finally taking her to see the new Batman film. 'Fantastic,' he tells her, 'our dating history is now – dinner, dinner, dinner, dinner – dinner, dinner, dinner, dinner – dinner, dinner, dinner, dinner – Batmaaaan!'

"I WAS MAKING LOVE TO THIS GIRL AND SHE STARTED CRYING. I SAID, 'ARE YOU GOING TO HATE YOURSELF IN THE MORNING?' SHE SAID, 'NO, I HATE MYSELF NOW.'"

RODNEY DANGERFIELD

A boy tells his friend, 'I went out with a girl last night.' 'Wow!' says his friend. 'How did it go?' 'Fantastic,' says the first boy. 'She put her arms round me 15 times.' 'Rubbish,' says the friend. 'You don't know anyone with arms that long.'

Jack had been going out with a cross-eyed woman. He ended the relationship because he thought she was seeing someone else on the side.

Girlfriends are like credit cards: you can't get one unless you already have one.

Harry decides it would be nice to go out with an old flame. He finds his old little black book of phone numbers, calls someone up and enjoys a romantic dinner for two with his plumber. He didn't mind paying for the meal but he thought having to pay a call-out charge as well was a bit much.

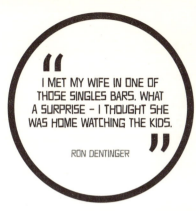

"I MET MY WIFE IN ONE OF THOSE SINGLES BARS. WHAT A SURPRISE – I THOUGHT SHE WAS HOME WATCHING THE KIDS."

RON DENTINGER

A girl turns up to meet her date at a quarter to nine. 'Sorry to have kept you waiting,' she says. 'Don't worry,' says the boy 'I've only been here five minutes.' 'Five minutes!' says the girl, outraged. 'You said you'd meet me here at eight!'

Danny and his girlfriend Daphne are babysitting her little brother Timmy. After Timmy has gone up to bed, the couple commence enjoying themselves in a full and frank manner on the sofa. After a few minutes Danny notices that Timmy has come back down and is watching them. He pulls up his trousers and chases the little boy back up to bed. When he comes downstairs again he says, 'If your brother tells your parents what he saw us doing, your dad's going to kill me. How much should I give him to make sure he doesn't say anything?' 'He usually charges a fiver,' says Daphne.

Two girls are talking. One asks the other how her blind date went last night. 'Terrible,' she says, 'my date turned up in a 1949 Rolls-Royce.' 'What was the matter with that?' asks her friend. 'He'd owned it since new,' says the first.

SINGLE MAN SEEKS KIND, CARING, COMPASSIONATE WOMAN WITH A BIG HAPPY HEART AND A WARM SOUL FULL OF LOVE. NO FAT CHICKS.

LONELY HEARTS AD

Freddie drives his new girlfriend out of town to lovers' lane for some hanky-panky. After they're done, the girl says, 'I should have told you that I'm a professional escort and I charge £50 for what we just did. So pay up.' 'OK,' says Freddie. 'That means you owe me £10.' 'How d'you work that out?' asks the girl. Freddie says, 'Because I should have told you that I'm really a cab driver and the fare back to town is 60 quid.'

A boy and his girlfriend are out on a date. 'Do you know what I love about you?' says the boy. 'My looks?' says the girl. 'No,' says the boy. 'My personality?' says the girl. 'No,' says the boy. 'I don't know then. I give in.' The boy says, 'That's the one.'

Jack runs into the family home and finds his dad. 'Father, I just met the woman I want to marry. She's just like Mum.' 'So what d'you want from me?' scowls Dad. 'Sympathy?'

Gerry goes on a blind date, but to be sure he has an escape plan in case things go sour he arranges for his friend to phone him at 9pm. The date turns out to be a disaster and Gerry can't wait to get away, so when his phone rings at the appointed time, he answers and puts on a look of shock. 'What's the matter?' says his date. 'Grandma just died,' says Gerry. 'I have to go.' His date lets out a sigh of relief. 'Well, thank God for that. If one of your relatives hadn't died, one of mine sure would have had to.'

I was in a restaurant the other day when a beautiful woman on the next table gave a huge sneeze and blew out her glass eye. It was sudden, but I was quick and before it could hit the floor I caught it in my hand. The woman was very grateful and invited me to join her. One thing led to another and we spent the night together. The next morning I said, 'Am I a lucky guy, or do most of your dates get treated this well?' 'Oh no,' she says. 'Not everyone. Just those who catch my eye . . .'

Sally is in bed with her new boyfriend. 'I have something to tell you,' says Sally. 'I used to be a hooker.' 'A hooker?' exclaims the boyfriend. 'That's a shock. When did you give it up?' 'After the sex change,' she says. 'I used to play for the London Irish.'

Why is New Year's Eve like a hot date? They both involve drink and going to bed making promises that will never be kept.

Nigel gets a call from an old flame. The last time he saw her she was a beautiful girl who was just starting out on a career as an international fashion model. Much to his surprise she asks him out for a romantic dinner. 'I'd love to come,' says Nigel. 'But you must make allowances for the passage of time. My hair's not as thick as it was and my waistline has expanded a little since the last time you saw me.' 'Don't be silly,' says the old flame. 'It happens to all of us. I might have put on a few pounds myself.' 'Oh,' says Nigel. 'In that case, forget it.'

Janice went to a computer dating agency to find a partner. They picked one out for her, but she was a little disappointed – she'd been hoping to get a man.

Nancy can't get a date to save her life, so her mother helps her write a seductive profile on a dating site and they upload a picture of Nancy's slightly better-looking workmate. The next day, they start to look through all the responses. Nancy clicks on the first message and bursts into tears. 'What's the matter?' asks the mother. Nancy sobs, 'It's from Daddy.'

Jack is engaged to a girl who has a really hot mother. One day the mother asks him over and when Jack rings on the door, the mother opens it wearing a sexy negligee. She pulls Jack into the house and closes the door. 'I can't resist you, honey. I'm all yours if you want me. What do you say we have some fun?' With that she starts to slink seductively up the stairs. 'Once you've made up your mind, I'll be waiting – in the bedroom.' Jack gulps, looks at the retreating derrière of his soon-to-be mother-in-law, opens the front door and steps outside. He finds his soon-to-be father-in-law waiting in the drive. 'Congratulations, son. You passed the test. There's not many men who could resist my wife and I'm glad that one of them is going to be marrying my daughter. Welcome to the family.' The moral of the story being – always keep your condoms in your car.

Larry goes up to his friend George, a long-term bachelor and says, 'I've found the perfect wife for you; she's young, rich and gorgeous.' 'But I'm a 50-year-old unemployed lavatory cleaner,' says George. 'She'd have to be insane to marry me.' Larry replies, 'I already told you she's young, rich and gorgeous. You can't have everything.'

Barry tells Gary, 'The girl I marry must have a sense of humour.' 'Well, that's lucky,' says Gary, 'because that's the only kind you're going to get.'

Gary's girlfriend starts calling him Amazon Prime. 'I know why that is,' says Gary. 'It's because I'm always there when you want me and I have an exciting package.' 'No it's not,' says his girlfriend. 'It's because you're cheap and you always come sooner than expected.'

Barry is very bad at dating. He phones up a girl to ask her to go and see a film with him that evening. 'OK,' says the girl. 'What about dinner before the movie?' says Barry. 'Yes, that would be a great idea,' says the girl. 'Right,' says Barry. 'I'll pick you up at nine. You should be finished eating by then.

Here's one surefire way to surprise your boyfriend this Valentine's Day. Introduce him to your husband.

A mate of mine set me up on a blind date. Just before I set off he said, 'There's one thing you should know. She's expecting a baby.' Well, I felt a right idiot waiting for her in the pub with a dummy in my mouth and dressed in nothing but a nappy.

Dave has a new girlfriend. She picks him up in her car one night to drive over and meet his parents but on the way they get a flat tyre. Dave calls his mum and says, 'Sorry, but we're going to be late. My new girlfriend's got a puncture.' 'Oh no, son!' says Mum. 'We actually thought you'd got a real one this time.'

Kevin tells his mate Barry, 'My new girlfriend likes it when I cover her with butter, jam, peanut butter or cheese spread and then lick it all off again. She really is a cracker.'

Gary goes out with a girl for the first time, but he doesn't find her very attractive. At the end of the evening she tells him, 'You ought to know, I never have sex on a first date.' 'No problem,' says Gary. 'But what about if it's the last?'

DEAD SEA

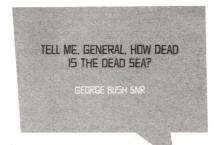

TELL ME, GENERAL, HOW DEAD IS THE DEAD SEA?

GEORGE BUSH SNR

DEAFNESS

I went to buy a hearing aid the other day. The man in the shop showed me one that was the size of a pea. It was brilliant, but it cost a fortune, so I asked for something cheaper. The next he brought out was the size of a small battery. It worked really well, but it was still too expensive, so I asked to see something cheaper. He reached under the counter and showed me one the size of a wallet. It sat in your top pocket and fitted to an earpiece with a wire that was so thin it was almost invisible. I quite liked it, but it was still a lot of money, so I asked for something cheaper. The man went out to the storeroom and came back with a big tin-box punched full of holes that had a pair of ancient headphones attached to it with an old curly telephone cord. The man said,
'This is the cheapest we've got. It's a fiver.'
'How does it work?' I said. 'It doesn't,' said the man. 'The box is empty.' 'Then what good is it?' I said. The man answers, 'When people see you wearing it, they shout.'

Dick's deaf wife packed her bags and left him for his best mate who was also deaf. Dick was furious afterwards. He said he should have seen the signs.

"I HAD A JOB SELLING HEARING AIDS DOOR-TO-DOOR. IT WASN'T EASY, BECAUSE YOUR BEST PROSPECTS NEVER ANSWERED."

BOB MONKHOUSE

Vic is stone deaf and it makes travelling on public transport extremely stressful. He is never entirely certain whether other passengers are yawning or screaming.

After years of deafness an old lady finally gets herself a hearing aid. It's so small it's virtually invisible. A friend asks her what her family thinks of it. 'I've not told them,' she says. 'It's interesting to listen to them talk to each other when they think I can't hear. I've changed my will half a dozen times since I bought it.'

Aunt Dot is showing her friend her new hearing aid. 'It's very tiny and quite expensive, but I demanded I get the very best available. You know me – I won't stand for anything second rate.' 'It does look very nice,' says the friend. 'What type is it?' Dot looks at her watch and says, 'Just gone five.'

Quentin is excellent at sign language. Sadly, he talks in his sleep, so he has to wear handcuffs in case he knocks out his wife.

Stan was worried he was becoming increasingly deaf, so went to the library and took out a book called 'How to Improve Your Hearing' by Alison Hard.

DEATH

Merv asks Vernon what he's been doing. 'I've been spending a bit of time on my wife's grave,' says Vernon. 'Oh dear,' says Merv. 'Sorry to hear that, mate. I didn't know she had passed away.' 'She hasn't,' says Vernon, 'she thinks I'm digging a garden pond.'

If you have a deep fear of dying alone, then being a bus driver may be the job for you.

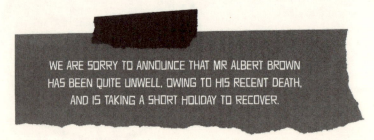

WE ARE SORRY TO ANNOUNCE THAT MR ALBERT BROWN HAS BEEN QUITE UNWELL, OWING TO HIS RECENT DEATH, AND IS TAKING A SHORT HOLIDAY TO RECOVER.

PARISH MAGAZINE

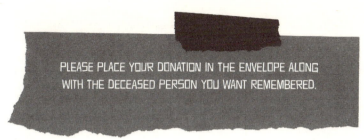

PLEASE PLACE YOUR DONATION IN THE ENVELOPE ALONG WITH THE DECEASED PERSON YOU WANT REMEMBERED.

PARISH NOTICES

A woman invites all her girlfriends out for a drink and informs them that she has just been diagnosed with AIDS. After the friends have gone home, the woman's daughter says, 'I thought the doctor told you you had cancer.' 'He did,' says the woman, 'but I don't want any of those bitches sleeping with your father after I'm gone.'

Mrs Smith is being interviewed over the fatal shooting of her husband. 'Do you remember the last words your husband said to you?' asks the detective. 'Yes,' sniffs Mrs Smith, 'He said, "Maureen, put down that bloody shotgun".'

My father was only 38 when he dropped off a scaffold and fell to his death. He wasn't a builder, they were hanging him for murder.

Q: Why do you only need two pallbearers at a lawyer's funeral?
A: Because a rubbish bin only has two handles.

Old Alf died doing the thing he loved most — making toast in the shower.

In the old days, the only things that were inevitable were death and taxes; now you usually have to include, shipping, handling and an extended warranty.

> LOOK AT THESE DIFFERENT PLACES AROUND THE WORLD WHERE THERE'S BEEN TREMENDOUS DEATH AND DESTRUCTION BECAUSE KILLERS KILL.
>
> GEORGE W. BUSH

DECISIONS

The judge tells a defendant in court, 'You have been found not guilty of bigamy. You are now free to go home.' 'Thank you, your honour,' says the prisoner. 'Which home should I go to?'

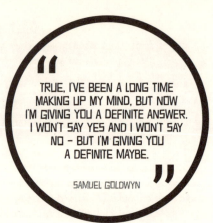

" TRUE, I'VE BEEN A LONG TIME MAKING UP MY MIND, BUT NOW I'M GIVING YOU A DEFINITE ANSWER. I WON'T SAY YES AND I WON'T SAY NO – BUT I'M GIVING YOU A DEFINITE MAYBE. "

SAMUEL GOLDWYN

DECOR

Harry visits a new bar in town and discovers that everything in it is coloured gold.
The walls, ceiling, windows, carpets, chairs, tables, the bar – they're all bright gold. Amazed by the sight, he orders a drink that is served in a golden glass. He finishes it and then goes to look for the men's room. He finds it hard to track down, but eventually he comes across a tiny room no bigger than a cupboard that has a single golden urinal standing in it. He relieves himself, then goes to have another couple of drinks. As he's leaving, the barman says, 'So what do you think of the place? Like the colour scheme?' 'It's very unusual,' says Harry. 'But I do like it. The only thing I'd change is the washroom. Why is it so small and why is there only one urinal in there?' The barman stares at Harry for a moment, then grabs him by the throat. He calls out into a back room. 'Hey, Pete. I just caught the bloke who peed in your saxophone.'

DECORATING

Tom goes to visit his friend Jock and finds him carefully stripping the wallpaper from the walls of his house. 'Are you decorating?' asks Tom. 'No,' says Jock, 'I'm moving.'

Tom finds Harry at home one day painting his living room wearing an anorak over a tweed jacket. 'Why have you got those on?' asks Tom. 'Because,' says Harry, 'the directions on the tin said to stir the paint and then put on two coats.'

Nigel and Betty decide to redecorate their house and Nigel makes a start by rolling paint across the kitchen ceiling. 'Have you got a tight hold on that paint roller?' asks Betty. 'Sure do,' says Nigel. 'Good,' says Betty. 'Because I'm taking the ladder into the front room.'

Janice spent a fortune redecorating her house. Sadly, when it was done, she had to divorce her husband. It turned out he clashed with the new curtains.

Sam is painting the outside of his house when a man comes up to admire his handiwork. 'Great stuff you're doing there. I doubt even the great Frank Jones could have done a better job.' 'Oh yes? Was this Frank Jones a professional house-painter?' asks Sammy. 'No,' says the man. 'But from what I've heard he was extremely good at it. He could also repair cars and household electrical goods. He was a whizz at plumbing and carpentry, was very good with money and was the perfect lover.' 'Wow,' says Sammy. 'You sure do know a lot about this Frank Jones. Is he a famous local character?' 'No,' says the man. 'But I'm married to his widow.'

> " MY WIFE DOES HER OWN DECORATING, BUT SHE OVERDOES IT. THE OTHER DAY I OPENED THE FRIDGE AND THERE WAS A LAMPSHADE ON THE LIGHT BULB. "
>
> TOMMY COOPER

DÉJÀ VU

Have I told you this déjà vu joke before?

A man is in the middle of having dinner when he suffers dijon vu. The sense that he has eaten mustard exactly like this before.

'Knock, knock.' 'Who's there?' 'Dejav.' 'Dejav who?' . . . 'Knock, knock.'

> " IT'S LIKE DÉJÀ VU ALL OVER AGAIN. "
>
> YOGI BERRA

DENTISTS

Always remember to be nice and polite to your dentist. Don't forget, he has fillings, too.

Norman comes out of the dentist's and bumps into a friend. 'I've just had to have all my teeth removed,' says Norman. 'I'll tell you what — never again!'

A man goes to the dentist and asks how much it is to extract a tooth. 'Eighty pounds,' says the dentist. 'No,' says the man, 'that's far too much. Are there any cheaper options?' 'Well,' says the dentist, 'I could do it without anaesthetic. That will knock £20 off the price.' 'It still sounds expensive,' says the man. 'OK,' says the dentist, 'I could save on electricity and equipment and just pull the tooth out with some pliers. That will knock another £20 off.' 'It's still too much,' says the man.' 'Right,' says the dentist, 'I could let get a student who has never done an extraction before to do the job and we'll just charge you a fiver.' 'Now you're talking,' says the man. 'Could I make an appointment?' 'OK,' says the dentist. 'What's your name?' 'No, it's not for me,' says the man, 'it's for my wife.'

> "HAPPINESS IS YOUR DENTIST TELLING YOU IT WON'T HURT AND THEN HAVING HIM CATCH HIS HAND IN THE DRILL."
>
> JOHNNY CARSON

A man is having a check-up at the dentist's. The dentist tells him he has an abscess which requires urgent treatment and he will have to use anaesthetic to put him to sleep. The man takes out his wallet and starts looking through it. 'Don't worry about the bill,' says the dentist, 'we can sort that out later.' 'I'm not worried about the bill,' says the man, 'I'm just checking how much money I've got in here in case any has gone missing when I wake up.'

A man goes to the dentist for root canal work. The man turns out to be allergic to all the anaesthetics the dentist has available. 'OK, there's nothing for it,' says the dentist, handing him some blue pills, 'you'll have to take these.' 'Is this another anaesthetic?' asks the man. 'No,' says the dentist, 'it's Viagra. It won't kill the pain. But at least it'll give you something to hang on to.'

ADVERT FOR A DENTIST IN HONG KONG

When we had our daughter's teeth seen to our dentist gave us a bill for £1,000. He said it was to cover lost earnings. He was only fitting her with a brace but she screamed so loudly all his other patients made a run for it.

A man goes to the dentist for a check-up. As he sits in the chair and opens wide, the dentist stares at him in shock. 'My God, that's the biggest mouth I've ever seen. That's the biggest mouth I've ever seen. The biggest mouth I've ever seen. Biggest mouth I've ever seen . . .' 'OK,' snaps the man. 'I get it, it's huge. Will you stop going on about it.' 'What do you mean, "stop"?' says the dentist. 'I only said it the once.'

A dentist is examining a woman patient. 'I'm sorry,' says the dentist, 'but I'm going to have to extract one of your teeth.' 'Oh no,' says the woman, 'I think I'd rather have another baby than go through this!' 'Well, make your mind up, love,' says the dentist, 'because that will mean I have to adjust the chair.'

DESCRIBING THINGS

The word 'indescribable' is the only word that cancels itself out. Thanks to the word 'indescribable' there is literally nothing that can't be described.

Why do the expressions 'fat chance' and 'slim chance' mean exactly the same thing?

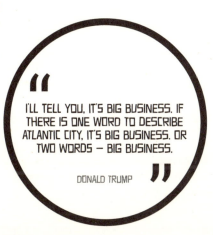

" I'LL TELL YOU, IT'S BIG BUSINESS. IF THERE IS ONE WORD TO DESCRIBE ATLANTIC CITY, IT'S BIG BUSINESS. OR TWO WORDS — BIG BUSINESS.

DONALD TRUMP "

DESERTS

A traveller is lost in the Sahara Desert and is desperate for water. He sees something in the distance and makes towards it, hoping it will be an oasis. It is however a little man with a table laid out with ties. 'Do you want to buy a tie?' asks the little man. 'No!' says the traveller. 'I'm dying of thirst. I need water! Of course I don't want a stupid tie!' 'OK,' says the little man, 'if you walk for about four miles over that next hill you'll find a restaurant run by my brother and he will give you all the water you want.' The traveller sets off. Three hours later he comes back. 'Did you find the restaurant?' asks the little man. 'Yes!' says the traveller. 'But your brother wouldn't let me in without a tie!'

A traveller is crossing the desert when he sees a man standing next to a tall chimney sticking out of the sand. The traveller says, 'That's a fine chimney you got there. What are you going to do with it?' 'That's not a chimney,' snaps the man. 'That's a well. The idiot who built it was holding the plans upside down.'

An English explorer is trekking across the Mojave desert with two Native American guides. Suddenly one of the guides runs off to a cave in a hill and calls into the darkness: 'Woooooo! Woooooo! Woooooo!' Hearing a reply from the cave: 'Woooooo! Woooooo! Woooooo!', the guide tears off his clothes and runs in. The English explorer asks the remaining guide why. 'It is mating time,' says the guide, 'if you see a cave and holler, "Woooooo! Woooooo! Woooooo!" and receive an answer back, a beautiful woman is waiting inside for you.' A few days later the English explorer comes across an enormous cave in the side of the hill. He hears the sound, 'Woooooo! Woooooo! Woooooo!' coming from the darkness so he rips off his clothes and runs in. The next day the newspapers report: 'Naked English Explorer Killed in Horrific Freight Train Accident.'

DETECTIVE WORK

Sherlock Holmes tells Doctor Watson, 'Watson, I deduce that the murderer came into the house through that yellow door.' 'How could you possible know that?' says Watson. 'My dear Watson,' says Holmes, 'it's a lemon entry.'

DIARRHOEA

A woman calls the doctor and says, 'Doctor, you've got to help me. My son has got a problem with diarrhoea.' 'What sort of problem?' says the doctor. 'It's come up in a test he's got for school,' says the woman, 'and he doesn't know how to spell it.'

PLEASE EXCUSE TOMMY FOR BEING ABSENT YESTERDAY. HE HAD DIARRHOEA AND HIS BOOTS LEAK.

SCHOOL ABSENTEE NOTE

Dick goes to the doctor because he is suffering from a nasty case of diarrhoea. 'Try taking this,' says the doctor, producing a packet of Bisto. 'Will that make it better?' asks Dick. 'No,' says the doctor,' but hopefully it will thicken it up a bit.'

PLEASE LET JEAN LEAVE THE ROOM IF SHE ASKS. SHE HAS BEEN SICK WITH DIRE REAR.

SCHOOL ABSENTEE NOTE

DICTIONARIES

Ron thinks he's in line for a job working on the new *Oxford Dictionary*. He says he's got a mate who's put a word in for him.

I bought myself a new thesaurus but it's terrible. And not only that, it's terrible.

Brenda bought Tom the world's cheapest and shortest dictionary. He literally couldn't find the words to thank her.

Have you ever thought, where did the person who wrote the first dictionary find all the words from?

DIET

Norman managed to lose 323 calories today. He went to the beach and a seagull stole his Snickers bar.

I'm not sure exactly what calories are but clearly they taste delicious.

Norma tells Nobby, 'Look! I lost 15 pounds.' 'Are you sure?' says Nobby. 'Look in the mirror, turn sideways and I think you might be able to find them again.'

"THE SECOND DAY OF A DIET IS ALWAYS EASIER THAN THE FIRST. BY THE SECOND DAY YOU'RE OFF IT."

JACKIE GLEASON

Norma goes to a dietician and asks for some advice to help reduce her obesity. The dietician says, 'Just try moving your head to the right and then to the left at particular times of day.' 'Which times of day?' asks Norma. 'At any time of day when somebody offers you something to eat,' says the dietician.

A woman bakes a cake for her husband but can't resist having a nibble and eventually eats the whole thing. She knows her husband will be furious when he finds out she ate a whole cake, so she bakes him a new one and only eats half of it.

> QUESTION MASTER: NAME SOMETHING YOU EAT TOO MUCH OF.
> CONTESTANT: FOOD.
>
> FAMILY FEUD

I'm slowly starving myself so I'll live longer – I call it a diet.

To encourage his wife to lose weight a man pastes a picture of a half-naked supermodel to the door of the fridge. It worked, up to a point: his wife lost half a stone, but he put on two more.

I'm going to try the garlic diet. Apparently you don't lose any weight but your friends all think you look thinner because they only view you from a distance.

Norman says his wife is very particular about what she eats to help maintain her figure. Mainly he says it involves cakes and pies.

DIFFERENT PERSPECTIVES

Events in life can seem very different from the point of view of others. For example, the sinking of the *Titanic* must have been like a miracle rescue for the lobsters in the ship's kitchen.

DINOSAURS

Q: What sound does a pterodactyl make when it goes to the toilet?
A: No sound at all because the 'P' is silent!

Dick was digging in his garden when he thought he'd uncovered part of a dinosaur. He ran inside in excitement and phoned the Natural History Museum, but unfortunately it turned out to be a fossil arm.

Palaeontologists have discovered the largest complete set of dinosaur teeth ever found. It's a mystery how they've been so perfectly preserved. They're also quite puzzled by the giant glass of water they found them in.

Harry calls up the RSPCA to report the Natural History Museum. He tells them, 'It doesn't look like they're feeding their Tyrannosaurus Rex at all.'

Q: Why did the dinosaur cross the road?
A: Because the chicken hadn't evolved yet.

DIPLOMATS

A diplomat is someone who can tell you to go
to hell and then make you look forward to the trip.

DISABILITIES

Old Jake said his wooden leg used to give him headaches. Whenever he had an argument with his wife, she'd start hitting him over the head with it.

Geoff stole his girlfriend's wheelchair after she split up with him. He says he's pretty sure she'll come crawling back to him soon.

George was disqualified from *Robot Wars* for cheating. When they unwrapped his robot, they found it was his gran in her wheelchair covered in Bacofoil and clutching a power drill.

DO YOU KNOW THEY HAVE EATING DOGS FOR THE ANOREXIC NOW?

PRINCE PHILIP (SPEAKING TO A BLIND WOMAN WITH A GUIDE DOG)

Great-uncle George had his tongue shot out of his mouth during the Battle of the Somme. He never talked about it.

Three sisters, Hettie, Henrietta and Harriet, are sitting on a bench when a cross-eyed old man approaches them. He looks at Henrietta: 'Hello, my dear. And what's your name?' 'My name's Hettie,' says Hettie. 'I wasn't talking to you, miss,' says the old man. 'But I didn't say anything,' says Harriet.

A preacher in America calls all those suffering with afflictions to come up on stage so he can cure them with prayer. A man comes up and the preacher asks him, 'What would you like me to pray about for you?' 'Preacher,' says the man, 'I need help with my hearing.' The preacher put his hands over the man's ears and prays intently. 'There!' says the preacher. 'Has that helped with your hearing?' 'I don't know,' says the man, 'I'm not having it until next Tuesday.'

An old man totters into a pub on two wooden legs. He buys a pint and then asks for the toilet. As the toilet is at the end of an unlit, muddy, cobbled old passage, the landlord offers to go with the old man as he thinks he is sure to fall. Nevertheless, the old man insists on going alone. Ten minutes later, the old man staggers back to the bar on his wooden legs, covered in mud and filth. 'I told you you'd fall,' says the landlord. 'I didn't,' says the man. 'I was sitting on the pot in the dark when the door opened and somebody bent down, grabbed my legs and said, "Who's left a flipping wheelbarrow in the khazi?"'

It is a well-known fact that if one of your senses is damaged, another of your senses will become enhanced to help compensate. And that is why people who have no sense of humour always have an incredibly well-developed sense of self-importance.

A man with no arms walks into a restaurant and orders a burger. Since he can't hold the bun, one of the waiters does it for him. He also orders a beer and the same waiter helps him drink it. Then he asks for his mouth to be wiped and the waiter does it for him with a napkin. 'Must be tough getting by without any arms,' says the waiter. 'It's not so bad,' says the man. 'People are normally very happy to help me out. By the way, is there a toilet here?' 'No,' says the waiter. 'You have to go five miles down the road to the library.'

DISASTERS

> "THEY SAY ANIMAL BEHAVIOUR CAN WARN YOU WHEN AN EARTHQUAKE IS COMING. LIKE THE NIGHT BEFORE THAT LAST EARTHQUAKE HIT, OUR FAMILY DOG TOOK THE CAR KEYS AND DROVE TO ARIZONA."
>
> BOB HOPE

Dave isn't one to flirt with disaster. He's in a serious long-term relationship with it.

For some reason an earthquake that happens thousands of miles away seems less of a catastrophe than the first time your new car gets a scratch.

Two businessmen are talking. One says to the other, 'I hear you've had some bad luck. Did your factory burn down last night?' 'Not so loud,' whispers the other, 'it's actually tomorrow!'

It has been reported that there has been a major gas explosion in Liverpool leading to the destruction of several buildings. It has been estimated that the disaster has caused over ten million pounds' worth of improvements.

Dick had a disaster when he went on a skiing trip in the Italian Alps. When people started screaming 'Avalanche!' he thought they were telling him it was time for a midday meal.

DISEASE

Our local department store had to quarantine their furniture showroom after several beds were found to have been nibbled by animals. They were worried it might be an outbreak of Futon Mouse disease.

A girl brings her boyfriend home for a night of passion. He starts taking his clothes off but when he drops his pants, she notices his knees are covered in spots. 'I know,' he says, 'when I was little I caught kneesles.' 'You mean measles,' says the girl. 'No,' says the boy. 'What I had was called kneesles.' Next he takes off his socks and she notices his feet look strange. 'I know,' he says, 'when I was little I had toelio.' 'You mean polio,' she says. 'No,' he says. 'What I had was called toelio.' Finally he removes his underpants. 'I don't believe it!' says the girl. 'You had smallcox as well.'

DISLIKES

There are three things I really dislike: 1. Negativity; 2. Irony; and 3. Lists.

DIVING

Harry goes scuba diving and his instructor shows him how to tip himself backwards out of the boat. Harry tries it but bangs his head. He also notices he's not very wet. 'What happened?' says Harry. 'You went the wrong way,' says the instructor. 'You're still in the boat.'

DIVORCE

Divorce is a bit like an espresso coffee. Expensive and bitter.

Brenda tells Tom they're getting divorced. 'Why?' says Tom aghast. 'Sum the reason up for me in two words!' 'OK,' says Brenda. 'Our marriage.'

Phil tells Tom that when he got divorced, he and his wife agreed to split the house between them. 'Which half did you get?' asks Tom. 'The outside,' says Phil.

Since his divorce three years ago, Ken has put on ten stone. The doctor tells him, 'You really must stop celebrating.'

Bill tells Arthur, 'I'm going to divorce my wife! She hasn't spoken to me in over six months.' 'OK,' says Arthur, 'but think about it very carefully. You know, women like that are very hard to find.'

A recent survey asked men and women why divorces cost so much. The most popular answer was, 'Because it's worth it.'

Betty is in court giving evidence. A lawyer approaches her and says, 'Are you married?' 'I'm divorced,' replies Betty. 'I see,' says the lawyer. 'And what did your husband do before you separated?' Betty says, 'A lot of stuff I only got to find out about later.'

A newly married couple go to court to apply for a divorce. 'What!?' says the judge. 'Why do you want a divorce so quickly?' 'Because,' says the husband, 'we've only been together seven weeks but we've found we don't agree about anything and she contradicts me all the time!' The judge turns to the wife and asks, 'What have you got to say about this?' 'Your honour,' says the woman, 'it's actually been eight weeks . . .'

After Zeke and Betty-Sue got divorced there was still some uncertainty about their legal status under Alabama law. Eventually it was sorted out. Although they were no longer husband and wife, they did remain aunt and nephew.

Three divorced men get chatting in a bar. One says, 'My wife left me for another man.' The second says, 'My wife left me because of my affairs.' The third one says, 'My wife left me for religious reasons – she worships money and I don't have any.'

Ruby and Janet are talking one day. 'All my husband wants to do is have sex,' says Ruby. 'That's why I'm divorcing him.' 'Isn't that a bit drastic?' says Janet. 'Most women would like that.' 'They do,' says Ruby. 'That's why I'm divorcing him.'

An engaged couple die on their way to their wedding. At the Pearly Gates they ask St Peter if they can be married in heaven. 'I'll see what I can do,' says the saint. Six months later St Peter comes to the couple's heavenly home and says, 'It's arranged. You can come to the church tomorrow and I'll have you married then.' 'Thank you so much,' says the groom-to-be. 'But we were wondering – if you can get married in heaven, can you get divorced in heaven too?' 'Divorced!' exclaims St Peter, 'Are you crazy? It just took me six months to find a priest. How long do you think it would take me to get a pair of lawyers?'

After 15 years of marriage Alice says she has learned that every argument has two sides: your side and the twit's.

Q: How many divorce lawyers does it take to change a light bulb?
A: Three – one to argue for the rights of the old bulb; one to argue for the rights of the new bulb; and a third to ensure suitable provision is made for the socket.

Once upon a time a fabulously rich couple decided to get divorced. And their lawyers lived happily ever after.

DIY

There are only two tools you should ever need: oil and tape. If something is supposed to move but doesn't, put some oil on it. If something moves but shouldn't, stick it down with tape.

Clive went into a bookshop and asked if they had a book that would teach him to do DIY. They sold him a blank notepad and a pen.

I was interested in doing some DIY, so I went to the library and asked if they had any books on shelves.

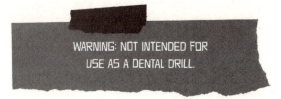

INSTRUCTIONS ON A DIY DRILL

The people from a television DIY show came to our town and appeared at the local theatre. It was quite good because before they came, we didn't have a local theatre.

If something jams – hit it; if it breaks you'd probably have needed a new one anyway.

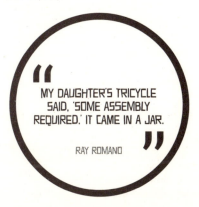

DNA

Q: What happens if you try mixing human DNA with goat DNA?
A: You get banned for life from the local petting zoo.

DOGS

Tom tells Dick he is thinking of getting a new dog. 'What sort?' asks Dick. 'A labrador,' says Tom. 'You don't want to get one of those,' says Dick. 'Have you seen how many of their owners go blind?'

Two dogs are talking. One says to the other, 'Rover, do you use a condom when you're having sex?' 'Durex,' says Rover. 'I asked you first,' says his friend.

I have a border collie. He's like any other dog except I only get to see him in the school holidays.

Bill's dog disappears one day so he wanders around the local park for ten minutes. He comes back and tells his wife he couldn't find the animal so she tells him to try looking a bit harder. Half an hour later Bill's had his head shaved and a couple of tattoos done but it doesn't seem to help him finding the dog.

Don't forget, if you're getting a puppy soon, you can give it any name you want but you'll then have to use this as the answer to security questions for the rest of your life.

Q: What do you get if you cross a labrador with a magician?
A: Labracadabrador!

Q: Why are we unable to hear dog whistles.
A: Because they can't.

Q: Why are dogs no good at playing poker?
A: Whenever they get a good hand their tails start wagging.

Two men are walking down the road when one says, 'Look at that dog with one eye!' His friend covers one of his eyes and says, 'OK. Where?'

It's been reported that a dog walker was found murdered in the park this morning. Police say they have located the dog but as yet have no lead.

Nobby saw a television programme about Battersea Dogs Home and it really opened his eyes. He took his dog straight down there the next day. He'd been wondering how to get rid of it for years.

Don and Phyllis got their new dog from the animal re-homing centre. The re-homing centre warned them that this dog had to be the only animal in the house and this turned out to be absolutely true. Which is why they haven't been able to get back into their house since.

> "A DOG BIT A CHUNK OUT OF MY LEG THE OTHER DAY. A FRIEND OF MINE SAID: 'DID YOU PUT ANYTHING ON IT?' I SAID: 'NO, HE LIKED IT AS IT WAS.'"
>
> TOMMY COOPER

Dick's dog is very stupid. The other day it spent the evening chewing away on a bone in front of the fire. When it was bedtime, it got up and hobbled away on three legs.

Tessa agrees to look after her neighbour's dog Tyson for a few days while his owner is away. She thinks that Tyson will be company for her own dog Fifi, but as soon as she leaves them alone and goes up to bed for the night she hears them moaning and howling and thrashing around. She rushes down and finds Tyson having his evil way with Fifi. Try as she might she is completely unable to get the two dogs apart. In desperation she phones her vet's after-hours number. The vet answers grumpily and she asks him what she can do to separate the two dogs. 'I'll tell you what,' says the vet, 'hang up the phone and I'll call you back. You'll then be able to separate the dogs because the sound of the phone ringing will make Tyson lose his excitement and cause him to withdraw.' 'Are you sure that will work?' asks Tessa. 'Well,' says the vet, 'it's just worked for me.'

A dog goes to send a telegram. He walks into the post office, takes a form and writes his message: 'Woof. Woof. Woof. Woof. Woof. Woof. Woof. Woof. Woof.' When he hands it in, the clerk tells him, 'You've only done nine words. You can add an extra 'Woof' to the message and it won't cost any more money.' 'Why would I want to do that?' says the dog. 'The message wouldn't make any sense at all then.'

Harry invites Tom round for dinner. During the meal Harry's dog keeps trying to climb up on to Tom's lap. 'Your dog seems to like me,' says Tom. 'No, it's not that,' says Harry, 'it's just that we were short of crockery tonight so you're eating off his plate.'

Clive reads an advert about a new test that will assess your dog's IQ. Clive is interested in finding out how clever his dog is so he writes a cheque for £20 and posts it off. A few days later he receives a note back that says, 'Your dog is definitely smarter than you are.'

> "ASTHMA DOESN'T SEEM TO BOTHER ME ANY MORE UNLESS I'M AROUND CIGARS OR DOGS. THE THING THAT WOULD BOTHER ME MOST WOULD BE A DOG SMOKING A CIGAR."
> STEVE ALLEN

Harry takes his dog into a bar. 'No dogs allowed in here,' says the barman. 'But,' says Harry, 'this is a special dog. He's able to talk.' 'If that dog can talk,' says the barman, 'I'll give you free drinks all night.' Harry places his dog on the bar and says, 'OK, Fido. What do you find on top of a house?' 'Ruff!' says the dog. 'A roof! That's right,' says Harry. 'OK, Fido, what do you find all round a tree?' 'Bark!' barks the dog. 'Bark! Quite right! And finally,' says Harry, 'what was the name of the greatest baseball player in US history?' 'Ruff!' woofs the dog. 'Babe Ruth is the correct answer once again!' says Harry. But the bartender is not impressed. 'Get out of here, idiot!' he shouts. 'Or I'm calling the police.' Outside the dog turns to Harry and says, 'Sorry about that, man. Should I have said Joe DiMaggio?'

Tom calls up Harry and says, 'I've just got a new dog this morning. Do you want to come over to have a play with it?' 'OK,' says Harry, 'but does the dog bite?' 'That's what I want to find out,' says Tom.

A man is in despair because for years he has been trying to train his dog but without any success. In the end he takes him to a preacher who says to leave the dog with him. The man comes back a few days later and the preacher demonstrates the commands that he has taught the dog to respond to. 'Fetch!' says the preacher, throwing a stick for the dog, and the dog goes and brings back the stick. 'Sit!' says the preacher, and the dog sits down. 'Shake hands!' says the preacher, and the dog offers a paw. 'Now you have a go,' says the preacher. 'Heel!' says the man, and the dog lifts one paw to the man's forehead and says, 'Oh Lord, I command this sickness to leave this sinner . . .'

Two farmers are talking. One claims that his dog can count. 'No he can't,' says the second farmer. 'OK, Fido,' says the first farmer, 'go and count the ducks in the pond.' The dog runs off for a moment and then comes back and barks four times. 'There! You see!' says the farmer. 'There are four ducks in the pond.' The other farmer goes and checks and there are indeed four ducks are in the pond. He still doesn't believe the dog can count however and wants to see him do it again. 'Go and do it again, Fido,' says the first farmer, and the dog runs off again. He returns and this time barks ten times. The second farmer goes to check and finds there are indeed now ten ducks on the pond. The second farmer is still not convinced and wants to see the dog count the ducks once more. 'OK, Fido,' says the first farmer, 'go and count the ducks one last time!' The dog runs off and this time returns and humps the other farmer's leg then seizes his walking stick and shakes it around. 'You see!' says the second farmer. 'He can't count at all! He's just gone mad!' 'Wrong!' says the first farmer. 'What he's telling you now is that there are more f***ing ducks on the pond than you can shake a stick at!'

A man is taking his new dog for a walk by the lake and throwing sticks across the water for the dog to fetch. The man is amazed to see that his new dog does not plunge into the water and swim to the sticks but instead is able to simply walk across the surface. The next day when he is out with the dog he meets a miserable pessimistic friend who he knows is never impressed by anything. 'Here! Watch this!' he says, and begins chucking sticks across the lake, confident that the sight of a dog walking on water will be something that will impress his friend. Each time he throws a stick the dog duly walks across the surface of the lake and brings it back. 'Notice anything unusual about my new dog?' says the man. 'I certainly do,' says the friend. 'He doesn't seem to be able to swim.'

I was out with my grandson in the park when we saw two dogs having sex. 'What's going on there, Grandpa?' asked my grandson. Embarrassed, I made up a story. 'Well, the dog on top has probably hurt his paw, so the one underneath is helping carry him to the vet.' My grandson shook his head. 'Unbelievable. Try to help someone out and you just get screwed.'

The dogs in our neighbourhood are very noisy. When one starts yapping they all get going, all through the night. It got so bad I went to see my doctor to get some sleeping pills. A week later I went back to the doctor covered in bites and scratches and threw the pills on his desk. 'This isn't working, doc. Do you know how hard it is to get a dog to swallow these things?'

Frank loses his champion poodle and puts an ad in the paper offering a £5,000 reward. No one comes forward, so the next week he put in an ad offering a £15,000 reward. There's still no luck, so the week after he doubles the reward to £30,000. Hearing nothing and getting desperate, he phones the newspaper to see about raising the reward even more. 'I'd like to speak to the editor about my advertisement,' says Frank. 'I'm sorry,' says the receptionist, 'he's out.' 'Can I speak to the head reporter?' asks Frank. 'Sorry,' says the receptionist, 'she's out too.' 'How about the advertising manager?' says Frank. 'Sorry,' says the receptionist, 'he's also out. In fact, everyone who works here is out except for me.' 'Well, where have they all gone?' asks Frank. The receptionist replies, 'They've all gone looking for a missing dog.'

Beryl takes her poodle to the groomer's and is appalled when they say the charge will be £200. 'That's outrageous,' says Beryl. 'The last time I had my hair done, it only cost £80.' 'That's as maybe,' says the groomer. 'But I bet you've never bitten your hairdresser.'

Larry had an incredible dog. It could do all sorts of things: roller-skate, juggle, handstands and back flips, play the accordion, do card tricks and impressions. Larry always reckoned they could make a fortune on the TV. But it wasn't to be, the dog was dead set on becoming a doctor.

A couple of dogs are taking a stroll. One says to the other, 'Hang on. I just want to check my messages.' Then he goes off and smells a lamp-post.

Two men pass each other in the graveyard. One says, 'Morning.' The other says, 'Nah. Just walking the dog.'

Phil gets a job as a dog walker. He goes to pick up a couple of dogs from the house of his first customer and they turn out to be a pekinese and a Rottweiler. The customer says, 'If the peke starts humping your leg, just shake him off.' 'OK,' says Phil. 'What if the Rottweiler does the same?' The customer says, 'You'd be wise to let him finish.'

If you pat a dog, he will wag his tail, but what will a goose do? Make him run like the clappers.

My dog was always chasing people on a bike. In the end there was nothing for it, we had to take his bike off him. But then he just sat in the garden all day barking. Then he started chasing people in a car. Which would have been OK except he kept wrecking the car when he tried to park it. Eventually we had to let him have his bike back because his park was worse than his bike.

Dick phones the RSPCA to tell them he has found a dog and some puppies all stuffed in a suitcase in the canal. 'Oh no,' says the RSPCA officer, 'can you tell if they are moving?' 'I presume so,' says Dick, 'at least that would explain the suitcase.'

Bill and Arthur are arguing about who has the better dog. 'My dog's best,' says Arthur, 'he wakes me up each morning, gets my slippers, goes to get my paper for me, collects some firewood for me, lights the stove, makes me a cup of tea and boils me an egg.' 'Mine's better,' says Arthur, 'he wakes me up, gets my slippers, gets my paper, collects the firewood, lights the stove, makes a cup of tea, boils me an egg and then stands on his head.' 'Why does he stand on his head?' asks Bill. 'I don't have an egg cup,' says Arthur.

A dog walks into a bar and says, 'Hello. Look, I'm a talking dog! That's good, isn't it? So how about a drink for a talking dog?' 'Certainly,' says the barman, 'just go down the corridor and the gents is the first on the right.'

Harry walks into a bar with his dog. 'Sorry,' says the bartender, 'but we don't allow dogs in here.' 'But this is a special dog,' says Harry. 'He can talk.' 'Rubbish!' says the bartender. 'It's true,' says Harry. 'Ask him a question.' 'OK,' says the bartender. 'What would you like to drink?' 'I'll have a pint of beer,' says the dog. 'No!' says the bartender. 'I don't believe it. That's just you doing some kind of ventriloquist trick.' 'No it's not,' says Harry. 'I'll tell you what. I'll go to the gents while you ask him again.' Once Harry has gone, the bartender says, 'OK, dog. Now what would you like to drink?' 'I told you before,' says the dog. 'A pint of beer!' 'Wow!' says the bartender. 'You really can talk! OK, I will give you £10 if you walk over to the bar across the street, order a beer from the landlord in there, drink it then spit it out in his face and tell him that you prefer my beer.' The dog takes the £10 and sets off across the road. A minute later Harry gets back from the gents. 'Where's my dog?' asks Harry. 'Don't panic,' says the bartender, 'I just sent him out on an errand and gave him £10 for his trouble!' Harry rushes outside where he finds his dog in the car park enjoying himself doggy fashion with a lady dog. 'What on earth are you doing?' says Harry. 'I've never seen you get up to this sort of thing before.' 'Well,' says the dog, 'I've never had £10 before.'

DOG FOOD

There's a new brand of luxury dog food available. It's called Postman Pâté.

The Woofy Chunks dog food company has just gone bust. Apparently they've had to call in the retrievers.

DOORS

Did you hear the joke about the glass door? I couldn't see it myself.

Barry sees Gary walking down the street carrying a door. 'What are you doing?' asks Barry. 'Oh,' says Gary, 'I lost my keys. I was worried someone would find them and be able to get into my house. So I've taken the door with me.' 'You stupid idiot,' says Barry. 'What if you lose the door somewhere? How are you going to get back into your house then?' 'I've thought of that,' says Gary. 'I left the window open!'

DOUGHNUTS

Elsie quit her job at the doughnut-making factory. She says she's had enough of the hole business.

DRINK DRIVING

What's the best way of avoiding a drunk-driving charge? Driving to a bar and getting so wasted you can't put the key in the ignition.

Harry tells Tom, 'I don't think I should have driven home from the pub last night.' 'Why not?' asks Tom. 'Because,' says Harry, 'when I went out, I was on foot.'

George is charged with drunk driving and has to defend himself in court. 'Your honour, it will mean a big change for me if I'm no longer allowed to drive lawfully,' says George. 'And what change is that?' asks the judge. George says, 'It'll mean I'll have to drive unlawfully.'

I'm a member of the AAAA. The society for drunk drivers.

A car slews off the road and cartwheels down a slope, flipping four times before crashing into a barn. The farmer rushes out of his house to find the driver climbing out of the wreckage with a bottle in his hand. 'My Lord,' says the farmer. 'Are you drunk?' 'Course I is,' slurs the driver. 'What d'you think I am, a bloody stuntman?'

Two drunks get lost while driving home from an evening drinking at a country pub. 'I think we might be getting closer to the town,' says the driver. 'How can you tell?' says the other. 'I'm hitting more people,' says the first.

Gary and Barry are driving home after a heavy session in the pub. 'Look out for that tree!' yells Gary, but it's too late and they crash straight into it. Later in hospital Gary says to Barry, 'You idiot! Why didn't you do something when I told you to watch out for that tree?' 'I would have done,' says Barry, 'but you were the one who was driving.'

Bert gets pulled over by the police for drunk driving. The policeman asks him to blow in a breathalyser. 'I can't,' says Bert. 'I have weak lungs. Blowing might injure them.' 'OK,' says the officer. 'In that case we'll have to take a urine sample.' 'Sorry,' says Bert. 'I have shy bladder syndrome. That would be impossible.' 'Very well,' says the officer. 'It will have to be a blood sample then.' 'Absolutely not,' says Bert. 'I have a severe phobia about needles.' 'OK,' says the officer. 'Then I'm going to tell you something you can do – you can get out of that car and walk in a straight line down the road.' 'Oh no, officer, I couldn't do that,' says Bert. 'Really?' says the policeman. 'And why can't you walk in a straight line?' Bert says, 'Because I am hopelessly drunk.'

Freddie gets pulled over for drunk driving. 'I've not had a drop, officer. I've been dry all night and sober all week.' 'Very well, sir,' says the policeman. 'But I'll still need to see your licence.' 'It's in my glove compartment,' says Freddie. 'I'll just reach over and get it out. Here, can you hold my hip flask?'

DRIVING

There are some people in the world who simply do not know how to drive. My name for these people is 'everybody except me'.

Bill tells Tom, 'My wife drives like lightning.' 'Oh,' says Tom, 'so you mean she drives quite fast?' 'No,' says Bill. 'She keeps crashing into tall buildings.'

Ron is a lorry driver but he isn't too bright. When he gets his new lorry he decides to test the air brakes by driving over a cliff.

Did you hear about the man who reversed into a car boot sale and accidentally sold his car engine for ten quid?

DRIVING OFFENCES

I got pulled over by the police for eating while I was driving. On reflection, perhaps a barbecue wasn't the best choice.

Betty and Barry are taking a trip in their car when Barry drives it the wrong way down a one-way street. 'Do you have any idea where we're going?' asks Betty. 'No,' says Barry. 'But it doesn't look like anyone likes it there. They're all leaving.'

Bobby gets pulled over by a traffic cop who asks to see his driving licence. 'Will you guys make your minds up?!' says Bobby. 'You took it off me last week and now you want to see it again!'

A teenager gets pulled over by the police after doing 80mph through a speed trap. As the policeman writes a ticket he says, 'Boy, I've been waiting all day for you.' The kid replies, 'Yeah? Well I got here as fast as I could.'

A policeman stops Glenda's car for speeding. He goes up to her window and says, 'I'd guess you were going on 60.' 'How dare you,' says Glenda. 'I was 52 last birthday.'

I am going to complain about the policeman who asked me to pull over in my car this morning. I thought it was very rude. I was in the middle of a phone call at the time.

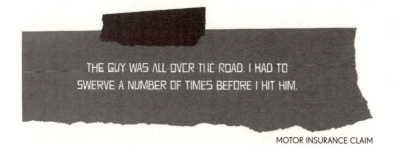

THE GUY WAS ALL OVER THE ROAD. I HAD TO SWERVE A NUMBER OF TIMES BEFORE I HIT HIM.

MOTOR INSURANCE CLAIM

DRIVING TEST

A young man is having a driving lesson. 'OK,' says the driving instructor, 'when we get to the top of this hill I want you to change gear.' 'What's your game?' asks the pupil. 'You never told me I had to bring some other clothes with me.'

Nigel is doing his driving test. The examiner tells him, 'When we get to the next roundabout, I want you to leave by the first exit.' So when they reach the roundabout, Nigel opens the car door and jumps out.

A driving instructor asks his pupil, 'What do you do at a traffic light?' 'Pick my nose for a few minutes,' says the pupil.

Rufus is taking a driving test. The examiner says, 'If you were driving through thick fog, what would you use?' Rufus thinks for a bit and scratches his head. 'I dunno. A car?'

Fred is doing his driving test. His examiner asks, 'What would you do if a blind man held up his stick and crossed the road in front of us?' 'I'd put my foot down on the accelerator,' says Fred. 'Why would you do that?' asks examiner. 'What's the problem?' says Fred. 'It's not like he'd be able to take my registration.'

Norma gets back from her driving test. 'How did you get on?' asks Nobby. 'The rotten swine failed me,' says Norma. 'Oh no,' says Nobby. 'What did he pull you up on?' 'A rope,' says Norma. 'Our car's at the bottom of the Thames.'

The traffic is terrible round here. Last week my son had to abandon his vehicle and complete his driving test on foot.

DRUGS

People are so negative. Why do they always have to say, He's addicted to drugs'? Why can't they say, 'He's passionate about drugs'?

Two men decided to inhale some recreational drugs. Unfortunately, their supplier gave them a sachet of curry powder instead of the class A drugs they were expecting and they both ended up in hospital. One of them was in a korma and the other had a dodgy tikka.

The drug ecstasy was discovered by a German pharmaceutical company in 1912. Nobody else got to hear about it until the 1980s. That's because the employees of the German pharmaceutical company had been off their tits dancing and having a huge party for the previous 70 years.

Barry is stopped by the police one night by a policeman and a sniffer dog. 'I'm going to have to search you, sir,' says the policeman, 'because my dog has just told me that you are on drugs.' 'You're telling me that I'm on drugs!' says Barry, 'and yet you're the one who's talking to a dog.'

Lenny was found guilty of smuggling 15lb of cannabis into the country. He was sentenced to a total of seven years – two for the drugs and five for contravening the decimal weights and measures regulations.

Dick managed to smuggle some coke through airport security by shoving it up his backside. He was gutted when he found he could buy another can of the stuff in the departure lounge.

Q: What do you get when you combine cigarette papers, marijuana and Viagra?
A: Stiff joints.

DRUNKENNESS

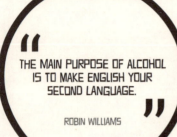

"THE MAIN PURPOSE OF ALCOHOL IS TO MAKE ENGLISH YOUR SECOND LANGUAGE."

ROBIN WILLIAMS

The definition of alcohol: the anaesthetic that helps us endure the operation of life.

If there's one thing I can't stand when I'm drunk, it's up.

I don't think of myself as an alcoholic. I prefer the term soberphobic.

I blame my wife for driving me to drink. Well, to be more precise she gave me a lift to the pub last night.

Two drunk guys are trying to find their way home along a train track. 'This is a long set of stairs,' says one. 'I know,' says the other, 'and the handrails have been put on far too low.'

It's terrible when you realise you're the only drunk person at a party. It completely ruined my son's sixth birthday for me.

Nobby gets home from the pub and his wife says, 'I can't believe how drunk you are each time you come home.' 'That's rubbish,' says Nobby, 'I'm not drunk.' 'Yes you are,' she says. 'No I'm chuffing not,' he replies. 'Prove it!' she says. 'Can you tell the time?' 'Of course I can!' says Nobby. He walks over to the clock and says, 'I'm not flipping drunk!'

I woke up at six o'clock this morning and lay there with a terrible hangover. Already my next-door neighbour was out mowing his front garden. At first I thought I'd smack him in the mouth. But then I thought, 'No! Blow it! He'll just have to mow around me.'

I asked my doctor what the best thing for a hangover was. He told me the only sure way was to drink vast quantities of alcohol the night before.

One night in bed Norma tells her husband Nobby, 'You only want sex when you're drunk.' 'That's not true,' says Nobby, 'sometimes I want a kebab.'

There's a new warning they're printing on bottles of alcohol. It says, 'Warning – drinking alcoholic beverages before pregnancy can result in pregnancy.'

My dad's answer to everything was alcohol. He wasn't a hard drinker but he was very little help in quizzes.

Ted went out drinking for the evening. At the end of the night, he realised he was over the limit so he did something that he'd never done before and took a bus home. The bus got him home safely and without incident, which was a bit of a surprise as he'd never driven one before.

Ron gets home drunk. He knows his wife won't let him in because he's been drinking so he decides to pretend that he has brought her some flowers. He knocks on his front door and when his wife looks out of the bedroom window above, he calls, 'I have flowers for the pretty lady!' A moment later, his wife is opening the front door to let him in. 'Where are the flowers?' she snarls. 'Where's the pretty lady?' asks Ron.

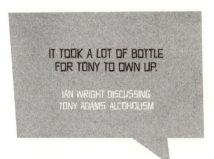

IT TOOK A LOT OF BOTTLE FOR TONY TO OWN UP.

IAN WRIGHT DISCUSSING TONY ADAMS ALCOHOLISM

The police stop two men who are drunk. 'Where do you live?' asks the policeman. 'No fixed abode,' says the first drunk. The policeman turns to his friend and asks, 'And where do you live?' 'In the flat downstairs from him,' says the second drunk.

Norman staggers in from the pub and his wife is furious with him. 'Why do you come home half-drunk like this every night?' she yells. 'Sorry, love,' says Norman. 'I keep running out of money.'

Two men are talking. One has had a terrible night. 'I was so drunk last night,' he says, 'I didn't realise I'd managed to find my way home. I climbed up the stairs, got into bed and then in the morning I still didn't realise I was at home with my wife and when I woke up I handed her a £20 note.' 'So what's the problem?' asks his friend. 'She reached in her bedside drawer,' says the first man, 'and got me £10 change.'

Harry is complaining to Dick about his wife: 'She spends every night going from one pub to another.' 'Does she stop when she's blotto?' asks Dick. 'No,' says Harry, 'she stops when she finds me.'

Brenda is concerned her husband Tom is an alcoholic so she goes to the doctor, who gives her a powder to put in his tea which he says should put him off drinking. A week later, the doctor asks her, 'Did it work? Has it cured him?' 'Well,' says Brenda, 'it's cured him of drinking tea.'

> "I TOLD MY GIRLFRIEND LAST NIGHT HOW MUCH I LOVED HER AND SHE SAID THAT I MUST HAVE BEEN OUT DRINKING AGAIN. I ASKED HER WHY SHE'D SAY THAT AND SHE SAID, 'BECAUSE I'M YOUR FATHER.'"
>
> DAVE GEORGE

A woman is fed up with her husband coming home drunk every night but rather than yelling at him again, she decides to use some reverse psychology. When he staggers in, she's waiting for him in a sexy nightie. 'Come on, big boy,' she says, 'let's go up to bed.' 'We might as well,' says the husband, 'I'm going to be in trouble when I get home, anyway.'

Did you see the survey they did about the way most people choose to go home after a long night in the pub drinking? The results were staggering.

Frank and his pals roll out of the pub and stagger off into the night. They end up in the middle of the road and start singing and shouting. Eventually one of the windows is flung open and an angry woman calls out. 'Can't you shut up and go to bed!' One of the drunks calls back, 'Are you Frank Smith's wife?' 'Yes I am,' she shouts. 'Oh good,' says the drunk. 'I thought we had the right street. Can you come down here and pick him out? Then the rest of us can get home.'

Larry tells Nobby he has bought a bag off the internet that can tell him exactly how much he's had to drink. 'I've got a bag that can do that too,' says Nobby, 'but I married mine.'

Vince goes to the doctor's and asks, 'Do you treat alcoholics?' 'Yes, I do,' says the doctor. 'Thank God for that,' says Vince. 'Let's go down the pub. I'm flipping skint.'

One night Hamish collapses on the way home from the pub. The next morning a woman comes by and finds him sleeping it off under a hedge. Hamish is wearing his kilt and the woman takes a quick peek under it. She quickly discovers that Hamish is not wearing any underwear and, as a joke, she ties a blue ribbon round his pecker. A few hours later Hamish wakes up. He stands to have a pee and is surprised when he finds the blue ribbon tied round his organ. 'Hoots,' says Hamish. 'I don't know what you've been up to, wee feller. But I'm as pleased as punch you won first prize.'

A police officer watches a drunk stagger across a busy road. As he gets to the pavement the officer approaches the man. 'Drinking, sir?' he says. The drunk peers at him and says, 'Depends. What have you got?'

If you're going out for a night on the town be sure to line your stomach with some green beans, mango, blueberries and orange. It won't stop you getting drunk, but if you throw up it will look more colourful.

Alcohol can cause severe problems for both your long- and short-term memory, so doctors are developing a new drug that will help restore them. Or you could just get married, in which case your spouse will always be ready to remind you about every idiotic thing you've ever done.

Herbert walks into a bar and shouts, 'A beer for me, a beer for every customer here and a beer for the barman!' Everyone cheers and the drinks are served, but when the barman asks for the money, Herbert says he is broke. The barman responds by beating Herbert up and throwing him into the street. The next day the same thing happens. Herbert walks into the bar and shouts, 'A beer for me, a beer for every customer here and a beer for the barman!' The barman figures Herbert wouldn't risk another beating, but when he's served the drinks and asks for the money, Herbert confesses he hasn't got any. The furious barman pounds Herbert's nose flat and throws him into the street again. The next day, Herbert is back yet again, except this time he has a large wad of money in his hand. He shouts out, 'A beer for me and a beer for every customer here!' 'Hey!' shouts the barman. 'What about me?' Herbert shakes his head. 'Nah! You turn nasty once you've had a drink.'

DUCKS

A duck is standing by the side of the road. A chicken comes along and stands next to him looking left and right. 'Don't do it, mate,' says the duck, 'you'll never hear the end of it!'

A couple of ducks book into a motel. Later that evening, one of the ducks goes to the reception desk and asks if they sell condoms. 'Yes,' says the clerk. 'I have some here. Would you like me to put them on your bill?' 'Hey,' exclaims the duck. 'What gave you the idea I'm kinky?'

Barry is walking through the local woods when he comes across a white duck covered in poop. He has a packet of tissues in his pocket so he uses a couple of them to wipe the duck clean. He lets the duck go and is astonished to see another poop-smeared duck waddle round from behind a tree. Again, Barry wipes the duck off and lets it go. Amazingly, a third dirty duck appears from behind the tree and Barry uses the last of his tissues to clean it up. As he sends the duck on its way he hears a low, gravelly voice comes from behind the tree. 'Oi. Got any more tissues?' 'N . . . N . . . No,' stammers Barry nervously. There's a pause, then the voice rumbles. 'You couldn't find me some more ducks, could you?'

A duck walks into a shop and says, 'Got any duck feed?' 'No,' says the shopkeeper, 'we have no call for it so we don't stock it.' 'OK,' says the duck, and leaves. A few minutes later the duck returns and says, 'Got any duck feed?' 'No,' says the shopkeeper. 'I told you before. We don't sell duck food.' 'OK,' says the duck, and leaves. A few minutes go by and the duck comes back yet again. 'Got any duck feed?' he asks. 'No!' says the shopkeeper. 'I've told you twice, we don't have duck feed, we've never had duck feed and we never will have duck feed. If you ask me again, I will nail your feet to the floor.' The duck leaves. A few minutes later he comes back. 'Got any nails?' asks the duck. 'No,' says the shopkeeper. 'OK,' says the duck. 'Got any duck feed . . . ?'

DYSLEXIA

I've got a friend who has dyslexia. He's been applying for jobs recently and asked me to check his application forms. One of the questions asked if he had any special needs. He'd written: 'I need to be given a bit more time than others as I have sex daily.'

After a long battle with leukaemia and a failed attempt at suicide, Kevin finally overcame his dyslexia and passed his school spelling test.

" OLD MCDONALD WAS DYSLEXIC, E-O-I-O-E. "

BILLY CONNOLLY

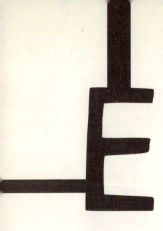

EASTER

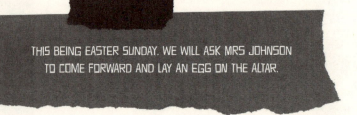

THIS BEING EASTER SUNDAY, WE WILL ASK MRS JOHNSON TO COME FORWARD AND LAY AN EGG ON THE ALTAR.

PARISH NOTICES

ECONOMICS AND ECONOMISTS

The definition of materialism – buying things you don't particularly need, with money you don't actually have, to impress people who don't really matter.

The economics teacher asks the class, 'What do we mean when we say, "It takes money to make money"?' One of the pupils puts his hand up. 'Please, miss,' he says, 'is it because you have to have some real money to look at so you can copy the design exactly?'

Good news – it is possible for two to live as cheaply as one. Bad news – probably only for half as long.

The average salary increase is large enough to bump up your tax bracket, but too small to make any difference to your take-home pay.

Yesterday I was privileged to meet the richest man in Greece. Say what you like about his country's economy, I have to say he did an excellent job polishing my shoes.

Two economists are shipwrecked on a desert island. They have no money with them but nevertheless over the next few years they make millions of pounds selling their hats to one another.

> "SPARE NO EXPENSE TO MAKE EVERYTHING AS ECONOMICAL AS POSSIBLE."
>
> – SAMUEL GOLDWYN

A physicist, an engineer and an economist are shipwrecked. The only food they have is a can of beans but they have no way of opening it. 'I know,' says the physicist. 'We can put the can in a fire and the content will expand to the point where the can bursts.' 'Good idea,' says the engineer. 'And I can design a rig that will trap the beans before they're thrown clear.' 'Nah,' says the economist. 'Too much like hard work. Let's assume we have a can-opener and take it from there . . .'

The council decide to build a monument outside the town hall. The job is put out to tender, three builders put in their bids and are called in for interview with the town clerk. 'Explain your tender,' the town clerk asks the first builder. 'Well,' says the builder, 'the job will cost £3,000. £1,000 for me, £1,000 for materials and £1,000 for my men.' The town clerk calls in the second builder and asks him the same question. 'Well,' says the second builder, 'the job will cost £6,000. That's £2,000 for me, £2,000 for materials and £2,000 for my workmen.' The town clerk calls in the third builder who says, 'The job will cost £9,000.' 'Oh dear!' says the town clerk. 'That sounds very expensive. How do you come to that figure?' 'Well, says the third builder, 'it's £3,000 for me, £3,000 for you and then we get the first guy to do the job for us!'

EDUCATION

Last year the school in our area became an academy sponsored by IKEA. Results have improved but the kids are always complaining now about how long assembly takes.

In a significant relaxation of eligibility criteria, the government has announced it will recruit school teachers from the ranks of the completely unsuitable.

I went to see a live production based on the Texas Chainsaw Massacre. Personally I think my daughter's primary school should just do a normal nativity play.

Tom's son is a bit soft. Tom worries that his wife has not prepared the boy for his first day at school. So before the lad sets off for his first day, Tom beats him up and nicks his dinner money.

Jake has been doing an English exam. 'Were there any difficult questions?' asks his mum. 'Yes,' says Jake, 'it asked what was the past tense of "think". I thought and I thought and I thought but I just couldn't come up with it, so in the end I wrote "thunk".'

"ON MY FIRST DAY OF SCHOOL MY PARENTS DROPPED ME OFF AT THE WRONG NURSERY. THERE I WAS . . . SURROUNDED BY TREES AND BUSHES."

KEN DODD

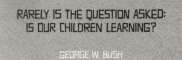

RARELY IS THE QUESTION ASKED: IS OUR CHILDREN LEARNING?

GEORGE W. BUSH

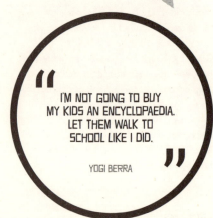

"I'M NOT GOING TO BUY MY KIDS AN ENCYCLOPAEDIA. LET THEM WALK TO SCHOOL LIKE I DID."

YOGI BERRA

> "MY FATHER WANTED ME TO HAVE ALL THE EDUCATIONAL OPPORTUNITIES HE NEVER HAD. SO HE SENT ME TO A GIRLS' SCHOOL."
>
> KEN DODD

Definition of teaching: the greatest act of optimism performed by mankind.

Education might show us how things work, but experience teaches us how they fail.

My son did a multiple-choice test at school today. I think he did really well. He said he got all 'A's.

Tom's son has graduated in both psychology and philosophy. No one will give him a job but at least he knows why.

My school was very select. In fact it was so posh we had to refer to the gym as James.

EXCUSE NOTES FOR ABSENCE FROM SCHOOL

▶ Gloria was absent yesterday as she was having a gangover.

▶ My daughter was absent yesterday because she was tired. She spent a weekend with the Marines.

▶ Please excuse Jennifer for missing school yesterday. We forgot to get the Sunday paper off the porch and when we found it on Monday, we thought it was Sunday.

▶ Please excuse Jimmy from being. It was his father's fault.

▶ Please excuse Mary for being absent yesterday. She was in bed with gramps.

EFFICIENCY

Pete took a course in business efficiency and time management and practised his new skills by looking at improvements he could make to his wife's household routines. He's made remarkable progress since then; it used to take his wife at least 30 minutes to cook his dinner, now he does it in 10.

ELECTRICAL GOODS

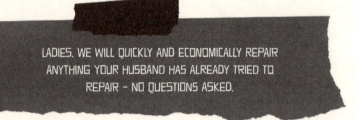

LADIES, WE WILL QUICKLY AND ECONOMICALLY REPAIR ANYTHING YOUR HUSBAND HAS ALREADY TRIED TO REPAIR – NO QUESTIONS ASKED.

SIGN IN THE WINDOW OF HARDWARE SHOP

ELECTRICITY

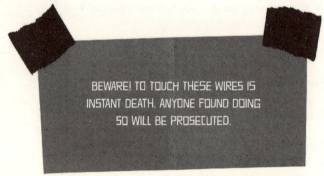

BEWARE! TO TOUCH THESE WIRES IS INSTANT DEATH. ANYONE FOUND DOING SO WILL BE PROSECUTED.

WARNING NOTICE AT A RAILWAY STATION

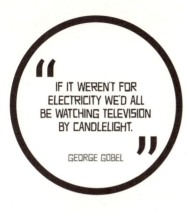

"IF IT WEREN'T FOR ELECTRICITY WE'D ALL BE WATCHING TELEVISION BY CANDLELIGHT."

GEORGE GOBEL

Q: How many electricians does it take to screw in a light bulb?
A: One. They're pretty good at that sort of thing.

Q: How did the electrician lose all the power in his home?
A: He got married.

ELEPHANTS

An elephant dies at the zoo. The local news go to interview the keeper and find him in floods of tears. 'You're clearly very upset at your old friend dying,' says the reporter. 'It's not that,' says the keeper, 'it's just that now I've got to bury the flipping thing.'

An elephant is taunting a mouse about its tiny size. 'Look how minuscule and puny you appear next to my magnificent, muscular bulk,' says the elephant. 'Hey, gimme a break,' says the mouse. 'I've been sick.'

Basil rings up his pal, Larry, and offers to sell him an elephant for £5,000. 'What do I need an elephant for?' says Larry. 'And where would I put it? My apartment is so small I can't even keep a dog.' 'OK,' says Basil. 'Make it £4,000.' 'No,' says Larry. 'Don't be ridiculous.' 'OK,' says Basil. '£4,000 and I'll throw in a giraffe.' 'Well,' says Barry, 'now we have a deal.'

A man is about to poach an elephant. But when he looks at it he thinks, 'I'm never going to fit it in this saucepan.'

Jerry tried to cross his poodle with a circus elephant, now he's got a cross-eyed dog that has to sit on an inflatable ring.

Q: How do you get down from an elephant?
A: You don't get down from an elephant. You get down from a duck.

Q: Why do elephants paint their toenails red?
A: So they can hide in cherry trees.

Q: Why is an elephant big, grey and wrinkly?
A: Because if it was small, white and hard it would be an aspirin.

Q: What do you get if you cross an elephant with an apple?
A: A pie that never forgets.

EMAIL

The Pope has appointed someone to be the official patron saint of email. He's called St Francis of a cc.

EMERGENCIES

Captain Jack has to abandon ship. He calls the coastguard on his mobile phone. 'Help,' he shouts. 'We had to ditch our boat and now we're in the water.' The coastguard says, 'Capsize?' Jack says, 'Seven and a quarter.'

I just saw a traffic warden drowning so I immediately reported it to the emergency services. I hope they come soon otherwise it will be a complete waste of a stamp.

EMERGENCY SERVICES

This morning I thought a pipe had burst in my house so I called out the plumber and the water board and the emergency services. But it was really embarrassing because after they'd all arrived I realised it was just my tummy making a noise.

Donald Trump tried to call out the emergency services by dialling 911 on his phone. He found the nine easily enough, but then couldn't find the eleven anywhere.

An old lady calls the fire brigade and says, 'Come quickly! Two naked men are trying to climb up to my bedroom window.' 'I think you need the police,' says the fireman. 'No, it's you I want,' says the old lady. 'Their ladder isn't big enough.'

EMISSIONS TEST

I recently failed an emissions test. It was quite embarrassing because I wasn't even in my car at the time.

ENCOURAGEMENT

ONCE AGAIN WE GOT A GOOD KICK UP THE BACKSIDE. MAYBE IT'S THE SHOT IN THE ARM WE NEEDED.

ALAN BORDER

END OF THE WORLD

If you ever hear that the world is about to end, the best advice is to go to the Isle of Man. Apparently everything happens 50 years later there.

ENEMIES

The enemy of my enemy of my enemy of my enemy of my enemy is Kevin Bacon.

ENERGY EFFICIENCY

I've started using those energy-efficient light bulbs and I've found they really do save energy. They screw in much more easily.

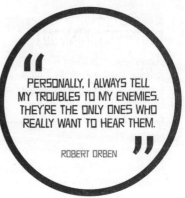

> PERSONALLY, I ALWAYS TELL MY TROUBLES TO MY ENEMIES. THEY'RE THE ONLY ONES WHO REALLY WANT TO HEAR THEM.
>
> ROBERT ORBEN

ENGAGEMENT

Ben and Kirsty are a young couple who want to get married. Kirsty knows that Ben has been saving for an engagement ring despite still being a student and having little money. What he really needs is a new computer for his work and she keeps telling him he should spend his money on that and they can then wait to get engaged. But one night Ben reaches in his pocket and produces a sparkling diamond ring for her. Kirsty is stunned and says, 'Wow! Do you have something to ask me?' 'Yes I do,' says Ben, getting down on one knee. 'Will you buy me a new computer?'

A guy invites his mother to a small party he's holding at his house. When he greets her at the door, he says, 'I have a surprise for you, Mum. There are seven girls at this party and I've decided to propose to one of them. You don't know her, but have a chat with each girl in turn and see if you can guess which one it is.' The mother does so and towards the end of the evening her son comes over and asks if she can guess who will be her future daughter-in-law. 'Yes,' says Mum. 'It's the brunette in the red dress.' 'That's amazing,' says the guy. 'How could you tell?' Mum says, 'Because I don't like her.'

ENTERTAINMENT

After the success of the Fringe at the Edinburgh Festival, they've decided to have the same sort of thing at the Cheltenham Festival. This year thoroughbred race horses from all over the world will be taking to the stage to perform stand-up, comedy sketches and a little-known early play by Bertolt Brecht.

> "LAST TIME I ACTED MY NAME WAS SO LOW ON THE PROGRAMME I WAS GETTING ORDERS FOR THE PRINTING."
>
> FRANK CARSON

Bert always wanted to be a big hit on Broadway — so he jumped off the Empire State Building.

Gerry wants to be a stand-up comedian and finds out that his local hospice is always looking for acts to help entertain their patients. Gerry goes along to try out some of his material, but his jokes are met with stony silence. Eventually he has to give up — no one is laughing at all. They hate him. 'Sorry, folks,' says Gerry. 'It's been great to be here, but have to go. I hope you get better soon.' And a voice from the audience shouts back. 'Yeah. And the same to you.'

I've been in the comedy business for years. I started so long ago I can't remember the time I got my first laugh; unfortunately, I can't remember the time I got my last one either.

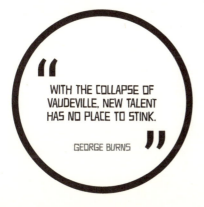

> "WITH THE COLLAPSE OF VAUDEVILLE, NEW TALENT HAS NO PLACE TO STINK."
>
> GEORGE BURNS

> "WHEN I GIVE CONCERTS, THE TICKETS SELL FOR $5 TO $100, BUT FOR MY CONCERTS THE $5 SEATS ARE DOWN IN FRONT ... THE FURTHER BACK YOU GO, THE MORE YOU HAVE TO PAY. THE $100 SEATS ARE THE LAST TWO ROWS AND THOSE TICKETS GO LIKE HOTCAKES! IN FACT, IF YOU PAY $200 YOU DON'T HAVE TO COME AT ALL."
>
> JACK BENNY

A comedian goes to entertain the residents at the local old people's home but finds them a difficult audience. They refuse to respond to his knock-knock jokes unless he can show them some ID.

EPILEPSY

A man goes to the vet and produces a goldfish. 'What's the matter with him?' asks the vet. 'He's got epilepsy,' says the man. 'He looks all right to me,' says the vet. 'Wait a minute,' says the man. 'I haven't taken him out of his bowl yet.'

EQUALITY

> WHEN MY SISTER AND I WERE GROWING UP THERE WAS NEVER ANY DOUBT IN OUR MINDS THAT MEN AND WOMEN WERE EQUAL – IF NOT MORE SO.
>
> AL GORE

ESCALATORS

Uncle Bernie will sue anyone for anything. He even tried to sue our local department store – he claimed that calling an escalator that took you anywhere but up was false advertising.

ESCAPE

During the Second World War three prisoners of war manage to escape and run away into a forest. The German guards are after them so they escape by climbing up trees. The guards run up to the tree where the first POW has hidden and shout, 'We saw you come this way! Come down and give yourself up.' But the POW makes a noise like a bird. The Germans hear 'toowit, toowit, toowit' and give up and move on to the next tree. Again they call, 'We saw you come this way! Come down and give yourself up.' But the second POW also makes a noise like a bird and goes, 'tweet, tweet, tweet'. Again the Germans are fooled so they move on to the third tree and call out again, 'We saw you come this way! Come down and give yourself up.' The third POW thinks for a moment before going: 'Mooo, mooo, mooo!'

ESKIMOS

In the frozen north, an Inuit couple get married and settle down in their igloo for their first night together. They get up the next morning and the bride finds out she's six months pregnant.

ETERNAL LIFE

It has been announced that we are now one step nearer to eternal life. A scientist has just developed a vaccine that makes people immune to dying on Tuesdays.

The people who yearn for an endless afterlife are usually the same ones who get bored stiff on a wet Sunday afternoon.

EUROVISION SONG CONTEST

It's great they now have the Paralympics for sport. And of course the Eurovision song contest. Which is like the Paralympics of music.

EXAGGERATION

If I had a pound for every time someone accused me of exaggerating, I'd now have five zillion pounds.

EXAMINATION

A doctor is called in to a clinic by a distraught nurse who had been preparing a patient for examination. The doctor explains to the patient, 'When the nurse asked you to strip to the waist, she meant from the neck downwards. Not from the toes upwards!'

EXERCISE

Dick had to break up with his gym. Apparently things just weren't working out.

Harry read that you should exercise both your mind and your body every day. Now he thinks about jogging on a daily basis.

Stan goes out for a jog but two minutes later he's back home. 'Did you forget something?' asks his wife. 'Yes,' says Stan. 'The fact that if I run for more than two minutes I will collapse and die.'

One day at the gym, Clive asks Bob, 'Why do you keep bending your knees, tucking them into your chest and tipping yourself forward like that?' 'Oh, you know,' says Bob. 'that's just the way I roll.'

Tom asks Harry, 'What was your New Year resolution last year?' 'To join the local gym,' says Harry. 'Oh yes,' says Tom. 'And what's your resolution this year?' 'To start going to it,' says Harry.

Norman's doctor told him to start his exercise programme very gradually. So this afternoon he drove past the gym.

Barry has found a machine at the gym which he can use for all his requirements. Apparently you can get Mars Bars, Bounty, Kit Kats, M&Ms and cans of Coke from it.

Norman isn't particularly athletic. He gets out of breath playing chess.

Martha used to perform tantric pelvic bouncing to tone her buttocks while she was working out. And that is why she was one of the most popular maths teachers in the school.

According to medical studies sex is a great way to give yourself a cardiovascular workout. Can that really be true? Is two minutes every six weeks really going to have that much impact?

Tom's mother-in-law took up skipping in order to get some exercise. In the end she was ordered to stop by the local council because she was registering seven on the Richter scale.

Jane Fonda released a number of very popular aerobics exercise videos in the 1980s. Recently she put out a new one. Although to save money you could just watch one of the old ones with the speed slowed down.

Jane Fonda released 20 exercise videos between 1982 and 1995. In 2010 at the age of 73 she made a new exercise video. She'd make another one but she's been stuck in a squatting position ever since.

Barry and Cynthia go to a pre-natal class. The instructor recommends that they both take exercise together by going on slow, gentle walks. Barry sticks his hand up, 'Will it hurt the baby if my wife carries a golf-bag?'

Healthy eating and exercise can add years to your life; the trouble is, they're always added on at the crappy end.

George's exercise regime has not got off to a good start – he bought himself a treadmill, but so far he's only managed widths.

Larry does ten sit-ups every morning – that's the maximum number of times the clock lets him use the snooze button.

Glenda always goes jogging in hot pants – they're not shorts, it's the friction from her thighs.

When Beryl signed up for her Pilates class they told her to come in wearing loose clothing. Trouble was, she didn't have any, which was the reason for the Pilates in the first place.

Sammy's mother-in-law says she's been trying to burn off some calories. So for Christmas Sammy bought her a flame-thrower.

Bert is 75 years old, is as fit as a fiddle and has never set foot a gym. 'What do you do for exercise?' asks his doctor. 'Mostly I act as a pallbearer,' says Bert. 'Really?' says the doctor. 'Do you go to a lot of funerals?' 'Yes,' says Bert. 'Mostly my mates who died while they were trying to exercise.'

If God wanted me to touch my toes he'd have put them higher up on my body.

Gertrude goes to her exercise class. She spends a whole hour bending, twisting, stretching and jumping up and down. And when she's finally got her leotard on, she finds the class finished ten minutes ago.

Norman goes to the gym and asks his trainer which machine he should use if he wants to impress women. 'The cash point in the lobby,' says the trainer.

EXPERIENCE

Experience might not prevent you from making mistakes, but at least the ones you do make will be new and interesting.

EXPERTISE

Experts are people who get to know more and more about less and less. The best of them know all there is to know about nothing at all.

EXPLORERS

" EXPERTS HAVE SPENT YEARS DEVELOPING WEAPONS THAT CAN DESTROY PEOPLE'S LIVES BUT LEAVE BUILDINGS INTACT. THEY'RE CALLED MORTGAGES.

JEREMY HARDY "

The explorer and adventurer Commodore Wilkins is waiting in his hotel room for his literary agent to phone him. Wilkins is on a book-signing tour to promote his autobiography that details all the adventures of his life – such as the time he spent three weeks tramping over frozen tundra through a blizzard to rescue a party of tourists trapped on a glacier; or the time he had to endure the blistering sun of the Qatar desert to find water after his jeep blew a tyre and turned over; or the time he had to swim the freezing Arctic waters in his underwear to reach a lifeboat full of shipwrecked orphans and lost three toes to frostbite. The agent calls him and asks Wilkins if he'd like to meet him round the corner at a coffee house. Wilkins looks out the window and says, 'No. It's raining.'

An anthropologist visits a colleague on a remote tropical island. The colleague tells him he's made an extraordinary breakthrough in translating the language of the natives. 'Look,' he says. 'If I point to that palm tree, listen to what the natives call it.' He points and a group of natives all call out the word 'Unlagoo'. 'Now watch this,' says the man. He points to the sky and the natives all cry out 'Unlagoo'. Next the man points at his own leg. Again all the natives say 'Unlagoo'. 'It's incredible,' says the man. 'My theory is that they have chosen the exact same word to represent everything they see around them. It's remarkable.' 'It is indeed remarkable,' says the anthropologist. 'Even more so because on the neighbouring island the exact same word means "index finger".'

EYESIGHT

Q: How many optometrists does it take to change a light bulb?
A: One . . . or two. One . . . or two.

I had that laser eye-surgery treatment where they shoot a laser beam in your eye to make your eyesight better. And I can see perfectly now. But out of both the front and back of my head.

I had terrible trouble when I first got contact lenses. It was incredibly painful, very messy. So . . . tip for you: they're meant to go on the *outside* of the eyeball.

Harry tells Tom, 'Can you guess who I bumped into at the opticians today?' 'Who?' asks Tom. 'The receptionist, the other people in the queue, the optician, everybody basically,' says Harry.

The number of elderly, retired people in Bournemouth has skyrocketed; it's got to the point where nearly all the store windows are now fitted with prescription glass.

I've just bought a new book that shows me lots of kinky new positions I can trying wearing my glasses in. It's called 'The Joy of Specs'.

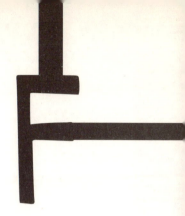

FACTS OF LIFE

A little girl comes up to her daddy one day and says, 'Daddy, what is "sex"?' The dad is shocked but realises the time has come to explain the facts of life. He sits the little girl down and tells her all about the intricacies of sexual reproduction before moving on to exactly how men's and ladies' genital equipment work and even draws her a few diagrams to illustrate the whole process. When he's finished he says, 'So why did you ask about this?' 'Because,' says the little girl, 'Mummy told me to tell you that dinner would be ready in a few secs.'

A computer nerd has a son who is also obsessed with computers. One day the son asks his dad how he was born and dad explains: 'One day your mother and I got together in a chat room, we swapped emails and agreed to meet at a cyber café where we went into a private room where your mother downloaded something from my memory stick. Unfortunately we then realised we had forgotten to activate a firewall and as it was too late to hit the delete button, nine months later we had a little computer virus.'

Johnny asks his daddy where he came from and Dad launches into a long lecture about human reproduction and the birds and the bees. Billy's jaw drops. 'Wow,' he said, 'That beats my pal, Billy. When I asked him where he came from, he said Birmingham.'

FAILURE

A friend asked me if I'd ever won anything. I replied 'Me, I couldn't win an argument!' In the end he convinced me that I could.

FAIRY TALES

An evil witch held a beautiful young girl in captivity. Despite her radiant beauty, she was dressed in a skirt of a particularly unpleasant pattern and design. She waited night and day for a knight to come and free her but time and again those that came were driven away by the sight of her disgusting dress. 'You see,' said the witch, 'I told you no knight would rescue a damsel in this dress!'

A fairy goes to see a football match between two teams of mythical creatures. She's familiar with most of the entities on the pitch, but sees a half-man half-horse creature that she doesn't recognise. She points out the animal to her friend and says, 'What's that thing?' The friend says, 'That's the centaur forward.'

FAITH HEALING

Last night I went to see the worst faith healer I've ever seen. He was so bad a guy in a wheelchair got up and walked out.

FAMILIES

A man becomes a new father and claims his household now represents the entire United Kingdom. He is English, his wife is Irish, the midwife is from Scotland and the baby wails.

A reporter is interviewing a woman who has 20 children. When he asks her why she's had so many, she says, 'It's partly the fault of my deafness. When my husband would come to bed, he'd say, "Do you want to go to sleep, or what?" And I always used to say, "What?"'

I have two brothers. To be honest, it's actually three brothers. But one of them is particularly poor at maths. So he doesn't really count.

George applies for a loan and has to give details of his father's profession. 'How long has he had his current position?' asks the manager. 'Four months,' says George. 'And what does he do?' asks the manager. George says, 'Right now, he's doing two years.'

Janet does not complain about her brother-in-law's shortcomings. His long-stayings are a bit of a problem though.

FAMILY PLANNING

FOR FAMILY PLANNING ADVICE – PLEASE GO ROUND BACK AND USE REAR ENTRANCE.

SIGN ON DOOR OF CLINIC

FANCY DRESS

My wife has decided to go to a fancy dress party as a Rastafarian. She's asked me to help her with her hair and I'm dreading it.

FAREWELL

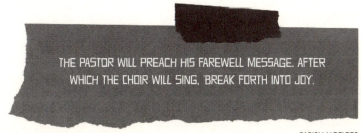

THE PASTOR WILL PREACH HIS FAREWELL MESSAGE, AFTER WHICH THE CHOIR WILL SING, 'BREAK FORTH INTO JOY.'

PARISH NOTICES

FARMING

Harry and his family are on holiday staying on a farm in the countryside. One day his little daughter comes running in and says, 'Daddy, I know why that pig in the farmyard is so enormous.' 'Why's that?' asks Harry. 'She's got loads of little pigs next to her,' she says, 'and it looks like they're all blowing her up.'

> QUESTION MASTER: NAME SOMETHING MADE OF WOOL. CONTESTANT: A SHEEP.
>
> FAMILY FORTUNES

Farmer Giles' wife finds him in the barn rigging up a vat of whisky to the chickens' drinking supply. 'What do you think you're doing?' she asks. 'It's going to be brilliant,' he says, 'this way we'll be able to get them to lay Scotch eggs.'

> QUESTION MASTER: NAME A FARM ANIMAL THAT THE FARMER MAY GROW SO FOND OF, HE MIGHT NOT WANT TO EAT IT. CONTESTANT: DOG.
>
> FAMILY FEUD

Farmer Giles goes out and ploughs one of his fields with a steamroller. 'What are you doing?' asks his wife. 'Isn't it obvious?' he says. 'I'm growing mashed potatoes.'

Farmer Smith buys a talking sheep dog. He sends the dog out to gather in his flock and asks it how many sheep he managed to catch. The dog says, '30.' 'That's impossible,' says Farmer Smith. 'I only have 27 sheep.' 'So?' says the dog. 'I thought you wanted me to round them up for you.'

Zeke and Darla are watching the cattle in the field by their house. One of the bulls starts to mount a cow and Zeke nudges Darla in the ribs. 'Boy,' he says. 'I'd sure like to be doing what that bull is doing.' 'Well, no one's stopping y'all,' says Darla. 'And it is your cow.'

> ARTIFICIAL INSEMINATION IS WHEN THE FARMER DOES IT TO THE COW INSTEAD OF THE BULL.
>
> SCHOOLBOY HOMEWORK ANSWER

FATHER'S DAY

A girl meets her boyfriend. 'Happy Father's Day!' she says. 'Thanks,' he says, 'but I'm not a father.' 'Yes,' says the girl. 'I need to have a word with you about that . . .'

FEAR

A little girl asks her daddy, 'Daddy, are you frightened of dogs?' 'No,' says Daddy. 'Are you frightened of wasps?' 'No,' says Daddy. 'Are you frightened of lightning?' 'No,' says Daddy. 'Oh,' says the little girl, 'so basically you're not frightened of anything apart from Mummy.'

FEMALE IMPERSONATION

Gerry tells a friend about his Uncle Jimmy. 'He's spent the last ten years as a female impersonator.' 'Really?' says the friend. 'Is he on stage?' 'No,' says Gerry. 'He's in prison.'

FERTILITY TREATMENT

Nigel and his wife are trying to have a baby, but Nigel's sperm turn out to be pretty lazy. His doctor suggests a new treatment based on injections from virile male chimpanzees. It works and nine months later Nigel calls his doctor to tell him that his wife has just given birth. 'Well done,' says the doctor. 'Is it a boy or a girl?' 'Beats me,' says Nigel. 'But we'll have a better idea once we've got it down from the curtain rail.'

Two women are talking. One has been trying without success to have a baby. 'I had that problem,' says the other, 'but then I went to Pedro. The big, dark, swarthy faith healer. After a couple of sessions with him I was pregnant.' 'My husband went to him,' says the first woman, 'but it still didn't work.' 'Try going on your own,' says her friend, 'it's much more effective that way.'

An old lady uses fertility treatment to have a baby. She takes it home and her neighbour pops by to see it. 'We'll have to wait till the baby starts crying, then I'll show it to you,' says the old lady. 'Why does it have to be crying?' asks the neighbour. The old lady gestures around her. 'Because it's in here somewhere, but I forgot where I put it.'

FIGHTING

A little boy runs to find a policeman and says, 'Come quick! My dad is in a fight at the pub.' The policeman comes with him and finds three men wrestling with each other. 'OK,' says the policeman, 'which of them is your father?' 'That's what they're fighting about,' says the boy.

FILING

The Hollywood film producer Sam Goldwyn was asked by his secretary if she should get rid of some old documents to make space in the filing. 'Yes,' he said, 'but keep copies.'

FIRE AND FIRE SERVICES

Bill is walking through the town centre when he sees a building on fire. Without fear for his own safety, he plunges in and manages to pull three men out to safety. 'You idiot,' says one of them, 'we're the firemen!'

The options to improve firemen's response times have been revealed. 1: grease the poles a bit more; 2: get rid of the poles and have a hole in the floor to jump through; 3: take the drinks machine downstairs and put it next to the fire engine.

Some members of the local fire brigade come to a school to talk to the children. One of the men asks them, 'Who knows what it means if the smoke alarm in your house goes off?' 'I do,' says a little boy. 'My dad's cooking dinner!'

Freddie's son wanted to become a fireman, so Freddie installed a practice pole for him in the garage. As it turned out, Freddie's son became a cop, but Freddie hadn't wasted his time; he has two daughters and they both became strippers.

Nobby calls the emergency services and says his living room is on fire. 'OK,' says the operator, 'so can you tell us how we get to your house?' 'I should have thought that's obvious,' says Nobby, 'you slide down your metal pole and drive here in your big red engine.'

A huge fire breaks out at a factory. The head of the company says he has vital documents in a vault in the centre of the plant and will pay £100,000 to anyone brave enough to go through the fire and retrieve them. Several fire engines turn up but none of the fire fighters can get through. Finally an engine crewed by elderly volunteers comes careering down the road straight into the middle of the inferno. The other firemen can't believe what they are seeing as the old-timers emerge a few minutes later with the documents safe and sound. 'What will you guys do with the money?' asks the head of the company. 'Well,' says one of the old-timers, 'the first thing is going to be to get the flipping brakes fixed on that engine of ours.'

Why has no one ever explained to the head of the fire service that everyone else uses steps to go downstairs not a metal pole?

FIRING SQUAD

An Englishman, an Irishman, a Welshman and Scotsman are captured during the war. They are told they are going to be lined up and shot but are offered a final request. The Englishman says, 'I'd like to sing "God Save The Queen" followed by "Rule Britannia".' The Irishman says, 'I'd like to sing "Danny Boy" and then do a 10-minute *Riverdance* routine.' The Welshman says, 'I'd like to sing "Men of Harlech" followed by a medley of hit songs by Welsh performers including "It's Not Unusual", "Hey Big Spender" and "If You Tolerate This Then Your Children Will Be Next". The Scotsman says, 'Is there any chance you could shoot me first?'

Three men are sentenced to death by firing squad. The first man is brought forward, the firing squad raise their guns and just as they take aim, the man shouts, 'Tornado!' The firing squad all look round to see if there is a tornado and when they turn back the man has run away. The second man is brought forward, the firing squad raise their guns and just as they take aim, he shouts, 'Avalanche!' The firing squad all turn to look for the avalanche and when they look back the second man has run away. Finally the third man is brought forward, the firing squad raise their guns and just as they take aim, he shouts, 'Fire!'

FISH AND FISHING

Harry has too much salmon in his diet. You can't usually tell but if he ever sees an escalator, he tries to run up it in the wrong direction.

Two fishermen are at the side of a river. 'Is this river good for fish?' asks the first. 'It's great,' says the second. 'In fact it's so good that very few of them are prepared to leave it.'

Remember the ancient lesson – give a man a fish and you will feed him for a day; teach him to fish and you'll completely get rid of him every weekend.

One rainy day, Tom finds Dick by the river standing under a bridge fishing. 'What are you doing fishing under the bridge?' asks Tom. 'Well,' says Dick, 'I figured this is where the fish would go to keep out of the rain.'

I've never been any good at fishing but the other day I found out there was a fishing helpline. I phoned them to get some advice and the operator asked me, 'Can you hold the line.' 'No,' I said, 'that's the reason I called you.'

Q: How many fishermen does it take to change a light bulb?
A: Just one but the bulb was THIS big!

Two fishermen, Steve and Mike, hear about an incredible new fishing ground far out to sea; it's full of fish but the only way they can tell if they're in the right place is to taste the water. When it stops tasting salty, they've arrived. The pair set off and, after an hour, Steve dips a bucket into the sea and tastes the water. 'It's salty,' he says. After another hour he tastes the water again. 'Too salty,' he says. After another hour, he tastes it again. 'Nah,' he says. 'Still very salty.' Another hour passes and Mike says, 'Is it about time to taste the water again?' Steve says, 'I can't. The bucket's empty.'

Beryl liked fishing so much, she changed her name. She's now known as 'Annette'.

Tina and Jackie are talking. 'So your husband tells you he goes fishing every weekend,' says Tina. 'Do you think that really he might be having an affair?' 'No,' says Jackie, 'I know he's definitely fishing because he never comes back with any fish.'

FLAMINGOS

It was after Brian's wife complained about the way he kept pretending to be a flamingo that he finally had to put his foot down.

FLATULENCE

Fred says his wife reminds him of a luxury German car. She keeps emitting gases but denies it.

An old lady goes to the doctor. 'I've got a slightly embarrassing problem,' she says. 'Although it doesn't smell at all and makes no noise whatsoever, I can feel myself passing wind constantly.' The doctor reaches in his drawer and hands the old lady some tablets. 'Take these for a few days,' he tells her. 'And then come back and see me again.' A few days later, the old lady is back at the surgery. 'Well, doctor,' she says, 'your tablets have made the situation even worse. I'm still passing wind constantly, it still makes no sound but now it all whiffs to high heaven.' 'Very good,' says the doctor. 'That seems to have fixed your sense of smell. Next, we have to sort out your hearing.'

Daphne is hosting a luncheon at her country house. Simpkins, the butler, is serving the vicar his soup, when the vicar suddenly lets off a huge fart. To spare the reverend any embarrassment, Daphne says, 'Simpkins. Stop that immediately.' Simpkins says, 'As you wish, madam. Did you see which way it went?'

FLIRTING

Dick managed to drown his Geordie mate after shoving him into the local swimming pool. Dick now wonders whether he misinterpreted the Geordie's last words: 'I'm really good at flirting.'

I have found that there is a fine line between being a bit flirty and being creepy. And that line is called being good-looking.

FOOD

Tom is at Harry's house when he notices an empty milk bottle in the fridge. 'What's that in there for?' asks Tom. 'Oh,' says Harry, 'that's in case any visitors asks for a black coffee.'

> **ENGLAND IS THE ONLY COUNTRY IN THE WORLD WHERE THE FOOD IS MORE DANGEROUS THAN THE SEX.**
>
> JACKIE MASON

> **DOES THE EXPIRATION DATE ON SOUR CREAM MEAN THE DATE IT BECOMES GOOD?**
>
> LARRY KING

Gus and Bill are arguing. Gus claims that an onion is the only fruit or vegetable that makes people cry. 'That's not true,' says Bill. 'OK. Prove it,' says Gus. 'I will,' says Bill, and chucks a coconut in his face.

Q: What do you call it when a chicken looks at a lettuce?
A: Chicken Caesar salad

Many people advise you not to eat late at night. But if that's right, why do they always have a light in the fridge?

Q: What contains a sandwich and a packet of crisps and swings round French cathedrals?
A: It's the lunch-pack of Notre Dame.

> **FRENCH COOKING'S ALL VERY WELL, BUT THEY CAN'T DO A DECENT ENGLISH BREAKFAST.**
>
> PRINCE PHILIP (AFTER ENJOYING AN ENGLISH BREAKFAST AT A RESTAURANT OWNED BY A FRENCHMAN CALLED IL PUNTO)

A man goes to the doctor's and says, 'Doctor, I've eaten something that disagrees with me.' 'Oh no you haven't,' says a voice from his stomach.

> QUESTION MASTER: NAME A FOOD THAT MAKES A NOISE WHEN YOU EAT IT. CONTESTANT: A REALLY LOUD HAMBURGER.
>
> FAMILY FEUD

> HOW MUCH CHICKEN IS THERE IN CHICK PEAS?
>
> CONTESTANT ON BIG BROTHER

Lord Winton goes to the kitchen of his stately home to have a word with his cook. 'My wife's mother is coming to stay with us next week,' he says. 'This is a list of all the meals that she particularly likes. If I catch you serving any of them while she's here, you're fired!'

Harry buys a pack of sausages which have a picture of a famous TV chef on the packaging. Underneath the label it reads, 'prick with fork'. 'I can see that,' thinks Harry, 'but what's it got to do with the sausages?'

> I LOVE ENGLAND, ESPECIALLY THE FOOD. THERE'S NOTHING I LIKE MORE THAN A LOVELY BIG BOWL OF PASTA.
>
> NAOMI CAMPBELL

Q: What do you call it when you think you've lost an Italian sausage but then you find it again?
A: A falsalami.

Vernon tells Barry, 'I had crab for dinner last night and ever since I've had a terrible pain in my stomach.' 'Oh dear,' says Barry, 'did it smell all right when you took it out of its shell.' 'What do you mean – "took it out of its shell"?' asks Vernon.

'Knock, knock.' 'Who's there?' 'Dana.' 'Dana who?' 'Dana talk with your mouth full!'

It's tragic getting older. Food has replaced sex in my life, which means that these days I'm not even able to even get into my *own* pants.

Nobby's wife asks him if he would like a frozen pizza for his dinner. 'Well,' says Nobby, 'I'd prefer it if you heated it up a bit first?'

For a change, Tom made dinner for his wife. After she finished eating he asked, 'What would you like for pudding?' 'The antidote,' she replied.

A bagel is essentially a doughnut with rigor mortis.

Gary asked the deli guy where he could go to weigh a pie. The guy said, 'Somewhere over the rainbow.'

Two men are complaining about their grandmother's kitchen skills. 'I can't stand another of her meals,' says one. 'It tastes like raw sewage.' 'Be fair,' says the other. 'She does cook it.'

Tom forgets to close the fridge door properly one night and in the morning he finds everything inside it has gone bad. Brenda is furious and yells at him, 'What am I going to do with all this food!' 'All right!' says Tom. 'No need to make a meal out of it.'

You hear lots of jokes about white sugar, don't you? But brown sugar jokes? Demerara!

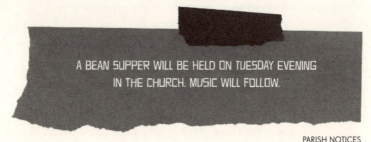

A BEAN SUPPER WILL BE HELD ON TUESDAY EVENING IN THE CHURCH. MUSIC WILL FOLLOW.

PARISH NOTICES

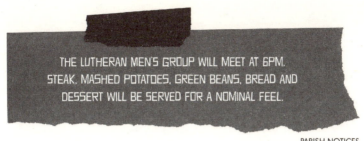

PARISH NOTICES

A teacher asks her class, 'Can you name the four main food groups?' One of the students puts his hand up and says, 'Is it canned, frozen, instant and lite?'

Jack gets an email warning him about the danger of catching salmonella from tins of ham. He thought he'd better delete it in case it was Spam.

FOOLS

It is very difficult to make any product completely foolproof because, ironically, fools have repeatedly proved themselves to be highly ingenious.

FOOTBALL

Q: Who is the most hated man in football?
A: The man who shouts, 'Give us a B!' at Borussia Moenchengladbach games.

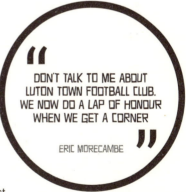

"DON'T TALK TO ME ABOUT LUTON TOWN FOOTBALL CLUB. WE NOW DO A LAP OF HONOUR WHEN WE GET A CORNER"

ERIC MORECAMBE

It has been reported that burglars broke into Leeds United's ground at the weekend and stole the entire contents of the trophy room. Police have asked members of the public to contact them if anyone tries to sell them a white carpet.

> ONE MOMENT I'M PLAYING FOOTBALL AND THE NEXT – WHACK – I WAKE UP IN HOSPITAL UNCONSCIOUS.
>
> ALAN BRAZIL

The Nigerian team gets knocked out of the World Cup and the manager goes on TV to say he is so disappointed with his team's performance that he will personally refund all the expenses of the fans who travelled out to support them. All he needs is their bank details, sort codes and pin numbers and he will transfer the money straight to them.

Nobby gets home from his Sunday morning football game with a bruised and bloody leg. 'Oh, Nobby,' says his wife, 'you play football too roughly! How exactly did this happen?' 'I don't know,' says Nobby, 'in fact to be honest I don't even know whose leg that is!'

A Conservative MP was found dead in a hotel room wearing a Leeds United football shirt. Apparently the police had to dress him in fishnet tights and stilettos to save the family from the embarrassment.

> HE HELD HIS HEAD IN HIS HANDS AS IT FLASHED PAST THE POST.
>
> ALAN BRAZIL

The manager of Nottingham Forest gets a call from the police. 'I'm sorry to tell you,' says the policeman, 'that the club has been broken into.' 'Oh no,' says the manager, 'did they get any valuable cups?' 'Don't worry,' says the policeman, 'they only went in the trophy room. They didn't get as far as the kitchen.'

Tom says he went to see Liverpool play at Anfield yesterday and it really lived up to all his expectations. When he came out, he found his car had been nicked.

> ALL THE LEEDS TEAM ARE 100 PER CENT BEHIND THE MANAGER, BUT I CAN'T SPEAK FOR THE REST OF THE SQUAD.
>
> BRIAN GREENHOFF

People complain about having women linesmen officiating at football games, but that's ridiculous. If there's one thing that woman are really good at, it's spotting men's mistakes.

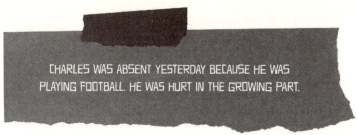

CHARLES WAS ABSENT YESTERDAY BECAUSE HE WAS PLAYING FOOTBALL. HE WAS HURT IN THE GROWING PART.

SCHOOL ABSENTEE NOTE

Before 1961 the maximum wage for a Manchester United player was £50 a week. So back then 100 quid would not only buy you a replica kit, you could afford the actual player to put in it as well.

Q: How many Manchester United fans does it take to change a light bulb?
A: Three. One to change the bulb, one to buy the official merchandise celebrating the event and one to drive them all back to Bedfordshire.

The local football team are playing another disastrous match. The captain goes to the referee and asks if they can introduce a ball. 'What do you mean?' says the referee. 'There's already a ball on the pitch.' 'I know,' says the captain. 'But the other team are using that one.'

SHIN PADS CANNOT PROTECT ANY PART OF THE BODY THEY DO NOT COVER.

WARNING ON A PAIR OF SHIN PADS

FOREIGN LANGUAGES

A Polish woman marries an Englishman, but doesn't make much progress with the language and has to rely on sign-language most of the time. One day she goes into a butcher's shop to ask for a leg of ham; she does this by pointing at her leg and making a sound like a pig. Next she wants to buy some chicken breasts, so she points at her chest and makes a sound like a chicken. Next she wants to buy some sausages, which has her stumped, until she goes out and drags in her husband.

Tom and Harry are on a walking tour of Germany. They meet a Swiss tourist who needs directions. *'Entschuldigung, koennen Sie Deutsch sprechen?'* asks the Swiss tourist. Tom and Harry stare at him. The Swiss man tries again, *'Excusez-moi, parlez vous Francais?'* Tom and Harry still look blank. *'Parlare Italiano?'* asks the Swiss man. *'Hablan ustedes Espanol?'* he asks finally, but still gets no response from Tom and Harry, so he goes away looking frustrated. 'I think maybe we should learn a foreign language,' says Tom. 'I don't see why,' says Harry, 'that bloke could speak four languages and it didn't do him any good.'

When Charles de Gaulle retired, a dinner party was held in his honour by the British ambassador. At the dinner table the ambassador's wife said to Madame de Gaulle, 'Your husband has been such a prominent public figure for so many years! How quiet retirement will seem in comparison. What are you most looking forward to?' 'A penis,' replied Madame de Gaulle. The other guests were all shocked and fell silent. A huge hush fell over the table. De Gaulle leaned over to his wife and said, 'I believe ze English pronounce zat word, 'appiness!'

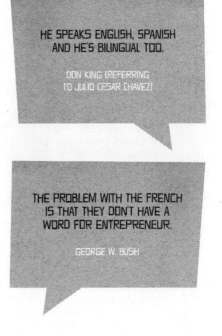

> HE SPEAKS ENGLISH, SPANISH AND HE'S BILINGUAL TOO.
>
> DON KING (REFERRING TO JULIO CESAR CHAVEZ)

> THE PROBLEM WITH THE FRENCH IS THAT THEY DON'T HAVE A WORD FOR ENTREPRENEUR.
>
> GEORGE W. BUSH

FOREIGN TRAVEL

Mavis and Doris decide to take their little old car on a touring holiday through France. They are both very excited by the trip but a couple of days before they set off, Mavis comes home and tells Doris they can't go. 'What's the matter, dear?' asks Doris. 'It's this business about driving on the right,' says Mavis. 'You said it would be easy,' says Doris. 'I know,' says Mavis. 'But I just had a practice run round the town centre today and caused 15 accidents.'

> "I ONCE SPENT A YEAR IN PHILADELPHIA. I THINK IT WAS ON A SUNDAY."
>
> W.C. FIELDS

Quentin's return flight from Majorca has been delayed since 1980. He says it's been the holiday of a lifetime.

Angus is on holiday in Canada. He goes into a bar, notices something hanging on the wall and asks the barman, 'Hey, laddie! What is that huge animal's head with the antlers?' 'That's a moose,' says the barman. 'Hoots!' says Angus. 'How big are your cats round here?'

I went on holiday to Antwerp. When you're driving into the city there's a big sign that says, 'Antwerp – twinned with Dectwerp.'

Maurice is a Jewish businessman who has sent his son to Israel for a few months to absorb the culture. He tells his friend Isaac, 'Can you believe it! When he came back he had converted to Christianity.' 'It's funny you should say that,' says Isaac, 'because I also sent my son to Israel and he came back a Christian as well. I think we should ask the rabbi about this.' So Maurice and Isaac go to the rabbi, who says, 'It's funny you should say that, because I also sent my son to Israel and he came back a Christian as well. I think the only thing to do is to pray to the Lord for guidance.' So they all begin praying and a voice from the heavens comes down to them: 'It's funny you should say that, because I also sent my son to Israel . . .'

> I'VE NEVER REALLY WANTED TO GO TO JAPAN, SIMPLY BECAUSE I DON'T REALLY LIKE EATING FISH AND I KNOW THAT'S VERY POPULAR OUT THERE IN AFRICA.
>
> BRITNEY SPEARS

MY WIFE...

▶ 'My wife's gone to the West Indies.' 'Jamaica?' 'No, she went of her own accord.'

▶ 'My wife has just been to a dreadful music concert in Southeast Asia.' 'Singapore?' 'Yes he was, and the band wasn't much better either.'

▶ 'My wife's gone to Northern Italy.' 'Genoa?' 'Of course I do. We've been married for over ten years.'

▶ 'I took my wife on a trip to Indonesia.' 'Jakarta?' 'No, we went by plane.'

▶ 'I've just taken my wife for a romantic weekend in North Wales.' 'Bangor?' 'Do you mind? That's a bit of a personal question.'

▶ 'My wife fell over while walking up a volcano in Indonesia.' 'Krakatoa?' 'No, she broke her entire leg actually.'

▶ 'My wife's gone somewhere just south of London.' 'Surrey?' 'I SAID MY WIFE'S GONE SOMEWHERE JUST SOUTH OF LONDON!'

▶ 'My wife's going to the extreme northeast of the USA?' 'Alaska.' 'Why? Don't you believe me?'

▶ 'My wife's off to St Petersburg.' 'Is she Russian?' 'No, she's got plenty of time.'

▶ 'My wife's gone on a plane to North America.' 'Chicago?' 'No, she passenger.'

▶ 'My wife's gone mad in Venezuela.' 'Caracas?' 'Yes, I'm afraid she's gone completely loopy.'

▶ 'My wife recently went on a sailing course in Poole.' 'In Dorset?' 'Oh yes, she'd thoroughly recommend it.'

▶ 'My wife wants us to go on safari to Africa.' 'Kenya?' 'No, we can't afford it.'

Neville and Janice are waiting at the airport, queuing up to check in their luggage. 'I wish I'd bought my leather jacket,' says Neville. 'What do you mean?' says Janice. 'We're going to Bermuda. What do you want with a leather jacket?' 'I don't want it,' says Neville. 'But I still wish I had it.' 'But why?' says Janice. Neville says, 'Because the plane tickets are in the inside pocket.'

I went on holiday to Spain last year and my hotel overlooked the sea. Sadly, the other things it overlooked were hygiene, good service and adequate sanitation.

FORESTRY

Billy goes for a job as a lumberjack. The interviewer is reading his application when he looks up and says, 'This must be a spelling mistake, it says here that you previously worked for ten years as a tree feller in the Sahara Forest.' 'That's right,' says Billy. 'Don't you mean the Sahara Desert?' says the interviewer. 'No,' says Billy, 'I'm a fast worker. They changed the name after I left.'

FORGERY

Sammy was probably the world's worst forger. He used to buy 50p pieces then grind the edges off them to turn them into 10p pieces.

FRED ASTAIRE AND GINGER ROGERS

Fred Astaire and Ginger Rogers go out to dine. They are just sitting down at their table when a waiter trips over and splatters Fred with jelly, trifle, apple pie and spotted dick. 'Oh no!' says Ginger. 'Just look at you now.' 'I know!' says Fred. 'I've got pudding on my top hat, pudding on my white tie, pudding on my tails . . .'

FREEDOM

Many people believe that the colours red, white and blue are symbolic of freedom. But this is ironic if you see them in your rear-view mirror flashing towards you.

FREEDOM OF SPEECH

I think freedom of speech is an important right. Another equally important right is the freedom not to listen, to put your fingers in your ears and go, 'La la la la la la!'

> WE SHOULD SILENCE ANYONE WHO OPPOSES THE RIGHT TO FREEDOM OF SPEECH.
>
> SIR BOYLE ROCHE

FRIDGES

Gary's taken to leaving his cans of beer out on the porch to cool down. He got the idea from the old lady next door – she does it with her milk bottles.

Harry has an old sofa that needs replacing. When the new one arrives he puts the old one on his drive with a sign saying 'Free'. After three weeks it still hasn't gone, so he changes the sign to 'For sale: £100 or nearest offer'. Within half an hour, it's been stolen.

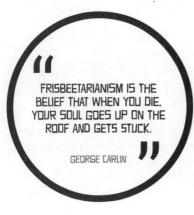

> "FRISBEETARIANISM IS THE BELIEF THAT WHEN YOU DIE, YOUR SOUL GOES UP ON THE ROOF AND GETS STUCK."
>
> GEORGE CARLIN

FRISBEE

It has been announced that the world Frisbee champion died today. Apparently he caught something that was going around.

FRUGALITY

To cut costs, Larry has to decide which magazine subscription he's going to drop: *National Geographic* or *Playboy*? Then his wife tells him to drop both, since they're both full of places he's never going to visit.

What do you call it when you buy something you don't need for a price you can't resist – a bargain.

Jim comes home from work early and sees a plumber's van parked in front of his house. 'Oh God!' he says. 'Let's hope he's my wife's lover.'

Angus is out in the town centre with his wife and children. He hails a taxi and asks how much it will be to drive them back home. 'I'll offer you a special rate,' says the driver. 'Ten quid for you and your missus and I'll take the kids for free. How does that sound?' 'Excellent,' says Angus. 'OK, kids, hop in the taxi and the nice man will drive you home while me and your mother catch the bus!'

Did you hear about the Scotsman who kept making obscene phone calls? They managed to catch him because he always tried to reverse the charges.

A miser is told he has only days to live, so he gathers all his money and stuffs it into a big sack. He then tells his housekeeper to carry the sack into the attic. 'Whatever for?' asks the housekeeper. 'When I die, I'll drift up to heaven,' explains the miser. 'On the way up I can grab the sack and take it with me.' The housekeeper shrugs and goes about her business. The next day, she knocks on the miser's bedroom door and discovers he's died in the night. Curious, she goes into the attic and finds that the sack is still there. 'I knew it,' she says. 'The old fool should have put it in the cellar.'

Maurice the miser used to stuff all his money in his mattress. One day he won the lottery and the next morning he jumped out of bed and broke his neck – they estimate he fell 40 feet.

Jasper might have been a terrible miser, but every year he always withdrew £5,000 from his bank account for a two-week holiday. When it had finished its holiday, he put it back.

Hamish saves money on toilet paper by wiping his backside on old newspapers. Aside from every second Sunday that is, because that's the day the local minister comes round for tea. On those days, Hamish rents a toilet roll from the pub.

Last night my friends were all saying how stingy I was. So I decided to prove them wrong and bought them a beer. They still weren't grateful though. It turned out they wanted one each.

Aunt Madge can never resist buying canned food that comes with 'money off' labels. By scrimping and saving like that she's managed to save enough to redecorate her front room. She'd like to do the same with the other rooms, but unfortunately they're all stuffed from floor to ceiling with tins.

Dick has just bought a new book called 'An Idiot's Guide to How to Save Money'. He paid £49.99 for it.

FRUIT

Q: What did the green grape say to the purple grape?
A: BREATHE!

A barman tells his wife, 'Ugh! The lemons we had sitting on the bar have all gone off. I just picked up one and it had gone all furry.' 'You stupid idiot,' says his wife, 'you've just squeezed my canary into somebody's drink.'

For years, food scientists had been trying to formulate an orange squash that tasted just like freshly squeezed oranges; then they gave up and did the next best thing – they bred a new type of orange that tastes just like squash.

FUEL

Dick has come up with a scheme to make himself rich. He has imported a million tonnes of sand from Saudi Arabia and piled it up in his back garden. Now he says he's going to start drilling for his own oil.

Dick tells Harry, 'I saw a film star at the petrol station yesterday.' 'Well, who was it?' asks Harry. 'The human torch guy from the *Fantastic Four* film,' says Dick. 'I asked for his autograph but he just kept screaming at me and rolling around on the floor.'

FUNERALS

What exactly are funeral directors worried about when they decide to nail down the lid of a coffin?

It was poor Trevor's funeral today. He died after being struck on the head by a ball at Wimbledon. His wife said it was a lovely service.

A traffic warden is being buried. As the coffin is lowered into the ground, a voice comes from inside the box: 'Help! Stop! I'm not really dead! Let me out of here!' 'Sorry, there's nothing I can do now,' says the priest, 'I've already done all the paperwork.'

Q: Why was the hearse horse hoarse?
A: Because of the coffin.

I couldn't believe the charges when I saw them. £100 for five years in the ground; £150 for ten years. Apparently it's the country's first ever pay-and-display cemetery.

They just doubled the price of plots at the local cemetery. The cost of living is going through the roof.

I've discovered that funeral costs can be extremely high. For example, at my mother-in-law's funeral after we'd paid for the bouncy castle and the donkey rides there was hardly anything left to pay for the disco.

Ted is at his mother-in-law's funeral. Halfway through the service his wife hisses at him, 'When we get home later, I'm going to make you pay for this!' 'What's the matter?' asks Ted. 'Is it because I'm not sharing my popcorn?'

> "ALWAYS GO TO OTHER PEOPLES' FUNERALS, OTHERWISE THEY WON'T GO TO YOURS."
> — YOGI BERRA

> QUESTION MASTER: NAME SOMETHING PEOPLE WANT TO BE BURIED WITH.
> CONTESTANT: THEIR HOME.
> — FAMILY FEUD

Did you hear about the idiot who asked to be buried at sea? Four of his mates drowned trying to dig a hole.

A vicar is giving a funeral service and telling everyone about the saintly nature of the deceased, of all the good works that he'd done, about his kindness and happy nature, his warmth of heart and generosity of spirit. Suddenly the dead man's wife gets out of her pew, goes to the coffin, lifts the lid and looks inside. 'Is everything all right?' asks the vicar. 'Yes, thanks,' she says. 'I was just making sure I was at the right funeral.'

The American baseball player Yogi Berra was asked by his wife where he would like to be buried. He replied, 'Surprise me!'

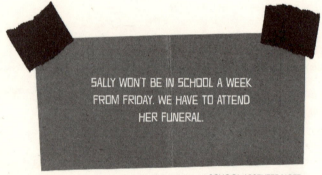

SCHOOL ABSENTEE NOTE

FUR COATS

Tony bought his girlfriend a fur coat made out of hamster skins. He came to regret it. That weekend they went to a funfair and she spent three days on the Big Wheel.

Glenda is walking down the street wearing a leopard-skin coat. A passer-by says, 'What poor dumb animal had to die to get you that?' Glenda replies, 'My husband.'

FURNITURE

JANET SMITH HAS VOLUNTEERED TO STRIP AND REFINISH THE COMMUNION TABLE IN THE SANCTUARY.

PARISH NOTICES

One day at the furniture factory, Arthur fell into the upholstery machine. Luckily he's fully recovered now.

Did you hear about the time the tallboy and the kitchen unit decided to have a race? It all ended in a drawer.

Q: What did the blanket say when it slipped off the bed?
A: Oh sheet!

What you call a desk, I call a trashcan with drawers.

FUTURE

The definition of the future – the time when you will wish that you'd done the things that you're not getting round to doing now.

GAMBLING

Dick organises a mystery tour and gets everyone going on the trip to pay in to a sweepstake to guess where they are going. When the big day comes and everyone's on board the coach, Dick gets up and announces that the driver has won £56.

A man tells a friend, 'I've just been playing cards with some people from Africa.' 'Zulus?' asks the friend. 'No,' says the man, 'actually most of the time I won.'

A man walks into a betting shop and asks the manager, 'Can I back horses in here, mate?' 'Of course you can,' says the manager. 'OK,' says the man, turning to the door and beckoning with both hands: 'Come on, then! In you come, lad!'

My addiction to gambling cost me my marriage. Or as I prefer to look at it, my addiction to gambling won me a divorce.

My girlfriend thinks I'm addicted to gambling. She hasn't ever mentioned it but I bet that's what she thinks.

The bookies have offered odds on nuclear war being the most likely thing to cause the end the world at 1,000 to 1, closely followed by asteroid impact at 50,000 to 1 and a superbug outbreak at 250,000 to 1. Dick thought there was a chance they might all happen and took out an accumulator on it.

Jack, Fred and some other friends are playing when Jack loses £1,000 on a single hand. The shock is so much that he clutches his chest and drops dead at the table. Fred looks round and asks, 'Who is going to tell Jack's wife?' So they draw straws and Fred has to go and impart the news. So Fred goes to see Jack's wife, knocks on the door and when she answers, he comes straight to the point, 'Jack has just lost £1,000 playing cards.' Jack's wife is furious. 'That swine!' she yells. 'You go back and tell him to drop dead.' 'Yes,' says Fred, 'I'll go and do that and tell you what happens.'

It's Jack's 33rd birthday, which coincidentally falls on the third day of the third month. He notices that his alarm clock has stopped at 3.33am and that the weather forecast is for temperatures of 33 degrees. He then notices that a horse called 'Triple Chance' is running in the 3.30. It's clearly a sign, he thinks. So he phones up the bookmaker, places a bet of £333 and, sure enough, his horse comes in third.

A monk is walking through a monastery garden when he hears a booming voice from the clouds shout, 'Dig!' The voice obviously belongs to God so the startled monk finds a spade and starts digging in the spot he was standing. After a few moments the monk unearths a small metal box. The voice shouts, 'Open!' The monk opens the box and sees a bundle of money inside. The voice shouts, 'Casino!' so the monk runs to the nearby casino. The voice shouts, 'Blackjack!' so the monk goes to the blackjack table and puts the cash down. The dealer gives the monk a king and a nine. The voice shouts, 'Hit!' The dealer gives the monk a queen. The dealer says, 'Bust.' The voice says, 'Damn!'

George goes up to Larry and says. 'I'll bet you £20 I can make you yell out without laying a finger on you. All you have to do is try to hit me.' 'OK,' says Larry, 'that sounds like easy money.' So George holds his hand out at his side and says, 'Punch the palm of my hand.' Larry takes a swing and, at the last second, George drops his hand out of the way. Sadly for Larry, George's hand is in front of a metal post and Larry thumps it with a yell of pain. George takes his winnings and goes off. Larry is determined to make his money back to he goes over to visit his friend, Frank, and makes the same bet. Frank says, 'Sounds like a doddle. What do I have to?' Larry looks around for a metal post, but can't see one, so he puts his hand over his face. 'Just punch my palm . . .'

Harry has bet a fortune that nuclear war will break out. Now he won't go more than half a mile from the bookies in case it happens and he needs to get there in under four minutes to collect his winnings.

Bob's wife left him because of his insatiable gambling. Now all he can think about is trying to win her back.

Nobby sees a sign in the local bookie's window that says 'Open Sunday 11–2.' He's pretty sure they do open on Sundays so he goes in and puts a tenner on it.

I no longer see my wife and family and it's all because of my gambling. I won a stack of money and moved to the Bahamas.

Harry comes home from the pub four hours late and his wife Vera isn't happy. 'Where have you been?' she asks. 'I've been in the pub,' says Harry, 'playing poker with Tom and Dick.' 'That's the last straw,' says Vera. 'I've had enough of you and your gambling. Pack your bags and get out of our house.' 'Yeah. There's just one thing,' says Harry. 'Unfortunately this isn't our house any more.'

They say one in every group of seven people will be addicted to gambling. I bet it's my mate Dave.

GAME SHOWS

Tom appears on an episode of *Who Wants to Be a Millionaire* and is set to win the jackpot if he can answer the question, 'Which of the following birds does NOT build its own nest: a sparrow; a thrush; a magpie; or a cuckoo?' Tom isn't sure so he asks to phone a friend and calls up Dick. Dick tells him that the answer is cuckoo and Tom gives this as his final answer. 'Cuckoo is the correct answer,' says the presenter, 'you've just won one million pounds!' Later Tom asks Dick how he knew the answer to such a difficult question. 'It's obvious,' says Dick, 'a cuckoo lives in a clock, doesn't it?'

Nobby goes on a TV quiz show. The host asks him to name two of Santa's reindeer. He thinks for a moment and then says, 'Rudolph and Olive!' 'Well,' says the host, 'Rudolph is correct but where do you get Olive from?' 'You know,' says Nobby. 'In the song where they say, "Olive the other reindeer, used to laugh and call him names . . ."'

GAMES

It's really annoying when people play that game where they knock on your door but by the time you get there, they've run away. I think the game is called Yodel.

Frank and Benny are playing Trivial Pursuit. Benny asks, 'If you were in a vacuum and someone called to you, would you hear them?' Frank thinks for a bit, then says, 'I don't know. Is it on or off?'

GANGSTERS

An English businessman fell foul of the notorious Glasgow Mafia. They made him an offer he couldn't understand.

Q: How many mafioso does it take to change a light bulb?
A: Three. One to do it, one to watch him do it and a third to shoot the witness.

Bernie, a vicious East End gangster, is killed carrying out an armed robbery. His brother, Jimmy the Razor, promises to give £5,000 to charity if the local vicar will lie and say something nice about him at his funeral. The service begins, but rather than saying anything pleasant, the vicar starts to relate all the thefts, beatings, mutilations and murders Bernie was ever involved with. He finally recounts the last of Bernie's sinister escapades, then says: 'Mind you, having said all that, Bernie was an absolute saint compared to his brother . . .'

GARDENING

Tom and Harry are waiting at the bus stop with his mate when they see a lorry go by with the back loaded up with rolls of turf. Tom is very impressed. 'When I win the lottery that's what I'm going to do,' he says. 'What are you going to do?' asks Harry. 'Send my lawn away to be cut,' says Tom.

Young Sandra is having trouble with her gardening and can't seem to get her tomatoes to ripen. She notices her neighbour has had no such problem and has a load of big red ripe tomatoes. 'How do you manage it?' asks Sandra. 'Well,' says the neighbour, 'my secret is that first thing every morning I go out and I stand naked in front of my tomatoes. Then they all turn red from blushing.' Sandra decides she will try the same tactic. A few days later the neighbours asks if it's worked. 'No,' she says, 'I've come out here every morning and I exposed myself but none of the tomatoes have turned red at all. On the other hand, my cucumbers seem to have gone absolutely enormous.'

Harry's lawnmower breaks and his wife keeps hinting to him to get it fixed. Harry keeps putting it off until his wife gets so fed up she decides to make a point and goes out in the garden and starts snipping the grass with a pair of sewing scissors. A few minutes later Harry comes out with a toothbrush and says, 'When you've finished cutting the grass, could you sweep the driveway as well?'

An old colonel notices his lawn is covered with molehills. He summons his gardener and asks him to do something about it. The next day he says to the gardener, 'Did you sort that mole problem out?' 'Oh yes. You don't have to worry about that any more,' says the gardener, 'I caught him, took him to the bottom of the garden and buried him alive.'

Tom's elderly neighbour kept complaining about the state of Tom's garden. In the end Tom had to have his patio completely relaid. He reckons they'll never find the old sod under all that paving.

An elderly Muslim man has a house in the UK. He plants a vegetable plot in his back garden but when it comes time to dig up his potatoes, he finds he is too old and weak to do it on his own. He emails his son in Pakistan to tell him about his problem. The son replies, 'Don't worry. I'll sort something out for you.' Five minutes later a squad of special forces arrive, push through the old man's house and spend the next few hours digging up his potato patch. The old man is baffled but then notices his son had sent him a second email shortly after the first which says: 'The material is buried in your potato patch. You know what to do with it.'

Tom is working in the garden, but can't find the rake. He sees his wife in a neighbour's garden, but since she's a bit deaf he doesn't bother shouting. Instead he waves to get her attention then points to his eye, then his knee and then makes a raking motion. His wife doesn't get it at first but he repeats the gestures and she understands: 'Eye – Kneed – The Rake!' She then signals back to him and points to her eye, next to her left boob, then to her backside and then to her crotch. Finally he gets it: 'Eye – Left Tit – Behind – The Bush!'

WARNING ON A LAWNMOWER

GENEALOGY

I come from a long line of people all waiting to get in.

Harry is tracing his genealogy. He discovers that he is descended from a very ancient and famous line. He can't believe his mother fell for it.

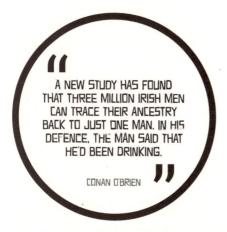

" A NEW STUDY HAS FOUND THAT THREE MILLION IRISH MEN CAN TRACE THEIR ANCESTRY BACK TO JUST ONE MAN. IN HIS DEFENCE, THE MAN SAID THAT HE'D BEEN DRINKING. "

CONAN O'BRIEN

GEOGRAPHY

> QUESTION MASTER: WHERE DO YOU THINK CAMBRIDGE UNIVERSITY IS?
> CONTESTANT: GEOGRAPHY ISN'T MY STRONG POINT.
> QUESTION MASTER: THERE'S A CLUE IN THE TITLE.
> CONTESTANT: LEICESTER?
>
> BEG, BORROW OR STEAL

Kevin failed his geography exam at school. He couldn't find the room where it was being held.

A teacher asks her class, 'Who can tell me what an island is?' A boy puts his hand up and says, 'It's an area of land which is entirely surrounded by water except for one side.' 'What do you mean "except for one side"?' says the teacher. 'The top side,' says the boy.

> I'VE READ ABOUT FOREIGN POLICY AND I'VE STUDIED. I NOW KNOW THE NUMBER OF CONTINENTS.
>
> GEORGE WALLACE (A CANDIDATE DURING THE 1968 US PRESIDENTIAL CAMPAIGN

> QUESTION MASTER: WHERE IS THE TAJ MAHAL?
> CONTESTANT: OPPOSITE THE DENTAL HOSPITAL.
>
> FAMILY FORTUNES

> STEVE WRIGHT: WHAT IS THE CAPITAL OF AUSTRALIA? I'LL GIVE YOU A CLUE, IT ISN'T SYDNEY.
> CONTESTANT: SYDNEY.
>
> THE STEVE WRIGHT SHOW

Q: What is the capital of Greece?
A: About £4.50.

GEORGE BEST

> SO, THIS MOVIE YOU STAR IN, *THE LIFE STORY OF GEORGE BEST*, TELL US WHAT IT'S ABOUT.
>
> GEORGE GAVIN INTERVIEWING THE STAR OF A NEW BIOPIC ON SKY SPORTS

> " OUR TALKING POINT THIS MORNING IS GEORGE BEST, HIS LIVER TRANSPLANT AND THE BOOZE CULTURE IN FOOTBALL. DON'T FORGET, THE BEST CALLER WINS A CRATE OF JOHN SMITH'S. "
>
> ALAN BRAZIL

> " I SPENT A LOT OF MONEY ON ALCOHOL, WOMEN AND FAST CARS. THE REST I JUST WASTED. "
>
> GEORGE BEST

GHOSTS

A psychic investigator goes to an old house that is renowned for being haunted. The investigator has brought a load of photographic equipment and is determined to take a picture of his ghost. He waits all night and eventually a ghostly apparition appears. Not only that but the ghost is more than happy to have his picture taken and stands posing for several minutes while the investigator snaps away. When he gets home and develops his photos, however, the results turn out to be very disappointing. The pictures are all underexposed and so dimly lit that it's impossible to make anything out. 'I don't believe it,' says the investigator, 'the spirit was willing, but the flash was weak.'

GOLF

Ken plays golf very badly which, as he says, takes an awful lot of balls.

Two old men are playing a round of golf. One of them says he is going to Mr Smith the dentist to get a new set of dentures later that day. The other says he had dentures from Mr Smith a couple of years before. 'Were they any good?' asks the first. 'Put it this way,' says his friend, 'I was on the golf course yesterday when I got hit right in the groin by a ball travelling at about 200mph.' 'What's that got to do with your teeth?' asks the first. 'That was the first time in two years I didn't notice them hurting,' says his friend.

A woman is playing golf. She tees off and watches as her ball hurtles towards a man at the next hole. Upon impact, he falls to the ground clasping his hands between his legs. The woman races over to the injured man and explains that she is a professional physical therapist and can relieve his pain. Despite his initial resistance, she insists on helping, and loosens his trousers and begins massaging his groin. 'How does that feel?' she asks. 'Absolutely fantastic,' he says. 'But I've still got this massive bruise on my hand where the ball hit me.'

Dick bets the pro at his local club £500 that he can beat him in a round of golf. 'But,' says Dick, 'clearly you're a much better player than I am. So to even things up, you have to allow me two "gotchas".' The golf pro isn't sure what a 'gotcha' is but agrees to the bet anyway. Later he has to pay Dick his £500. 'What happened?' asks the barman in the club house. 'Well,' says the pro, 'I was just teeing up for the first hole when that idiot stuck his hand between my legs, grabbed my crotch and shouted "Gotcha!" Have you ever tried to play 18 holes of golf waiting for the second "gotcha"?'

Barry and Jim are on the golf course when they see a woman drop her pants to go to the toilet in the bushes. 'My goodness,' says Barry, 'I think that's Mrs Fitzgerald from the golf committee. She's been taken short in the bushes. Twenty quid says she doesn't wipe her bum.' 'Don't be ridiculous,' says Jim, 'she's a very respectable woman. She will definitely wipe her bum. I'll take the bet.' 'OK,' says Barry, and then shouts across at the bushes, 'Lovely morning, Mrs Fitzgerald!'

A man comes running from the golf course into the clubhouse looking very upset. 'I've just been on the first hole,' he says, 'and I sliced the ball but it hit a tree and bounced off over the road where it hit a man on a motorbike who fell off in front of a lorry, which crashed and spilled oil all over the carriageway, which caused a pile-up with hundreds of smashed cars and people lying all over the place. What should I do?' The club president thinks for a moment and then says, 'I'd try taking it a bit easier on the backswing in future.'

A man is out playing golf. He says to his caddy, 'This golf course is the most rough and difficult I've ever played on.' 'What do you mean?' says the caddy. 'We left the course over an hour ago.'

A married couple are playing golf. They reach the sixth hole when the wife has a heart attack. 'Fetch a doctor!' she gasps before passing out. When she comes round, she sees her husband lining up a putt. 'I thought I told you to fetch a doctor!' she yells. 'Don't worry,' says the husband. 'I found a doctor. He's just on the fourth hole.' 'What do you mean?' says his wife. 'He's playing the fourth hole while I'm lying here with a heart attack on the sixth!?' 'It's OK,' says her husband. 'The people on the fifth are going to let him play through.'

James takes every opportunity to get in a round of golf. One Sunday morning he slips out of bed before dawn and heads for the local course, but on the way a terrific thunderstorm opens up and he reluctantly heads for home. It's still early, so he slips into bed next to his wife, who he thinks will still be asleep. 'Hello, darling,' she mumbles. 'Hello, dear,' he whispers. 'The rain's terrible.' 'Yes,' mumbles his wife. 'And can you believe my fool of a husband is out playing golf in it?'

Tom, Dick, Harry and Gus are out golfing. 'It's really difficult for me to get out here,' says Tom. 'I had to promise my wife that I would paint the house next weekend.' 'That's nothing,' says Harry, 'my wife wouldn't let me come until I promised to build a new patio in the garden.' 'My wife,' says Dick, 'wouldn't let me come until I promised to fit a new kitchen for her. What about you, Gus? What did you have to do to get your wife to let you come out for a round of golf?' 'I just set the alarm for 5:30,' says Gus. 'When it goes off I roll over and ask her, "Golf or sex?" And she says, "Don't forget to take your umbrella".'

GOOD DEEDS

A man is going out of a shop when a boy runs up and says, 'Excuse me, sir. I believe you dropped your wallet.' The boy presents the wallet and the man says, 'That is very honest of you.' He then looks inside the wallet and says, 'That's funny. I had a £50 note in here before. But now I have four tenners and a couple of fivers instead.' 'I know,' says the boy, 'I got you a bit of change. The last time I returned a wallet, the man told me he didn't have anything small enough to give me as a reward.'

GORILLAS

A man comes home and finds a gorilla in a tree in his garden. He looks in the phone book and luckily a gorilla removal service is listed. He phones them up and they send out one of their officers, who turns up with a shotgun, a stick, a pair of handcuffs and a Chihuahua. 'Now listen carefully,' says the gorilla removal expert, 'I will climb up the tree and poke the gorilla with this stick. The gorilla will then fall to the ground. The Chihuahua will then sink its teeth into the gorilla's sensitive regions. When the gorilla crosses his hands to protect himself, you slap on these handcuffs.' 'OK,' says the homeowner. 'But what's the shotgun for?' 'If things go wrong,' says the gorilla removal expert, 'and I fall out of the tree before the gorilla, take the gun and shoot the Chihuahua.'

GRANDPARENTS

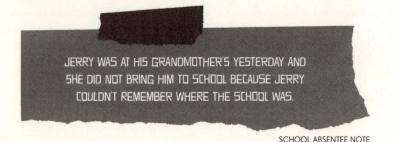

JERRY WAS AT HIS GRANDMOTHER'S YESTERDAY AND SHE DID NOT BRING HIM TO SCHOOL BECAUSE JERRY COULDN'T REMEMBER WHERE THE SCHOOL WAS.

SCHOOL ABSENTEE NOTE

Barry is planning a visit to his elderly grandmother. He calls her and she gives him directions to the apartment complex where she lives: 'Come to the main door. I am in flat 14T. You'll see a panel of buttons in front of you. With your elbow push button 14T and I'll buzz you in. Then go to the lifts and press the button for floor 14 with your elbow.' 'That's fine,' says Barry. 'I can do all that. But why do I have to press the buttons with my elbows?' 'What!?' says his grandmother. 'You mean you're coming empty-handed?'

GRAVEYARDS

George is coming back drunk from the pub when he takes a detour through the graveyard. Unfortunately an open grave has been left uncovered and George falls in. It's a cold night and George is soon calling for help. 'Can somebody get me out of here?! It's freezing cold!' Another drunk is passing by and he staggers over to look down on him. 'No wonder you're cold, mate,' he slurs. 'You must have woken up and kicked off all the dirt.'

Fred is walking through a graveyard when he comes across a man lying across one of the plots clutching the headstone. 'Why did you leave us?' he sobs. 'Why did you have to go? I'd do anything to bring you back. Anything.' 'I'm terribly sorry,' says Fred. 'Is that your wife's grave?' 'No,' sniffs the man. 'Her first husband's.'

Tom was walking through the graveyard when he saw something that turned his hair white. It was a flock of pigeons.

We've got a ghost in our local cemetery who always appears wearing a raincoat. We call him Max Bygraves.

GREEN ENERGY

Billy-Bob had to take down one of his windmills. The salesman had convinced him to buy two, but it turned out there was only enough wind for one.

I don't think they should build any more of those offshore wind farms. This country seems windy enough as it is.

GREETINGS CARDS

Tom walks into a card shop and asks, 'Do you sell bereavement cards?' 'Yes,' says the assistant. 'Excellent,' says Tom. 'Can I get one in exchange for this "Get Well Soon" card I bought yesterday?'

Mum takes her little boy to choose a birthday card for Dad. The little boy spends a long time going through all the cards in the shop, opening each one before shoving it back into the display. 'Don't you like any of them?' asks Mum. 'Yes,' says the boy, 'but I'm trying to find one of the ones that have money in them.'

NOT SUITABLE FOR CHILDREN 36 MONTHS OR YOUNGER.

WARNING ON A BIRTHDAY CARD FOR A ONE-YEAR-OLD

GULLIBILITY

Henry never realised he was completely gullible, till his friend told him he was.

GUNS

It has been reported that a stash of guns and explosives has been found behind a job centre in Liverpool city centre. Local people say they are shocked. They had no idea they had a job centre.

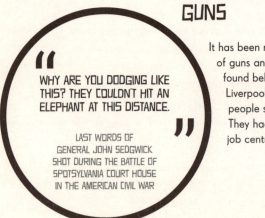

"WHY ARE YOU DODGING LIKE THIS? THEY COULDN'T HIT AN ELEPHANT AT THIS DISTANCE."

LAST WORDS OF GENERAL JOHN SEDGWICK SHOT DURING THE BATTLE OF SPOTSYLVANIA COURT HOUSE IN THE AMERICAN CIVIL WAR

GYMNASTICS

June had to give up on yoga. She tried standing on her head, but could never get her feet high enough.

GYNAECOLOGY

A gynaecologist decides to switch careers and become an car mechanic. He goes to college to study and takes all the exams. He gets a special commendation. Not only did he manage to take apart the engine, clean and repair it and put it all back together, he did the whole job through the exhaust pipe.

Q: If tennis players get tennis elbow, skiers get skiers' thumb and golfers get golfers' wrist, what do gynaecologists get?
A: Tunnel vision.

> "A MALE GYNAECOLOGIST IS LIKE AN AUTO MECHANIC WHO NEVER OWNED A CAR."
>
> CARRIE SNOW

HABITS

Tom tells Harry, 'My wife has got into a terrible habit. Each night she won't go to bed until two or three o'clock.' 'Oh no,' says Harry. 'What's she doing staying up till that time?' 'Waiting for me to come home,' says Tom.

HAIR

I always wanted to be a barber, but I just couldn't cut it.

At school everyone used to make fun of me because I had bog-brush hair. I didn't question it at the time, but now I do wonder why didn't my mum and dad didn't just buy themselves a proper toilet brush?

Harry lost in a pub quiz. It all came down to the last question: 'Where do women mostly have curly hair?' The answer obviously should have been 'Africa'.

You should not be tempted if you see adverts for cheap hair removal. It'll probably end up being a complete rip-off.

Do you think the man who invented the Mohican had really just got carried away while trying to trim his sideburns the same length?

Bob goes into the barber's and asks if he can have his hair cut just like Tom Cruise. 'OK,' says the barber, and gives him a couple of cushions to sit on.

It has been reported that the first ever all-night, open-air festival for people with brightly coloured luminous hairdos has ended in tragedy after a Boeing 747 mistook them for a landing strip.

Last week my girlfriend did a charity event doing hairdressing nonstop for 24 hours. By the end she was completely lacquered.

I get my hair done by the world famous Irish hairdresser – Tim O'Tay.

A barber runs out of his shop to find a policeman. 'Have you seen a man run by here, officer?' asks the barber. 'He just ran out of my shop without paying me!' 'Does he have any distinguishing features?' asks the policeman. 'Yes,' says the barber. 'He's carrying one of his ears in his left hand.'

HALLOWEEN

Len hates it when trick-or-treaters knock on his door at Halloween. So now he turns the lights off and pretends he isn't in. The only problem is he's the local lighthouse keeper.

HANDWRITING

A teacher says to a little boy in her class, 'Your handwriting is terrible!' 'I know,' says the boy, 'but look on the bright side. If it was any better you'd find out I can't spell anything.'

HANDYMEN

Brian sees an opening for a handyman at the local hospital and decides to apply. He's asked to fill out a form and ticks off all the skills he has. When the interviewer looks at the form he says, 'According to this, you can't do brickwork, cleaning, electrical work, decorating, gardening, plumbing, gas repairs or carpentry.' 'That's right,' says Brian. 'So why do you think you'd make a good handyman?' asks the interviewer. Brian says, 'Because I only live next door.'

HARDWARE

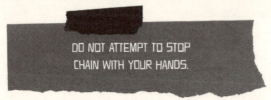

DO NOT ATTEMPT TO STOP CHAIN WITH YOUR HANDS.

INSTRUCTION GIVEN ON PACKAGING FOR A CHAINSAW

Did you hear the joke about the deep-sea drilling equipment? It was boring in the extreme.

Alice is decorating her house and goes to a DIY store to buy a new door-knocker. The sales assistant says, 'Do you want a screw for that?' Alice says, 'No, but I'll give you a kiss and cuddle for a can of paint.'

Nobby comes home with a huge black eye. 'What on earth happened to you?' asks his wife. 'I got chatting to the man next door,' says Nobby, 'and I started complaining about how muddy our garden is. He told me I needed decking, so I thought I'd better get the first punch in.'

HEAD LICE

I had to do my son's hair with head-lice shampoo. It got rid of the lice but the shampoo contains pesticides so it does have side effects. Now he's got sweetcorn growing out of his ears.

HEADACHES

Every morning Betty used to wake up with a nagging headache. She soon found a cure though – she divorced him.

Bert goes to the doctor with a headache. The doctor tells him, 'I wouldn't worry about your headache.' 'I know you wouldn't,' says Bert. 'And if you were the one who had it, I wouldn't worry about it either.'

HEALTH

Dick tells Harry, 'I went for a routine check-up on the NHS this morning.' 'How did it go?' asks Harry. 'Fine,' says Dick, 'until he got me to drop my trousers and stuck his finger up my bum!' 'Isn't that a routine sort of check?' says Harry. 'No!' says Dick. 'Not at the dentist's, it's not.'

Norman goes to the doctor because he has fluid on the knee. 'This can be a problem at your age,' says the doctor. 'You need to try aiming at the toilet a bit more carefully.'

I treasure my EpiPen because my best friend gave it to me as he lay dying. I'm not quite sure what he was trying to say to me but it seemed very important to him that I should have it.

A man is on holiday in the wilds of Scotland. He remarks to a local that the air is so fresh and the countryside is so invigorating that this must be a very healthy place to live. 'It is,' says the local. 'There's been only one death in the last ten years. And that was the local undertaker, who died of starvation.'

I was told the seaside was a good place to go for rheumatism. And it was true because I went there and, sure enough, I got it.

Tom feels unwell so he calls the doctor. 'The earliest appointment we have,' says the receptionist, 'is in two weeks' time.' 'That's no good,' says Tom, 'I could be dead by then!' 'Don't worry about that,' says the receptionist, 'just ask your wife to give us a call and we'll cancel the appointment.'

Norman goes to the doctor with a pain in his left knee. 'That's just old age,' says the doctor. 'What do you mean?' says Norman. 'I've had my right knee just as long and I've got no pain in that at all.'

My doctor is very considerate. I couldn't afford the treatment I needed last year so he kindly touched up my X-rays for me.

My dad always said fresh air was the best medicine. And that is why me and my brother spent our childhood in hospital being treated for pneumonia.

Fred goes into the living room and joins his wife, Beryl, on the sofa. 'Well?' says Fred. 'Well, what?' asks Beryl. 'Aren't you going to ask me how I'm feeling?' says Fred. 'All right,' says Beryl. 'How are you feeling?' Bert says, 'Don't ask.'

My father was asked to resign as a town councillor last week. He came down with a touch of gastroenteritis at the planning meeting and passed the wrong kind of motion.

Harry tells Tom, 'I've just been given two weeks to live.' 'You mean you're ill?' asks Tom. 'No,' says Harry. 'My wife's going away to her sister's for a fortnight.'

HEALTH FOOD

How much 'Too Good to Be True – Healthy Choice' Ice Cream is it possible for someone to eat before it isn't too good to be true or a healthy choice any more?

Fred has started taking a 100 per cent natural organic herbal extract that makes him feel fantastic. It's called opium.

Last week I held up a health food shop armed with nothing but a bag of gluten.

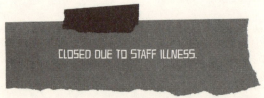

SIGN IN THE WINDOW OF A HEALTH FOOD STORE

HEARTS AND HEART CONDITIONS

Dick has the heart of a lion. And that's probably the reason he got a lifetime ban from Longleat Safari Park.

A man goes to the doctor worried he might be suffering from heart trouble. 'Don't worry about your heart,' says the doctor, 'I can promise you it will keep working right up until the day you die.'

> IF SOMEBODY HAS A BAD HEART, THEY CAN PLUG THIS JACK IN AT NIGHT AS THEY GO TO BED AND IT WILL MONITOR THEIR HEART THROUGHOUT THE NIGHT. AND THE NEXT MORNING, WHEN THEY WAKE UP DEAD, THERE'LL BE A RECORD.
>
> MARK S. FOWLER
> (CHAIRMAN OF THE US FEDERAL COMMUNICATIONS COMMISSION)

My next-door neighbour had to have a pacemaker fitted. I don't know where he got it from, but every time he makes love, my garage door opens.

A doctor tells a patient that because of his heart problems he should not attempt to engage in sexual activity until he is capable of climbing two flights of stairs without becoming short of breath. 'OK,' says the patient, 'but what if I just looked for a woman who lives on the ground floor?'

A car mechanic and a heart surgeon are talking. 'What I don't understand,' says the mechanic, 'is why I don't get paid as much as you when I do just as complicated a job. I have to open up an engine, take out valves, replace them and put them back so it's working like new. It's just like surgery.' 'Yes,' says the surgeon, 'but have you ever had to do it while the engine is running?'

HEROISM

Tom and Harry are on holiday in Wales. They go into a working men's club and notice a man sitting in the corner who has such a massive cauliflower ear and extraordinarily flat head that they can't help but laugh. 'I hope you're not laughing at Evan,' says another man at the bar. 'He's the bravest man here. He saved the lives of hundreds of local miners when the shaft collapsed.' 'But how did he get such a flat head?' asks Tom. 'He used it to hold up the roof of the mineshaft,' says the man. 'And what about the cauliflower ear?' asks Harry. 'Oh,' says the man, 'that's where we had to hit him with a hammer to wedge him in.'

HIDE AND SEEK

The world hide-and-seek champion said it was his intention to get married this year but his perfect woman would be hard to find.

HIPPOS

Q: What's the difference between a hippo and a Zippo?
A: One is very heavy but the other is a little lighter.

HIPSTERS

How many hipsters does it take to change a light bulb? Two. One to change the bulb and another to hold his fedora.

HISTORY

Historians have been examining the life of the legendary figure William Tell. They've discovered that his ancestors were not archers or crossbowmen, but that he was descended from a long line of crown green bowlers. Unfortunately, all the records of their bowling triumphs and details of the teams for which they played were lost in a fire. It seems we may never know for whom the Tells bowled.

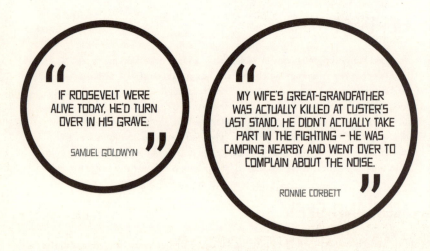

"IF ROOSEVELT WERE ALIVE TODAY, HE'D TURN OVER IN HIS GRAVE."

SAMUEL GOLDWYN

"MY WIFE'S GREAT-GRANDFATHER WAS ACTUALLY KILLED AT CUSTER'S LAST STAND. HE DIDN'T ACTUALLY TAKE PART IN THE FIGHTING – HE WAS CAMPING NEARBY AND WENT OVER TO COMPLAIN ABOUT THE NOISE."

RONNIE CORBETT

SCHOOLBOY HISTORY HOMEWORK ANSWERS

▶ Charles Darwin was a naturist who wrote *The Organ of Species*.

▶ Francis Drake circumcised the world with a 100-foot clipper, which was very dangerous to all his men.

▶ Magna Carta decreed that no man should be hanged twice for the same offence.

▶ The sun never set on the British Empire because the Empire was in the east and the sun sets in the west.

▶ Lincoln's mother dies in infancy and he was born in a log cabin that he built with his own hands.

PRESENTER: WHAT HAPPENED IN DALLAS ON NOVEMBER 22, 1963?
CONTESTANT: I DON'T KNOW, I WASN'T WATCHING IT THEN.

GWR FM BRISTOL

I THINK WE AGREE, THE PAST IS OVER.

GEORGE W. BUSH

PAUL WAPPAT: HOW LONG DID THE SIX-DAY WAR BETWEEN EGYPT AND ISRAEL LAST?
CONTESTANT: . . . FOURTEEN DAYS.

RADIO NEWCASTLE

Bill and Gladys go on a guided history walk to Runnymede, where King John was asked to sign the Magna Carta. 'When was that exactly?' asks Bill. The guide tells him, 'Twelve fifteen.' Bill looks at his watch and turns to Gladys, 'Would you believe it,' he says. 'We only missed it by 20 minutes.'

A few years ago you would go into a shop to buy cigarettes then slyly ask for a pack of condoms as well. These days, it's the other way round.

Q: Which king of England was also a qualified chiropodist?
A: William the Corn-curer.

HITCHHIKERS

For years Norman thought that, everywhere he went, his driving was greatly admired by strangers on the side of the road. Eventually someone told him they were hitchhikers trying to thumb a lift.

Benjamin was the world's worst hitchhiker. Aside from looking like a serial killer and never holding up his thumb, he used to sleep in late to avoid the traffic.

Barry is driving along a country road out in the middle of nowhere. In the distance he sees a young hitchhiker desperately running along with three huge dogs snapping at his heels. Barry races up to the young man, throws the door open and shouts, 'Come on! Quick! Jump in the car!' 'Hey, thanks, man!' says the young guy. 'That's really good of you. Usually no one will stop when they see I've got my dogs with me.'

HOAXES

As it's now the fourth time this week I've awoken at King's Cross station with concussion, I'm beginning to think my Hogwarts acceptance letter might be a hoax.

HOLD-UPS

There is a hold-up at an Indian restaurant. A criminal walks in, pulls out a gun and tells the manager, 'I want everything you've got in the till.' 'Is that to take away?' asks the manager.

A man is walking home when a mugger attacks him. He fights back and they struggle for half an hour until the mugger overpowers him and takes his wallet. Inside, the mugger finds just a few pence in loose change. 'Why did you put up such a fight when you've only got a few pennies in your wallet?' says the mugger. 'Well, to be honest,' says the man, 'I thought you were after the 100 quid I've got hidden in my shoe.'

Following an attempted mugging a few years ago Vince thought he'd better start carrying a knife when he goes out. Since then he's been mugging people much more successfully.

Barry is held up by a man with a gun. 'Your money or your life,' says the robber. 'You'd better take my life,' says Barry, 'I'm saving my money for my old age.'

It has been reported that a gang of thieves were responsible for a hold-up last month in which a lorry loaded with 1,000 tins of prunes was stolen. The men have been on the run ever since.

A robber walks into a bank, pulls out a gun and tells the cashier, 'Hand over the money or you're geography!' 'Don't you mean history?' says the cashier. 'Don't change the subject,' says the robber.

Neville was holding up a bank when one of the tellers sounded the alarm. The police quickly arrived on the scene and blocked all the exits – so Neville left by the entrance.

HOLES

Two men are out walking. One of them falls into a deep hole. 'Is it very dark down there?' calls his friend from the top. 'I'm not sure,' says the other, 'I can't see a thing.'

A man discovers a deep dark hole in the ground while out walking in the country. He picks up a small pebble and throws it into the hole but hears no sound. He then finds a bigger pebble and throws that into the hole, but again hears no sound. So he picks up a rock and throws that in, but there's still no sound. Finally, he finds an enormous boulder and rolls it along the ground and drops it into the hole. He listens for any sound from the hole but instead hears a goat charging down towards him. He jumps out of the way and the goat disappears into the hole. A minute later a farmer appears and asks, 'Have you seen my goat? I can't understand how he's disappeared. I left him tied to an enormous boulder.'

HOLIDAYS

A travel agent looks up from his desk and sees an old man and an old lady looking at the adverts in the window for exciting glamorous holidays all around the world. The travel agent feels sorry for the old couple so he goes out and tells them, 'Hey, I know that a lot of these holidays might be a bit expensive for anyone on a pension so I'd like to make you a special offer. I will give you a pair of tickets to stay in Rio de Janeiro for seven nights.' He takes them inside, makes the booking for them in a five-star hotel and tells them to come back to let him know how they enjoyed their holiday.' Sure enough, a few weeks later, the little old lady calls by and tells him, 'I had the holiday of a lifetime. It was absolutely marvellous. But there's just one thing that's been puzzling me. Who was that old man I had to share the room with?'

> "THE LAST TIME I WAS IN SPAIN I GOT THROUGH SIX JEFFREY ARCHER NOVELS. I MUST REMEMBER TO TAKE ENOUGH TOILET PAPER NEXT TIME."
>
> BOB MONKHOUSE

Bill is at the luggage carousel at the airport. The first bag comes down the chute and Bill picks it up. His wife says. 'What are you doing? That doesn't belong to us.' 'I might as well,' says Bill. 'The first bag never seems to belong to anyone.'

After a nice holiday you feel good enough to go back to work – and so poor that you've got no choice.

Did you hear about the cannibal who went on a self-catering holiday?
He ate himself.

Harry tells Tom that he's been arguing with his wife about where to go on holiday this year. 'I want to go to the Canary Islands,' says Harry. 'So what's the problem?' asks Tom. 'Vera wants to come with me,' says Harry.

I booked a holiday and got two weeks in Ibiza debating the reform of the workhouses, the Corn Laws, the Electoral Reform Bill and the early work of Charles Dickens. That wasn't what I thought they meant when they advertised an 1830 holiday.

HOME

Home is the place where you can say anything you like without fear of recrimination. And that's because home is the place where absolutely nobody listens to a word you say.

The definition of home: a place where one or more members of a family wait until other members of the same family bring the car back

HOME ENTERTAINMENT

I've got a massive home entertainment system: widescreen, DVD, Dolby surround sound, everything. The audio is incredible, an assault on the senses, a big powerful thumping noise, crashing all round you from every part of the room. And that was just the sound of me trying to get the damn thing set up and working.

HOMELESSNESS

Harry is walking through the city centre when he notices an attractive young homeless girl. He walks over and asks if he could take her home. The girl agrees, Harry says thanks very much, picks up her cardboard box and walks off with it.

HOMESICKNESS

Brenda tells Tom, 'I'm feeling homesick.' 'But you are at home,' says Tom. 'I know,' says Brenda, 'and I'm sick of it.'

HONESTY

Honesty might be the best policy, but I don't mind settling for second best – dishonesty.

> EIGHT MORE DAYS AND I CAN START TELLING THE TRUTH AGAIN!
>
> CHRIS DODD (A US SENATOR TALKING TOWARDS THE END OF A POLITICAL CAMPAIGN)

HONEYMOONERS

Gerry surprises his wife with breakfast in bed – a huge plate of bacon and eggs with pancakes and syrup and toast and coffee on the side. 'Quite a spread,' says Gerry. 'It looks wonderful,' agrees his wife. 'I know,' says Gerry. 'And from now on, that's how I want it every morning.'

HORROR MOVIES

Ed tells Bob, 'Last night I saw that new horror film about a killer teabag.' 'A killer teabag?' says Bob. 'Was it scary.' 'No,' says Ed. 'It was only a PG.'

HORSE RACING

Geoff's ambition was always to ride in the Grand National, but sadly he was run over by a steamroller. After that he had to settle for being a flat jockey.

Frank is one of Britain's most obese jockeys. Last year he converted almost 40 race horses into ponies.

A female teacher takes a group of primary school children to Cheltenham Races so they can learn about thoroughbred horses. After lunch, she takes the children to the toilets. One of the boys comes out of the gents and tells her that none of them can reach the urinal. The teacher has no option but to go into the loo and lift the boys up one by one so they can wee into the urinal. After a few minutes of this, she notices one of them is particularly well endowed. 'Are you in Year 4?' she asks. 'No,' he says, 'actually I'm riding Kilburn Lad in the 2:15.'

A trainer is watching a jockey get ready for a race. 'Are you sure you're a qualified jockey?' asks the trainer. 'You've just put the saddle on the wrong way round.' 'I haven't,' says the jockey. 'You don't know which direction I'm going in.'

There are plenty of signs that will tell you when you're betting on the wrong horse – the worst one is when you see your horse trying to place a bet on another horse.

HORSES

A horse walks into a bar. 'Why the long face?' asks the barman. 'Because,' says the horse, 'my alcoholism is destroying my family.'

Bert asks Ted, 'What happened to the horse you bought last week?' 'It died,' says Ted. 'Oh no!' says Bert. 'So what did you do?' 'Well,' says Ted. 'I thought that it would be difficult trying to sue the previous owner, so I held a raffle for it at £1 a ticket.' 'But it was for a dead horse!' says Bert. 'Didn't anyone complain?' 'Only the winner,' says Bert. 'So I gave him his pound back.'

Q: How many legs does a horse have?
A: Six – forelegs at the front and two at the back.

Q: Why do other horses regard shire horses as being unfashionable?
A: Because they're the ones who wear flared trousers.

Gerry goes to a local farm to see a horse they have for sale. The horse is a fine animal and Gerry is surprised to find that the asking price is only £50. 'That's very cheap,' says Gerry. 'Is there anything wrong with it?' 'Arrrr, no,' says the farmer. 'Only, he don't look very good.' 'He looks fine to me,' says Gerry. 'Mind if I take him out for a ride?' 'Course,' says the farmer. 'But remember, he don't look very good.' Gerry still can't see anything the matter with the horse, so he saddles up and goes for a gallop. Three hours later, he returns with his arm in a cast. He comes up to the farmer and says, 'That horse almost killed me. It ran straight into a wall. I had a vet examine it and he said it was completely blind.' The farmer shrugs, 'Well I did tell you it don't look very good.'

A farmer finds that birds keep building their nests in his horse's thick long mane. He asks the vet what he should do. The vet advises putting some baker's yeast in the horse's feed as this will cause an odour that will deter the birds. Sure enough, it works perfectly and a few days later the farmer asks the vet where he got the idea from. 'It's common knowledge,' says the vet. 'Have you never heard? Yeast is yeast and nest is nest and never the mane shall tweet!'

Did you hear about the tragic horse? He had a terrible tale of whoa!

A horse walks into a bar. The barman asks, 'Why the long face?' The horse replies, 'Because I've heard you tell the same flipping joke every time I come in here.'

HOSPITALITY

The definition of hospitality – the art of making your guests feel at home even when you wish they were.

Tom tells his wife Brenda that he's invited a new work colleague round for dinner that night. 'What did you do that for?' says Brenda. 'The house is a mess. I've got nothing in. We haven't got round to doing the dishes from breakfast yet and I don't feel like cooking a fancy meal! What possible reason could you have for inviting this person round to see all this chaos?' 'That's just it,' says Tom, 'the poor guy is thinking about getting married.'

HOSPITALS

A young man wakes up in hospital following a drunken car accident. The nurse tells him, 'I'm afraid you may not feel anything from the waist down.' 'OK,' he says, 'so can I feel your boobs instead, then?'

Ted and Bill are in hospital. Ted asks Bill, 'What are you in for?' 'Camera down the throat,' says Bill. 'Oh, I see,' says Ted, 'an endoscopy.' 'That's right,' says Bill, 'what about yourself?' 'Camera up the backside,' says Ted. 'Oh,' says Bill, 'a colonoscopy.' 'No,' says Ted, 'the woman next door was sunbathing and my wife caught me taking a photo.'

Dick is going into the hospital for surgery when he sees a sign that says 'Thieves operate here'. 'That's terrible,' he thinks, 'wouldn't it be better to leave it to medically qualified professionals?'

Gary is waiting in the hospital for news about his granddad. A doctor tells him, 'I'm afraid we're going to have to switch off his life support.' 'OK, I get it,' says Gary. 'Then you're going to try switching him straight back on again to see if that fixes the problem.'

A man is in hospital after a road accident. He wakes up covered in plaster with his legs hoisted up. 'How do you feel?' asks the doctor. 'Not too bad,' says the man, but then suddenly leans to his left. The doctor quickly grabs him and props him upright again. Later a nurse asks, 'How are you getting on?' 'Not too bad,' says the man, but again he leans over to one side. The nurse grabs him and props him upright. The next day the man's wife visits him. 'How are you?' she asks. 'Not too bad,' says the man, 'the only problem is that no one here will let me fart in peace.'

> "A HOSPITAL IS NO PLACE TO BE SICK."
>
> SAMUEL GOLDWYN

Q: Who is the coolest person working in the hospital?
A: The ultrasound guy.

A hospital doctor is checking on his patients. He comes to the first patient and asks the nurse on the ward, 'Did you give this patient the medication I prescribed. Two tablets every eight hours?' 'Oh no!' says the nurse. 'I thought you said eight tablets every two hours!' At the next bed the doctor asks, 'Did you give this patient the treatment I advised? One tablet every 12 hours.' 'Oh no!' says the nurse. 'I thought you said 12 tablets every one hour.' At the third bed, the doctor finds a man with an anguished look on his face. 'With this patient,' says the doctor, 'I didn't prescribe any medication but I did ask you to prick his boil.' 'Oh no!' says the nurse.

Nigel accidentally swallowed an immersion heater. After a brief spell in hospital, he's now all right, but does get occasional hot flushes.

Q: Who is the coolest person in the hospital when the ultrasound guy is away on holiday?
A: The hip replacement doctor.

Gary goes to visit his granddad in hospital. Gary is pleased to see that the hospital has provided games and leisure activities for the patients to enjoy while they are there. His eye is particularly taken by the big bright orange space hopper which he finds his granddad sitting on when he arrives. He climbs on with granddad and spends a happy few minutes bouncing up and down the ward with him until a doctor takes him aside and says, 'That's not a space hopper. That's the growth your granddad is due to have removed in the morning.'

Tom goes to visit Harry in hospital before his operation but finds him getting dressed and packing his things. 'You've got to get me out of here,' says Harry. 'The nurse just said, "You must stop trembling and sobbing and worrying. The operation will be fine."' 'What's the matter with that?' asks Tom. 'She was trying to put you at ease.' 'She wasn't talking to me,' says Harry, 'she was talking to the surgeon.'

The Secretary of State for Health officially opened London's first hospital entirely devoted to bellybutton-piercing-related conditions. He performed the ceremony using a ten-foot cotton bud to dislodge a six-foot-diameter ball of blue fluff from the entrance lobby.

HOSTAGES

It has been announced on the news that police have finally ended the recent hostage crisis at the local football stadium by means of a penalty shoot-out with the kidnappers.

HOTELS

THE FLATTENING OF UNDERWEAR WITH PLEASURE IS THE JOB OF THE CHAMBERMAID.

SIGN IN AN EASTERN EUROPEAN HOTEL

Barry is away on business. He asks the receptionist at his hotel if she'll give him a wake-up call. At six o'clock the next morning, Barry's phone rings and he hears the receptionist asking, 'What the hell do you think you're doing with your life?'

A man is booking into a hotel. The receptionist says, 'Would you mind making your own bed?' 'No problem,' says the man. 'OK,' says the receptionist, and hands over a hammer, nails and a few planks of wood.

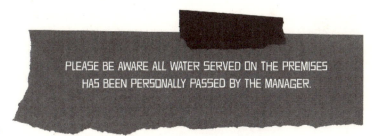

PLEASE BE AWARE ALL WATER SERVED ON THE PREMISES HAS BEEN PERSONALLY PASSED BY THE MANAGER.

SIGN ON THE MENU AT A FOREIGN HOTEL

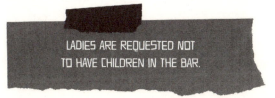

LADIES ARE REQUESTED NOT TO HAVE CHILDREN IN THE BAR.

SIGN IN A NORWEGIAN HOTEL

> **WHAT A HOTEL. THE TOWELS WERE SO FLUFFY I COULD HARDLY CLOSE MY SUITCASE.**
>
> HENNY YOUNGMAN

Harry walks up to the hotel reception and says, 'Can I check myself out, please.' 'Of course, sir,' says the receptionist. 'There's a mirror just behind you.'

A man is booking into a hotel when he notices an attractive woman in the lobby who is clearly looking for business. The man calls her over and says to the receptionist, 'Fancy that! I've just bumped into my wife. Please show us to our room.' The next morning, the man's lady companion has gone and he is stunned when the hotel receptionist hands him a bill for £10,000. 'How can it be that much?' asks the man. 'I've only been here one night.' 'I know,' says the receptionist, 'But your wife has been here for two months.'

Freddie gets a job as the manager of a large hotel. His first job is to stop the guests stealing things. 'Easy,' says Freddie. 'We'll tell them that every guest can take their pillows home with them.' 'What good will that do?' says the owner. 'We'll just lose all our pillows.' 'Yes,' says Freddie. 'But once their suitcases are full of cheap pillows they won't have room for all the other stuff they've been nicking.'

Poor Beryl was trapped in her hotel room for three days. She couldn't get out. There were three doors in her room and she couldn't use any of them: one led to a closet, one led to a bathroom and the last one had a 'Do not disturb' sign hanging off the handle.

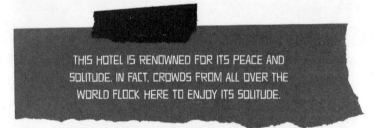

THIS HOTEL IS RENOWNED FOR ITS PEACE AND SOLITUDE. IN FACT, CROWDS FROM ALL OVER THE WORLD FLOCK HERE TO ENJOY ITS SOLITUDE.

EXTRACT FROM AN ITALIAN HOTEL BROCHURE

SIGN BY A HOTEL LIFT IN FRANCE

Henry books into a hotel on a business trip. He finds he has to share a room with another guest and is appalled to discover the man snores like crazy. Henry doesn't get a wink of sleep and complains to the manager. Unfortunately, there are no other rooms, so Henry is stuck with the man for a second night. The next day, Henry books out and the manager apologises for the inconvenience. 'That's OK,' says Henry. 'I slept fine the second night.' 'Did you find a way to stop the snoring?' asks the manager. 'Yes,' says Henry. 'When I went to bed, I kissed the guy goodnight and he spent the whole night watching me.'

HOUSE HUNTING

A couple go to see a house that they are thinking about buying. The owner greets them at the door and shows them round. 'It smells funny in here,' say the couple. 'I know,' says the man, 'this house is bordered on the north by the gasworks, on the south there's a rubber factory, to the east is the cat food plant and over on the west is the local sewage treatment plant.' 'Oh dear!' say the couple. 'That doesn't sound very nice. Does the house have any redeeming features?' 'Well,' says the man, 'you can always tell which way the wind is blowing.'

HOUSEHOLD PRODUCTS AND APPLIANCES

INSTRUCTIONS ON AN ELECTRIC KETTLE

Tom tells Harry he has bought a new non-stick frying pan. 'Is it any good?' asks Harry. 'I don't know,' says Tom, 'I haven't been able to get the label off it yet.'

I bought a bottle of cream cleaner. I tried using it to clean the pint of gold top I had in the fridge, but to be honest it left a bit of an aftertaste.

INSTRUCTION ON A CAN OF AIR-FRESHENER

I bought my wife a new fridge yesterday. She's really pleased with it. When she opened the door, you should have seen her little face light up.

Tom bought a new can opener but it's useless – it won't open anything. He calls it a can't opener.

Q: Which dance do tin openers do?
A: The can-can.

HOUSEWORK

Young children are always getting under your feet wanting to help with the housework. So why, as soon as they get old enough to be any use at it, do they stop offering?

Alice sees a bottle of household cleaner in the supermarket which has the slogan: 'Loves the jobs you hate!' Next time her husband asks for a bit of nookie, out comes the bottle.

Harry was in the middle of cleaning when the Grim Reaper came to collect him. Harry had to shoo him out with the vacuum cleaner. He was Dyson with death.

Bill calls Larry, his recently divorced friend. 'How are you coping?' asks Bill. 'Can you manage on your own.' 'Yes,' says Larry. 'But do you know where the washing goes after it comes out of the machine?' 'I'm not sure,' says Bill. 'Where did your wife put it?' 'That's what I'm trying to find out,' says Larry. 'I load the washer, but when I pull the chain all the clothes disappear.'

My wife picked a bad time to take up housework. Yesterday, she cleaned the kitchen and wiped out some very important telephone numbers written in the window dust.

> "CLEANING YOUR HOUSE WHILE YOUR KIDS ARE STILL GROWING IS LIKE SHOVELLING THE WALK BEFORE IT STOPS SNOWING."
>
> — PHYLLIS DILLER

George was tired of living in a messy house, with no clean clothes and nothing but lousy food to eat, so he got married. Ironically, around the same time his friend Brian got divorced for exactly the same reasons.

A man gets fed up with going to work every day so he says a prayer: 'Dear Lord, I have to do eight hours at work each day while my wife just stays at home looking after the house. Let her see what I have to go through by swapping her body with mine for one day. Amen'. And sure enough, the man's prayer is answered and the next morning he wakes up in his wife's body. He gets up, makes breakfast for all the family, gets the kids up and ready for school, makes their packed lunches, cleans the house, does the laundry, gets the shopping, changes the cat litter, walks the dogs, makes the beds, picks the kids up from school, makes dinner for everyone, does the ironing, gives the kids a bath and collapses exhausted into bed where he is expected to provide a bit of night-time entertainment for his partner. The next morning he gets up and prays: 'Dear Lord, I don't know what I was thinking. Obviously it's even harder work staying at home. So please let us swap our bodies back.' 'OK,' says God, 'you have learned your lesson. The only problem is you're going to have to wait nine months, because you got pregnant last night.'

Gladys finds her husband watching TV. 'There's so much DIY to do round here,' she says. 'When are you going to think about painting the shed?' He says, 'After I've finished thinking about fixing the gutters.'

Brian comes home and finds the house is a complete mess: the carpets are dirty, the windows need cleaning, there's dust everywhere, the sink is full of washing up and the laundry basket is full. He goes into the bedroom and finds his wife under the covers having a snooze. He wakes her up and says, 'What on earth is going on?' His wife says, 'You know all that stuff I normally do? Well, today I didn't do it.'

HUMILITY

Donald Trump has sought psychiatric help. Apparently he fears he may be suffering from delusions of humility.

HUMOUR

Things are always funny until somebody gets hurt. Once that happens, it's absolutely hilarious.

HUNTING

An explorer is hacking through the jungle when he finds a tiny native standing next to an enormous dead lion. 'Wow!' says the explorer. 'Did you kill that?' 'Yes I did,' says the little man. 'But,' says the explorer, 'how did a little fellow like you kill an enormous beast like that?' 'Simple,' says the little man, 'I killed it with my club.' 'Really?' says the explorer. 'How big is your club?' 'There's about 100 of us,' says the little man.

A woman goes into a hunting shop in the USA to buy her son a rifle for his birthday. She picks one out, but is clueless as to whether it's suitable, so goes to the counter to ask the salesman's advice. To her surprise she finds the salesman is completely blind. 'Could you cock the gun for me?' he asks. 'What will that do?' asks the woman. 'I can tell which gun it is just by the sound of it,' he replies. The woman does so and the man says, 'Mmmm. A Raider 22, with the standard sights and hickory stock. That's a very good choice for a beginner. And it's a bargain at $200.' The woman is impressed and reaches down to get to her bag and find her purse. Unfortunately, as she does so, she lets out a fart. 'That's a total of $245,' says the salesman. '$245?' says the woman. 'Just now you said $200.' 'Yes, ma'am,' he replies. 'But the duck call is $30 and the skunk bait is $15.'

HYGIENE

I don't think it's a big deal that I dislike soap, yet everyone else just seems to want to rub it in my face.

> LOUIS PASTEUR DISCOVERED A CURE FOR RABBIS.
>
> SCHOOLBOY HOMEWORK ANSWER

I gave my pet chimp his bath yesterday. He went 'Ah-ah-ha-eek-eek-who-hah-eek'. So I added a bit more cold water.

Grandpa was never much on bathing. He used to say that if God had meant us to take showers he would have put our armpits on the top of our shoulders, not underneath.

HYPNOTISM

Nigel's first appearance as a theatre hypnotist did not go well. He got 30 people up on the stage and put them in a deep trance, then he dropped his watch, accidentally stood on it and said, 'Crap!' It took a week to get the smell out of the auditorium.

HYPOCHONDRIA

What's the best way to make a hypochondriac happy? Tell them they look awful.

I have found the hardest thing about Hypochondriacs Anonymous is admitting that you don't have a problem.

HYPOCRISY

The definition of a hypocrite is someone who publishes a book about atheism and then prays to God that it will be a bestseller.

ICE CREAM

Nobby's little boy keeps begging him for an ice cream. In the end Nobby gives in and hands the little lad a Magnum. 'I'll show you how to take the safety catch off,' he tells him, 'then you can use it to hold-up an ice-cream van.'

IDENTITY THEFT

I am worried about identity theft. When I die I don't want to be buried or cremated. I want to be shredded.

Sid was the victim of ID theft last year. Ever since he's just been called 'S'.

ILLNESS

A man walks into the doctor's and says, 'Doctor, can you tell what's wrong with me?' 'Well,' says the doctor, 'first of all your eyesight is pretty poor, because this is the vet's.'

Did you know that you can have flu in both an affirmative and a negative manner? Sometimes the eyes have it and sometimes the nose.

An old man falls over in the street and a passer-by stops to help. 'What happened?' asks the passer-by. 'I had a dizzy spell and fell over,' says the man. 'Oh dear,' says the passer-by. 'Have you got vertigo?' 'No,' says the man. 'I live just around the corner!'

Uncle Bert worked at the docks for 40 years and never had a single day's illness in his life. He always managed to stretch it out to a week or two.

Ted's wife is seriously ill and confined to bed. One night she says to him, 'Is there anything I can do to help you so I'm not just a burden all the time?' 'Well,' says Ted, 'you could do a few of these funeral invitations for me.'

SCHOOL ABSENCE NOTES

▶ Please excuse Jason for being absent yesterday. He had a cold and could not breed well.

▶ Please excuse Lisa for being absent. She was sick, so I had her shot.

▶ Please excuse little Jimmy from missing school yesterday. His father is gone and I could not get him ready because I was in bed with the Doctor.

▶ Please excuse Tommy for being absent. He was out with the swan flue.

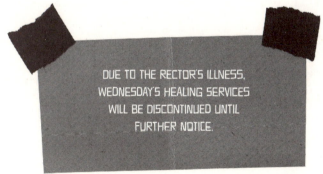

DUE TO THE RECTOR'S ILLNESS, WEDNESDAY'S HEALING SERVICES WILL BE DISCONTINUED UNTIL FURTHER NOTICE.

PARISH NOTICES

IMAGINATION

All my friends laughed at me when they found out my girlfriend was imaginary. But the jokes on them. Because they are too.

> " I HAD A MONUMENTAL IDEA THIS MORNING, BUT I DIDN'T LIKE IT. "
>
> SAMUEL GOLDWYN

IMMATURITY

How many immature people does it take to change a light bulb?
Your mum.

IMMIGRATION

Apparently there are immigrants coming here from around the world to steal my job. But they're in for a bit of a surprise — I don't have one.

IMPORTS

> IT IS CLEAR OUR NATION IS RELIANT UPON BIG FOREIGN OIL. MORE AND MORE OF OUR IMPORTS COME FROM OVERSEAS.
>
> GEORGE W. BUSH

IMPOSSIBILITY

It is not true that nothing is impossible, as anyone who has ever tried to slam a revolving door will know.

INBREEDING

Dale was born and raised in Norfolk and, despite all the things people say about the place, he looks reasonably normal and has eight perfectly formed fingers and two thumbs. Admittedly, they're on his foot.

There are three reasons why it's hard to solve a redneck murder: first, no one talks to the cops; second, their DNA is pretty much the same; third, no dental records.

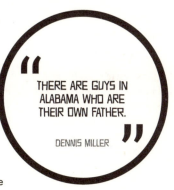

> THERE ARE GUYS IN ALABAMA WHO ARE THEIR OWN FATHER.
>
> DENNIS MILLER

INCONTINENCE

Harry phones up the Incontinence Hotline. The first thing he hears is a voice telling him, 'Can you hold, please?'

INDIA

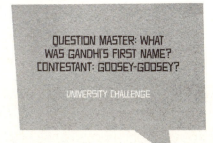

QUESTION MASTER: WHAT WAS GANDHI'S FIRST NAME?
CONTESTANT: GOOSEY-GOOSEY?

UNIVERSITY CHALLENGE

I have a friend who is half-Indian. He's called Ian.

INFLATION

Old Norman tells his grandson, 'I remember when I was your age I used to be able to go down to the shops with just a shilling in my pocket and come back with all my shopping for the week. I can't do that any more.' 'Why not?' asks the little boy. 'They've put up surveillance cameras,' says Norman.

INGRATITUDE

I think women can be very ungrateful. This morning I took her breakfast in bed but instead of saying 'Thank you' or 'That's a nice surprise' she just kept asking 'Who are you?' and 'How did you get into my house?'

" A FRIEND GOT ME SEATS TO THE WORLD SERIES. FROM WHERE I SAT, THE GAME WAS JUST A RUMOUR. "

HENNY YOUNGMAN

INHERITANCE

Vernon tells Harry, 'I've just had a letter through the post. It says that a relative I've never heard of before has died and left me a gold watch in her will.' 'Oh no,' says Harry, 'what if it's a wind-up?'

I will never forget the day my little brother was born. It sticks in my mind because it was also the day I lost half my inheritance.

Barry finds out that his elderly, wealthy aunt is growing increasingly infirm. In an attempt to make her think well of him, he volunteers to take her poodles for a walk each time he visits. In the end the old lady dies and Barry is thrilled when her lawyer informs him that she has indeed remembered him in her will. 'So what did she leave me?' he asks. 'Her poodles,' says the lawyer.

Brenda is clearing the attic out when she finds a wig-weaving machine. She goes to put it in the bin but Tom stops her and says, 'Hey! Don't throw that away! That's an old family hair loom.'

Harry's aged Uncle Reginald passed away and left him 392 antique clocks in his will. Harry has spent the last few weeks trying to wind up the estate.

A young Swedish man called Bjorn Bjornson receives a letter from a lawyer. The letter informs him that his long-lost Uncle Juan from Spain has died. The old man's will stipulates that Bjorn should now change his name to become Juan's namesake and once he has done so he will inherit old Uncle Juan's fortune. However, Bjorn does not want to change his name permanently so he finds a lawyer who will arrange for him to become Juan temporarily. That evening he goes to meet his girlfriend's parents for the first time where he has to introduce himself as 'Juan' rather than the Bjorn they have heard so much about. 'Don't worry,' explains his girlfriend. 'He was Bjorn yesterday and he'll be Bjorn again next week.' 'Thank goodness for that,' says her father, 'otherwise there'd be Juan Bjorn every minute.'

Mississippi has some very strict laws on inheritance: for example, a widow can't touch her dead husband's estate until she turns 15.

Fred is on his deathbed and his wife and children are gathered around him. The old man has also called for a legal witness to be present and with his last few breaths begins to speak: 'My son Jack, I want you to have the houses in Mayfair; my son Vince, I want you to have the office buildings in the city; my daughter Sandra, I want you to have the apartments in the East End; and my wife Ursula, I want you to have all the residential property along the banks of the river.' After he has passed away, the legal witness says, 'Wow! He must have been a very wealthy man to have owned all that property.' 'He didn't own any property,' says Fred's wife, 'he had a window-cleaning round.'

The sale of my late grandmother's estate was a big success. I got £1,000 just from flogging her leftover pills down the pub.

INJECTIONS

A doctor is about to give a little girl an injection. The little girl screams when she sees the needle, 'No, no, no!' 'Really!' says her mother. 'That's not very polite behaviour, is it?' The doctor tries again and this time the little girl screams, 'No, thank you! No, thank you! No, thank you!'

INSECTS

A woman picks up a can of fly spray in a hardware shop and asks, 'Is this any good for flies?' 'Not really,' says the assistant. 'It tends to kill them.'

I'm feeling a bit embarrassed that I didn't win the nation's largest butterfly contest when I'd told everyone I had a prize specimen. Honestly. Me and my big moth.

> QUESTION MASTER: WHAT INSECT IS COMMONLY FOUND HOVERING ABOVE LAKES?
> CONTESTANT: CROCODILE?
>
> THE WEAKEST LINK

An insect flew into my house last night, went twice round the light bulb in the living room and exploded crying, 'Death to the infidels!' I think it might have been a jihadi long legs.

A man walks into the doctor's and says, 'Doctor, I keep thinking I'm a moth. This morning I woke up and found myself in my wife's wardrobe eating her clothes.' 'It sound like you need a psychiatrist,' says the doctor. 'Why did you come here instead?' 'I don't know,' says the man, 'I just wandered in when I saw your light was on.'

Two boll weevils grew up in South Carolina. One went to Hollywood and became a famous actor. The other stayed behind in the cotton fields and never amounted to much. The second one, naturally, became known as the lesser of two weevils.

A teacher is taking a class in medicine and hygiene. 'How can we stop flies spreading disease?' asks the teacher. 'Keep them zipped up,' says a voice from the back.

Henry rushes into an emergency clinic with a huge red lump on his nose. 'I got stung by a bee. Please help me!' The nurse hands Henry a tube of cream, 'Put some of that on it.' 'Are you crazy?' says Henry. 'That bee must be miles away by now.'

Maud invents a new type of fly spray that's twice as efficient as the old ones. 'So what's the secret?' asks a journalist. 'Is it twice as poisonous?' 'No,'' says Maud. 'But it contains an aphrodisiac, so you're always sure to get two at a time.'

It has been reported that a gigantic bluebottle has escaped from a secret science facility and is threatening to destroy Washington DC. The police are sending in a SWAT team.

INSECURITY

Worry is a bit like having a rocking chair. It gives you something to do but it doesn't get you anywhere.

INSOMNIA

Bill's doctor is useless. He went to see him about his insomnia and was told to get plenty of bed rest.

Reginald has found the perfect cure for his wife's insomnia. He's an accountant and when she can't sleep he just tells her about his day in the office.

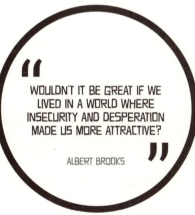

"WOULDN'T IT BE GREAT IF WE LIVED IN A WORLD WHERE INSECURITY AND DESPERATION MADE US MORE ATTRACTIVE?"

ALBERT BROOKS

It has been announced that a cure for insomnia is on the way. However, it's not something that is going to happen overnight.

INSULTS OF A GENERAL NATURE

▶ Something is clearly eating you. And when it's finished, it's going to suffer horribly.

▶ I think it's very admirable that you've come here today specially to humiliate yourself in public.

▶ I'm not sure exactly what your problem is, but I bet it's very difficult to pronounce.

▶ One of these days, you're going to find your true self. And once you find it, you'll go, 'Ughhhhhh!'

▶ I think we have met in a previous life. And you were a pain in the neck then as well.

▶ Your problem is that you seem unable to laugh at yourself. Luckily there is no end of volunteers to do the job for you.

▶ Your finest hour lasted a minute and a half.

▶ Why did your parents never encourage you to run away from home?

▶ I promise I will miss you. Now will you please go away?

▶ This would be an ideal moment for you to become a missing person.

▶ If you get the chance to life your live again, could you do it as far away from me as possible.

▶ See if you can pull your lip right up over the top of your head and then do your very best to swallow!

▶ There are only a few people in this world that I find obnoxious but unfortunately you are all of them.

INSURANCE

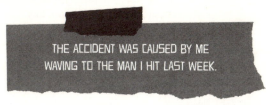

THE ACCIDENT WAS CAUSED BY ME WAVING TO THE MAN I HIT LAST WEEK.

MOTOR INSURANCE CLAIM

Bert's bed is destroyed in a fire so he fills in an insurance claim. However, the company tell him they will not pay because they have learned from the fire brigade that the fire started because Bert had got drunk and dropped a lit cigarette he was smoking in bed. 'That's got nothing to do with it,' Bert tells them, 'that bed was already on fire when I got into it.'

Someone asked US baseball player Yogi Berra why he had bothered buying life insurance. He replied, 'I'll get it when I die.'

Jack visits his local car dealership and asks about his insurance cover. 'I bought the car six months ago. Am I still insured against breakages?' The salesman reassures him that he is. 'That's good,' says Jack. 'Because the front bumper is broken. As is my neighbour's bicycle, his leg, two fences and a lawnmower.'

My family were worried about what would happen to them if I died, so I took out full insurance cover that would put them in the lap of luxury. Now they're more worried about what will happen to them if I stay alive.

Chris and Rita are discussing whether to buy holiday insurance. 'What's the point?' says Chris. 'We get it every year and it never seems to make any difference.'

INTELLIGENCE AND THE LACK OF IT

The male brain is like the prison system. There aren't enough cells per man.

On the downside, no man is quite as clever as his mother thinks he is. On the plus side, no man is quite as dumb as his mother-in-law thinks he is.

> "GIVE ME A SMART IDIOT OVER A STUPID GENIUS ANY DAY."
> — SAMUEL GOLDWYN

Betty the blonde sees another blonde standing on a surfboard in the middle of a field. Betty goes up to the fence and calls out, 'Hey, dummy. What are you doing? It's girls like you that give us blondes a bad name.' 'Tough luck,' says the other girl. 'If you don't like it, why don't you come out here and stop me?' 'I would,' says Betty. 'Only I can't swim.'

Tom, Dick and Harry go for a job interview. As part of the application they have to undergo an intelligence test. The interviewer asks Tom, 'How many d's are there in Dambusters?' 'One,' says Tom. When the interviewer asks Harry the same question, he has to think for a moment before answering, 'One.' Finally the interviewer asks Dick, 'How many d's are there in Dambusters?' Dick spends some time thinking and counting on his fingers. Finally, he says, '139.' 'How do you work that out?' asks the interviewer. 'I counted them, 'says Dick. 'You know how *The Dambusters* goes. Dee dee, dee dee dede dedee. Dee dee, dee dee dede dedee . . .'

> "I DON'T REALLY THINK, I JUST WALK."
> — PARIS HILTON

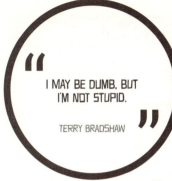

> **I MAY BE DUMB, BUT I'M NOT STUPID.**
>
> TERRY BRADSHAW

Gerry is visiting Beryl. He uses her bathroom and notices there's a portrait of Beryl hanging over the sink. 'What's up with the painting in the bathroom?' he asks. Beryl says, 'I broke the mirror yesterday, so I'm using that till I get a new one.'

Zeke is driving his truck through the Alabama badlands when a cop pulls him over for speeding. The cop says, 'Got any ID?' Zeke says, 'About what?'

How many idiots does it take to change a light bulb? Three. One to hold the light bulb and two to turn the chair he's standing on.

'My husband has a mind like concrete,' says Glenda. 'Really?' says Janice. 'You mean he's hard-minded and resilient?' 'No,' says Janice. 'He's completely mixed up and as dumb as a stone.'

The face is familiar but I can't quite remember my name.

While he was at work, Frank got hold of the wrong end of the stick. Which wouldn't be so bad, except he has a job at the sewage farm.

Norman takes his wife Elsie to the doctor's. The doctor examines her and says, 'I'm afraid your wife's mind has completely gone!' 'Well that's no surprise,' says Norman. 'She's been giving a piece of it to me every day for the past 25 years.'

> **I WONDER WHAT THE MOST INTELLIGENT THING EVER SAID WAS THAT STARTED WITH THE WORD 'DUDE'. 'DUDE, THESE ARE ISOTOPES.' 'DUDE, WE REMOVED YOUR KIDNEY. YOU'RE GONNA BE FINE.' 'DUDE, I AM SO STOKED TO WIN THIS NOBEL PRIZE. I JUST WANNA THANK KEVIN AND TURTLE AND ALL MY HOMIES.'**
>
> DEMETRI MARTIN

INTELLIGENCE AND THE LACK OF IT – INSULTS

▶ Are you the result of an experiment into Artificial Stupidity?

▶ Did you ever stop to think. And then forget to start again?

▶ I don't believe you have enough brains to give yourself a headache.

▶ Some people have drunk deep from the fountain of knowledge. You on the other hand seem to have just swished a bit round your mouth and spat it out again.

▶ I like you. You remind me of when I was young and incredibly stupid.

▶ You are an exceptional specimen. People could use you as a blueprint to build an idiot.

▶ You have a lightning mind. One big flash and it's all over.

▶ You seem a nice enough person but I wouldn't be comfortable to see you working in the nuclear industry.

▶ If you had another brain exactly the same as the one you've got now, you would still be classified as a half-wit.

▶ Your eyes sparkle but I think it might just be the lights shining in through your ears.

▶ You must be a wonder of medical science. The world's only surviving brain donor.

INTERNET

We live in an extraordinary age. Today more people are concerned with deleting history than they are with making it.

When people are on the internet they are able to adopt any persona and be whatever they want. So why do so many of them choose to be stupid?

Harry bought himself a game of computer tennis. He broke his wrist trying to hit the monitor over the net.

Tom says the internet is incredible. He finds it amazing that he can sit in his back bedroom at home and visit places all around the world. His family aren't impressed. They're insisting he takes them on a proper holiday.

I know internet businesses are notoriously volatile but I really thought there would have been a market for my website aimed at all the people who aren't online yet. I just can't understand why www.i-haven't-got-a-computer.com didn't take off.

Q: What's the similarity between women and putting a search into Google?
A: Neither of them will let you finish before they chip in with a suggestion.

Give a man a fish and you feed him for a day, give him a computer and an internet connection and you'll never see him again.

Phil is giving his grandmother some instructions on doing Google searches, but she doesn't really understand how it works. 'It's easy,' he says. 'Type in a question like you were asking one in a letter to a friend.' So Grandma types: 'Hello, Maureen. How are your piles today?'

> "DON'T TALK TO ME WHILE I'M INTERRUPTING YOU."
>
> SAMUEL GOLDWYN

INTERROGATION

Two British officers are captured by the Germans. One listens while the other is taken in for interrogation. He hears through the door, 'Answer ze question!' Slap! 'Tell us ze answer to ze question!' Slap! Slap! 'Tell us vot ve vant to know!' Slap! Slap! Slap! 'Will you stop hitting me and just answer ze question!'

INTOLERANCE

If there's one thing I just will not put up with for a minute, it's intolerance.

INTRUDERS

A celebrity gets home and finds a photographer snooping round his house taking pictures. So he grabs the photographer, shouts and swears at him, throws him to the ground and breaks all his equipment. Only then does he remember agreeing to do that spread for *Hello* magazine.

A businessman is held up on his way home one night and doesn't manage to get back until early in the morning. Up in the bedroom he finds his wife looking rather put out. She tells him, 'After I'd gone to bed and switched the light off, a burglar climbed into the house and came up the stairs into the bedroom.' 'Oh no!' says the businessman, 'did he get anything?' 'Well, I thought it was you coming home,' says his wife. 'So, yes, he did!'

INVENTIONS

Jimmy made a fortune out of his safety sign business. His most popular one was a 'Stop' sign to put at the top of ladders.

It is a little-known fact that the man who invented the umbrella actually meant to call it a 'brella', but unfortunately he hesitated while he was at the patent office.

INVISIBILITY

Tom asks Harry, 'If you were invisible what would you do?' Harry says, 'I'd go to Paris, I'd find a mime artist performing in the street and I'd beat him to death. Imagine the round of applause he'd get!'

For ten years Gary labours night and day to successfully develop the world's first genuine invisibility cloak. Unfortunately when he gets up the next morning he can't find where he put it.

INVITATIONS

George Bernard Shaw once wrote to Winston Churchill: 'I am enclosing two tickets to the first night of my new play; bring a friend . . . if you have one.' Winston replied, 'Cannot possibly attend first night, will attend second . . . if there is one.'

IT WORKERS

Q: How many IT support workers does it take to change a light bulb?
A: I'm not sure but have you tried just turning the bulb off and then on again?

Q: How many Microsoft employees does it take to change a light bulb?
A: Six. One to change the bulb and five to collect the worldwide royalties.

Two computer programmers are talking. One says, 'Guess what! Last night after work I met this gorgeous woman and she seemed to really like me so we had a few drinks and then went back to my office. We locked the door and she started to take all her clothes off and lay down on my desk next to my new laptop.' 'Wow!' says his friend. 'A new laptop? What model is it?'

JACK-IN-THE-BOX

I bought a cheap Jack-in-the-box from the market but it turned out to not work very well. It didn't surprise me.

JEHOVAH'S WITNESSES

A man hears a knock at the door and finds a woman from the Jehovah's Witnesses standing outside in the rain. He feels sorry for her and invites her in. 'So,' he asks, 'what were you going to tell me about this Jehovah's Witness business?' 'I don't know,' says the woman. 'I hadn't really planned on ever getting this far.'

JEWELLERY

RINGS DISPATCHED BY MAIL. PLEASE WRITE WITH CHEQUE STATING SIZE REQUIRED OR ENCLOSE PIECE OF TAPE TIED ROUND FINGER.

NEWSPAPER CLASSIFIED ADVERTISEMENT

Beryl goes into a fancy jewellers and asks to try on a pearl necklace. 'It suits you, madam,' says the sales girl. 'Would you like to make a purchase?' 'Well, that will depend on your returns policy,' says Beryl. 'How so, madam,' asks the sales girl. 'If I didn't like it, would you take it back?' 'Of course, madam,' says the sales girl. Beryl then asks, 'And if my husband didn't like it, can I be sure that you would refuse to take it back?'

JOB APPLICATIONS

Bob goes for an interview for a job at IKEA. They show him into the interview room, give him a screwdriver and some bits of wood and say, 'OK. Build yourself a chair and sit down.'

Nobby goes for a job interview. The interviewer asks him, 'What do you think is your greatest weakness?' 'Plain speaking and honesty,' says Nobby. 'They don't sound like weaknesses to me,' says the interviewer. 'Oh yeah?' says Nobby. 'Well, I don't give a monkey's what you think, big nose!'

Justin goes for an interview for a job working in a restaurant and the owner asks him, 'What do you see yourself bringing to the table here?' 'Doesn't that depend on what the customers order?' says Justin.

Gary gets a new job. His boss tells him, 'I will pay you £8 an hour starting from today and after six months your pay will go up to £12 an hour. So, when would you like to start?' 'In six months,' says Gary.

Barry always puts on his CV that he is great at working under pressure and against tight deadlines. It sounds a whole load better than admitting he leaves everything until the last possible minute.

Dick tries applying for a job at a new office. 'Sorry,' says the manager, 'we don't need much help here.' 'That makes me ideal for the job,' says Dick. 'I'm not much help at all.'

Nobby is filling in a job application. At the bottom of the form, it says, 'Sign here.' So Nobby writes, 'Capricorn'.

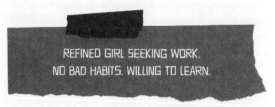

REFINED GIRL SEEKING WORK.
NO BAD HABITS. WILLING TO LEARN.

NEWSPAPER CLASSIFIED ADVERT

Ben goes in for his first day in a new job. His new boss tells him, 'There are two things I expect from my staff here. Cleanliness and honesty. So tell me honestly, did you wipe your feet on the mat in the entrance lobby when you walked in?' 'Yes I did,' says Ben. 'Get out of here! You're sacked!' says the boss. 'There is no mat in the entrance lobby!'

Jack has got a new job at the recycling factory squashing all the fizzy drink cans. He says he finds it soda pressing.

Jack goes for a job as a butcher's delivery boy, but the butcher tells him he's too young. A few weeks later Jack comes back and applies again. 'What are you doing?' asks the butcher. 'I told you I was looking for someone older.' 'I am' says Jack. 'It's been over a month . . .'

Sandra goes for a job interview and is asked to give an example of problem-solving she has done. 'Well,' she says, 'I do a lot of crossword puzzles and Sudoku.' 'That's good,' says the interviewer, 'but can you give me any examples you've done at work.' 'Yes,' says Sandra, 'that's where I do them.'

Sally applies for a job at a retail outlet. The owner looks at her CV and says, 'I don't understand. It says here that you worked in a clothing store for 30 years.' 'That's correct,' says Sally. 'How can that be true when you're only 35 years old?' asks the owner. 'Well,' says Sally, 'I did a lot of overtime.'

I've just seen a job opportunity advertised on a lamp-post round the corner saying you can earn lots of money working from home if you have a mobile phone and a skylight in your roof. So I applied for the job and I'm officially now one of my local airport's privatised air traffic controllers.

Nigel applies for a job as a model masseur and bikini-line waxer for a famous glamour photographer. He rings up and is told to come in for an interview. 'Do you know the big park by the ice-rink?' asks the photographer. 'Yes,' says Nigel. 'Well, you'd better wait by the boating lake in the middle,' says the photographer. 'Are the interviews being held in the park?' asks Nigel. 'No,' says the photographer, 'The interviews are being held in my studio on the other side of town. The queue starts in the park.'

Billy gets a job as apprentice to the local blacksmith. The blacksmith says, 'I can't afford to pay you anything for the first year and for the next five years you'll be doing nothing but helping me out with the donkey work. Do you understand?' Billy says he understands. 'Good,' says the blacksmith. 'Let's get started. Now I'm going to take this horseshoe out of the fire and put it on the anvil. When it's cooled off a little, I'll nod my head and you hit it. OK?' Billy says he understands. So the blacksmith takes the shoe from the fire, puts it on the anvil, nods his head and Billy hits it with the hammer. And now Billy is the village blacksmith.

My brother Dean is applying for a job he saw advertised for the headmaster of a college in the USA. He says it's got his name all over it.

JOBS

Frank has got a new job and tells everyone that in his new position he's got literally hundreds of people under him. He cuts the grass in the local cemetery.

A teacher is asking her pupils what their parents do for a living. A little boy sticks up his hand and says, 'My daddy just sits in a chair all day.' 'Doing what?' asks the teacher. 'Nothing,' says the boy. 'He just sits.' 'But he must do something,' says the teacher. 'No, he doesn't do anything,' says the boy. 'He's a consultant.'

I had to let my masseur go today. He was a nice-enough guy but he kept rubbing me up the wrong way.

I had a job working as a lumberjack, but they gave me the axe.

JOURNALISM

A journalist is a media professional who carefully separates the cold, hard facts from the fantastical made-up garbage, then prints the garbage.

JUMBLE SALES

LADIES, DON'T FORGET THE RUMMAGE SALE. IT'S A CHANCE TO GET RID OF THOSE THINGS NOT WORTH KEEPING AROUND THE HOUSE. DON'T FORGET YOUR HUSBANDS.

PARISH NOTICES

JUNGLE

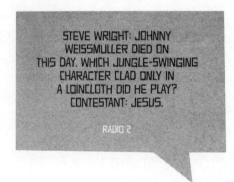

STEVE WRIGHT: JOHNNY WEISSMULLER DIED ON THIS DAY. WHICH JUNGLE-SWINGING CHARACTER CLAD ONLY IN A LOINCLOTH DID HE PLAY? CONTESTANT: JESUS.

RADIO 2

KEY RINGS

Definition of a key ring: a simple handy device that enables you to lose all of your keys in one go.

KIDNAPPING

Stig and Ken were the world's worst kidnappers. They kidnapped a rich heiress then sent her back to her parents to deliver the ransom note.

KLEPTOMANIA

A man goes to the doctor and says, 'Doctor, please help me. I'm a terrible kleptomaniac. I can't stop walking into shops and stealing things.' 'OK,' says the doctor, 'take these pills for a week and if they don't work, could you get me an HD television and an iPhone?'

It's hard to explain puns to kleptomaniacs. They always seem to take things very literally.

KNOCK KNOCK! WHO'S THERE? . . .

- . . . 'Doorbell Repairman!'

- . . . 'Boo!' 'Boo who?' 'OK. No need to cry. It's only a joke!'

- . . . 'Eva.' 'Eva who?' 'Eva you're deaf or your doorbell isn't working!'

- . . . 'Biggish.' 'Biggish who?' 'No thanks, I just bought one.'

- . . . 'Ivor.' 'Ivor who?' 'Ivor good mind not to tell you.'

- . . . 'Joanna.' 'Joanna who?' 'Joanna come and answer the door?'

- . . . 'Few.' 'Few who?' 'Yeah, it stinks. Have you farted?'

- . . . 'Atch.' 'Atch who?' 'Bless you!'

- . . . 'Bless.' 'Bless who?' 'Thanks, but I didn't sneeze!'

- . . . 'Shirley!' 'Shirley who?' 'Shirley you must know me by now!'

- . . . 'Adam.' 'Adam who?' 'Adam up and give me the total!'

- . . . 'Danielle' 'Danielle who?' 'Danielle so loud, I heard you the first time!'

- . . . 'Alfred.' 'Alfred who?' 'Alfred the needle if you sew!'

- . . . 'Des.' 'Des who?' 'Des no bell, that's why I'm knocking!'

- . . . 'Chester.' 'Chester who?' 'Chester minute, don't you recognise me?'

- . . . 'Gus.' 'Gus who?' 'That's what you're supposed to do!'

- ... 'Harriet.' 'Harriet who?' 'Harriet all my lunch, I'm starving!'

- ... 'Harry.' 'Harry who?' 'Harry up and open this door!'

- ... 'Howard.' 'Howard who?' 'Howard I know?'

- ... 'Emma.' 'Emma who?' 'Emma bit cold out here, will you let me in?'

- ... 'Ivan.' 'Ivan who?' 'Ivan infectious disease!'

- ... 'The postman.' 'The postman who?' 'Do you want this parcel or not?'

- ... 'Isabel.' 'Isabel who?' 'Isabel broken, because I had to knock!'

- ... 'Alex.' 'Alex who?' 'Alex plain later!'

- ... 'Little old lady.' 'Little old lady who?' 'I didn't know you could yodel!'

- .. 'Me.' 'Me who?' 'I didn't know you had a cat!'

- ... 'Shirley.' 'Shirley who?' 'Shirley you know who I am?'

- ... 'Signor.' 'Signor who?' 'Signor light on, so I knocked!'

- ... 'To.' 'To who?' 'No, no, no; to whom!'

- .. 'Toby.' 'Toby who?' 'Toby or not Toby, that is the question!'

- ... 'Woo!' 'Woo who?' 'Don't sound so excited, we're Trick or Treaters dressed as ghosts. Now give us cash.'

- ... 'Police.' 'Police who?' 'Police stop telling these bad knock knock jokes!'

LADDERS

I had to go to accident and emergency yesterday because I'd just fallen off a 50-foot ladder. They told me there wasn't too much need to worry as I'd been on the bottom rung at the time.

The builder noticed that someone had stolen his ladder. So he put a sign on his shed door telling them to bring it back or further steps would be taken.

LANDMINES

A friend of mine walked into a minefield. I'm going to go and help him find his feet again.

LANGUAGE AND GRAMMAR

The teacher asks the class, 'Who can give me an example of something that goes without saying?' A voice calls from the back of the class: 'A mute incontinent.'

It is important to understand the correct way to use capital letters. Particularly when being asked to help your Uncle Jack off a horse.

When I was at school my English teacher always used to write on my report that my grammar was useless and I would never get anywhere. Just wait till I proof him wrong.

LAP DANCING

Harry tells Tom that he went to a lap-dancing club last night. 'How was it?' asks Tom. 'Well,' says Harry, 'a woman spent the evening taking all my money while leaving me sexually frustrated. I don't know about you, but I can get all that at home.'

LATE HOME

Two women are talking. 'My husband's very late home from work,' says one, 'I'm beginning to think he might be having an affair.' 'Why do you immediately presume the worst?' says the other. 'Maybe he's just been in a car crash.'

Tina is out late one night and her husband George is getting worried. He texts Tina's four closest friends to ask if she is staying the night with any of them. A minute later, Tina walks through the door saying she got held up at work. A minute after that, George receives four texts from her friends all saying, 'Yes, she's staying here with me tonight.'

LAUNDRY

Jimmy was the dirtiest boy on the block. In fact, he was so dirty, his clothes were cleaner on the outside than they were on the inside.

Ken comes home and finds his wife has used a couple of bricks to prop their washing machine up on one side. 'What do you think you're doing?' asks Ken. 'What it says on the instructions,' says his wife. 'Wash at 30 degrees!'

Glenda did herself an injury yesterday. She tried putting herself in the tumble drier to see if she would come out three sizes smaller and wrinkle-free.

A man gets out of prison after a ten-year sentence. Before he walks out, he is given his old suit back. He checks inside the pockets and, to his surprise, finds a wrinkled old laundry ticket for a second suit which he left at the dry-cleaner's just before he was convicted. He goes back to the cleaners, goes up to the counter and presents his ticket. The assistant looks at it and tells him, 'That'll be ready on Friday.'

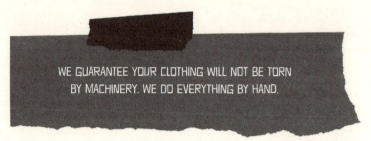

SIGN AT A DRY-CLEANER'S

Jerry wants to put his sweatshirt in the washer but is worried it will shrink. He calls to his wife to ask what temperature it should be set to. She replies, 'What does it says on the label?' Jerry checks and then shouts back to her, 'FCUK.'

SIGN ON A LAUNDERETTE WASHING MACHINE

Phil goes home and finds his wife washing their laundry in the bath. 'It saves money,' she explains. 'By doing it here instead of the launderette, I just made us £10.' 'You did?' says Phil. 'Quick, do it again.'

SIGN IN WINDOW OF A LAUNDRY IN ITALY

Sam drops off his dry-cleaning at the store. The owner says, 'Y'know, I wish I had ten more customers like you.' 'You do?' says Sam. 'I always figured I was a bit fussy. I seem to complain a lot.' 'You do,' says the owner. 'I wish I had ten of you; instead I have around 100.'

George goes to a dry-cleaner's to complain about a huge tear he's found in a pair of trousers he collected the day before. 'I want a refund,' says George. 'Sorry,' says the store owner, 'I can't help you.' 'But the sign in your window says "money back if not completely satisfied",' says George. 'I know,' says the owner. 'And when we took your money we were completely satisfied with it.'

LAW AND LAWYERS

In the UK, everything not prohibited by law is allowed. In Germany, everything that is not allowed by law is prohibited. In China, everything is prohibited, even if it is allowed by law. In the Netherlands, everything is allowed, even if prohibited by law. In North Korea, everything not prohibited by law is obligatory.

The longest trial in recent history lasted seven months. It should only have taken a day or two, but when the first witness was asked to hold the Bible and read from the card, he got mixed up. He held the card and read the Bible.

Two lawyers get together to discuss a case with which they are both involved. 'OK,' says the first, 'the best thing will be if we are both completely honest with one another. Who wants to go first?' After several hours in complete silence, they give up and go home.

A lorry driver sees an elderly priest by the side of the road and stops to give him a lift. Further along the road, he sees a lawyer also by the side of the road. He drives straight at the lawyer, meaning to run him over but then thinks, 'I can't do this. I've got a priest in the cab.' So instead he swerves around the lawyer and misses him. Nevertheless, as he passes by, he hears a thump and looks back in the mirror to see the lawyer lying in a puddle and rubbing his head. The lorry driver turns to the priest and says, 'Sorry about that, Father. I thought I'd missed that lawyer.' 'You nearly did, my son,' says the priest, 'but I managed to get him with my door instead.'

A lawyer decides to get into black magic and summons up the Devil. The Devil says to him, 'I can offer you a proposition. I will give you the satanic magical ability to win every case you take. You will become the richest and most famous lawyer in the entire world, admired by all your peers. But what you must give me in exchange is your soul and the souls of your wife, your children and all your other relatives.' 'OK,' says the lawyer, 'but what's the catch?'

Q: What's the difference between a lawyer and a prostitute?
A: The prostitute will stop screwing you after you die.

A man goes to see a lawyer and asks him what rates he charges. 'It's £250 for three questions,' says the lawyer. 'Isn't that quite expensive?' asks the man. 'Yes, it is,' says the lawyer, 'and what is your third question?'

A lawyer dies on the same day as the Pope. Both of them go up to heaven and St Peter greets them and shows them their rooms. First, the Pope is shown to his room, which is very small and bare with a small bed and desk. Next, the lawyer is shown his room, which is huge with a luxurious bed and a pool table. 'Is there a mistake here?' asks the lawyer. 'Why am I getting this room and not the Pope?' 'No mistake!' says St Peter. 'We've got hundreds of popes here. But you, my friend, are our first ever lawyer.'

> "A VERBAL CONTRACT ISN'T WORTH THE PAPER IT'S WRITTEN ON."
>
> SAMUEL GOLDWYN

Clifford applies for a job as a corporate lawyer. 'Honesty and integrity are the cornerstones of our organisation,' says the interviewer. 'Can you give me an example of your integrity?' 'Yes,' says Clifford. 'I borrowed £100,000 to complete my law degree and paid it all back after my very first case.' 'I see,' says the interviewer. 'And what is an example of your honesty?' 'To be honest, I'd have to tell you that I lost my very first case.' 'Wait a minute,' says the interviewer. 'I thought you said your first case earned you £100,000?' 'No,' says Clifford. 'My first case was the bank suing me to get the money back.'

No one can accuse Jake of misrepresenting himself: on his business card it says 'Criminal Lawyer' and that's just what he is.

Sammy goes to a lawyer and says he wants to sue the local airport. He puts a battered holdall on the table. 'That was brand new when I took it on my last flight. Look what their baggage handlers did to it.' The lawyer pokes the bag with his finger and says, 'I'm sorry. But your case simply isn't strong enough.'

Why is arguing with a lawyer like mud-wrestling with a pig? After a while you realise they both enjoy it.

Nigel wins a court case to recover some money he'd lent to his ex-business partner. His friend asks him how he did it. 'I thought you said you had no proof you ever lent him anything? You said it was all done on a handshake.' 'It was,' says Nigel. 'I lent him £5,000, but I wrote him a letter demanding he pay me back £10,000. He wrote back to say he only owed me half that. And that's what I showed to the judge.'

Gary's lawyer will charge for anything – making paper copies, text messages, sending emails. Last night he had a dream about Gary and sent him a bill.

A pair of lawyers are on a flight when they discover that the man in the seat next to them is a lawyer from a rival company. The rival, Bill, stands up to get a Coke from the galley and offers to bring back a couple more for his new friends. While he's gone, the other lawyers play a practical joke on him and hide his headphones. Bill comes back and eventually finds his headphones under his seat. A short while later, he offers to get some more Cokes. While he's away, the other lawyers hide his mobile phone in the storage locker. Bill comes back and eventually manages to hunt down his missing device. A little later he offers to get yet more Cokes. He leaves and the lawyers hide his blanket in another row of seats. Bill comes back and sees that, yet again, something has gone missing. 'Come on, guys,' he says. 'We have to stop these endless practical jokes: the headphones, the mobile phone, the blanket, the spitting in Cokes . . .'

A judge is just about to pronounce sentence on a defendant when the man's lawyer rushes into the court room and demands a retrial. 'A retrial?' says the judge. 'Why? Has new evidence come to light?' 'No,' pants the lawyer. 'I was just looking through his financial records and I found he's got £15,000 he never told me about.'

YOU SHOULD THINK ABOUT GETTING A NEW LAWYER IF...

- ... the defence team start high-fiving each other as soon as they see him.

- ... you notice he keeps flicking through Tinder during the trial.

- ... he plonks a large sign in front of himself that says, 'No Refunds' as soon as the case begins.

- ... just as the trial is starting, he leans over and asks, 'The judge is the one in the funny wig, right?'

- ... whenever the judge tells him his objection is overruled, he says, 'What ever!'

- ... you discover he also runs the court's shoe-shine franchise.

- ... he brings your trial papers to court in a Tesco's bag.

- ... he decides to argue your case through the medium of interpretive dance.

- ... he's introduced as the council for the defence, and asks, 'Which fence?'

- ... he confuses 'motions' with bowel movements.

LAZINESS

Norman goes through the supermarket check-out and asks an assistant to carry his shopping to his car for him. The assistant duly obliges. When they get to his car, Norman says, 'Sorry to make you carry my shopping all this way. I could have done it myself, but I'm afraid I'm a bit of a lazy so-and-so.' 'Yes, I gathered that,' says the assistant. 'Here's your Mars Bar.'

A squad of soldiers is on the parade ground. The sergeant tells them, 'I've got a nice easy job here for whichever one of you can prove he is the laziest man here. So which of you thinks they are the laziest?' All the men put their hands up apart from one. 'So,' the sergeant says to the man who didn't raise his hand, 'you're the one person here who isn't lazy?' 'No,' says the soldier, 'I just couldn't be bothered putting my hand up.'

Sammy's ambition was to be a procrastinator, but he could never quite get round to it.

I joined a self-help group for procrastinators a couple of years ago. We still haven't got round to meeting up though.

Elsie says her husband, Norman, is getting lazier as he gets older. He used to cut his toenails every week. Now he just does them every few months but keeps a series of increasingly bigger shoes ready in the cupboard.

Ted's wife tells him, 'I'm sick to death of you being so lazy. Pack your bags and get out!' 'Could you pack them for me?' says Ted.

LESSONS IN LIFE

The early bird always gets the worm. So remember – you'd be an idiot to be an early worm.

It's probably never a great idea to perform card tricks for the guys you play poker with.

It's never a good idea to bite your fingernails. Particularly not if you use the same hand to scratch your backside.

If people get you down, remember that not all of them are annoying – some of them are dead.

Blessed are they who can laugh at themselves for they shall never cease to be amused.

Always remember that, if life gives you lemons, they're very handy to stick down your bra to make your boobs look bigger.

> **SEIZE THE MOMENT. REMEMBER ALL THOSE WOMEN ON THE *TITANIC* WHO WAVED OFF THE DESSERT CART.**
>
> ERMA BOMBECK

Life is like a box of chocolates. It doesn't last as long for fat people.

Never knock on Death's door. Just ring the bell and run away. He hates that.

If you help someone in trouble, they'll surely remember you the next time they're in trouble.

Here is a way to make sure you always hit your target. Shoot first and then, whatever you hit, tell people that was what you were aiming at.

Many people say that hard work never hurt anybody. It is, however, slightly more certain that no one has ever relaxed themselves to death.

According to ancient wisdom people who live in glass houses should not throw stones, and have their toilet built in the basement.

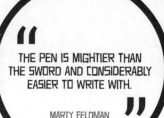

> **THE PEN IS MIGHTIER THAN THE SWORD AND CONSIDERABLY EASIER TO WRITE WITH.**
>
> MARTY FELDMAN

Always love your enemies. Because there's every possibility your friends will turn out to be a right shower of b*stards.

Things written in very small print seldom include good news.

Life may often seem like an uphill climb. But on the plus side, at the same time you'll be mooning everyone coming up behind you.

Top shopping tip – never buy expensive jewellery from someone on foot and out of breath.

It is true that a fool and his money are soon parted, but it can also be true that a fool and his money are soon partying.

It doesn't matter how old you get, it's never too late to learn something stupid.

An important lesson to remember – if you attempt to achieve the impossible and succeed, your boss will add it to your regular duties.

Remember – things are never impossible for those who don't have to do them.

> " SILENCE IS NOT ONLY GOLDEN, IT'S SELDOM MISQUOTED. "
>
> BOB MONKHOUSE

Always give 100 per cent whatever you're doing. Unless, obviously, you're donating blood.

The best time to add insult to injury is when you're signing someone's plaster cast.

You can pick your friends and you can pick your nose. It is, however, inadvisable to try and pick your friend's nose.

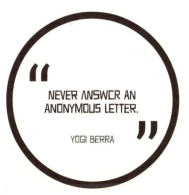

> " NEVER ANSWER AN ANONYMOUS LETTER. "
>
> YOGI BERRA

> WE ALL KNOW THE LEOPARD CAN'T CHANGE HIS STRIPES.
>
> AL GORE

> **IF THE WORLD WERE PERFECT, IT WOULDN'T BE.**
>
> YOGI BERRA

After all's said and done, it usually turns out that a lot more was said than was actually done.

Every time I walk into a singles bar I hear my mother's voice in my ear: 'Janice, don't pick that up. You don't know where it's been.'

Three little words that are never true: 'Easy to Open'.

The next time you think the world sucks, remind yourself that we'd all fall off if it didn't.

Life is a bit like being a husky pulling a sledge — if you're not at the front of the pack the scenery never changes.

> **NEVER MAKE FORECASTS, ESPECIALLY ABOUT THE FUTURE.**
>
> SAMUEL GOLDWYN

> **IT'S A FUNNY OLD WORLD. A MAN'S LUCKY IF HE GETS OUT OF IT ALIVE.**
>
> W.C. FIELDS

> **EXPECTING THE WORLD TO TREAT YOU FAIRLY BECAUSE YOU'RE A GOOD PERSON IS A LITTLE LIKE EXPECTING THE BULL NOT TO ATTACK YOU BECAUSE YOU'RE A VEGETARIAN.**
>
> DENNIS WHOLEY

You can divide people into three types: the ones who get things done; the ones who watch things getting done; and the ones who wonder what the hell just happened.

Everything is easier said than done. With the exception of speaking, which is just about the same.

LIBRARIES

A Scouser walks into a library and says, 'Have you got "An Introduction to Urdu".' 'Are you going to India on holiday?' asks the librarian. 'No,' says the Scouser, 'I want to learn how to be a hairdresser.'

A librarian slips over at work. She should have been more careful. She was in the non-friction section at the time.

A man walks into the library and asks for a book on indecent exposure. 'Sorry, sir,' says the librarian, 'but someone's already taken it out.'

Harry thinks the lady who works at his local library must be Italian. Every time he takes a book back she says, 'Hey! That's a fine!' So he says, 'Grazie,' and walks out.

A man walks into a library and asks the librarian if they have any books on cliff-hangers in stock. 'Interesting that you should ask that,' says the librarian, 'because. . . . .'

LIFE

In the modern world, the pace of life can be extremely frantic. But it's the sudden stop at the end that really bothers me.

Life either keeps passing me by or keeps trying to run me over.

Don't forget – as far as you are concerned you will be the last person to die in your lifetime.

LIFE-SAVING

Last night in the pub the barman suddenly called, 'Does anyone know CPR?' I replied that I knew the whole alphabet and everyone laughed. Well, apart from this one bloke . . .

LIFTS

Nobby gets a job in a company that manufactures lifts. 'How's business?' asks Tom. 'Oh, you know,' says Nobby, 'it's up and down.'

Tom, Dick and Harry all book into the tallest hotel in the world. The receptionist tells them, 'I'm afraid there's only one room left for you to share. It's on the 90th floor and the lift is broken.' To pass the time on their trek up the stairs, the three men decide to tell each other the saddest story they can think of. The winner will be the one who they all agree has told the saddest story of all. On the 30th floor Tom tells his story and they all agree it is quite sad. On the 60th, Dick tells his story and they all agree that this is even sadder. And then when they reach the 90th floor Harry says, 'Well, I think you're all going to agree that my story is the saddest story of them all.' 'Why? What is it?' ask the others. 'I left the key to the room at reception,' says Harry.

LINGERIE

An old man decides to spice up his love life, so he goes to an expensive lingerie shop to buy his wife a see-through nightie. They show him several nighties at increasingly higher prices and he chooses the one that is the most expensive and most see-through of all. That night he gives his wife her present and tells her to go upstairs and try it on. However, she notices the ridiculous price on the receipt and decides to wrap the nightie up and take it back for a refund. She reasons that the nightie is so see-through and her husband's eyesight is so poor, he will not be able to tell if she is wearing it or not. So she strips off and strikes a pose at the top of the stairs. 'What do you think?' she asks. 'Very nice,' he says, 'but for £500 you'd think at least they'd have ironed it.'

LIONS

Sven and Kurt are two explorers on an expedition through the jungle. They are hacking their way through the undergrowth when Sven pulls up a tree branch and throws it into the bush. A moment later, they hear a deep roar. 'Oh no!' says Sven. 'It looks like the branch woke up a sleeping lion. We're going to have to run for our lives!' 'I don't see why I've got to run anywhere!' says Kurt. 'You're the one who threw it at him!'

Carruthers and Jenkins are trying to hunt down a vicious man-eating lion. They come across some lion tracks leading into dense undergrowth. 'There's only one way to handle this,' says Carruthers. 'We'll split the work 50/50. Jenkins, you find out where the beast has got to and I'll find out where it came from.'

LISTENING

If you think someone is a good listener, think again. You might have just bored them so much they're now thinking about something else.

LITERACY

I read a news story that said 10 per cent of adults are illiterate. Actually, I didn't really read it. I just got the gist from the pictures.

Freddie's not that bright. He can't read or write and takes offence at the smallest thing. Last week he tried to sue the local supermarket for forging his signature on a pallet of hot-cross buns.

For many years Gilbert has lived an impoverished, ignorant life. He's as poor as a church mouse and can barely read and write. But one day he wins the lottery and he and his wife are catapulted into a world of riches. A month after his big win, Gilbert's bank manager asks to see him about some irregularities in his account. 'I'd just like to clear something up,' says the manager. 'For years you always signed your cheques with a pair of crosses.' 'Yes,' says Gilbert. 'So what?' 'Well, now you appear to be signing them with three crosses,' says the manager. 'Oh that,' says Gilbert. 'That's on account of me and the wife having gone up in the world. She thought I ought to start using my middle name.'

LITERATURE

Last week, Rob was crushed underneath a great pile of books. He says he's only got his shelf to blame.

> AGATHA CHRISTIE IS SUCH A WELL-KNOWN NAME; HER BOOKS SELL ALL OVER THE WORLD – AND OTHER PLACES AS WELL.
>
> MICHAEL GRADE

Charles Dickens walks into a bar. 'Alas! All inspiration has forsaken me!' he says. 'I have no idea what I should write for my next book. Barman, prepare me a martini!' 'Very good, sir,' says the barman. 'Olive or twist?'

A writer tells his friend he became a full-time professional over a year ago. 'That's great,' says his friend, 'have you sold anything yet?' 'Yes,' says the writer, 'my TV, my furniture, my house . . .'

A lion, a witch and a wardrobe walk into a bar.
'Get out of here!' says the barman. 'I'm serving Narnia!'

I started watching the great Shakespearian tragedy *Othello* and I couldn't break away. I ended up watching the entire play over and over again. It's true what they say. *Othello* is very moor-ish.

> "I READ A BOOK TWICE AS FAST AS ANYBODY ELSE. FIRST, I READ THE BEGINNING AND THEN I READ THE ENDING, AND THEN I START IN THE MIDDLE AND READ TOWARD WHATEVER END I LIKE BEST."
>
> GRACIE ALLEN

I've read a lot of autobiographies. I don't want to give away any spoilers but they all seem to end with the person deciding to write their life story.

> **PRESENTER:** COMPLETE THE TITLE OF THE RUDYARD KIPLING POEM – GUNGA...
> **CONTESTANT:** HO.
>
> *THE WEAKEST LINK*

> **QUESTION MASTER:** NAME THE PLAYWRIGHT KNOWN BY THE INITIALS GBS?
> **CONTESTANT:** WILLIAM SHAKESPEARE.
>
> *NATIONAL LOTTERY JET SET*

> **QUESTION MASTER:** WHAT WAS CHARLES DICKENS' FIRST NOVEL?
> **CONTESTANT:** WHITE CHRISTMAS?
>
> *THE VAULT*

> "THIS BOOK HAS TOO MUCH PLOT AND NOT ENOUGH STORY."
>
> — SAMUEL GOLDWYN

> **GIRL:** NAME A BOOK WRITTEN BY JANE AUSTEN.
> **BOY:** CHARLOTTE BRONTE.
>
> *BLIND DATE*

SCHOOLBOY HISTORY HOMEWORK ANSWERS

▶ Homer was not written by Homer, but by another man of the same name.

▶ Milton wrote 'Paradise Lost', then his wife died and he wrote 'Paradise Regained'.

▶ Shakespeare wrote tragedies, comedies and hysterectomies – all in Islamic pentameter.

LOANS

A man walks into a bank in central London and tells the cashier he is going away for a couple of weeks on holiday and needs to borrow £1,000. The cashier checks his details and agrees to give the man the loan but tells him he will need to provide some collateral. 'OK,' says the man, 'I've parked my Rolls-Royce outside. It's worth £250,000. Will you accept that?' The cashier readily agrees and the man brings his Rolls to the bank's secure car park. He takes his £1,000 loan and sets off on his trip. The cashier and his manager have a good laugh at someone taking out a loan for £1,000 and leaving a £250,000 car as collateral. Two weeks later, the man is back, he repays his £1,000 loan plus the £20 interest due. As he hands over the keys, the bank manager says, 'Thank you for your business. But we notice from your details that you are a multimillionaire. Why did you need to take out a loan for £1,000?' 'I didn't,' says the man, 'but how else could I park my car in central London for two weeks for just £20 and be absolutely certain it'd still be here when I got back?'

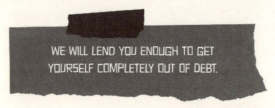

WE WILL LEND YOU ENOUGH TO GET YOURSELF COMPLETELY OUT OF DEBT.

ADVERT AT A LOAN COMPANY

LOBSTERS

A man says to a waiter, 'Waiter, this lobster has only got one claw.' 'Sorry, sir,' says the waiter. 'It must have been in a fight.' 'Well,' says the man, 'any chance you could take this away and bring me the winner instead?'

LOGIC

Logic – the ability to be wrong with confidence.

LONGEVITY

Before he passes away, a 100-year-old man tells his grandson the secret of his great age. 'Every morning when you have your porridge, sprinkle a tiny bit of gunpowder over it.' The boy follows his advice and does this every day for the rest of his life. Finally, he dies aged 120 leaving three wives, 14 children, 40 grandchildren, 78 great-grandchildren, 167 great-great-grandchildren and a hole half a mile wide where his local crematorium used to be.

LOQUACIOUSNESS

Tim's mum tells him, 'You should never use two words when one will do.' 'In that case, Mother,' says Tim, 'why don't you just say, "Avoid verbosity"?'

Barry goes to the school parent's evening to see his daughter's teacher. 'She's a clever girl,' says the teacher, 'but she talks too much in class. I've got an idea I want to try which I think will help break the habit.' 'That sounds great,' says Barry. 'If it works can you let me know and I'll try it on her mother.'

Freddie says his first wife was highly educated. She could talk for hours on any subject you chose. He says his second wife is exactly the same — only, she doesn't need a subject.

Chris finds a magazine article that says that in an average day, a man will say around 25,000 words and a woman will say 50,000. He shows it to his wife, Rita. 'There!' he says. 'I always told you that women chatter twice as much as men.' 'That's because men never listen,' says Rita. 'So women have to say everything twice.'

LOST

An exhausted explorer is lost in the jungle. After several days he finds another explorer. 'Thank goodness,' he says, 'I've been lost here for three days.' 'Don't get too excited,' says the second explorer, 'I've been lost here for three weeks.'

Harold asks Betty to help find his glasses. 'Where did you last see them?' she asks. 'If I knew that,' says Harold, 'I wouldn't be asking!'

LOTTERY

Nobby is in bed with Norma. He looks at her and says, 'You know what — you remind me of the lottery.' 'Aw!' says Norma, 'you mean I'm worth millions?' 'No,' he says. 'I wish you'd flipping roll over!'

I think I might start doing the Arctic lottery, although I'm a bit put off by their slogan: 'You've got to be Inuit to win it . . .'

Nobby gets home and asks Norma, 'What would you do if I told you that I'd won the lottery?' 'I'd take my half,' says Norma, 'and get out of this dump and you'd never see me again.' 'That's what I thought you'd say,' says Nobby, reaching in his pocket. 'This morning I won ten quid. Here's a fiver. Now, get lost!'

Beryl wins £5 million on the lottery. Unfortunately, under the new rules, she gets £1 a year for the next five million years.

Sammy wins £25 million on a lottery rollover. After he's collected his winnings he goes back to the family home and gives his old dad £100 in cash. 'This means a lot to me, son,' says Dad, clutching the notes. 'I've been broke my whole life. We never told you this, but your mother and I couldn't even afford to get married.' 'What?' exclaims Sammy. 'Do you mean I'm a bastard?' 'Yes,' says Dad, holding up his 100 quid. 'And a tight one too.'

A teacher asks the class to write a story about what they'd do if they won a fortune on the lottery. After the children hand in their papers, she finds that little Johnny has submitted a blank page. 'What's the matter?' she asks. 'Couldn't you think of anything?' Johnny points to the empty page. 'No. If I came into money, that's just what I'd do – nothing at all.'

The odds of getting knocked over by a bus are around the same as winning a million on the lottery, but no matter how hard Granddad tries he can't find a bookie willing to take the bet.

Q: What's the difference between a man buying a lottery ticket and a man arguing with his wife?
A: The man buying a lottery ticket has a chance of winning.

Bill wins the lottery. As a railway nut, the first thing he does is buy a big house and install a locomotive and carriages in his back garden. One day, his friend drops by to see him. It's raining and he finds Bill shivering in his garden having a cigarette under an umbrella. 'What are you doing?' says his friend. 'I thought you'd be enjoying your new train set.' Bill shakes his head and points to the carriages. 'I can't,' he says. 'They're all non-smoking.'

LOVE

If you've ever wondered who loves you more, your partner or your dog, there is a useful test to find the answer. Try locking both of them in the boot of your car for a few hours. Then, when you let them out, see which of them is happiest to see you again.

There is a tingly sensation you get when you meet someone you really like. Apparently, it's the feeling of common sense suddenly leaving your body.

They say that love is all about chemistry. And that's why my wife will only touch me while wearing protective gloves.

A man writes to his girlfriend, 'Dearest, if I were far away could you love me still?' He gets a reply saying: 'Yes. In fact, I think I'd love you more, the further away you were.'

According to surveys, most men will choose love over wealth and health. So presumably the majority of men willing to enter into loving relationships are poor and sick.

A survey found that 10 per cent of women say 'I love you' to a man in order to lure him into bed; the other 90 per cent say it to get rid of him afterwards.

Ralph told me that he fell in love with his wife at second sight. It would have been first sight, but at the time he didn't know her father was a billionaire.

Ted says that when he met his wife it was love at first sight. Unfortunately, he's had a second look since then.

A couple are drinking in the pub. The man suddenly says, 'Do you know what? I love you!' 'Oh yes,' says his wife. 'So is that you, or is it the beer talking?' 'It's me!' says the man. 'Talking to the beer!'

Brenda tells Tom, 'You never tell me how much you love me.' 'I know,' says Tom, 'but I wouldn't want to upset you.'

LOWPOINTS IN LIFE

YOU KNOW YOU'VE REACHED A LOWPOINT WHEN . . .

▶ The Salvation Army declines your donated clothing.

▶ The telemarketers hang up when they realise who they're speaking to.

▶ You start going to church and your priest becomes an atheist.

▶ You walk your dog and it spends the whole time pretending not to be with you.

▶ The neighbour's dog has sex with your leg and you start sending it flowers.

▶ Your favourite crisp manufacturer say they are going to announce a new flavour and you lose sleep wondering what it will be.

▶ You discover your house is part of a Jehovah's Witness 'no-go' area.

▶ You realise you're really not too proud to fish out the 5p coin you accidentally dropped in a public toilet.

▶ Your blind date turns out to be a clinically obese ex-convict with halitosis and Tourette's Syndrome, and when she visits the bathroom she gets stuck trying to climb out of the window.

▶ A tramp asks you if you have any spare change, you say no, and he gives you 50p.

▶ The local loan shark keeps making excuses why you shouldn't come round and pay back the money you own him.

▶ You take your mother out for a Sunday lunch and she insists on wearing a burkha in the restaurant just so she won't be recognised with you.

LOZENGES

The inventor of the throat lozenge died recently. The family have asked that there should be no coffin at his funeral.

LUCK

A doctor examines a man and tells him it's bad news. 'I'm afraid you've got a new virus called Yellow 24,' says the doctor. 'It's called Yellow 24 because your skin will go yellow and you only have 24 hours to live. Currently there is no known cure so the only thing you can do is go home and enjoy your last few hours in peace.' The man goes home and tells his wife. To take their minds off the terrible news, they go out to the local bingo hall. With his first card the man gets four corners and wins £35. Next, with the same card, he gets a line and wins £320. And finally he gets a full house and wins £1,000. Then, unbelievably, he wins the National Game as well and nets a prize of £380,000. The bingo caller calls him up on stage and says, 'I've never seen anyone do that before. You must be the luckiest man on earth!' 'Not really,' says the man, 'I've got Yellow 24.' 'Blow me down!' says the bingo caller. 'He's only gone and won the raffle as well!'

LUGGAGE

Neville has worked all his life as a railway porter. At his retirement party, his boss presents him with a farewell gift – a luxury set of leather luggage. 'What am I meant to do with these?' says Neville. 'Pick them up and take them home,' says the boss. 'Pick them up yourself,' says Neville. 'What do you think the flippin' trolleys are there for?'

LYING

> "HALF THE LIES OUR OPPONENTS TELL ABOUT US ARE UNTRUE."
>
> SIR BOYLE ROCHE

Arthur goes to the doctor and says, 'Doctor, you've got to help me. I feel like everyone thinks I tell lies all the time.' 'I don't believe that for one minute,' says the doctor.

My wife says I'm always making things up. But what does she know? I'm not even married.

The vicar gets up in church and says to the congregation, 'My sermon today is about lying. There is an important lesson about this in the Gospel of St Mark, Chapter 17. Hands up, all those of you who are familiar with Mark, Chapter 17!' Several people in the congregation put up their hands. 'Right,' says the vicar, 'you're the ones who really need my sermon, because the Gospel of Mark only goes up to Chapter 16.'

Two men are talking. One says, 'My wife is a filthy liar.' 'How do you know?' says the friend. 'She told me she spent last night at her sister's,' says the man. 'How do you know that's a lie?' asks the friend. 'Because,' says the man, 'I was spending last night with her sister.'

Father Bertie sees a group of teenage boys from the local school and asks what they're doing. 'We were just playing a game,' says one of the boys. 'We're competing to see which of us can tell the biggest, whopping lie about our love life.' Father Bertie is shocked and says, 'Dear me, lads! Me and my pals would never have talked about that sort of thing when we were at school. In fact, when I was the same age as you, I never thought about sex once.' 'OK! Game over, everyone!' says the boy. 'Father Bertie's won!'

MAGIC

Dick thinks his wife has picked up a few tricks from her years working as a magician's assistant. The other night he came home and found her in bed. She said, 'Abracadabra!' and his best friend, Pete, walked of the wardrobe. Dick looks at Pete and says, 'You must be wondering what on earth is going on.'

Nigel buys a magic book with the intention of becoming a professional conjurer. For his main trick he chooses the 'Incredible Vanishing Egg', then books himself into the local theatre to put on his first performance. Nigel goes through his act, then reaches the finale and puts an egg on his head. He covers it with a cloth and asks a member of the audience to come on stage and hit it with a hammer. A month later, Nigel wakes up in hospital, jumps out of bed with his arms out and cries, 'Ta-daaa!'

Gary and Bob come out of a sweetshop. 'Guess what!' says Gary. 'While we were in there I slipped three bars of chocolate into my pocket and the shopkeeper didn't notice. I bet you can't do anything as crafty as that.' 'OK,' says Bob, and they march back inside. 'Excuse me,' says Bob to the shopkeeper, 'would you like to see an incredible magic trick?' The shopkeeper agrees, so Bob asks for a bar of chocolate. The shopkeeper hands over a bar, Bob eats it and asks for another. The shopkeeper hands another over, Bob eats it and asks for a third bar of chocolate. The shopkeeper hands this over and Bob eats this as well. Finally, the shopkeeper says, 'OK. So what's supposed to be so magical about this?' 'Now,' says Bob, 'take a look in my friend Gary's pocket and see what you find!'

Gavin is celebrating his birthday. He has long heard the old family legend that his father, grandfather and great-grandfather all have the ability to walk on water when it is their birthday, but when he tries to walk across the lake to the local pub for a birthday drink, he sinks and almost drowns. The next day in hospital, he finds his father at his bedside. He asks, 'Why can't I walk across the water on my birthday? You, Granddad and Great-granddad all managed it?' 'Because,' says Dad, 'your birthday is in August, you twit. The rest of us were all born in December when the lake is frozen!'

An old tramp finds a rusty can on the beach. He picks it up, gives it a rub and out pops a genie. 'Wow!' says the tramp. 'You have to grant me a wish – I want a lovely big house on the coast with a stable at the back and a huge swimming pool and spa all set in a huge, beautiful garden.' 'Tough luck, mate,' says the genie. 'If I could do that, do you think I'd be living in a rusty flipping can?!'

MAGNETS

I've got a friend who is endlessly fascinated by magnets. Personally, I can't see the attraction.

MAKE-UP

Ken's wife tells him, 'I've put some lipstick on today.' 'I don't think it's worked,' says Ken, 'you still seem to be able to move them.'

MANNERS

Vera asks Harry, 'What do you think you're doing?' 'I'm holding the door open for you,' says Harry. 'I thought it was good manners.' 'For the last time,' says Vera, 'will you go away while I'm on the toilet.'

A child who is brought up to be polite and courteous will be welcome in any home; on the downside, when they grow up they will never be able to muscle-in on heavy traffic.

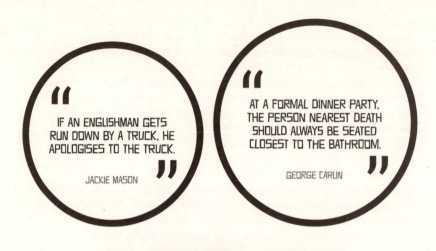

> IF AN ENGLISHMAN GETS RUN DOWN BY A TRUCK, HE APOLOGISES TO THE TRUCK.
>
> JACKIE MASON

> AT A FORMAL DINNER PARTY, THE PERSON NEAREST DEATH SHOULD ALWAYS BE SEATED CLOSEST TO THE BATHROOM.
>
> GEORGE CARLIN

CUSTOMERS WHO FIND OUR WAITRESSES RUDE OUGHT TO SEE THE MANAGER.

SIGN IN A KENYAN RESTAURANT

Two grand Southern ladies are taking the air on the veranda of a fine mansion. One says, 'You see that there Rolls-Royce? Well, my husband gave that to me on our fifth wedding anniversary.' Her friend says, 'Well, isn't that fine.' The woman points to some horses in a paddock. 'And on our tenth wedding anniversary he bought me a string of race horses.' Her friend says, 'Well, isn't that fine.' The woman points to a huge swimming pool at the side of the house. 'And for our fifteenth anniversary, he built me this beautiful pool and spa, all for me.' Her friend says, 'Well, isn't that fine.' 'So tell me,' says the woman. 'Does your husband buy you nice things?' 'Why, yes,' says the friend. 'Only last year he sent me to a charm school to improve my vocabulary.' 'Your vocabulary?' says the woman. 'Yes,' says the friend. 'I used to say, "I don't give a rat's ass." But now I say, "Well, isn't that fine".'

Norman lacks any table manners. Even the family dog can't watch him eating without gagging.

Aunt Hortense has a face that would crack a mirror. One day she visits her niece and is shown into a sitting room where her niece's daughter is waiting to keep her company. The niece doesn't say a word, and after a while Hortense asks what's the matter. 'I can't think of anything to say,' says the daughter. 'Not after mother told me not to mention your huge conk and missing teeth.'

MANURE

Kevin sees a sign at a local farm saying they are giving away horse manure free of charge. He goes in and enquires about the offer but, just as he expected, it turns out to be bull.

MARGARET THATCHER

A new film about Margaret Thatcher is coming out. Apparently it's going to be an 18 certificate because it's upsetting for miners.

Meryl Streep won an Oscar for her portrayal of Margaret Thatcher in *The Iron Lady*. Apparently in the sequel she will be going head to head with Robert Downey Junior as Iron Man.

MARINE LIFE

Harry phones up his friend Dennis in Australia. Dennis tells him that he went to the beach a week ago and there was a sign up warning of shark attacks. Dennis ignored the warning and, sure enough, he ended up having his leg bitten off by shark. 'Oh no!' says Harry. 'Which one?' 'I don't know!' says Dennis. 'All sharks look the same to me!'

Harry phones up a branch of Sea World. Before his telephone call can be answered he hears a message saying, 'Your call will be monitored and recorded for training porpoises.'

MARRIAGE

Two women are talking. 'Do you know,' says one, 'if something ever happened to my husband, I don't think I would ever want to get married again.' 'I know exactly what you mean,' says her friend. 'Once is quite enough.'

Marriage brings enlightenment. Particularly with regards to finding out the kind of man your wife would rather have married.

Before marriage, a man will lie awake all night thinking about something a woman has said to him. After marriage, he's fast asleep before the woman has even finished saying it.

MARRIAGE IS . . .

▶ . . . the moment when a man and woman decide to become one. The trouble starts when they have to decide which one it's going to be.

▶ . . . like a deck of cards. At the start, all you need is two hearts and a diamond, but after a while you're longing for a club and a spade.

▶ . . . a mutual relationship. It works as long as both those involved know when to stay mute.

▶ . . . like having a bank account. You put it in and you take it out, but eventually you lose interest.

If men behaved the same way after they got married as they did beforehand, half of all divorces wouldn't take place. Mind you, if women behaved the same before they got married as they did afterwards, half of all marriages wouldn't happen in the first place.

> QUESTION MASTER: NAME SOMETHING A GIRL SHOULD KNOW ABOUT A MAN BEFORE SHE MARRIES HIM.
> CONTESTANT: HIS NAME.
>
> FAMILY FEUD

A man will fail to understand a woman on two occasions: the first is before marriage; the second is after marriage.

At the start of a marriage, the husband speaks and the wife listens. After a few years, the wife speaks and the husband listens. Soon after that, the husband and wife both speak and the neighbours listen.

An unmarried woman expects a husband; a married woman suspects her husband; a widowed woman respects her husband.

A couple have been married for 50 years during which time they have had 25 children. 'That's extraordinary,' says a newspaper reporter. 'How have you managed to stay together so long?' 'Well,' says the man, 'early on, we came to an agreement – whichever of us walked out first got the kids.'

Tom has begun treating discussions with his wife as though they were user agreements on the internet. He just tells her to skip straight to the end so he can tick 'I agree'.

Harry gets home from work at five o'clock only to find his wife is in a bad mood. Everything Harry says and does makes her even more cross. By eight o'clock, he has had enough so he says, 'I'll tell you what I'm going to do. I'm going to walk out of the front door and then I'm going to come back in and we'll restart the evening from scratch.' Out he goes and then, a few seconds later, he opens the front door and calls brightly, 'Honey, I'm home!' 'And where the bloody hell have you been?' says his wife. 'It's after eight o'clock!'

Never blame your wife for not being perfect. If she was, she would have married someone much better than you.

Harry says he married his wife for her looks. Just not the ones she's been giving him recently.

Asking someone to marry you because of the opportunity for sex is like buying an airliner because you like the little packets of peanuts.

Marge and Peter were happily married for years. It was only after they bought a waterbed they began to drift apart.

Ken and Jackie are newlyweds. One evening Jackie says, 'I've been thinking. Now we're married, you don't need to go out for a drink with your friends so much any more, you don't have to play football every Sunday and you don't need to have a round of golf every Saturday morning.' Jackie then notices the horrified look on Ken's face. 'What's the matter?' she asks. 'I'm sorry, love,' says Ken, 'but for a moment there you were beginning to sound like my ex-wife.' 'What do you mean, your ex-wife?' asks Jackie. 'I thought this was your first marriage.' 'It is,' says Ken.

> QUESTION MASTER: NAME A PHRASE SOME HUSBANDS DREAD HEARING.
> CONTESTANT: 'HONEY, I'M HOME.'
>
> FAMILY FEUD

After several years of marriage, Sally is beginning to think her love life has become a bit boring. One night she tells her husband, 'Do you know what? I can't remember the last time we had sex.' 'What do you mean?' he yells back. 'We're having it right now!'

> "HIS PREVIOUS WIVES JUST DIDN'T UNDERSTAND HIM."
>
> JAN CHAMBERLAIN (MICKEY ROONEY'S EIGHTH WIFE)

Two women are talking. 'My husband reminds me of the sea,' says one. 'Oh,' says the other, 'you mean he's wild, tempestuous and unpredictable.' 'No,' says the first, 'he makes me sick.'

Harry gets in from the pub, staggers upstairs, opens the bedroom door and whispers to his wife, 'I think I'd better just sleep in the spare room tonight, love.' 'That's very considerate of you,' says his wife. 'You've come in a bit tipsy and you don't want to disturb me.' 'No,' says Harry. 'Actually I've brought a woman home with me.'

Keith tells Barry, 'My wife's an angel.' 'You're lucky,' says Barry. 'Mine's still alive.'

Vera asks Brenda, 'Is your husband a bookworm?' 'No,' says Brenda, 'he's just an ordinary one.'

Betty says to Nancy, 'My husband is very hard to please. Is yours like that?' 'I wouldn't know,' says Nancy. 'I've never tried.'

Ken's wife told him that it was a long time since he'd done anything that took her breath away. So he grabbed her inhaler and chucked it out of the car window.

Tom's wife is rushed into hospital and it looks like she is going to be in for some time. Tom spends the night anxiously pacing round in the corridor until he finally manages to get hold of a doctor. 'Doctor,' says Tom, 'I hoped I would never have to ask this question but – do you have any idea how to use a Hotpoint washing machine?'

Bob is complaining to Jack about his wife. 'It's really annoying,' he says, 'she goes on and on to me about her first husband.' 'Mine's worse,' says Jack. 'She goes on and on to me about her next husband.'

A man goes to see his boss. The secretary tells him, 'He's on the phone. I think he must be speaking to his wife.' 'How do you know it's his wife?' asks the man. 'He's been on half an hour,' says the secretary, 'and so far I've only heard him say "Hello" and "Yes".'

A young couple are talking. The girl tells her boyfriend, 'I am going to help you with all your trials and troubles.' 'I don't have any trials and troubles,' says the boy. 'I know you don't have any now,' says the girl, 'but I'm talking about after we're married.'

Definition of a husband – a man who vacuums the hall carpet then declares he has cleaned the whole house.

> "THROUGHOUT OUR MARRIAGE, MY WIFE HAS ALWAYS STOOD BY MY SIDE. SHE HAD TO. WE'VE ONLY GOT ONE CHAIR."
>
> TOMMY COOPER

Nigel spent all last night poring over his marriage licence. Try as he might, he couldn't find a loophole.

Everyone should try living with a partner. After all, happiness isn't the only thing in life.

Gladys has been married so many times, she's had a wedding dress made of non-wrinkle wash'n'wear nylon.

Paula has only just got married but is already on the phone to her friend, Tina, in a flood of tears. 'Frank and I have had a furious argument,' sobs Paula. 'Don't worry,' says Tina. 'Most newlyweds have these little tiffs, but it soon passes.' 'OK. Fine,' says Paula. 'But what am I going to do with the body?'

Jenny's husband has stuck with her through all her bad patches and personal disasters. Mind you, he caused most of them.

Jeff is the richest man in town. One day he's out with his wife, Katy, when they pass a man selling hot dogs from a stall. The man says. 'Katy! Remember me? We used to go out when we were at school.' Katy says hello and they carry on walking. 'Just think,' says Jeff. 'If you'd chosen that guy, you'd be married to a hot-dog vendor.' 'No,' says Katy. 'If I'd chosen him, I'd still be married to the richest man in town and you'd be a grease monkey in your dad's garage.'

Nigel always has the last say when he argues with his wife. Usually it's, 'Yes, of course, dear.'

Frank has installed a strobe light in his bedroom ceiling. It does to tend to give him a headache, but on the plus side, it makes it look like his wife is moving around a bit when they're having sex.

Mrs Crabtree was always complaining to her husband that he hadn't taken her anywhere in years. Finally, the neighbours saw them leaving the house together. Unfortunately, it was the day their gas cooker exploded.

Fred is watching TV when he hears his wife call sweetly from the kitchen: 'What do you fancy for your dinner tonight, my darling? Succulent chicken, tasty beef or lamb in a rich sauce?' 'I'll have the lamb,' calls Fred. 'I was talking to the cat!' says his wife. 'You're having chips.'

A teacher asks her class about marriage and what sort of partner they would like to live with when they are grown-up. 'I'd like a wife who is like the moon,' says one little boy. 'That's very romantic,' says the teacher. 'You mean she would be beautiful and serene.' 'No,' says the boy, 'I'd want her to arrive each night and then leave again first thing in the morning.'

Many people think marriage and death are similar, but they are wrong. The two conditions are very different. For a start, when you're dead, you don't spend all your time wishing you were married.

Nobby and his wife are arguing again. 'All you do is keep pushing my buttons,' she tells him. 'I wish that was true,' says Nobby. 'I might have found the mute by now.'

My wife kept telling me that she wanted me to be more like her ex. So I divorced her.

Nobby says he and his wife have been happily married for two years. One was 2010 and the other was in the early 1990s.

Two old men are talking. One tells the other that he's getting married. 'Is she good-looking?' asks his friend. 'No,' says the old man. 'Is she a good cook?' asks his friend. 'No,' says the old man. 'Does she have any money?' asks the friend. 'No,' says the old man. 'Then why the hell are you getting married to her?' asks the friend. 'Because,' says the old man, 'she's still got a driving licence.'

MARRIAGE GUIDANCE

Nobby tells Tom that he's going to *How to Train Your Dragon*. 'You mean you're going to the cinema?' says Tom. 'No,' says Nobby, 'that's what I call marriage guidance counselling.'

MARTIAL ARTS

I saw a man in the park practising the ancient oriental art of Tai Chi. It was either that or he was doing slow-motion Kung Fu against a mass of small flying insects.

I beat a black belt at Karate yesterday. My next opponent will be a green sock.

Did you hear about the Karate champion who joined the army? On his first day on parade, he saluted and knocked himself out.

MASSAGE

A married couple are sitting on the sofa one night when the wife feels her husband fondling her back. He massages around and down her spine then reaches over to grasps her thighs and rub her bottom. 'That was nice,' she says, 'why have you stopped?' 'It's OK,' says the man, 'I've found the remote now.'

MATHS

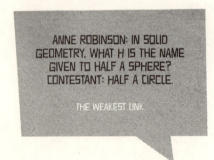

ANNE ROBINSON: IN SOLID GEOMETRY, WHAT H IS THE NAME GIVEN TO HALF A SPHERE?
CONTESTANT: HALF A CIRCLE.

THE WEAKEST LINK

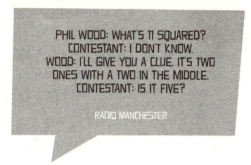

PHIL WOOD: WHAT'S 11 SQUARED?
CONTESTANT: I DON'T KNOW.
WOOD: I'LL GIVE YOU A CLUE. IT'S TWO
ONES WITH A TWO IN THE MIDDLE.
CONTESTANT: IS IT FIVE?

RADIO MANCHESTER

When he was at school Barry was terrible at maths. He says he can't count the number of times he failed the exam.

Pythagoras walks into a bar, trying to work out a geometrical problem. 'In a right-angled triangle,' he mutters to himself, 'the square of the hypotenuse Z is equal to the sum of the short side X and . . . what?' 'Y, the long face?' says the barman.

Who likes Roman numerals? I for one!

A Roman soldier walks into a bar, holds up two fingers and says, 'Five beers please.'

Ten out of nine people are completely baffled by fractions.

Q: Why was six afraid of seven? **A:** Because seven was a registered six offender.

MECHANICS

FREE PICK-UP AND DELIVERY. TRY US ONCE. YOU'LL NEVER GO ANYWHERE AGAIN.

ADVERT FOR AN AUTO REPAIR SERVICE

A doctor is picking up his car from the garage and cannot believe the bill he's been given. 'This is more than I get paid as a doctor,' he tells the mechanic. 'Maybe,' says the mechanic, 'but don't forget, every few months there'll be a dozen new models I have to learn how to repair. You doctors get to work on the same basic bodywork, year after year.'

Q: How many garage mechanics does it take to change a light bulb?
A: Five. Four to salvage one from a scrapyard and one to try and force it into place.

Betty took her car in for a service. She was worried that her motor mechanic might rip her off and was very relieved when the bill came to only £200: £100 for the new seat springs; £75 for the anti-crash spray; and £25 for washing the petrol.

A motorist walks into a garage in a filthy temper. 'You put a new battery in my car six months ago and told me that it would be the last battery the car would ever need!' he yells. 'Now six months on, the battery is dead!' 'Sorry, mate,' says the mechanic, 'but I didn't think your car would last that long.'

Larry goes into a garage and asks for a 710 cap for his car. 'A 710 cap?' replies the mechanic. 'Never heard of one of those.' 'But all cars have them,' says Larry. 'Look, I can show you.' So saying, he pops the bonnet on a car and points to the 710 cap. 'OK,' says the mechanic. 'Now take the cap off and turn it round.' Larry does so. 'What does it says now?' asks the mechanic. Larry squints at it and says, 'OIL'.

MEDALS

In a controversial move, the army announced they are replacing medals with stickers that say, 'I was very brave at the war today.'

MEDICINE

A good rule of thumb is to refuse any medication that has more side effects than you have symptoms.

It can be very dangerous to mix medications. Particularly if the medications involved are sleeping pills and laxatives.

Norman's doctor pumped him full of antibiotics to help him get over a severe infection. In fact, he gave him so many, when Norman sneezed on a bus he cured five other passengers.

Why aren't any scientists working to find a cure for natural causes?

Vince went on the TV show *Embarrassing Bodies* last week. He was told that sort of thing required a lot of balls. Luckily he had three, so the producers put him straight on.

Tom tells Harry proudly, 'Of course, you know my son is now at medical school.' 'I heard,' says Harry. 'So which area of medicine is he studying?' 'He's not,' says Tom. 'The rest of them are studying him.'

Tom goes to the doctor with a lingering cold. 'There's nothing I can do about this,' says the doctor, 'in fact I'm not even sure what you've got?' 'Come on, doctor,' says Tom. 'You've got to do something for me?' 'OK,' says the doctor, 'what I recommend is that you camp out in your garden for the next three nights and pour cold water over yourself every three hours.' 'But I'll get pneumonia if I do that,' says Tom. 'I know,' says the doctor, 'and I can cure pneumonia.'

Harry gets home from the doctor's and tells his wife the bad news. 'He's given me this little bottle of pills and told me I'll be on them for the rest of my life,' says Harry. 'Well, that's not too bad,' says his wife. 'Yes, it is,' says Harry, 'the label on the bottle says, "No repeat prescriptions"!'

Try as he might, Bert couldn't take his pills every two hours like his doctor told him. It took him at least three hours to get the top off the bottle.

MEMENTOES

Two women are talking. 'What's in that locket you're wearing?' asks the first. 'It's a lock of my husband's hair,' says her friend. 'I keep it as a reminder of happier days,' says her friend. 'But your husband's still alive,' says the first. 'I know,' says her friend, 'but he's gone bald.'

MEMORABILIA

Tom is showing Harry some of his grandfather's prized possessions. 'This is his knife,' says Tom, 'apparently he used it to stab a German.' 'Wow!' says Harry. 'So was that during the Second World War?' 'No,' says Tom, 'it was last year in Benidorm. They were having a row over a sun lounger.'

MEMORY

A man goes to the doctor and says, 'Doctor, you've got to help me. My memory is terrible. I can't remember anything. I can't remember how I got here today. I can't remember my way home. I can't remember if I'm married or what I do for a living. Is there anything you can do to help?' 'Yes, there is,' says the doctor, 'but I am going to require payment in advance.'

Vince tells Dick, 'My wife has a dreadful memory.' 'Oh,' says Dick, 'so she keeps forgetting things.' 'No,' says Vince, 'it's worse than that. She remembers absolutely everything.'

Chris and Rita celebrate their 50th wedding anniversary in a fancy restaurant. They have a nice meal, but on the way home Rita realises that she's left her purse behind. Chris tells her she's going senile, turns the car around and moans at her the whole way back. They stop outside the restaurant and Rita gets out. Chris calls through the window, 'And make sure you didn't forget anything else! I'm not coming back again! Oh, and pick up my glasses while you're at it . . .'

At the old people's home, Ernie and Jasper are talking. 'My memory is shot,' says Jasper. 'I forget everything.' 'Me too,' says Ernie. 'I can't even remember the name of that guy who died yesterday. Was that Fred, or you?'

MEN AND WOMEN

All men have one, but some have ones that are longer than others. A man will give his to his wife when he gets married, and the Pope doesn't use his at all. What is it? A surname.

Whenever a man calls something a silly, childish game, he means it's something a woman can beat him at.

If you talk to a man and he listens, he's gay. If you talk to a man and he pretends to listen, he's straight and single. If you talk and he doesn't listen at all, he's your husband.

A man of few words, is usually married.

Nobby thinks his wife has a really odd way of starting conversations. She always begins: 'Have you been listening to a single word I've been saying?'

> " GUYS ARE LIKE DOGS. THEY KEEP COMING BACK. LADIES ARE LIKE CATS. YELL AT A CAT ONE TIME . . . THEY'RE GONE. "
>
> LENNY BRUCE

Men are like ice-cream sundaes – they're smooth and sweet and head straight for your hips.

Scientists have made a startling discovery about male brains. The left hemisphere has nothing right in it, while the right hemisphere has nothing left in it.

> " WOMEN NOW HAVE CHOICES. THEY CAN BE MARRIED, NOT MARRIED, HAVE A JOB, NOT HAVE A JOB, BE MARRIED WITH CHILDREN, UNMARRIED WITH CHILDREN. MEN HAVE THE SAME CHOICE WE'VE ALWAYS HAD: WORK, OR PRISON. "
>
> TIM ALLEN

> **MEN WANT THE SAME THING FROM THEIR UNDERWEAR THAT THEY WANT FROM WOMEN: A LITTLE BIT OF SUPPORT, AND A LITTLE BIT OF FREEDOM.**
>
> JERRY SEINFELD

My girlfriend and I often laugh about how competitive we are. However, I'm definitely the one who laughs more.

My wife and I have very different views on the nature of sexual relationships. She wants a relationship without any unnecessary sex, whereas I want sex without any unnecessary relationship.

Q: Why did the woman cross the road?
A: Who knows why they do anything?

After many years of research, scientists have identified exactly what makes women happy. Absolutely nothing.

Women don't have such dirty minds as men, but there's a reason for that — they change them more often.

It is possible for a man to discern a woman's mood by examining her hands. If you find a loaded gun in either of them, she may not be happy.

> **WOMEN ARE CURSED AND MEN ARE THE PROOF.**
>
> ROSEANNE BARR

For all the men who think a woman's place is in the kitchen – just remember, that's where the knives are kept.

Men and women agree on one thing. Neither of them trust women.

WE SPECIALISE IN WOMEN AND OTHER DISEASES.

SIGN AT A DOCTOR'S SURGERY IN ITALY

MENTAL PROBLEMS

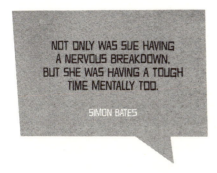

NOT ONLY WAS SUE HAVING A NERVOUS BREAKDOWN, BUT SHE WAS HAVING A TOUGH TIME MENTALLY TOO.

SIMON BATES

I have often questioned my sanity, but each time it turns out to have had a watertight alibi.

A man goes to the doctor and says, 'Doctor, there's something wrong with my wife. For the past few weeks she's become convinced she's a horse.' 'My goodness,' says the doctor. 'It sounds as though she has a very serious mental condition. She'll need a long course of therapy and I'm afraid it could be very expensive.' 'Don't worry about that,' says the man. 'Money's no object. I had 15 to 1 on her yesterday when she won the Gold Cup!'

A man tells his doctor, 'Doctor, I keep thinking I'm a pony.' 'No, don't be ridiculous!' says the doctor. 'You're just a little hoarse.'

A man tells his doctor, 'Doctor, I keep thinking I'm a sheep.' 'How do you feel?' asks the doctor. 'Quite baaa-aad,' says the man.

A man tells his doctor, 'Doctor, sometimes I think I'm a wigwam and sometimes I think I'm a tepee.' 'I'll tell you what your problem is,' says the doctor, 'you're two tents!'

Eddie and Melvyn are patients in a secure mental hospital. One day Eddie throws himself into the pond in the hospital grounds and sinks to the bottom. Melvyn jumps in to save him. Later that day Melvyn is called into the hospital director's office. 'Melvyn,' says the director, 'I've good news and bad news. The good news is that we're letting you go home as you have proved your sanity by rescuing another patient from drowning. The bad news is that your friend Eddie went back to his room and hanged himself from the ceiling. 'No, he didn't,' says Melvyn, 'that was just where I left him to dry.'

Three patients in a mental institution are being examined by the head psychiatrist. He tells them that if they pass the exam, they will be free to leave, but if they fail they will be kept in the institution for another ten years. He takes them to a high diving board over an empty swimming pool and asks them to jump. The first patient jumps headfirst into the pool and breaks both his arms. The second patient jumps and breaks both legs. Finally, the third patient looks over the side and refuses to jump. 'Congratulations!' says the psychiatrist. 'You are free to go home. But before you go, just tell me why didn't you jump.' 'I can't swim,' says the patient.

A government inspector visits an asylum to investigate their admission policy. 'How do you decide if someone's insane?' asks the inspector.' 'We show them a bathtub full of water,' says the Head Doctor. 'We give them a choice between a bucket and a spoon and ask them to empty the bath.' 'I understand,' says the inspector. 'Anyone who chooses the spoon is classified as insane.' 'No,' says the doctor. 'Anyone who doesn't pull out the plug is insane. What size strait-jacket do you take?'

I had a mental breakdown after buying my new deck of cards. Some of the pack was round, some square and some rectangular. I just couldn't deal with it.

Yes, it's true, I am schizophrenic, but looking on the bright side I will always have each other.

A man tells his doctor, 'Doctor, I think I have an inferiority complex.' 'No,' says the doctor, 'I've examined you all over and I can tell you for certain, you really are inferior.'

A man goes to the doctor and says, 'Doctor, I keep thinking I'm a small bucket.'' 'No,' says the doctor, 'you're just a little pail.'

A man goes to the doctor and says, 'Doctor, I keep thinking I'm turning into a wheelbarrow.' 'No,' says the doctor, 'your problem is you let people push you around.'

Dr Smith visits the local asylum and finds a patient with his ear pressed to the wall. 'What are you listening to?' asks the doctor. The patient beckons for the doctor to join him. The doctor listens for a few moments then turns to the patient and says, 'I can't hear anything.' 'I know,' whispers the patient. 'It's been like that for weeks.'

Nigel rings the mental home in a panic and asks the duty nurse to check who's in room 25. The nurse goes to have a look, then returns and says that the room is empty. 'Thank God for that,' says Nigel. 'so I really have escaped.'

Brian goes to the chief psychiatrist at his mental home and says, 'I've stopped hearing those voices in my head.' 'Very good,' says the psychiatrist. 'So do you want me to release you?' 'No,' says Brian. 'I want you to give me a hearing aid.'

There are consistently more men in mental hospitals than there are women. So I think that tells us something. Mainly it tells us exactly who is driving who crazy.

METRIC SYSTEM

God did not intend for man to use the metric system. If he had, Jesus would have only had ten disciples.

MEXICANS

Martin went for a winter break in Mexico and came back covered in peck-marks all over his body. He thought someone had told him that the Mexicans use chickens for heaters. But he may have misheard.

How many Mexicans does it take to change a light bulb? Just Juan.

A Mexican magician tells his audience that he will disappear on the count of three. He counts, 'Uno, dos . . .' And POOF! He disappears without a tres.

MIDDLE EAST

Reuben is reading an Arab newspaper. A friend asks, 'What are you doing? Why don't you read a Jewish newspaper?' 'That's what I used to read,' says Reuben, 'but it was always full of stories of Jews being persecuted, Jews being harassed and people planning to attack Israel. Now I read this and it's full of stories about how the Jews own all the banks, the Jews control the media, the Jews are all rich and powerful. It's a much less depressing read.'

MILK

Where does condensed milk come from? Do they have to milk very tiny cows?

Teacher asks the class to name six things that have milk in them. Little Johnny puts up his hand. 'Yoghurt, an ice-cream sundae, and four cows.'

MIMES

Larry was beaten up by a troupe of mimes. It was terrible. The things they did to him were unspeakable.

Brian the mime was arrested last week. He opted for the right to remain silent.

MIRACLES

A woman finds a magic lamp. She rubs it and a genie pops out and offers to grant her a wish. The woman says, 'I want my boyfriend to only ever think about me. I want him to always have me by his side day and night. I want him to take me everywhere he goes and I want to be the first thing he grabs when he gets up in the morning.' 'Your wish shall be granted!' says the genie, and turns her into an iPhone.

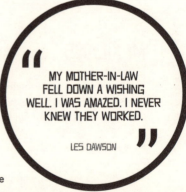

"MY MOTHER-IN-LAW FELL DOWN A WISHING WELL. I WAS AMAZED. I NEVER KNEW THEY WORKED."

LES DAWSON

A western preacher is helping to mend the fence on a ranch when his Bible falls out of his pocket. He looks for it for days, but can't find it anywhere. Three weeks later, he's visiting the same ranch when a cow walks up to him with something in its mouth and drops it at his feet – it's his Bible. The preacher picks up the good book and says, 'Lord, this must be some kind of miracle.' The cow says, 'Not really. Your name's written on the inside cover.'

A man is having a drink when he notices a man with a massive round orange head sitting at the bar. The man is intrigued so he goes over and buys the man with the massive round orange head a drink. 'So you noticed my massive round orange head,' says the orange head man, 'and I bet you want to hear the story. You know, I've gone over it in my mind many times. But it all goes back to a day years ago when I was walking along the beach and stubbed my toe on something. I looked down and there in the sand was an ancient brass lamp. I picked it up and dusted it and, all of a sudden, out pops a genie. The genie says, "You have released me from centuries of imprisonment in the lamp. Now I am in your debt and will grant you three wishes as a token of my gratitude." "That's great," I said. "My first wish is to be fabulously rich." And the genie says, "Your wish is granted." And all of a sudden my wish came true and I was living in a beautiful mansion with an expensive sports car in the drive and millions in the bank. "Fantastic!" I said. "For my second wish, I want to be married to the most beautiful woman in the world." And the genie says, "Your wish is my command." And into the mansion walked the most gorgeous woman I had ever seen. She took my hand and we fell in love and the genie married us right there. Then the genie said, "You still have one wish remaining." And this might be the point where I went wrong, because then I said, "OK. For my third wish I want . . . a massive round orange head."'

MIRAGES

Two starving Mexicans have spent days wandering the desert when they come across an incredible find – a tree that has juicy rashers of bacon hanging off every branch. 'We are saved, amigo,' says one of the men, 'we have found a bacon tree!' But as he runs towards it, gunshots ring out and he takes a bullet. As he falls to the ground, he calls to his friend, 'Go back, amigo! It's not a bacon tree after all. It's a ham bush!'

MIRRORS

Terry goes to the Job Centre. 'What sort of work are you looking for?' asks the clerk. 'I'd like a job cleaning mirrors,' says Terry. 'Really?' says the clerk. 'Why's that?' 'No reason,' says Terry, 'it's just something that I could really see myself doing.'

The headmistress of a school notices that the sixth-form girls have got into the habit of putting on lipstick in the girls' toilets and then pressing their lips against the mirror to leave prints. She gets all the girls to assemble in the toilet and tells them how it takes the cleaning lady hours to remove these prints each day. To demonstrate how difficult it is, she brings out the cleaning lady, who dips her mop into one of the toilet bowls and uses it to scrub the mirror clean. From that day on, the girls never kiss the washroom mirror again.

MISHEARD

Bill goes into the kitchen and finds his wife frying something odd in a pan. He stares at the thing and says. 'Why are you doing that?' 'Because when you got in last night this is what you asked me to do,' says his wife. 'I know I'd had a few drinks,' says Bill, 'but I don't remember asking you to cook my sock?'

MISSING PERSONS

Janet's husband goes missing. After two weeks, the police tell her she'd better prepare for the worst. So she goes to the Oxfam shop to ask for all his clothes back.

Barry tells Stan that his wife left him last Wednesday. 'She said she was just going out for some milk,' says Barry. 'But she never came back.' 'Oh no,' says Stan. 'So have you managed?' 'It's been OK really,' says Barry. 'I found some of that powdered stuff in the cupboard.'

Sammy phones the police to report that his wife is missing. 'How long has she been gone?' asks the desk sergeant. 'Two weeks,' says Sammy. 'Why wait so long to report it?' asks the sergeant. 'I didn't notice at first,' says Sammy. 'For the first 13 days I just thought I was having a happy dream.'

MISSING THE POINT

Two old ladies are talking. 'I was in the park yesterday,' says one, 'and a man came up and showed me the lining of his mackintosh.' 'Are you sure he wanted you to look at the lining?' asks her friend. 'Yes,' says the first old lady. 'He wasn't wearing anything else.'

MISTAKES

It's never nice getting things wrong, but if you want to look on the bright side, it does bring a lot of pleasure to those around you.

My wife says I never seem to learn from my mistakes. Coincidentally, most of my previous seven wives used to say something very similar.

MISTRESSES

A woman is suing for divorce after discovering that her millionaire husband has not only had a mistress for the past ten years but that he also bought her a house. The husband's lawyer explains that the affair is now over and the house has been sold for a profit of two million pounds, which the millionaire is offering to his wife as a divorce settlement. 'I didn't realise it was possible to make that sort of money,' says the woman. 'Can we sue him for not having more mistresses?!'

A successful businessman has been married for years. One night he and his wife are out having dinner when a stunning young woman comes over, gives the husband a kiss and tells him that she will see him later. 'Who was that?' asks the wife angrily. 'That's my mistress,' says the husband. 'I'm not standing for this,' says the wife. 'I want a divorce.' 'OK,' says the husband. 'But that means no more shopping trips to Paris, no more holidays in Barbados and Tuscany and you won't have the sports car to drive any more.' Just then one of the husband's business colleagues walks in with a young girl on his arm. 'Who's that girl with him?' asks his wife. 'That's his mistress,' says the husband. 'Ours is prettier,' says the wife.

MOBILE PHONES

Barry calls his friend Gary on his mobile. 'What are you doing at the moment?' asks Barry. 'Failing my driving test,' says Gary.

Over the past 15 years mobile phones have kept getting thinner and smarter. Unfortunately, over the same time period their owners have been heading in the opposite direction.

Mobile phones are one of the few things men will boast that they have the smallest one around.

Oddly enough, ever since everyone has had a camera on their mobile phone, the number of UFO sightings has dramatically plummeted.

Before the introduction of modern mobile phones, you used to have to carry round a thing the size of a house brick if you wanted to talk to people. I used to throw it through their windows and talk to them through the hole.

If I forget where I left my phone, the only way I can find it is to ring my own number and listen for it. I don't know why I have it anyway. Only one person ever calls me. And that's me trying to find my phone.

In view of moves to legislate against the millions of people who still insist on using their mobile phones while driving their cars, a company has at last developed the world's first completely hands-free car.

Martha gets a new sim card for her phone. She puts it in and decides to play a trick on her husband, who is in the next room. She calls him up with her new number and says, 'Hello, darling! What are you doing tonight?' The husband whispers back, 'Hi, sexy. I'd better call you back. My wife's just in the next room.'

Dick is out one day when his mobile rings. He answers and asks, 'How the hell did you know I was here?'

A man yells at Nobby because he's texting while driving. Nobby yells back, 'Shut up! Mind your own business! And get off my flipping bonnet!'

MOBILITY

My gran always loves a practical joke, so I put her walking stick just out of reach. I can't believe she fell for it.

MONEY

It's true that money cannot buy you happiness. Nevertheless, it's a bit more comfortable to cry in a Rolls-Royce than on a bicycle.

Money may not buy you happiness, but then again it does give you the option of looking for it in a wider range of places.

Harry claims he earns a seven-figure salary. That's true although, sadly, there is a decimal point in front of the last two figures.

Nobby always wanted to be filthy, stinking rich. So far he's managed two out of three.

> "MY GRANDFATHER ALWAYS SAID, 'DON'T WATCH YOUR MONEY; WATCH YOUR HEALTH.' SO ONE DAY WHILE I WAS WATCHING MY HEALTH, SOMEONE STOLE MY MONEY. IT WAS MY GRANDFATHER."
>
> — JACKIE MASON

The gas company phone up Harry because he hasn't been paying his bills. 'We fitted a new boiler for you last year, but you still haven't paid us for it,' says the gas man. 'Why should I?' says Harry. 'When you put it in, you told me that in 12 months it would pay for itself.'

> "I PAID TOO MUCH FOR IT, BUT IT'S WORTH IT."
>
> — SAMUEL GOLDWYN

The US baseball player Yogi Berra was asked what we would do if he found a million dollars. He replied, 'I'd find the fellow who lost it, and, if he was poor, I'd return it.'

Kevin is in court for getting into debt. He gets up and says, 'As God is my judge, I do not owe this money.' The judge responds, 'Unfortunately he's not, I am, and you do.'

Vince got into money problems. He did some research and found 30 organisations that offered to consolidate all his debts into a single monthly repayment at a phenomenal rate of interest. He's now taken out loans from all 30 of them.

I pay all my bills by card and by direct debit now. It's so long since I've seen any cash that, to be honest, I'm not sure if we ever switched over to the Euro or not.

Harry's boss asks him, 'How much of your wages do you usually take home and give to your wife?' 'None of it,' says Harry. 'None of it!' says the boss, astounded. 'How do you get away with that?' 'I don't,' says Harry. 'She comes to meet me on payday and takes the money home herself.'

Money is like fat. There's plenty of it about, but it always seems to be in the wrong places.

> "MONEY IS NOT THE MOST IMPORTANT THING IN THE WORLD. LOVE IS. FORTUNATELY, I LOVE MONEY."
>
> JACKIE MASON

Gary's credit record was so bad, when he went in to fill in a loan application, the bank wouldn't even lend him a pen.

Tom bumps into Gary and notices he's looking a bit nervous. 'I've got a meeting at the bank in ten minutes,' says Gary, 'I think it's going to change my life forever.' 'That sounds exciting,' says Tom. 'Yes, it is,' says Gary. 'Could you help me put on this balaclava?'

Mr Smith rings his stockbroker and tells him to sell all his stocks. 'All of them?' says the broker. 'It's really not a good time right now. Wait a month or two and you'll get a better price.' 'I can't wait,' says Mr Smith. 'I need all the cash now. When I got married, I promised my wife I'd never gamble on stocks and shares. I told her I had all our money hidden under the mattress.' 'So,' says the broker, 'do you need the money now because you're making a large purchase?' 'No,' says Mr Smith. 'I need it now because my wife is buying a new bed.'

A man is driving through London when he sees a kid sitting crying on the kerb. He gets out to see what's the matter. The kid holds up a £50 note. 'See this money? I used to have two £50 notes. It's all the money my Mum saved up for Christmas. She sent me out to take it to the bank, but when I was walking along this guy came up to me, stole one of the notes and ran off with it.' 'Oh dear,' says the man. 'And didn't anyone help you?' 'No,' sniffs the boy. 'The people on the street just acted like it didn't happen.' 'Well, you should have learned your lesson by now,' says the man, and grabs the 50 quid and runs for his car.

Tom asks Harry, 'What would you do if you had Richard Branson's money?' 'I'd spend it all quickly before he noticed it was gone,' says Harry.

Maurice was the world's worst loan shark. He loaned five people a total of £60,000 at outrageous interest, then skipped town before they could pay him back.

MONSTERS

Have you heard about the Transformer who can change from an enormous robot into an outfit of clothes that costs under a tenner? He's called Optimus Primark.

Q: What's big and furry and spends all day doing sit-ups?
A: The abdomenable snowman.

MORMONISM

Q: Why did the Mormon cross the road?
A: To get to the other bride.

MOTHERS

A man calls his elderly mother. 'How are you, Mum?' asks the man. 'Very weak,' says the mother. 'Oh no,' says the son, 'what's happened?' 'I haven't been able to eat for a month,' says his mother. 'Oh no,' says the son, 'why haven't you been able to eat?' 'Because,' says the mother, 'I didn't want to have my mouth full of food in case you called.'

MOTHERS-IN-LAW

Nobby's mother-in-law is in hospital. He asks Norma if there is any news. 'They say she's not looking too good,' says Norma. 'Well, we all know that,' says Nobby. 'But did they say anything about her condition?'

Ken's mother-in-law phones him up. 'Come over quickly,' she says, 'I think I might be dying.' 'OK, I'll tell you what,' says Ken, 'call me back when you're a bit more sure.'

Brenda comes home and finds her mother standing in a bowl of water holding a finger up to the light socket and her husband, Tom, reaching for the switch. 'You're just in time, dear,' says the mother. 'Tom has come up with a brilliant idea for curing my arthritis.'

Ted's mother-in-law came round unexpectedly yesterday. He says that's the last time he buys cheap chloroform.

Brenda asks Tom, 'Can my mother come down for the weekend?' 'I'm not sure,' says Tom. 'Oh, go on!' says Brenda. 'She's been up on that roof for a week now.'

Larry is having a cup of tea with his mother-in-law. 'I've decided,' she says, 'I want to be cremated.' 'No problemo!' says Larry. 'You get your coat, and I'll start the car!'

Nobby thinks he is a proper gentleman because he always holds the door open for his mother-in-law. Mind you, he does it when he's doing 70 down the motorway.

It's Christmas and Tom is simmering with anger. Finally he goes to have a word with his wife, Brenda. 'It's no good,' he says, 'I can't stand having that miserable, interfering old woman here any longer. She comes to us every Christmas and spends the whole time complaining about everything. She bosses me around and criticises everything I do. I'm sorry, but I don't want your mother coming here again.' 'What do you mean, *my* mother?' says Brenda. 'I thought she was *your* mother!'

MOTOR RACING

ANYTHING HAPPENS IN GRAND PRIX RACING, AND IT USUALLY DOES.

MURRAY WALKER

A protest march passes by chanting, 'What do we want? Race car noises! When do we want them? Neeeeeyyyyoowww!'

When they win, racing drivers are always opening bottles of champagne that fizz everywhere. With the money they spend on those cars, you'd think they'd have better suspension.

MOTORING OFFENCES

Tom drives past a speed camera too quickly and a few days later he receives a letter telling him he is being fined £90, along with a photograph of his speeding car. Tom decides to be a bit cheeky and sends back a photograph of £90. A few days later Tom looks in his letterbox and finds the police have sent him a photograph of a pair of handcuffs.

Tom is out in his car when he gets pulled over by the police. A policeman walks over, taps on Tom's window and says, 'Would you blow in this bag for me please, sir?' 'Why? Do you think I've been drinking, officer?' says Tom. 'No,' says the policeman, 'it's just that my chips are a bit hot.'

The police pull over an old lady in a car. She has a passenger, an old man whose face is frozen in a rictus of fear. The policeman says, 'Madam, I just pulled you off the motorway for driving at 25 miles an hour. Why were you driving so slowly?' 'I wasn't,' says the old lady. 'I was doing what the sign told me. It said the "M25", so I drove at 25 miles an hour.' 'That's not how it works, madam,' says the policeman. 'Couldn't your friend here have told you that?' He looks at the old man, who's not moved a muscle since they stopped. 'Is he all right?' asks the policeman. 'I'm not sure,' says the old lady. 'He's been like that since we got on the A150.'

MOUNTAINS

It has been reported that an attempt to scale Mount Everest by the Sir Alfred McAlpine company has been abandoned. Three-quarters of the way up, they ran out of scaffolding.

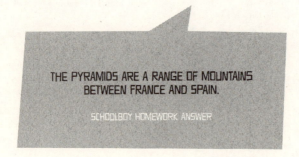

THE PYRAMIDS ARE A RANGE OF MOUNTAINS BETWEEN FRANCE AND SPAIN.

SCHOOLBOY HOMEWORK ANSWER

MUD-WRESTLING

For a long time, Tina had a serious addiction to mud-wrestling. Thankfully, for the last five years she's managed to stay clean.

MUSIC AND MUSICIANS

Little Billy is at home practising on his violin. Every time he starts playing a new tune, the dog lifts its head and starts howling painfully. When he stops playing, the dog stops howling. As soon as Billy finds another tune, the dog starts up again as well. After half an hour of scraping, screeching and howling, Dad has had enough. He stomps across to Billy and says, 'For goodness' sake, can you please try and find a piece of music that the dog doesn't know!'

Q: What was Jay-Z's wife called before they got married?
A: Feyoncé.

A man is travelling through the USA when he sees a shop that sells only two products, drum kits and guns. Intrigued, he goes inside to find out more. 'Why do you specialise in just these two things?' he asks. 'Well,' says the shopkeeper, 'it seems to work pretty well. Every time a guy comes in here to buy a drum kit, pretty soon afterwards, his neighbour will drop by to choose a gun.'

A man goes into an antiques shop. 'This is my son's violin,' he says, taking the instrument from its case. 'How much would you give me for this?' '£100,' says the antiques dealer. 'Never mind,' says the man, 'someone has offered me twice as much as that for it.' 'Was that someone from another antiques shop?' asks the dealer. 'No,' says the man, 'it was my next-door neighbour.'

Maisie's dad is listening to her singing practice. 'You know what,' says Dad. 'I think you should be on the telly.' 'Because I sing so well?' asks Maisie. 'No,' says Dad. 'Because then I'd be able to switch you off.'

As I get older, I keep having an urge to burst into song and sing, 'The lion sleeps tonight'. It's only ever just a whim away . . . a whim away, a whim away.

A famous violinist goes to Africa to prove that music can be used to tame animals. He stands in the jungle and begins to play, and gradually the most savage, dangerous animals come out of the trees and settle down around him, transfixed by the beautiful sound. But then a lion comes tearing out and bites the man's head off. 'Hey!' says a gorilla. 'I was just enjoying that!' The lion cups his paw to his ear and says, 'What did you say, sonny?'

Last night I had a dream where Gloria Gaynor was standing over my bed, looking down at me. Well, of course, at first I was afraid, I was petrified . . .

Did you hear about the man who bought an old satnav from Bonnie Tyler? It keeps telling him to turn around, and every now and then it falls apart.

The mafia had a word with Rick Astley because they were sick of only ever hearing him sing 'Never Gonna Give You Up'. He soon changed his tune.

Q: What's the difference between a rock guitarist and a jazz guitarist?
A: A rock guitarist plays three chords in front of 1,000 fans . . .

Marti Pellow from 'Wet Wet Wet' is suffering from frostbite after an attempt at Mount Everest. Apparently, now he doesn't feel it in his fingers, and he doesn't feel it in his toes . . .

I went round to see MC Hammer. He has some lovely ornaments in his house, but you wouldn't believe how precious he is about them.

I rarely hear anything from Rick Astley nowadays. I'm beginning to think he may have given me up and let me down . . .

Despite now all being over 70 years old, Led Zeppelin are getting back together to perform a reworked version of one of their classic songs. They call it 'Stair-Lift to Heaven'.

Elvis Presley never seemed to want me as a friend. I think the reason might have been that I ain't never caught a rabbit . . .

Rick Astley's wife would really like him to buy her favourite Pixar movie on DVD, but he keeps categorically refusing.

I lost my pet mouse Elvis last night. He was caught in a trap and couldn't get out . . .

I'm considering putting all my old John Lennon records on eBay. Imagine all the Paypal . . .

Stevie Wonder is on stage playing his greatest hits. An old hipster man in the front row shouts out, 'Play a jazz chord! Play a jazz chord!' Stevie plays him a jazz chord, but the old man is still shouting, 'Play a jazz chord! Play a jazz chord!' Stevie tries again and plays a complex jazz riff. Still, the old man is not satisfied and shouts, 'Play a jazz chord! Play a jazz chord!' Stevie shouts back, 'I don't get it, man? What jazz chord?' 'Your big song,' calls the man. 'Play a jazz chord!' 'I still don't get it,' says Stevie. 'Sing some of it. Maybe I'll figure it out.' So the old man starts singing, 'A jazz chord . . . to say, I love you.'

It has been reported that Miley Cyrus has split up with her boyfriend. Apparently their relationship just wasn't twerking.

My friend Jasper once produced Earth, Wind and Fire. He's got nothing to do with the music industry. He just likes really strong curries.

Phil Spector hasn't been doing so well recently. But that's not the case with his brother Crispin. Apparently, he's the head of quality control at Golden Wonder.

The other day I got a call from Cher on my mobile phone. Unfortunately, she kept breaking up. It had nothing to do with the signal reception, it turned out to be a problem with her cosmetic surgery.

Q: If Justin Bieber challenged Kanye West to a fight to the death, who would be the ultimate winner? **A:** Society.

I've got a favourite new indie band. They're called 'Dog Whistle'. You probably won't have heard them.

Have you heard about the tribute band called 'Jar Lid'? They cover 'The Jam' and 1960s band 'Marmalade'.

I've formed a new band. We're called 'Duvet'. We do covers.

A warning has been issued. Apparently, if you play Justin Bieber's records backwards you will hear terrifying satanic messages. But if you play them forwards it's even worse. Because then you hear Justin Bieber.

When I was younger, I was in a rock band. We weren't very good. Our audiences always encouraged us to smash up our instruments *before* our gigs.

A mystery occurred during the middle of this year's Proms. Apparently the Bermuda Philharmonic Orchestra were performing a concert when, halfway through, their triangle player disappeared.

> STEWART WHITE: WHO HAD A WORLDWIDE HIT WITH 'WHAT A WONDERFUL WORLD'?
> CONTESTANT: I DON'T KNOW.
> WHITE: I'LL GIVE YOU SOME CLUES. WHAT DO YOU CALL THE PART BETWEEN YOUR HAND AND YOUR ELBOW?
> CONTESTANT: ARM.
> WHITE: CORRECT. AND IF YOU'RE NOT WEAK, YOU'RE . . .?
> CONTESTANT: STRONG.
> WHITE: CORRECT - AND WHAT WAS LORD MOUNTBATTEN'S FIRST NAME?
> CONTESTANT: LOUIS.
> WHITE: WELL, THERE WE ARE THEN. SO - WHO HAD A WORLDWIDE HIT WITH THE SONG 'WHAT A WONDERFUL WORLD'?
> CONTESTANT: FRANK SINATRA?
>
> BBC NORFOLK

Q: How many jazz musicians does it take to change a light bulb?
A: Three. One to change the light bulb and two to click their fingers and say, 'Nice'.

Q: How many disco dancers does it take to change a light bulb?
A: Two. One to boogie up the ladder and one to say, 'Get down!'

It has been reported that Ken Dodd is going to form a new super-group with the American rock star Jon Bon Jovi. It's going to be called 'By Jovi'.

Karl Gustav von Krug, the well-known conductor, was sent to the electric chair for murdering his wife. Three times they threw the switch, but Karl was not affected at all. Eventually they had to release him on the grounds that, while he was a conductor, he was just not a very good one.

Crazy Jimmy was a dyslexic heavy-metal guitarist. One day he choked to death on his own Vimto.

Harry claims he can turn a duck into a soul singer. He puts it in the oven until it's Bill Withers.

What did the blues singer want engraved on his headstone? 'I didn't wake up this morning. Didn't get out of bed . . .'

Q: Which singer loves biscuits the most?
A: Lionel Rich-Tea.

Nigel spent millions at a music auction on a small, brown, dried-up lump. He's now had it authenticated by an expert as being Beethoven's first movement.

Q: What's the difference between a podiatrist and a heavy-metal drummer?
A: The podiatrist bucks up your feet.

Q: What's the difference between a drum maestro and a drum novice?
A: Less than a week.

Q: What's the difference between a rock guitarist and a government bond?
A: The bond eventually matures and makes money.

Q: What's the difference between a puppy and a boy-band songwriter?
A: The puppy will eventually stop whining.

Q: What's the difference between dropping an anvil on an accordion and dropping one on an onion?
A: People cry when you squash an onion.

Q: How can you tell if a plane is full of sopranos?
A: When the engines stop, the whining carries on.

Q: Where do classical composers live?
A: In A Flat

Q: How does Liam Gallagher prefer his soup?
A: He likes a roll with it.

Q: What do you call a gorgeous woman on the arm of a trombonist?
A: A tattoo.

Q: What's the similarity between a drummer and a philosopher?
A: They both perceive time as an abstract concept.

It's terrible when the day comes when a singer realises he is no longer able to sing. It's even worse if the day comes and the singer doesn't realise it.

A singer is on stage. She sings her first song and the audience clap and shout, 'Once more!' She sings the song again and, again, the audience shout, 'Once more!' She sings it a third time and still the audience call for her to sing it again. 'Thank you,' she says, 'but why do you want to just hear the same thing again and again?' 'It's gradually getting better,' says a voice from the audience.

Tom tells Harry, 'I do backing vocals.' 'What?' says Harry. 'Are you a singer?' 'No,' says Tom. 'But you know when you hear that voice from a lorry saying "vehicle reversing"? That's me!'

My neighbours listen to some great music. Usually whether they want to or not.

I think the record companies have been doing a great job in the battle against piracy. Mainly they do it by only releasing music no one would ever want to steal.

THE SENIOR CHOIR INVITES ANY MEMBER OF THE CONGREGATION WHO ENJOYS SINNING TO JOIN THE CHOIR.

PARISH NOTICES

MYSTERIES

Q: How many thriller writers does it take to screw in a light bulb?
A: Two: One to screw the bulb almost all the way in and the other to give it a surprising twist right at the end.

MYSTERIOUS FLYING OBJECTS

Q: Why are men like UFOs?
A: You don't know where they've come from, you don't know what their mission is and you don't know what time they're going to take off again.

> Q: WHAT IS THE DEFINITION
> OF A MYTH?
> A: A FEMALE MOTH.
>
> SCHOOLBOY HOMEWORK ANSWER

NAILBITING

Nobby tells his friend, 'I finally managed to cure my son of biting his nails.' 'How did you manage that?' asks the friend. 'I knocked his teeth out,' says Nobby.

NAMES

It isn't until you have to think of a name for your child that you begin to realise just how many people you have met in your life to whom you've developed an enormous dislike.

Tom, Dick and Harry are talking about their children. 'My son was born on St George's Day,' says Tom, 'so I decided to call him George.' 'That's a coincidence,' says Harry, 'my son was born on St Valentine's Day, so I decided to call him Valentine.' 'That's a coincidence,' says Dick, 'because exactly the same thing happened with my son Pancake.'

The film producer Sam Goldwyn was told by a friend that he had named his son Sam. Goldwyn replied, 'Why did you do that? Every Tom, Dick and Harry is named Sam!'

Tom introduces Dick to his friend 'Einstein'. 'Why do you call him Einstein?' asks Dick. 'Is it because he's very clever.' 'No,' says Tom, 'it's because he gets drunk after just one pint of lager.'

When my brother was born, my mum and dad couldn't agree on a name for him. In the end they had to toss a coin to help them decide. And that's why my brother is called Tails.

The Court of Human Rights has ruled that it is illegal for parents to punish their children by changing their names to something stupid. The court was responding to a case brought against Mr and Mrs Peter Johnson of Spalding by their eight-year-old son, Master Davros Spanktablet the third.

I don't understand that song 'New York, New York (So Good They Named It Twice)'. Surely the thing that was so good they named it twice was 'twice'.

Texas Pete married a beautiful Navaho woman named 'Three Horses'. All she did was nag, nag, nag . . .

WHAT DO YOU CALL . . . ?

▶ **Q:** What do you call a man with his right arm in a shark's mouth?
A: Lefty.

▶ **Q:** What do you call a man with a seagull on his head?
A: Cliff.

▶ **Q:** What do you call a man with a plank on his head?
A: Edward.

▶ **Q:** What do you call a man with two planks on his head?
A: Edward Wood.

▶ **Q:** What do you call a man with three planks on his head?
A: Edward Woodward.

▶ **Q:** What do you call a man with four planks on his head?
A: I don't know but Edward Woodward would.

▶ **Q:** What do you call a woman with a tortoise on her head?
A: Shelley.

▶ **Q:** What do you call a woman tied up by the riverbank?
A: Maud.

▶ **Q:** What do you call a man who has a shovel on his head?
A: Doug.

▶ **Q:** What do you call a man without a shovel on his head?
A: Douglas.

▶ **Q:** What do you call a man who has no shins?
A: Tony.

▶ **Q:** What do you call a woman from Ireland who likes sitting out in the sunshine?
A: Pattie O'Furniture.

▶ **Q:** What do you call a man who's terrified of Christmas?
A: Noel Coward.

▶ **Q:** What do you call a man with a flat-bodied, cartilaginous fish on his head?
A: Ray.

▶ **Q:** What do you call a taxi driver in Ancient Egypt?
A: Tootandcomeout.

▶ **Q:** What do you call a guy in a hole in the ground?
A: Phil.

▶ **Q:** What do you call a man who has a nose but no body?
A: Nobody knows.

NAPKINS

Q: Which country was once run by napkins?
A: The Serviette Union.

NARCISSISM

I used to be a narcissist. But now look at me!

NATIVE AMERICANS

A Scottish woman moves to the USA and gets married to a Native American. Their first child is called Hawkeye the Noo.

Q: Why did the Native American put a hat on? **A:** To try and keep his wigwam.

NEIGHBOURHOOD WATCH

The Neighbourhood Watch has eight million members in the UK. They've proved to be a very effective organisation. Over the years, they've managed to convict all of their 16 million neighbours.

I can't understand it. My local neighbourhood watch has called a meeting to discuss some weird creepy guy who lives in the road, and everyone's been invited except me.

NEIGHBOURS

Simon goes to visit his neighbour, George, and finds his wife is in tears. 'George is dead,' she says. 'There was a fire at the local orphanage. George broke down the door and helped the orphans climb out, but then he had to run back inside and rescue the caretaker who was trapped in the attic. George was terribly burned but, once he got the caretaker out, he ran back into the flames to help an old nurse who was trapped under a fallen roof timber. He pulled it off her and threw her down to the firemen waiting outside, but when he jumped after her, he broke his neck. I was at his bedside at the hospital when he passed away.' 'Oh dear,' says Simon. 'Did you manage to speak to him before he died?' 'Yes. He said a few last words,' sobs the wife. 'Oh good,' says Simon. 'That's actually the reason I came round. Did he say anything about the lawnmower he'd borrowed off me?'

I've had the latest of a series of massive rows with my next-door neighbours. Apparently they've now arranged for a TV show called *Neighbours from Hell* to come and make a programme about our ongoing dispute. I was furious. I'd already signed a contract with *Neighbours at War* on the other channel to do exactly the same thing.

Bert gets up in the middle of the night to go to the toilet. As he passes the window, he notices a man climbing into his neighbour's garden. Then he sees his neighbour, holding a spade, come from the bushes behind the man. The neighbour uses the spade to whack the intruder on the head and carries on hitting him until he's dead. Bert then sees his neighbour dig a hole, bury the body and cover it over at the end of his garden. Bert goes back to bed looking stunned. 'You'll never believe what I just saw,' Bert tells his wife. 'That old git next door has still got my spade.'

I've got new neighbours and they are loud and obnoxious. Now I know how Canada feels.

NEWSPAPERS

Did you hear about the man who was arrested for having a wee in the middle of the newsagents? It was all over the papers.

Harry asks his teenage son Josh, 'Have you got a newspaper?' 'Of course I don't have a newspaper,' says Josh, 'I use my iPad for everything. Here. Try it.' Harry takes the iPad and goes into the next room. A moment later there is the sound of smashing and tinkling. Harry returns with the iPad in bits. 'Thanks, son,' says Harry. 'That fly never knew what hit it.'

One of the most astonishing things about the world is that the amount of news that occurs every day always fits exactly into the same-sized newspaper.

I phoned the newspaper to check how much it was to advertise in the classifieds. They said it's £2 per inch. It's going to cost me a bomb! I'm selling a 40-foot ladder.

The only time when people stop to consider if stories in the newspaper seem genuinely plausible or not is April Fool's Day.

NOAH

If Noah took two of every animal on to the Ark, does that mean he also took two woodworms with him? And if he did, how did he keep the Ark from sinking?

Just before the Flood, God phones Noah and tells him there's been a change of plan. 'Forget about the two of every kind of animal. Just concentrate on saving all the carp.' 'That's a lot of carp,' says Noah. 'There must be tens of thousands of them. I'll have to add more tanks. They're going to be stacked up pretty high.' 'That's right,' says God. 'I want you to build a Multi-Storey Carp Ark.'

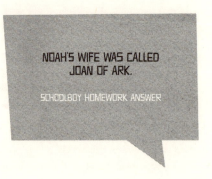

NOAH'S WIFE WAS CALLED JOAN OF ARK.

SCHOOLBOY HOMEWORK ANSWER

NOISE

Norman has worked for years in a noisy garage. He goes to the doctor and says, 'My work has affected my hearing so badly, I can't even hear myself fart any more.' The doctor gives him some tablets. 'Will these improve my hearing?' asks Norman. 'No,' says the doctor, 'but they will make your farts much, much louder.'

NON-CONFORMITY

Isn't it strange how all the non-conformists look exactly the same?

NORTH KOREA

I asked a friend in North Korea what it was like to live in that country. He said he couldn't complain.

NORTH POLE

Farmer Giles buys an area of land at the North Pole. He wants to get into the frozen-pea business and he thought this would be the best place to grow them.

NORTHERN IRELAND

The Prime Minister goes on a visit to Northern Ireland. A resident asks him, 'What do you think of County Down.' 'I like it,' says the Prime Minister, 'but, to be honest, it's never been the same since Carol Vorderman left.'

NOSES

A nose walks into a bar. The barman says, 'I can't serve you, you're off your face!'

NOSTALGIA

We shouldn't waste our time reliving the past. We should all spend it worrying about the future.

NUDITY

A Catholic priest and an Anglican vicar are at the gym. At the end of their session they are both in the shower when the fire alarm goes off. The priest and the vicar both have to run out of the gym stark naked. When the all-clear sounds, they have to go back through the main entrance still completely naked. As they pass through the crowds, the priest covers his private parts with his hands while the vicar holds his hands over his face. 'Why are you doing that?' asks the priest. 'Why not cover your privates like I'm doing?' 'I thought about that,' says the vicar, 'but I concluded most people here would recognise me by my face.'

Dave's mum writes and asks him to send a recent picture of himself. Unfortunately, the only one he has was taken on holiday at a nudist colony. So he takes a copy of the picture, cuts it in half, puts the top half in an envelope and sends it to his mum. A few days later he gets another letter saying the picture was so lovely that his grandmother wants a copy. He gets another copy of the picture, cuts it in half but then accidentally puts the bottom half of the picture in the envelope. A few days later, he gets a letter from his granny saying, 'Thank you for the lovely picture. However, I think you should stop having your hair permed like that as it makes your nose look too long.'

Bernice wants to go on a nudist holiday. Her husband is a bit shy about the idea, so to get some practice she suggests he does some nude sunbathing in their back garden. 'I can't do that,' protests the husband. 'What if the neighbours see me naked?' 'In that case,' says Bernice, 'they'll definitely know I married you for your money.'

If God had intended for me to run around naked, he would have made my skin a bit closer fitting.

Beware naturists! Your end is in sight.

NUISANCE PHONE CALLS

Nobby tells Trevor, 'I've been having a lot of problems with nuisance phone calls recently.' 'Are they about PPI?' asks Trevor. 'No,' says Nobby, 'usually it's this woman saying, "I thought you were going to be home from the pub three hours ago!"'

NURSING HOMES

I'm looking for a new nursing home for my mother. Ideally, what I need is one without phones or access to a letterbox.

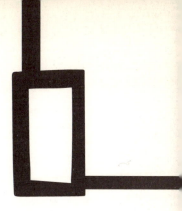

OBESITY

Nora is an exceptionally large lady. The other day she fell over and managed to rock herself to sleep before she could get up again.

Norman's doctor told him, 'I don't want to offend you by saying you're overweight, but if I had to choose five of my most obese patients, you would be three of them.'

Norman's wife Elsie fell down the stairs last night. 'Quick!' he shouted. 'It sounds as though *Eastenders* has started early!'

Everyone agrees, Gertrude is a big-hearted girl. And not only that, she's got the hips to match.

Vera has been in the bathroom for hours getting ready to go out. Finally, she opens the door and asks Harry, 'Tell me honestly, love. Do I look fat in this?' 'Well, a bit,' says Harry. 'But to be fair, it is quite a small bathroom.'

Norman thinks he may have put on weight. Now when he gets in the bath, the water in the toilet rises.

Norman is very overweight. He's got the only car in town that has stretch marks.

Harry's mother-in-law is a large and slow-moving woman. She got run over in the town centre last week. The driver said he would have tried going round her, but he didn't think he had enough petrol.

Barry is very overweight, so he decided to take up horse riding to help him shed a few pounds. After two weeks, he'd lost seven pounds but the horse was down five stone.

A man goes into a bar and sees a woman dancing on a table. 'Wow!' he says. 'Fantastic legs!' 'Do you really think so?' says the woman. 'Definitely,' says the man. 'Most tables would have collapsed under that weight.'

Elsie asks Norman, 'Why are you always talking behind my back?' 'Sorry, love,' says Norman, 'But by the time I get round the front, I've forgotten what I was going to say.'

Norman's doctor tells him, 'I'm afraid to tell you that you are morbidly obese.' 'That's terrible news,' says Norman. 'As if I didn't have enough on my plate!'

According to the latest study there are 10,000,000 overweight people in the country and 5,000,000 extremely overweight people. Obviously though, those are just round figures.

Old Nora is very overweight and very bossy. One day she was on a bus and had just got comfortable in her seat when she saw that the only standing passengers were three middle-aged women. She turned to the man sitting next to her and said, 'If you were a gentleman, you'd get up and let one of those women sit down.' 'If you were a lady,' said the man, 'you'd get up and let all three of them sit down.'

A fat lady is looking for a way to cross a busy road. She spots a boy scout on the other side and calls out, 'Hey. Can you see me across the road?' The scout calls back, 'Lady, I could see you from the edge of town.'

Norman's doctor examines him and says, 'You're quite overweight.' 'What should I do?' says Norman. 'Don't eat anything fatty,' says the doctor. 'You mean like cake or biscuits,' asks Norman. 'No,' says the doctor. 'I'll tell you once again – Fatty, don't eat anything!'

YOUR MUM IS SO FAT . . .

▶ Your mum is so fat, she has to put her belt on with a boomerang.

▶ Your mum is so big, her backside has to have its own Member of Parliament.

▶ Your mum is so fat, she had to apply for planning permission to sit down.

▶ Your mum is so fat, her school photo was an aerial shot.

▶ Your mum is so fat, when she goes out in heels, she comes home in flip-flops.

▶ Your mum is so fat, when she rang Weightwatchers to register they said, 'We want your weight not your phone number'.

▶ Your mum is so fat, she can go on holiday just by rolling over.

▶ Your mum is so fat, she has to use a toilet brush to clean out her bellybutton.

▶ Your mum is so fat, she has to put on her lipstick with a paint-roller.

▶ Your mum is so fat, she went out for dinner and got a group discount.

▶ Your mum is so fat, she sat on some memory foam and it forgot.

▶ Your mum is so fat, whenever she turns around they throw a welcome-home party.

▶ Your mum is so fat, it took five UFOs to abduct her.

▶ Your mum is so fat, you have to grease the door frame and hold a fairy cake on the other side just to get her through.

OBVIOUSNESS

Q: What do you call a person who points out the obvious?
A: A person who points out the obvious.

OCELOTS

Q: How do you titillate an ocelot?
A: You oscillate its tit a lot!

OCTOPI

Susan crossed a female octopus with a bull. Now she has a cow that can milk itself.

OINTMENT

A man goes to the doctor and says, 'Doctor, this ointment you gave me keeps making my arm smart. What should I do?' 'You could try rubbing some on your head,' says the doctor.

OMNISCIENCE

Q: What's the opposite of 'omniscient'?
A: I don't know at all.

ONLINE SECURITY

Nobby gets a new computer but has difficulty getting it working. 'I can't understand it,' he says, 'I'm putting in exactly the same password it shows in the instruction book.' 'What password is that?' asks his wife. 'Asterisk, asterisk, asterisk, asterisk!' says Nobby.

As a joke, Freddy tried to use the phrase 'mypenis' as his computer password, but it turned out it wasn't long enough.

I could never remember my computer password, so I changed it to 'incorrect'. Now if I ever forget, it reminds me: 'Your password is incorrect'.

ONLINE SHOPPING

Today is the birthday of the inventor of online shopping. I think we should all wish him Many Happy Returns.

Harry received a spam email for penis enlargement. He sent off a cheque for £100 and they sent him back a magnifying glass.

Henrietta bought a 40-year-old box of After Eights on eBay for £500. They were worth so much because they were still in mint condition.

Vernon always gets really annoyed when he buys something online and then finds exactly the same item being sold on a different site for a fraction of the price. He was particularly cross when it happened just after he'd married his Filipino wife.

Apparently the Pope was the first person to buy things off the internet. He used to pay for them using his papal account.

Nobby is doing some online shopping. He finds a horse being offered at a bargain price so he clicks the option 'Add to cart'.

Nobby's wife keeps going on eBay. So far, he says he's not had any bids on her.

Last night I went on eBay and bought 1,000 bottles of Tippex. That was a big mistake.

I just sold my homing pigeon on eBay. That's the 28th time this year.

OPEN-MINDEDNESS

If someone tells you to be open-minded, it's usually code for 'Why don't you agree with me?'

OPTIMISM AND PESSIMISM

Q: How many optimists does it take to change a light bulb?
A: None; if you just wait patiently a little longer the power is sure to come back on.

What's the difference between a pessimist and an optimist? A pessimist says, 'Things are terrible. They can't possibly get any worse.' And an optimist says, 'I think they can!'

Yesterday I wrote a short poem about being over-optimistic. I reckon it's definitely going to make me a million pounds.

A pessimist is a person who has had to listen to too many optimists.

Harry is an eternal pessimist. His definition of a good day is one when you wake up and no one has drawn a chalk outline around your body.

Mr and Mrs Smith have two twin boys, Kevin and Larry. Kevin is an eternal optimist, while Larry is a complete pessimist. On Christmas morning, Mr Smith fills Larry's room with all the latest toys and games. Kevin's room, on the other hand, is filled with horse manure. On Christmas morning, the boys wake up and Mr Smith finds Larry looking very sad. 'What's the matter?' asks Dad. 'I've got all these new toys and games for Christmas,' says Larry, 'but I'm really depressed. How am I ever going to read all the instruction manuals and learn to work them? And how am I going to find enough batteries to go in them? And even if I do, they're all bound to get broken and spoiled!' Mr Smith then goes next door to Kevin's room and finds him dancing for joy and digging around in his pile of horse manure. 'Why are you so happy with your present?' asks Dad. 'Because,' says Kevin, 'there's got to be a pony in here somewhere!'

ORGAN DONATION

When he was at the supermarket yesterday, Harry accidentally handed over his organ donor card instead of his loyalty card. He only realised his mistake when two shelf-stackers dragged him into the cold room and tried to remove his kidneys.

ORGANS

A little old lady plays the organ in the local church. One afternoon, the vicar comes to visit her and she sits him down in the front room next to her pride and joy, her own personal Hammond organ. As he is sipping his tea, the vicar notices a bowl of water with a condom floating in it has been placed on top of the organ. 'What in heaven's name is that?' asks the vicar. 'Oh. I found it in the park,' says the little old lady. 'The instructions said that if I placed it on the organ and kept it wet, it would prevent the spread of disease. And it's really worked. I haven't had a cold all winter.'

ORGIES

Q: Why don't polite people like orgies?
A: Writing all the thank-you letters afterwards takes too much time.

ORIGAMI

Norman used to be head of a business specialising in origami, but after a while it folded.

The finals of the 'International Origami Championships' are on TV tonight. But they're only available on paper view.

ORIGINS

A man is answering questions for a survey. 'Where were you born?' asks the interviewer. 'Manchester,' says the man. 'Yes. But which part?' asks the interviewer. 'All of me,' says the man.

PAIN

For eons, men and women have argued over which is more painful: being kicked in the gonads, or giving birth. The answer is however obvious. A year after giving birth, a woman will often say, 'Why don't we have another baby?' No man, however, has ever gone back to anyone, a year later, to say, 'I'll tell you what, Dave, I don't half fancy having you kick me in the nuts again.'

PAINT

A man comes out of Buckingham Palace covered in bits of wallpaper and emulsion. A policeman says, 'What happened to you?' 'I've just been decorated by the Queen,' says the man.

PANDAS

Did you hear about the Rock and Roll Panda? Apparently it only eats a 'Wop bop a lop bamboo'.

PANTO

Last night, the actor playing the lead in our local theatre's production of Aladdin was assaulted live on stage last night. To be fair, the audience did try to warn him.

PARACHUTES AND SKYDIVING

Q: What's the hardest part of skydiving? **A:** The ground.

Strictly speaking, a parachute is not really necessary if you want to go skydiving. A parachute is only necessary if you want to go skydiving again afterwards.

If you're skydiving and your parachute and reserve parachute fail to open, don't worry too much. You've still got all of the rest of your life to enjoy the experience.

A man is learning to skydive. His instructor takes him up in a plane and tells him, 'You jump out first then I'll come after you and we'll parachute down together.' The man jumps out of the plane and looks above to see his instructor jumping out after him. The man pulls his rip-cord and his parachute opens. He looks up and sees his instructor pull his rip-cord. The instructor's parachute fails to open and the man watches him plummet past. 'So that's the way it is, is it?!' says the man, undoing the straps of his parachute. 'Well, if he wants a race, I'll give him a flippin' race!'

Just because nobody complains doesn't mean all parachutes are perfect.

PARENTING

It's not easy being a mother. If it was, dads would do it.

A main part of the job description for being a dad is waiting in the car.

I had a very fond father, he was always telling me he loved me. It later turned out he loved everyone. He was on Prozac.

If you notice that all your kid's crayons come from 'Wetherspoons' it might be time to reconsider your approach to parenting.

Harry says his children treat him like he's God. They only ever talk to him when they want something.

When I was a little boy my parents kept moving house a lot. Usually though I managed to find them again.

Barry's girlfriend keeps telling him that she thinks he'll make a brilliant father one day. He doesn't believe her. Even worse, neither do their children.

PARROTS

A woman goes into a pet shop and sees a parrot. The parrot looks at her and says, 'Hello, missus. Blimey, you're ugly!' The woman is furious and storms out of the shop. The next day, she passes the pet shop again and the parrot is by the door. It sees her and says, 'Hello, missus. Blimey, you're ugly!' On her way home later that day, the parrot sees her again and says, 'Hello, missus. Blimey, you're ugly!' The woman has now had enough and goes in to complain in the strongest possible terms to the pet shop owner. 'If that bird ever uses those words again,' she says, 'I will sue the shop and have that parrot put down!' The shop owner promises that the parrot will never insult her like this again. The next day the woman passes the pet shop again. The parrot sees her and says, 'Hello, missus!' The woman stops and gives the bird an icy stare. 'What?' she demands. The bird pauses, struts back and forth on its perch then says, '*You* know . . .'

Larry is sitting in first class on a passenger jet and finds a parrot on the seat next to him. He calls the stewardess over to order a cup of coffee, but the parrot beats him to it and shouts, 'Give me a gin and tonic, fatso. And make it snappy!' The stewardess hurries away and returns with the parrot's drink. Larry is about to ask for a coffee again, when the parrot shouts, 'Hey, butt-breath. Get me some freaking peanuts. Go on, move that fat backside.' Again the stewardess hurries away and quickly returns with a bag of nuts. Once more, Larry opens his mouth to ask for a cup of coffee, but the parrot shouts, 'Doofus! I need a napkin with this drink. D'you think I'm some kind of pig, you moron?' The stewardess is about to hurry away when Larry says, 'Excuse me, but what do I have to do to get a goddam coffee around here?' At this, the stewardess freaks out, opens the emergency door and tips Larry and the parrot into the wide blue yonder. As they free-fall to the ground, the parrot looks at Larry and says, 'Well, that was pretty rude. You've got a lot of balls for a guy who can't fly.'

Big Gavin leads such a dodgy lifestyle, his parrot has managed to learn the phrase, 'Open up, Police!'

Barry has an idea to drive pet owners crazy. He goes into pet shops and tries to teach the parrots to say, 'Help, they've turned me into a parrot!'

The government has issued a warning about the danger of bird flu from parrots. If you hear someone go 'Atishoo!' there is no need for concern. If you hear someone go 'Atish-oo's a pretty boy then!' you should run like hell!

The Reverend Farquhar visits an elderly lady who is one of his new parishioners. She invites him into her drawing room and shows him a large cage containing a parrot. The parrot has strings tied to each of its legs. 'Listen to this,' says the old lady. She pulls the string on the right leg and the parrot starts to recite the Lord's Prayer. Then she pulls on the left string and the parrot starts to recite the Book of Genesis. 'Good heavens,' says the vicar. 'I wonder what would happen if you tugged both strings at once?' 'What d'you think would happen?' says the parrot. 'I'd fall off my flipping perch!'

Jane buys a parrot from a pet shop. Unfortunately, the parrot's previous owner used to be a madam in a brothel and the parrot has picked up some disgraceful language. As soon as Jane uncovers its cage, the parrot says, 'Well, well, a new madam and a new brothel.' 'I'm not a madam and this is not a brothel,' says Jane. Jane's teenage daughters walks in at this moment and the parrot says, 'Well, well, a new madam, a new brothel and new girls.' 'These are not working girls,' says Jane. 'These are respectable young ladies.' At that moment, Jane's husband walks in. The parrot says, 'Well, well, a new madam, a new brothel and new girls, but the same old customers. How y'doing, Mike?'

PARTIES

It was only when my mum and dad threw a surprise party for my brother's birthday that I finally realised that he was their favourite twin.

Norman arrives at a party at his next-door neighbour's house. 'I haven't brought any beer with me,' he says, 'because I couldn't be bothered walking all the way to the shop. Sorry about that. I'm a bit lazy.' 'Yes,' says his next-door neighbour. 'Your taxi driver just told me the same thing.'

A boy says to a girl, 'Are you the one I was snogging at the party last night?' 'I'm not sure,' says the girl. 'What time were you there?'

I'm a big fan of 1970s music. To indulge my passion I put up a marquee in my back garden every November, fill it with glitter-balls and flashing lights and spend the next few months boogying out there to funky music. It's the winter of my disco tent.

PAST, PRESENT AND FUTURE

The past, present and future walk into a bar. It was extremely tense in there.

PEACE

> THE PEACEMAKING MEETING SCHEDULED FOR TODAY HAS BEEN CANCELLED DUE TO A CONFLICT.

PARISH NOTICES

PEDANTRY

I'm getting sick of being told I'm pedantic. If I had a penny for every time I've been told I'm pedantic, I'd have 67 pounds and 34 pence.

A man wants to visit the library at his local university. He asks a student, 'Do you know where the library's at?' 'Yes,' says the student, 'But, don't you know, you're not supposed to end a sentence with a preposition like "at"?' 'OK,' says the man, 'let me put it another way. Do you know where the library's at, you pedantic twerp?'

PENGUINS

Two penguins walk into a bar. Which is pretty stupid of them. Surely the second one should have seen it.

A penguin walks into a bar, goes to the counter, and asks the bartender, 'Have you seen my brother?' The bartender says, 'I don't know. What does he look like?'

PENISES

Yesterday Barry discovered two interesting facts about himself. Firstly, his willy is exactly the same length as two of those little pens they have in his local branch of Argos. Secondly, he is no longer welcome in his local branch of Argos.

Larry goes to see a medical specialist about an embarrassing problem. 'I have a very petite penis,' says Larry. 'So promise not to laugh when you see it. I'm very sensitive about it.' The doctor promises, but when Larry drops his trousers the doctor almost has a fit of the giggles at the size of it. 'What seems to be the matter with it?' asks the doctor, trying to keep a straight face. Larry says, 'It's swollen.'

A man wakes up in a hospital and a doctor tells him that he's been involved in a terrible accident which has resulted in the loss of his penis. 'But don't worry,' says the doctor, 'you've got health insurance that will pay £9,000 that you can put towards a replacement penis. But these artificial penises don't come cheap. They work out around £1,000 per inch. So you should have a word with your wife to decide what sort of penis you both feel appropriate.' After ten minutes the man has discussed the matter with his wife. 'So what have you decided?' asks the doctor. 'We're getting granite worktops in the kitchen,' says the man.

Harry decides to have a penis extension. It costs thousands and his house looks pretty weird now.

Did you hear the joke about my penis? To be honest, it's a bit too long.

A survey asked 1,000 women what they would do if they had a penis for a day. The majority of them replied: 'Get a pay rise.'

Granddad wanders into the living room with his willy hanging out covered in shoe polish. He hadn't quite heard what we said when we said it was the night when we all had to turn our clocks back.

The government is thinking of introducing a penis tax based on length. They figure it's the only tax men will want to overpay.

" MY FINGERS ARE LONG AND BEAUTIFUL, AS, IT HAS BEEN WELL BEEN DOCUMENTED, ARE VARIOUS OTHER PARTS OF MY BODY.

DONALD TRUMP "

PENS AND PENCILS

Did you hear the joke about the blunt pencil? I couldn't see any point in it myself.

Teacher: 'Who were the first people to write with fountain pens?' Little Johnny: 'The Incas.'

My pencil isn't prone to making Freudian slips, but my penis.

PEOPLE

Some people bring happiness wherever they go. Others bring happiness whenever they go.

Some people are like Slinkys. Not very interesting until you push them downstairs.

PERFUME

It's always embarrassing when you compliment a woman on her unusual perfume — and she tells you she isn't wearing any.

Tom says he's got some new aftershave that smells like fresh breadcrumbs. Apparently the birds all love it.

PERSONAL SMELLS

You know what it's like when you're at home with the family and you fart but you think you'll get away with blaming it on the dog. But then the dog looks at you accusingly and everyone knows the truth. Something very similar happened to me yesterday. Unfortunately, I was in the elephant house at the zoo at the time.

If you've got bad breath, look on the bright side. It's better than no breath at all.

You know you have a body odour problem when the guys from the sewage works won't sit next to you on the bus.

PERVERSION

Barry is looking for something in his mum's bedroom when he looks in a drawer and finds a mask, handcuffs and a whip. 'Wow!' says Barry. 'I can't believe it! My mum must be a superhero!'

Nobby and Norma are flying off on holiday and start talking about kinky things they would like to try while they're away together. Norma tells Nobby she's always fantasised about being handcuffed. So Nobby fixes it for her by slipping a bag of drugs in her hand luggage.

Glenda decides to spice up her love-life. She puts on a negligee, greets her husband at the front door and hands him a pair of handcuffs. She says, 'Put these on me, then do whatever you want.' So he cuffs her to the radiator and goes to watch a football match.

I was talking to a woman about my interest in pet birds when she suddenly slapped me. All I did was ask if she wanted to come back to my place to have a look at the 12 finches I've got.

PETS

A man goes into his local pet shop and asks, 'Do you have any chameleons here?' 'To be honest,' says the manager, 'I'm not entirely sure.'

Harry reads that many pet owners find it comforting to have their pets sleep on the bed with them. He tries it with his goldfish, but it doesn't end well.

A drunk walks into a pet store and buys a tortoise. An hour later he comes back and buys another. An hour after that, he comes back again and buys a third. The next time he comes in, he reels over to the enclosure where the tortoises are kept and finds it's empty. He looks around in disappointment and confusion until the store owner comes and asks what he's looking for. 'You'll probably think I'm being greedy,' says the drunk. 'But I'm feeling a bit peckish again. Do you have any more of your delicious crusty meat pies?'

Freddie sees a competition for pet canaries – the best singing canary will win £1,000. Freddie doesn't have a canary but he does have a finch that sings beautifully. So he buys a can of yellow paint and covers the bird from head to foot. Sadly the finch becomes ill and Freddie takes it to the vet, where it dies. 'Was it the paint that killed it?' asks Freddie. 'Probably,' says the vet. 'But the fact you sanded it down between coats didn't help either.'

Little Toby asks his dad if his beloved pet tortoise will live forever. 'I'm afraid not, son,' says Dad. 'But don't be too upset because, when he dies, he will go to tortoise heaven and we will celebrate his passing with a lovely big party. All your friends can come round and we'll have loads of cake and jelly.' 'Ooo!' says Toby. 'I'll tell you what, can we just kill him now?'

> QUESTION MASTER: NAME A WAY YOU WOULD TREAT A PET LIKE A HUMAN. CONTESTANT: TAKE IT TO THE VET.
>
> FAMILY FEUD

Nobby broke into the local pet shop last night. Apparently he stole a rabbit before making a run for it.

An old man goes to buy a pet to provide himself with some company. He goes to the pet shop and looks at the dogs but they all seem too lively. 'I've got just the thing for you,' says the pet shop owner. 'It's a special breed of tortoise. It will do anything a dog will do and it even talks.' The old man is very pleased and takes the tortoise home. Sure enough, he finds he is able to engage the tortoise in simple conversation. He is still not convinced, however, that the tortoise can do everything a dog could do, so he takes the tortoise to the front door and says, 'Tortoise, go down to the newsagent's and get my paper for me.' Months go by and the tortoise does not return. The man is furious and writes a letter to the pet shop owner about his evidently false claim that the tortoise would do anything a dog would do. On his way to the letterbox the old man finds the tortoise not far from his garden gate. 'What's going on?' says the old man. 'I sent you out for my paper six months ago!' 'Hey!' says the tortoise. 'If you're going to be like that about it, I won't bother going at all!'

Vernon has a worm for a pet. He doesn't know if it's male or female so he calls out a worm-sexer to look at it. 'How can we tell if it's a male worm or a female worm?' asks Vernon. 'Simple,' says the worm-sexer. 'You tickle it in the middle.' 'Then what?' asks Vernon. 'If he laughs, it's a male worm,' says the worm-sexer. 'And if she laughs, it's a female worm.'

PHILOSOPHY

Jason has a first-class degree in philosophy. He spends each day locked in deep thought about what it means to be unemployed.

Q: What's the difference between a philosopher and an engineer?
A: About £50,000 a year.

Q: How many philosophers does it take to change a light bulb?
A: Three. One to change it and two to stand around arguing whether the light bulb exists or not.

Q: How many Marxists does it take to change a light bulb?
A: None. The light bulb contains the seeds of its own revolution.

PHONES

I didn't realise just how good I must be on the phone until they told me that my call to customer service might be used for training purposes.

A woman gets an obscene phone call. 'Hello,' says a voice, 'can you guess what I'm holding in my hand?' 'No thanks,' says the woman, 'if you can hold it in just one hand, it's of no interest to me.'

Phil is doing his shift at Directory Enquiries when he hears the man on the other end of the line doing lots of heavy breathing. 'I hope you're not some kind of pervert,' says Phil. 'No,' says the man. 'I'm calling from a phone box, only I haven't got a paper and pen, so I'm fogging up the glass to write the number with my finger.'

A couple are in bed when the phone rings. The husband answers and, after a moment, hangs up. 'I can't believe it,' he says, 'that's the third time this week someone's phoned us up thinking we're the coastguard.' 'What do you mean?' asks his wife. 'It's some stupid man,' says the husband. 'He keeps ringing to ask if the coast is clear.'

Harry has put his friend Richard on speed dial on his phone. He calls it his 'get Rich quick' scheme.

> "MY PHONE WILL RING AT TWO IN THE MORNING, AND MY WIFE'LL LOOK AT ME AND GO, 'WHO'S THAT CALLING AT THIS TIME?' I DON'T KNOW! IF I KNEW THAT WE WOULDN'T NEED THE BLOODY PHONE!"
>
> LEE EVANS

> QUESTION MASTER: NAME A PART OF THE TELEPHONE.
> CONTESTANT: THE BOTTOM PART.
>
> FAMILY FEUD

Barry's phone rings at three o'clock in the morning. 'Hello,' says Barry. 'Hello,' says a voice, 'is that Julie?' 'No,' says Barry, 'I think you've got the wrong number.' 'Oh dear,' says the voice, 'I'm sorry to have troubled you.' 'Don't worry,' says Barry, 'I had to get up anyway because the phone was ringing.'

PHOTOGRAPHY

In 1969, Neil Armstrong went to the moon and took five photographs. These days people do that every time they make cheese on toast.

Glamour-puss Wendy is having her photograph taken by a professional photographer. He asks her to open her shirt a little bit and then to slip the shirt half off, then to go completely topless. Before Wendy realises what's happening, the photographer has talked her into having her picture taken completely nude. Everyone agreed that it completely ruined her niece's wedding.

It's always embarrassing when you drop your wallet and a photo of your wife with nothing on falls out. I was talking to a friend the other day and exactly that happened. He dropped his wallet and out fell a picture of my wife with nothing on.

Edna goes to a photographer with a picture of her late husband wearing a hat. 'I always hated that hat,' she says. 'I'd rather see him without it. Can you airbrush it out?' 'No problem,' says the photographer. 'I just need to know his hair colour so I can fill in the space when it's gone.' 'Why d'you need to ask me that?' says Edna. 'You'll be able to see for yourself when you take the trilby off.'

PHYSIQUE

George has the body of a god. Unfortunately, it's Buddha.

PIANO TUNING

Dick calls a piano tuner out to look at his piano. The piano tuner works away all day but nevertheless his bill only comes to £3. 'Is that all?' asks Dick. 'You spent all day tuning my piano, and yet you only charge £3?' 'Pardon?' says the piano tuner.

A piano tuner turns up at Fred's house. 'What's up?' says Fred. 'I didn't call for a piano tuner.' 'You didn't,' says the piano tuner. 'Your neighbour did.'

PIGEONS

During the First World War a platoon of British soldiers are at the front waiting for orders which are being sent to them by carrier pigeon. They see the pigeon approaching with their message, but there's a shot and the bird falls into no-man's land. The captain says, 'I need a volunteer to go out there, find the pigeon and get the message.' One soldier volunteers, climbs out of the trench and runs off into a hail of bullets and explosions. His comrades think he has no chance of finding the pigeon and surviving his mission but, two hours later, he returns covered in dirt and blood. The captain asks, 'Did you find the pigeon?' 'I did, sir,' says the man. 'Did the pigeon have a message for us?' asks the captain. 'Yes it did, sir,' says the man. 'Excellent,' says the captain, 'so what was the message?' 'Coooooo!' says the soldier. 'Cooooooo!'

Larry has been trying to breed a new type of military carrier pigeon. Recently he's been trying to cross a pigeon with a woodpecker. He wants a bird that will deliver vital messages, but knock first.

My next-door neighbour told me he'd lost his homing pigeon. 'I don't mean to be pedantic,' I told him, 'but the official term for what you've lost is a pigeon.'

PILES

Vernon goes to the doctor to complain. 'I didn't like that pile cream you gave me last week,' says Vernon, 'I tried putting it on, and I got a very nasty reaction.' 'Oh dear,' says the doctor, 'exactly whereabouts did you apply it?' 'On the bus on the way home,' says Vernon.

A man walks into a chemist's in South Yorkshire to ask for an ointment for his piles. 'Does tha' sell arse cream?' asks the man. 'Aye, lad, we do,' says the chemist. 'D'you want a Magnum or a Cornetto?'

PIRATES

A pirate walks into a bar and the barman says, 'What's happened to you? You didn't used to have that wooden leg.' 'I know,' says the pirate, 'but I was in a battle and I got hit with a cannon ball.' 'And what about your hand?' says the barman. 'You didn't used to have the hook.' 'I know,' says the pirate, 'but then I was in a sword fight and my hand was cut off.' 'But what about your eye?' says the barman. 'You didn't used to have that patch.' 'I know,' says the pirate. 'But then I set sail again and a flock of birds flew over and one of them pooped straight in my eye.' 'Really?' says the barman. 'But you can't have lost your eye just from that.' 'No, I didn't,' says the pirate, 'but, unfortunately, it was my first day with the hook.'

I bought a copy of *Pirates of the Caribbean* on DVD and noticed there was a warning about piracy on the box. Surely the clue was in the title.

Have you heard about the dyslexic pirate? Everywhere he went, he had a carrot sitting on his shoulder!

Q: What certificate did they give the new pirate movie?
A: Arrrrrr.

Q: What musical instrument do pirates like best?
A: The arrrrrr-monica.

Q: What did the pirate say on his 80th birthday?
A: Aye, matey.

Q: What is a pirate's favourite letter of the alphabet?
A: Ye'd think it be 'R', but a pirate's first love will always be the 'C'.

Q: How much does a pirate pay for his earrings?
A: A buccaneer.

Q: What's a pirate's least favourite letter?
A: Dear sir, we are writing to you because we have evidence you have been violating copyright . . .

PLAGIARISM

Ed announces that he has just invented a brand-new word to be added to the English language. 'What is it?' asks Josh. 'Plagiarism,' says Ed.

PLATONIC RELATIONSHIPS

Jackie is worried about her friend Phyllis's affair with an 18-year-old toy-boy. 'Don't worry. It's a platonic relationship,' says Phyllis. 'How do you work that out?' asks Jackie. 'Well,' says Jackie, 'it's play for him, and a tonic for me.'

PLUMBERS

George the plumber knocks on the door of a house. A woman answers and George says, 'Mrs Smith? I've come about your leaking mains pipe.' 'I'm afraid they don't live here any more,' says the woman. 'The Smiths moved out about three months ago.' 'Typical,' says George. 'They call you out on an emergency, then when you turn up, they haven't bothered waiting in for you.'

Have you heard the joke about the plumber? I'll tell you it three weeks on Tuesday some time between 1 and 8pm.

POACHING

A gamekeeper catches a poacher at the side of the lake. 'I've got you!' says the gamekeeper. 'I've caught you red-handed plucking that bird!' 'You're wrong,' says the poacher, swiftly throwing the bird in the lake, 'that duck was my friend.' 'Oh yes?' says the gamekeeper. 'So why have I caught you standing in the middle of a pile of feathers?' 'My friend wanted to go for a swim in the lake,' says the poacher, 'so I said I'd mind his clothes for him!'

POISONING

Harry makes himself dinner and ends up in A&E with a terrible stomach problem. The doctor comes and tells him, 'We've got the results of your tests back and I'm afraid you're going to have to stay in hospital. It seems that what you thought was an onion was in fact a daffodil bulb. But don't worry! The good news is – you should be out in the spring!'

POLAR EXPLORATION

Gavin is an explorer who has travelled to both the Arctic and the Antarctic. Sometimes he is insanely proud of his achievement. Other times he gets very depressed about his life on the ice. His doctor suspects he may be bipolar.

POLICE INVESTIGATIONS

Billy-Bob wants to join the local police department and goes in for an interview. 'First we got to check your IQ,' says the Police Chief. 'What's one and one?' Billy-Bob says, 'Eleven.' 'OK,' says the Chief. 'What's the two days of the week that start with the letter T?' Billy-Bob says, 'Today and tomorrow.' 'OK,' says the Chief. 'Last question. Who shot JR?' 'Gee,' says Billy-Bob. 'That's hard. Can I think about it?' 'Sure,' says the Chief. 'You do that while I get a coffee.' Billy-Bob is left scratching his head when his mother calls his mobile to see how he's getting on. 'I'm doing good, Momma,' he says. 'I ain't been here more than an hour and I'm already working on a murder case.'

Nobby is called in for questioning by the police. 'Where were you between five and eleven?' asks the policeman. 'Where do you think I was?' says Nobby. 'At primary school.'

Barry hears a knock at the door and finds a policeman standing there with a pencil and a piece of thin paper. 'I was hoping you might be able to help me trace someone,' says the policeman.

I just saw a member of the local police force rolling around on the ground, howling like a dog and stripping off in the town square. Honestly, it was just PC gone mad.

For professional reasons, Big Tony always keeps his radio tuned to the police frequency; in fact, he's such an avid listener, he once committed a crime just so he could dedicate it to his girlfriend.

Q: What did the policeman say to his stomach? **A:** You are under a vest.

POLITICS

Q: What's the difference between a democratic and a feudal system?
A: In a democracy your vote counts; under a feudal system your count votes.

In the old days, we had empires ruled by emperors and kingdoms ruled by kings. These days, we have countries.

Q: What's the difference between a politician and a sack of fertiliser?
A: The sack.

To err may be human. But to blame someone else is politics.

The veteran left-wing MP Dennis Skinner once said in the House of Commons, 'Half the Tories opposite are crooks!' The Speaker of the House urged him to retract. So he said, 'OK, half the Tories opposite aren't crooks.'

A canvasser comes to Harry's door during the election. 'What do you think of the two candidates?' asks the canvasser. 'Well, put it this way,' says Harry, 'I'm glad only one of them can get in.'

Politicians may be OK but they shouldn't get involved in things they don't really understand. Like having to do a decent day's work for a living.

POLLUTION

Dick is appalled by the amount of pollution overtaking the world. The other day he found a load of dead fish lying in a pool of oil. Mind you, he had just opened a can of sardines.

POPULARITY

A man complains to his wife, 'Nobody loves me. Nobody cares about. Everybody hates me.' 'That's not true at all,' says his wife, 'some people haven't met you.'

Q: When George Osborne went to the London Olympics, why did 80,000 people start booing him?
A: Because that was the maximum capacity of the stadium.

I don't know if it's any reflection on my popularity, but in our next match my darts team have voted for me to go in goal.

Harry's speech at the local council meeting was greeted with boos from half those listening and loud applause from the rest. Unfortunately for Harry, the people clapping were applauding the people who were booing.

PORNOGRAPHY

Dave was watching a blue film last night when suddenly his mum walked in. Dave couldn't believe his eyes. This was the first time he'd found out what she did for a living.

Trevor rings up a saucy late-night adult TV channel to speak directly to the woman currently writhing naked on screen. 'Hi, big boy, what would you like me to do for you?' she asks. 'Could you get off screen and hide somewhere please,' says Trevor, 'my missus is due home any minute and I can't find the TV remote.'

The Home Secretary asks the Prime Minister, 'What are we going to do about the Pornography Bill?' 'Oh no!' says the Prime Minister. 'I think we'd better just pay it.'

Cuthbert wanders into a dodgy area of town. A seedy-looking individual sidles up to him and says, "Ere, mate. Do you want to buy some pornography?' 'Don't be ridiculous,' says Cuthbert, 'I don't even own a pornograph.'

POST

A letter comes through Dick's door and lands on the mat. The words 'Do Not Bend' are printed on the envelope in bold capitals. Dick stands there for the next four hours trying to work out how to pick it up.

A delivery man knocks on Harry's door and says, 'I've got a parcel here for your next-door neighbour.' 'Well,' says Harry, 'you've got the wrong house then, haven't you?'

Did you hear the joke about the letter that was lost in the post? I didn't get it.

A man walks into a stationery shop and says, 'Do you have an envelope that's five centimetres wide, five centimetres high and 75 metres long.' 'What do you need that for?' says the assistant. 'I've just sold my garden hose on eBay,' says the man.

Fred's neighbour, Tom, is going down to the shops, so Fred asks him to look in at the post office on the way to see if there's a parcel waiting for him. Tom agrees and half an hour later Fred sees him walking past his house carrying his shopping. Fred calls out to him. 'Did you get a chance to look for my parcel?' Tom calls back, 'Yes. It's there.'

A man brings a parcel in to the post office. The counter assistant tells him, 'This package is too heavy. You need to put more stamps on it.' 'Really?!' says the man. 'And that's going to make it lighter!?'

The postman knocks on Harry's door. 'I can't tell if this letter is meant for you or not,' says the postman. 'The name on it seems to be smudged.' 'It's definitely not for me then,' says Harry. 'My name's Smith.'

The Post Office recorded massive profits last year. Mostly it was generated by all the letters they received complaining about their service.

It has been announced that the carrier services Fed-Ex and UPS are going to merge. The new company will be called Fed-UP.

I gave the postman a fright this morning by coming to the door stark naked. He asked me, 'Why haven't you got any clothes on? And how did you know where I live?'

POSTURE

My boss says he will sack the employee who has the worst posture. I've got a hunch it will be me.

POTATOES

Q: What's 30ft long and has a diet of potatoes?
A: The queue at a Russian butcher's.

POVERTY

It would be good to experience what it's like to be really poor for one day. Of course, being poor for any more than one day would begin to get a bit annoying.

>
> THE PRIME MINISTER ANNOUNCED TODAY A NEW PLAN TO ENSURE THAT WE DON'T ALL SUDDENLY BECOME POOR WHEN WE REACH 60. HE'S GOING TO MAKE SURE WE'RE ALL POOR WHEN WE REACH 30.
>
> THE TWO RONNIES

The UN conducts a survey on the world food supply. They ask various representatives the answer to the following question: 'In your opinion what is the solution to the food shortage experienced by the rest of the world'. The survey was not a success. The Chinese didn't know what 'opinion' meant, Western Europe didn't know what 'shortage' meant, the Middle East didn't know what 'solution' meant, and the USA didn't have a clue about the 'rest of the world'.

Q: Where do poor meatballs live? **A:** In the spaghetto.

POWER CUTS

We had a power cut this morning. Everything stopped working. The TV, the internet, the phone, the DVD player, the radio. Plus, it then started raining and I couldn't go out. In the end there was nothing for it. I had to sit down and talk to my wife for two hours. She seems like a nice person.

PRAYERS

A man has to drive into the city centre for an important job interview, but he can't find anywhere to park. In the end he prays to heaven and says, 'Oh Lord, help me to find a parking space and I will never doubt you and devote my life to you from this moment on.' Just then a car pulls out from the kerb next to him, leaving a vacant parking space. 'OK. No need to worry after all, Lord!' says the man. 'I just found one!'

PREDICTIVE TEXT

It has been reported that the inventor of predictive text has just died. His funfair is going to be hello on Sundial.

Barry tries texting a girl he just met to tell her how much he likes her, but it all goes terribly wrong when predictive text changes his message to 'I wish you were nine'.

PREGNANCY

> "DO YOU MIND IF I SIT DOWN, 'CAUSE I'M PREGNANT?' A WOMAN SAID. I SAID IN REPLY, 'YOU DON'T LOOK IT. HOW LONG HAVE YOU BEEN PREGNANT?' SHE SAID, 'ONLY TEN MINUTES – BUT DOESN'T IT MAKE YOU FEEL TIRED?'"
>
> MAX MILLER

A little girl asks her daddy why Mummy's tummy has gotten so big. 'Because she's pregnant,' says Dad. 'She's got a baby growing in there.' 'Well, that explains that,' says the girl. 'But what's the story with her big fat bum?'

Play it safe – never even suggest that a woman might be pregnant unless she's actually giving birth in front of you

PREJUDICE

An Englishman, a Welshman and a Pakistani are waiting in a maternity ward. A doctor comes out and tells them that their three children have all just been born. 'Unfortunately,' says the doctor, 'there's been a mix-up and we're not sure which baby belongs to which parent.' The three new dads discuss the problem and agree they should all be able to recognise their own child. The Welshman opts to go in first and follows the doctor to see the three newborns. A few minutes later he comes back out cradling what is evidently an Asian child. 'Hang on a minute,' says the Pakistani. 'Are you sure that baby is really yours?' 'Not really,' says the Welshman, 'but one of the other two is definitely English. And I'm really not prepared to take the chance.'

> "I AM FREE OF ALL PREJUDICES. I HATE EVERYONE EQUALLY."
>
> W.C. FIELDS

I think my children are very biased. Every time we go to the shops all they say to me is 'bias' this and 'bias' that.

PRESENTS

Ted's wife thinks he's very generous. He frequently brings her home bunches of flowers and teddy bears for the children. He says living round the corner from an accident black spot has unexpected advantages.

PRISON

A man is sent to prison. On his first night, the lights go out and after a few minutes he hears someone in another cell call, 'Thirty-two!' He then hears all the other prisoners including his cellmate laughing like mad. After the laughter subsides, he hears another voice call, 'Seventy-six!' Again all the prisoners and his cellmate are in fits of laughter. He asks his cell-mate, 'Why is everyone laughing every time someone calls out a number?' 'Well,' says the cellmate, 'we've all been in prison so long we know all the jokes off by heart. So to save time we've written them all down in a big joke book and numbered them. Now instead of telling the whole joke we can just call out the number and it sets us all off laughing.' 'Can I have a go?' says the man. 'Of course,' says the cellmate. 'Right!' says the man and thinks of a good number. 'Forty-three!' he calls. But there is no response from the other cells. He tries again. 'Forty-three!' he shouts out more clearly. Again there is no response, but a moment later a voice from another cell calls, 'Forty-three!' and this provokes gales of laughter. 'Hey!' says the man. 'He said the same number as me. But when I said it no one laughed.' 'I know,' says the cell mate, 'but you see — it's the way he tells them!'

An 80-year-old man is found guilty in court and sentenced to 25 years in prison. 'I can't do all that!' says the old man. 'Don't worry!' says the judge. 'Just try and do as much as you can.'

During the war three soldiers are captured by the Germans. The men are told they will be put into solitary confinement for the next five years, but they will all be given one last request before they're locked up. The first asks to have five years' worth of beer, and the Germans oblige. The second asks for five years' worth of whisky and, again, the Germans oblige. The third asks for five years' worth of cigarettes and, once again, his request is fulfilled. Five years later, the men are released. The first comes staggering out blind drunk, the second is half-dead from acute alcoholism, and the third one sticks his head round the door and says, 'Have any of you chaps got a light?'

Big Ernie drowned while attempting to escape from jail. He'd been trying to dig his way out of a prison ship.

In a Missouri jail, three new prisoners get talking in the yard. Two of them are white and one is black. One of the white prisoners says, 'I got put away for five years for attempted arson. The judge said it would have been ten if I'd managed it.' The other white prisoner says, 'I got ten years for attempted murder. The judge said it would have been 20 if I'd actually killed him.' The black prisoner says, 'I got 20 years for riding a bicycle without lights. The judge said it would have been 40 if I'd been out at night.'

Nobby gets sentenced to ten years for his part in a time-share fraud. The judge told him he has to go to prison for two weeks every year in June.

PRIVILEGE

Q: How many Etonians does it take to change a light bulb?
A: Two. One to open a bottle of champagne; the other to ring the electrician.

PRIZES

An American traffic cop pulls a car over and tells the driver, 'Congratulations! We're having a competition for people who remember to wear their seatbelt and you've just won $50! What will you do with the money?' 'I don't know,' says the driver, 'I might use it to get myself a driver's licence.' 'Don't listen to him,' says a woman in the passenger seat, 'he always talks rubbish when he's drunk.' 'Don't tell him that,' says a man from the back seat, 'we'll be in real trouble if he finds out it's a stolen car.' At that moment there's a sound from the boot and a voice says, 'Why have we stopped? Are we over the border yet?'

Harry gets a text message telling him he's won an alternative of two prizes. The message says: 'Congratulations! You have won either £100 in cash, or a ticket to see an Elvis Presley tribute act. To claim your prize, press the following buttons on your keypad. It's a one for the money, it's a two for the show . . .'

PROOFREADING

It's critical to properly poop read a document to ensure are no spelling or missing words.

PROPERTY

I stayed with an old friend recently and he said to treat his house like it was my own. So while he was out, I sold it.

PROPOSALS

A man starts going out with a beautiful girl and asks her to marry him. He tries to entice her by telling her that his father is a 90-year-old multimillionaire. The girl says to call her in a week after she's thought about it. One week later, he phones up. 'Congratulate me!' she says. 'I'm your new step-mother!'

PROSTITUTES

A street-walker accosts a religious minister in the street and asks him if he wants a good time. 'Madam,' says the minister. 'May I ask if you are aware of the concept of Original Sin?' 'No,' says the street-walker. 'But I've got to tell you — if it's very original, I'll have to charge extra.'

Sally the street-walker is on her corner when the local vicar comes up to say hello. 'Good morning, Sally,' he says. 'Do you know that I was praying for you last night.' 'Blimey!' says Sally. 'It's easier to phone. I'll give you my number.'

Trevor is driving through a seedy area of town. He pulls up next to a lady of the night who has evidently had something of a rough life. She agrees to do anything he wants for £50 and climbs in the car. Half an hour later, she's back at Trevor's house creosoting his fence.

PROZAC

I've just heard that Prozac is no longer the best-selling anti-depressant on the market. For some reason that makes me feel very sad.

PSYCHICS

My last girlfriend was psychic; she left me before our first date.

I got sacked from my job as a psychic. I didn't see that coming at all.

Tom goes to see a psychic. 'What's your name?' asks the psychic. 'I want my money back,' says Tom.

If you ever want to embarrass and please a psychic at the same time, just throw them a surprise party.

A man goes to visit a fortune teller. He walks in and meets a jolly old lady who sits him down at her table and gazes into her crystal ball. 'You will live a long and prosperous life!' she tells him. 'You will come into great wealth! And you will marry the most beautiful woman you have ever seen! Isn't that nice?' she concludes, with a happy smile on her face. The man responds by jumping up and punching her right on her nose. 'Ow! I told you a lovely fortune!' says the jolly old lady. 'What did you hit me for?' 'Sorry,' says the man, 'but I always like to strike a happy medium.'

Vince asks Norman, 'Have you ever had a premonition?' 'No,' says Norman, 'but I have an eerie sense that one day, I will.'

Gary goes to see a fortune teller. She looks into her crystal ball and tells Gary to watch out because a large amount of money will be coming his way soon. Gary walks out feeling very pleased and is immediately run over by a Securicor van.

A man takes his wife to the funfair and decides to try a machine that tells both your fortune and your weight. The machine pops out a card, and the man shows it to his wife. 'Look!' he says. 'It says I'm intelligent, good-looking and a fantastic lover.' 'I know,' says his wife, 'and not only that, it's got your weight wrong as well.'

> **PREDICTIONS ARE DIFFICULT, ESPECIALLY ABOUT THE FUTURE.**
>
> YOGI BERRA

Why are fortune tellers always able to fit into one another's clothes? They're all mediums.

Victor is a waiter. Sadly, he dies after suffering a heart attack in the restaurant where he works. A few weeks later, his wife visits a psychic who tells her to sit opposite her and hold hands over the parlour table. 'Victor,' says the psychic. 'Can you hear me? Can you hear me?' A ghostly voice calls back, 'Yes. I can hear you.' 'Come to us, Victor,' says the psychic. 'Come to us.' 'I can't,' says the voice. 'Why can't you come to us?' asks the psychic. 'That's not my table,' says Victor.

Nigel goes to see a psychic perform at the local theatre. The psychic invites audience members to ask him questions to try and catch him out. Nigel sticks up his hand and says, 'What is my father's name and where is he right this minute?' The psychic concentrates for a moment, then says, 'Your father is a travelling salesman called Ron living in Aberdeen.' 'No he's not,' says Nigel. 'He's called Bert, and he's sitting at home right now.' The psychic replies, 'Bert might be sitting at home, but your father is Ron, and he's in Aberdeen.'

Q: One.
A: How many mind-readers does it take to change a light bulb?

PSYCHOLOGY

An ego and a super-ego walk into a bar and the barman says, 'I'm sorry, but I'm going to have to ask you for some id.'

PUBLIC SPEAKING

A member of the royal family arrives at a university to give a speech. Unfortunately, she discovers that she has forgotten to bring the printed text of the speech. 'Fax it up?' suggests the university professor. 'Yes,' she replies, 'it does rather.'

I wouldn't say Gary is a bad public speaker, but he delivers lines the way a one-armed postman delivers glass vases.

PUNCTUALITY

Kevin's boss calls him over and says, 'I notice you always seem to arrive late for work in the morning.' 'I know,' says Kevin, 'but don't worry. I make up for it in the afternoon by leaving early.'

Gary gets into work and his boss calls him into his office. 'This is the third time you've been late for work this week, Gary,' says the boss, 'so you know what this means, don't you?' 'Yes,' sighs Gary, 'I've still got two days till the weekend.'

"THIS IS THE EARLIEST I'VE EVER BEEN LATE."

YOGI BERRA WHEN ARRIVING LATE FOR A MEETING

Dick comes into work half an hour late. 'What happened?' asks the boss. 'Sorry,' says Dick, 'but on the way here, there was this man who'd lost a 50-pound note and couldn't find it anywhere.' 'Were you helping him to look for it?' asks the boss. 'No,' says Dick, 'I was standing on it.'

A man comes into work an hour late with his face covered in cuts and bruises. 'Sorry I'm late,' he tells the boss, 'I fell down two flights of stairs.' 'That took you a whole hour?' says the boss. 'How big were those stairs?'

Beryl is late for work and goes to her boss to apologise. 'Sorry I'm late,' she says, 'only I wanted to vacuum under the sofa and I had to wait till Jim had left the house.' 'Why did you have to wait?' asks the boss. 'Doesn't he like the sound of the vacuum cleaner?' 'He doesn't mind that,' says Beryl. 'But I can't lift the sofa when he's sitting on it.'

Our company has found a great way of making sure its employees get to work on time. There's 100 staff and they've reduced the number of spaces in the car park to 80.

PUNCTUATION

Two quotation marks 'walk into' a bar.

A group of asterisks are having a party. A full-stop walks through the door. The asterisks all stop chatting and stare in amazement. 'What's the matter with you lot?' says the full-stop. 'I've just gelled my hair!'

Q: What happened when the semicolon broke the law of grammar?
A: He was given two consecutive sentences.

PUSHED AROUND

Evadne tells her husband Bill, 'I'm fed up with you pushing me around all the time and constantly talking behind my back.' 'It's not my fault, is it?' says Bill. 'You're the one who's in a wheelchair.'

QUEUES

Why is it that when you're stuck at the back of an endless queue, you always feel a bit better if someone else comes and stands behind you?

Be careful never to stand behind the Devil in a queue at the post office, or you could be stuck there for ages. Apparently, the Devil can take many forms.

RABIES

A man goes to the doctor and is diagnosed with rabies. 'Doctor,' says the man, 'I must have a pen and paper immediately.' 'Do you want to write your will?' asks the doctor. 'No,' says the man, 'I want to make a list of people I want to bite.'

RADIO

Mary likes to listen to Radio WYZ as it offers a full hour of uninterrupted music. She especially likes the way the announcer reminds her she's listening to a full hour of uninterrupted music every ten minutes.

" MY AUNT USED TO SAY, 'WHAT YOU CAN'T SEE, CAN'T HURT YOU.' WELL, SHE DIED OF RADIATION POISONING A FEW MONTHS BACK! "

HARRY HILL

RADIOACTIVITY

My cousin won the Sellafield and District best-behaved child contest. She was so well-behaved, people used to call her Goody Three Shoes.

RAFFLES

Harry goes to the local stationery shop and buys a book of raffle tickets for just £1.99. 'This is a bargain,' he tells the shopkeeper, 'in the pub they charge 50p for just one of these.'

Brian's wife comes home after a night out with the girls. He notices she's wearing a diamond necklace. 'I won it in a raffle,' she explains. 'Now excuse me while I take a shower.' The next night, she comes home wearing a pair of new earrings. 'I won them in a raffle,' she explains. 'Now excuse me while I take a shower.' The next night, she has an expensive watch on her wrist. 'I won it in a raffle,' she explains. 'Now excuse me while . . .' 'Don't tell me,' says Brian. 'You want to take a shower.' His wife says, 'Actually, I might have a bath tonight.' 'Well don't put out too much water,' says Brian. 'You don't want to get your raffle ticket wet.'

RAMBLERS

Beryl hates phoning the 'Ramblers' Association' – they keep going on and on and on and on . . .

A rambler is out and about in the countryside. He asks a farmer, 'How far to the next village?' 'Ten miles,' says the farmer. 'But if you run you might do it in five.'

RECYCLING

SCOUTS ARE SAVING ALUMINIUM CANS, BOTTLES, AND OTHER ITEMS TO BE RECYCLED. PROCEEDS WILL BE USED TO CRIPPLE CHILDREN.

PARISH NOTICES

REDHEADS

Bert tells Ted that his wife is a natural redhead. 'You mean,' says Ted, 'she has a mass of lustrous auburn locks.' 'No,' says Bert, 'she is literally a redhead. Completely bald and badly sunburnt on top.'

REDNECKS

YOU KNOW YOU'RE A REDNECK IF . . .

- . . . your school prom night had a creche.

- . . . the reason your daddy walks you to school is because he's still a pupil there as well.

- . . . your beer can collection is considered one of the main tourist attractions in your local area.

- . . . the final words of any member of your family have been, 'Hey y'all! Watch this . . .'

- . . . your boat has not left your driveway in 15 years.

- . . . you have a home-made fur coat hanging up by your front door.

- . . . you've ever had to rake up leaves from your kitchen floor.

- . . . birds consider your beard an attractive nesting site.

- . . . your school song was 'Duelling Banjos'.

- . . . you've ever given a rat trap as a wedding anniversary present.

- . . . the dog catcher has to call for backup when he visits your house.

YOU KNOW YOU'RE A REDNECK IF...

▶ ... you've ever queued up to have your picture taken with a freak of nature.

▶ ... your mother has ever got into a fist fight during a high school sports event.

▶ ... you won't stop at a toilet if you have any empty beer cans in your car.

▶ ... you have ever participated in a 'who can spit tobacco the farthest' contest.

▶ ... your truck has curtains but your house doesn't.

▶ ... family reunions always end with a chewing tobacco spit-off.

▶ ... you consider a six-pack and a bug zapper to be enough for an evening's entertainment.

▶ ... you prefer to walk the excess length off your jeans rather than have them sewn up.

▶ ... you have at least one living relative named after a Southern Civil War general.

▶ ... you've ever climbed up a water tower holding a bucket of paint so you can defend your sister's honour.

REFEREES

If you have one child that makes you a parent. If you have two, that makes you a referee.

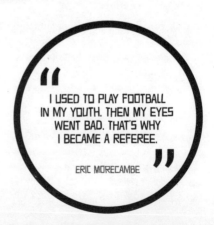

" I USED TO PLAY FOOTBALL IN MY YOUTH. THEN MY EYES WENT BAD. THAT'S WHY I BECAME A REFEREE. "

ERIC MORECAMBE

REINCARNATION

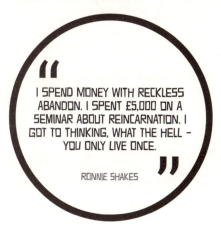

"I SPEND MONEY WITH RECKLESS ABANDON. I SPENT £5,000 ON A SEMINAR ABOUT REINCARNATION. I GOT TO THINKING, WHAT THE HELL – YOU ONLY LIVE ONCE."

RONNIE SHAKES

RELATIONS

Barry can't work out why he has only got three brothers, while his sister has got four.

My uncle was legendary for being big-hearted. He wasn't kind or generous, he just had hideously swollen ventricles.

Larry is telling George a riddle. 'Say my parents have a baby, and that baby is not my brother or my sister. Who would it be?' George thinks for a bit, then gives up. Larry says, 'It would be me.' 'Oh, I see,' says George. Next day, he tells the riddle to his wife. 'Say my parents have a baby, and that baby is not my brother or my sister. Who would it be?' His wife says, 'Well, that would be you, obviously.' 'No, you're wrong,' says George. 'It's my mate, Larry!'

RELATIONSHIPS

I brought a ten-year-long relationship to an end today. Looking on the positve side, it wasn't mine.

Relationships are like overweight people. They don't often work out.

> "RELATIONSHIPS ARE HARD. IT'S LIKE A FULL-TIME JOB, AND WE SHOULD TREAT IT LIKE ONE. IF YOUR BOYFRIEND OR GIRLFRIEND WANTS TO LEAVE YOU, THEY SHOULD GIVE YOU TWO WEEKS' NOTICE. THERE SHOULD BE SEVERANCE PAY AND, THE DAY BEFORE THEY LEAVE YOU, THEY SHOULD HAVE TO FIND YOU A TEMP."
>
> — BOB ETTINGER

RELIGION

> "I DO BENEFITS FOR ALL RELIGIONS. I'D HATE TO BLOW THE HEREAFTER ON A TECHNICALITY."
>
> — BOB HOPE

The good news, according to Jesus, is that we are all God's children. But then if that's true, what's so special about Jesus?

If the Pope genuinely believes that the almighty and omnipotent Lord, who controls all things on Heaven and Earth, has personally chosen him to lead the one true Holy Roman Catholic Church, why does he have to have a lightning conductor on the roof of the Vatican?

Tom tells Harry, 'My wife has converted me to religion.' 'Really?' asks Harry. 'Yes,' says Tom. 'Before we got married I didn't believe in hell.'

The fact that there's a highway to hell but only a stairway to heaven tells us a lot about the anticipated amount of traffic expected on each route.

Holy Joe is waiting at some traffic lights when he sees a 'Honk If You Love Jesus' sticker on the car in front. Joe gives a jaunty honk in response. A moment later, the driver leans out and yells back at him, 'Quit your honking, doofus! Can't you see the lights are still red?!'

Neville is a member of the Salvation Army, but he hardly ever attends any of their meetings. He tells everyone he's part of their Secret Service.

Once the meek inherit the earth, it'll be interesting to see just how long they'll be able to hold on to it.

During a religion lesson at school, a little boy is asked to draw a picture of a story from the Bible. A few minutes later the teacher comes round to see what he's done. 'You've done a picture of an aeroplane,' says the teacher. 'How is that meant to be a picture from the Bible?' 'It's the flight into Egypt,' says the little boy. 'And the man sitting at the front is Pontius the Pilot.'

> "I ADMIRE THE POPE. I HAVE A LOT OF RESPECT FOR ANYONE WHO CAN TOUR WITHOUT AN ALBUM."
>
> RITA RUDNER

Little Katy is in the art class at school and the teacher tells her to draw anything she wants. After a few minutes the teacher comes to her desk and asks her what she's doing. 'I'm drawing a picture of God,' says Katy. 'Well, that's nice,' says the teacher. 'But no one really know what God looks like.' Katy taps her paper and says, 'They will in a minute . . .'

Brian and Paddy are Catholic brothers who run a corner shop together. One day, Brian announces he's getting married. And, even worse, his fiancée is a Protestant. 'That's going to cause us nothing but trouble,' says Paddy. 'No,' says Brian, 'I've had a word with her and she's going to convert to Catholicism.' And so Brian gets married and his new wife becomes a Catholic. The next week he tells Paddy, 'My wife is taking this whole thing very seriously. She doesn't want me to work on Sundays any more because the Pope says it is a holy day of rest.' 'But that's one of our busiest days,' says Paddy. 'I told you that marrying a Protestant would cause nothing but trouble!'

The RE teacher at school tells the class, 'The Bible commands us to honour our fathers and mothers. But can anyone think of another one of the Ten Commandments that tells us how we should treat our brothers and sisters?' A little boy puts his hand up and says, 'Is it "Thou shalt not kill"?'

In school at Christmas the teacher asks if any of the children know any carols. A little boy says he knows the one about the baby Jesus going to the toilet. The teacher is shocked. 'What do you mean?' she asks. 'You know,' says the little boy, 'the one that goes – a wee in a manger . . .'

At Sunday School, the priest tells the children how Lot had to take his wife and flee from the city of Sodom. 'So Lot's wife got turned to salt?' asks Johnny. 'That's right,' says the priest. 'But Lot was OK,' says Johnny. 'Yes,' says the priest. 'He was fine.' 'OK,' says Johnny. 'So what happened to the flea?'

Our church is very liberal, it accepts all denominations, but prefers twenties . . .

One morning a Catholic priest, a Baptist minister and a rabbi all hike into the woods. Each of them has made a bet that they'll be the first to convert a grizzly bear to their faith. That evening, they return to the lodge they're sharing and tell how they got on. The priest stands up. He's in a bad way, with scratches and bite marks all over him. 'It was a struggle, to be sure,' he says. 'But I did it in the end. All I had to do was get him to drink some holy water. He'll be attending his first mass next week.' The minister stands up. He too is covered in scratches and bites. 'I also succeeded,' he says. 'I managed to drag a crazed bear into the river and baptised him there. Glory to God. He'll be coming to church next Sunday.' The rabbi stands up. He's in terrible shape, with black eyes, both arms in plaster and wearing a neck-brace. 'I admit it,' he says. 'I messed up. On reflection, perhaps I shouldn't have started with the circumcision . . .'

REMOTE CONTROLS

It has been reported that the inventor of the TV remote control has died. Paramedics tried unsuccessfully to revive him by twizzling his batteries round and banging him on the edge of the coffee table.

Do you know why they call the TV control a 'remote'? Because those are the odds of finding the damned thing you when you need it.

A woman is at the shops when the girl serving her notices she has her TV remote control in her handbag. 'Do you always go shopping with your TV remote?' asks the girl. 'No,' says the woman, 'but my husband refused to come with me. So I figured this was the worst thing I could do to him legally.'

REPAIRS

WE REPAIR ANYTHING. IF DOOR LOCKED PLEASE KNOCK HARD AS BELL ISN'T WORKING.

ADVERT IN A HARDWARE SHOP WINDOW

REPETITION

I've said it before and I'll say it again, I am not the sort of person who repeats myself.

RESCUE

Ten men and a woman have to be rescued off a mountain. They all end up dangling on a rope beneath a helicopter while it struggles to get airborne again. The pilot calls down that one of them will have to let go because otherwise the helicopter is carrying too much weight. The men all insist that they are far too important to their families, friends and workplaces to sacrifice themselves. In the end the woman says that she will have to give up her life because as a woman she is used to making sacrifices for her husband, her sons and for men in general. When she finishes speaking, the men clutching on to the rope with her are all so moved they burst into a spontaneous round of applause . . .

RESPECT

The government has announced plans to combine all the year's various 'minute silences' into one single silent afternoon every 5 August.

RESPONSIBILITY

The biggest problem in the world today is that nobody will take responsibility for anything. Don't quote me on that though.

> I AM RESPONSIBLE FOR ALL OF MY MISTAKES. AND SO ARE YOU.
>
> GEORGE W. BUSH

RESTAURANTS

Harry goes to an Indian restaurant and orders a meal. After a few minutes the waiter comes over and says, 'Curry OK?' 'If you must,' says Harry, 'but just one song and then leave me in peace.'

A notoriously aggressive chef has opened a new restaurant. I went in and asked what was on the menu and he chucked a prawn cocktail at me. He said, 'And that's just for starters!'

> JOB VACANCIES – PERSON REQUIRED TO WASH DISHES AND TWO WAITRESSES.
>
> ADVERT IN RESTAURANT WINDOW

An Englishman, an Irishman, a Scotsman, a Welshman, a Chinese man, a Russian, a Korean, a Japanese man, an Indian, an American, a Frenchman, a German, an Australian, a Dutchman, a Spaniard, a Latvian, a Brazilian, an Indian, an African and an Arab all walk into a restaurant and the manager says, 'I'm terribly sorry, but I can't let you in without a Thai.'

OPEN SEVEN DAYS A WEEK
AND ALSO AT WEEKENDS.

SIGN ON DOOR OF RESTAURANT

Jesus walks into a restaurant with his disciples and tells the waiter, 'I'd like a table for 26 please.' 'But,' says the waiter, 'there are only 13 of you.' 'I know,' says Jesus, 'but we still need a table for 26 because we're all sit down the same side.'

Bert is in a restaurant. The waiter asks what he would like. Bert indicates the next table and says, 'I'll have whatever that man is having.' 'You can't have that, sir,' says the waiter. 'Why not?' asks Bert. 'Because he's having it,' says the waiter.

Stan and Deirdre are walking through the town centre when they pass a brand-new swanky restaurant. 'Ooh!' says Deirdre. 'Did you catch the smell of the food coming from that place? It smelled absolutely gorgeous.' Stan thinks for a minute and says, 'You know what, love. We don't get out very often, but tonight I'm going to treat you.' And with that, he walks her past the restaurant again.

A man is eating in a restaurant when he accidentally knocks a spoon off the table. Quick as a flash a waiter is there to present him with a clean spoon from his pocket. 'Thank you,' says the man. 'So you carry spare spoons with you.' 'Oh yes,' says the waiter, 'according to an efficiency study, 20 per cent of customers will knock a spoon off the table each week, so all the waiters here keep a replacement spoon ready to hand out.' Later, as he's paying for his meal, the man says to the waiter, 'I hope you won't mind me mentioning, but did you know you have a piece of string hanging from your trouser zip?' 'Yes,' says the waiter, 'that also came up in our efficiency study. We were taking too long going to the toilet and washing our hands afterwards. So now all the waiters here have strings attached to their willies so they can pull them out and go to the toilet hygienically without touching it.' 'OK,' says the man, 'but how do you manage to get it back into your trousers when you've finished?' 'Well,' says the waiter, 'luckily we all carry a spoon in our pockets.'

A family go out to an all-you-can-eat restaurant, but the mum is embarrassed when her son goes back yet again to refill his plate. 'You can't go back for even more food,' she tells him, 'aren't you embarrassed that people have seen you go back five times now?' 'Not really,' says the boy, 'I just told them I was filling the plate up again for you!'

Did you hear about the two idiots who went to an expensive restaurant? They ordered a meal, then sneaked out without eating it.

"WHERE GOOD FOOD IS AN UNEXPECTED PLEASURE."

NEWSPAPER ADVERT FOR RESTAURANT

A Frenchman called Gervase owns a fresh seafood restaurant. His supplier arrives to restock the live fish tanks and produces an unpleasant-looking green squid with a little moustache on its lip. Gervase complains that none of his customers will want to eat such a weird-looking specimen but, nevertheless, he is left with the squid. It turns out that none of the customers ever fancy the squid and it takes up permanent residence in the tank. Gradually Gervase becomes attached to the moustachioed little creature until one day a bunch of yobs come in and demand the squid for their dinner. Gervase tells them that it isn't for sale but the yobs persist. In the end Gervase takes the squid into the kitchen to prepare it for cooking. He places it on the chopping board and raises a cleaver but, looking down at the little squid, he finds he cannot deal the fateful blow. Instead he asks his kitchen assistant Hans to dispatch the creature instead. Despite being a rough old army veteran, even Hans cannot resist the poor little squid looking up at him with a mournful tear in its eye. And so he too has to put down the cleaver and let the squid live. And this all goes to prove the old adage: 'Hans that do dishes can feel soft as Gervase with vile green hairy lip squid'.

I took my family out for a meal at one those new trendy open-air restaurants. It was very nice and surprisingly inexpensive, but for some reason all they served was soup, and for some reason all the waiters were dressed as members of the Salvation Army.

Gary has just got a new job as a waiter. He says the pay isn't great, but at least it puts food on the table.

WAITER!

▶ 'Waiter! What's this in my bowl?' says a customer. 'It's bean soup,' says the waiter. 'I don't care what it's been,' says the customer, 'I want to know what it is now.'

▶ 'Waiter! I can't eat this meat,' says a customer. 'It's rotten. Call the manager!' 'That's not going to help,' says the waiter. 'He won't eat it either.'

▶ 'Waiter, how often do you change the tablecloths in this restaurant?' asks a customer. 'I don't know, sir,' says the waiter, 'I've only worked here six months.'

▶ 'Waiter,' says a man, 'could you tell me what this fly is doing in my soup?' 'I think it's the breast stroke, sir,' says the waiter.

▶ 'Waiter,' says a customer, 'you've got your thumb is in my soup.' 'Don't worry, sir,' says the waiter. 'It's not hot.'

▶ 'Waiter,' says a customer, 'there's a live fly moving around in my soup.' 'Don't worry, sir,' says the waiter. 'He won't last long in that stuff.'

▶ 'Waiter, there's a fly in my soup,' says a man. 'Don't worry, sir,' says the waiter. 'The spider on your bread will get rid of him.'

▶ 'Waiter,' asks a customer, 'is my burger going to be long?' 'No, sir,' says the waiter. 'It's going to be round like normal.'

▶ 'Waiter!' exclaims a man. 'You've got your thumb on my steak!' 'Well, sir,' says the waiter. 'You don't want it to fall on the floor again, do you?'

▶ 'Waiter,' says a customer, 'there's a fly swimming about in my soup.' 'Look on the bright side,' says the waiter. 'If the portions here weren't so generous, he'd be paddling.'

RETAIL

A celebrity is asked to come and open a new supermarket. 'Is it because you've seen me on the television?' asks the celebrity. 'No,' says the manager. 'I've lost my keys and someone told me you had a crowbar handy.'

Bert walks into a grocery store and finds the shelves filled with boxes of salt everywhere he looks. He goes up to the counter and asks the owner why he has so much salt in his shop. 'It's a mistake, I know,' sighs the owner. 'I guess I'm just not a very good salesman.' 'Don't be so hard on yourself,' says Bert. 'No one could ever sell this much salt.' The shop owner shakes his head and says, 'No, that's not true! You should meet my salt wholesaler. Now *there's* a man who can sell salt!'

In business news, 'Poundstretchers' and 'Marks and Spencer.' are going to merge to beat the credit crunch. The new store is going to be called 'Stretchmarks'.

RETIREMENT

Old Arthur announces that he has decided to take early retirement and live off of his savings. Two weeks later he is homeless and looking for a new job.

I have a retirement plan in place. Unfortunately it depends entirely on me having at least one successful child.

RHUBARB

A boy from the town goes to visit his cousin who lives on a farm. As they're playing, he notices a big pile of horse manure in the corner of the farmyard. 'Yuk!' says the town boy. 'What's that for?' 'My dad puts it on his rhubarb,' says his cousin. 'Really?' says the town boy. 'My dad puts custard on his.'

RIDDLES

▶ **Q:** Arthur is a butcher who is six feet tall and of average build, what does he weigh? **A:** Meat.

▶ **Q:** What is exactly one foot long and very slippery? **A:** A slipper.

▶ **Q:** What happens if you dial 666? **A:** A few minutes later an upside-down policeman will turn up.

▶ **Q:** Seven is an odd number. What do you have to take away from it to make it even? **A:** The 's'.

▶ **Q:** What's brown and rhymes with 'snoop'? **A:** Dr Dre.

▶ **Q:** What floats on water and goes quick? **A:** A South African duck.

▶ **Q:** What's small, transparent and smells of worms? **A:** A blackbird's fart.

▶ **Q:** What's round and unpleasant? **A:** A vicious circle.

▶ **Q:** What's green, smelly and likes camping? **A:** A Brussels scout.

▶ **Q:** What's the meaning of 'acoustic'? **A:** It's what a Scotsman uses to keep his cattle under control.

▶ **Q:** What has handles and flies? **A:** A dustbin.

▶ **Q:** What's a hospice? **A:** Usually about three gallons a time.

▶ **Q:** What starts with 'T', ends with 'T' and has 'T' in the middle? **A:** A teapot.

▶ **Q:** What do you get if you cross a joke with a rhetorical question?

RIOTING

I saw footage of the riots in Greece on the news. It's terrible. It looks like the whole place is in ruins.

ROADS

I just scored a major victory over my town council. For years they've been trying to build a new road through my living room, but now they've backed down. They're going through the kitchen instead.

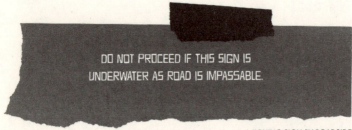

DO NOT PROCEED IF THIS SIGN IS UNDERWATER AS ROAD IS IMPASSABLE.

WARNING SIGN BY ROADSIDE

ROBIN HOOD

Robin Hood calls all his Merry Men to his bedside. 'I am dying,' he says, 'bring me my bow and an arrow and I will fire a final shaft. Wheresoe'er it lands, bury my body there.' The Merry Men do as Robin bids, he draws his bow and shoots and, true to his last request, they bury his body on top of the wardrobe.

ROUTINE

Two men are reminiscing about their younger days. 'Do you know what,' says one of them, 'for 30 years I was always up at six in the morning, worked solidly until five, had a simple dinner, did an hour's exercise and was in bed by nine.' 'Oh yes,' says the other. 'So what were you in for?'

"START EVERY DAY OFF WITH A SMILE AND GET IT OVER WITH."

W.C. FIELDS

ROWING

Ted tries to row the Atlantic single-handed, but had to stop after a few hours because he just kept going round in circles.

ROYALTY

I've seen stamps, coins, banknotes and that great big chair she has at Westminster and it's left me thinking: just who does the Queen think she is?

RUSSIA

Ivan is on an underground train in Moscow. He whispers to a fellow traveller, 'Comrade, do you work for the police?' 'No,' says the man. 'Do you work for the KGB?' asks Ivan. 'No,' says the man. 'Do you, or does anyone else in your family, work for the Communist Party?' asks Ivan. 'No,' says the man. 'I'm just an ordinary citizen.' 'Good,' says Ivan. 'In that case – get off my foot, you clumsy great oaf!'

Have you heard of Russia's greatest ever billiards player? Inoff the Red.

Russian dolls are terrible. I always find that they're completely full of themselves.

SACKED

Harry gets the sack from his job at the clock factory. He tells them he can't understand why they'd do this after all the extra hours he'd put in.

I was sacked from my job last week. Or, as I prefer to put it, I'm currently on eternity leave.

Nobby was once given a five-year prison sentence for falling asleep on the job. That wouldn't happen in many occupations, but Nobby was a burglar at the time.

I got sacked from my job feeding the giraffes at the zoo. Apparently they didn't think I was up to it.

SACRIFICES

A little boy is desperate to get a new PlayStation and his dad takes this as an opportunity to teach him an important lesson about life. 'We all have to make sacrifices to get the nice things we want,' says Dad. 'It's not fair . . .' says the little boy. 'That's enough, son,' says Dad. 'We're selling your kidney whether you like it or not.'

SAFETY

Quentin was nervous of being run over when he went out jogging and always dressed in white so that motorists could see him. He'd still be alive today if he hadn't been flattened by that snow plough.

SAMARITANS

Bill works for the Samaritans. If he tries to call in sick in the morning, they always manage to talk him out of it.

SANDWICHES

A man opens his lunch at work and starts eating the sandwich he's made for himself. 'This is disgusting,' says the man. 'What's in it?' asks a colleague. 'Crab paste,' says the man. 'Oh dear,' says the colleague. 'When did you buy it?' 'Only yesterday,' says the man. 'They were having a sale at the chemist's.'

SCALLIES

You know you're a scally, when you have to address your Father's Day card, 'To whom it may concern . . .'

George is driving his company car through the back streets of the city centre when the engine stalls. He gets out and pops the hood to see what's the matter, then hears someone doing something at the back end. He goes round and finds a scally trying to force open the boot with a crowbar. 'What the hell are you doing?' shouts George. 'This is my car.' The scally says, 'Calm down, mate. We'll split it. You do the front; I'll do the back.'

Scallies love pub quiz nights, but they always start with the same question – 'What are you looking at?'

Why did the scally cross the road? To nut a complete stranger, again.

SCARS

Norma asks Nobby if the scar from her appendix operation makes her look unattractive. 'Nah! Don't worry about it, love,' says Nobby. 'These days your boobs cover it nicely.'

SCHIZOPHRENIA

I am not a schizophrenic. And what's more, neither am I.

I went to a charity pantomime held on behalf of people with severe delusional paranoia. Things were going pretty well until someone shouted 'It's behind you!'

SCIENCE

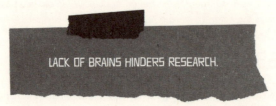

LACK OF BRAINS HINDERS RESEARCH.

HEADLINE IN US NEWSPAPER

I'm reading an interesting book about anti-gravity. I just can't put it down.

Schrodinger's cat walks into a bar. And also doesn't.

A maths student, a science student, and an art student are given the task of measuring the height of a steeple. The maths student measures the steeple's shadow and works it out using trigonometry. The science student uses a reflecting laser array. And the art student buys the vicar a beer and asks him, 'Exactly how high is your steeple?'

A photon checks into a hotel. The clerk asks him if he needs any help taking his luggage up to his room. 'No thanks,' says the photon, 'I'm travelling light.'

> EAMONN HOLMES: THERE ARE THREE STATES OF MATTER: SOLID, LIQUID AND WHAT?
> CONTESTANT: JELLY.
>
> NATIONAL LOTTERY BBC 1

And the barman says, 'Sorry. We don't serve your kind in here.' A faster-than-light neutron walks into a bar.

Scientists have now managed to attach a microscope to the end of a telescope. They believe they will now be able to see extremely small objects on very distant planets.

Genetic hybridisation has created a cross between a donkey and a scorpion. It can give you a really nasty sting, but on the plus side you can ride it to A&E.

Oxygen asks Potassium out on a date and Potassium says, 'OK!' But then Oxygen gets a date with Magnesium and says, 'OMg!' Later, Nitrogen asks to go out with Oxygen, but Oxygen gives him a definite, 'NO!'

Scientists say that the universe is made up of a range of building blocks including protons, neutrons and electrons. But the most common of all is, of course, morons.

I love the way the Earth moves. It really makes my day.

Neon walks into a bar and orders a beer. The barman says, 'Sorry, we don't serve noble gases here.' He doesn't react.

I would tell you a joke about the Periodic Table but all the good ones Argon.

Want to hear a joke about sodium? Na.

Want to hear a joke about potassium? K.

SCOTTISH DRESS

Angus announces he's getting married. He tells his proud parents that he will wear a kilt to the wedding. 'Och aye,' says his dad, 'and what's the tartan?' 'Dunno,' says Angus. 'I expect she'll have some sort of big white dress.'

SCRABBLE

Geoff was rushed to hospital after accidentally swallowing some 'Scrabble' tiles. The doctor told him that if he goes to the toilet it could spell disaster.

SEAN CONNERY

Sean Connery asks his driver to take him to a nightspot that's good for singles, so the driver drops him off at the all-night skincare clinic.

Q: Does Sean Connery enjoy eating all herbs equally?
A: No. Only partially.

Sean Connery's agent calls him at home. 'Sean, I've got this great role lined up for you. Come to the studio tomorrow morning and we'll meet the producer.' 'OK,' says Sean. 'What time do you want me there?' 'How about ten-ish?' says the agent. 'Tennish?' says Sean. 'I thought you shaid we were going to a shtudio?'

SEASIDE

> "I WENT TO BLACKPOOL ON HOLIDAY AND KNOCKED AT THE FIRST BOARDING HOUSE I CAME TO. A WOMAN STUCK HER HEAD OUT OF AN UPSTAIRS WINDOW AND SAID: 'WHAT DO YOU WANT?' 'I'D LIKE TO STAY HERE.' 'OK. STAY THERE!'
>
> TOMMY COOPER

A glamorous beach bunny is walking along the shore when she notices a man staring at her. She goes over to speak to him. 'Hey! Do you know that your swimming trunks match your eyes?' 'I know what you mean,' says the man. 'They're both blue.' 'No,' says the woman. 'They're both bulging.'

I took Grandpa on a beach holiday and we went paddling in the sea. When he took his socks off, I noticed how filthy his feet were. 'Don't you ever clean them?' I asked. 'It's not my fault,' he said. 'You didn't bring me last year.'

Gary tells Ken he was shocked by what he saw during his holiday in Blackpool. 'I saw this bloke and his missus having a right old shouting match down on the seafront,' he says. 'And then the woman just smacked the guy in the head and they started hitting each other over and over in front of everyone. Then this copper turned up but, instead of calming things down, he just started to hit the guy with his truncheon. Then the guy takes the truncheon off the policeman and starts hitting him with it.' 'My God!' says Ken. 'So how did it all end?' 'In a really weird way,' says Gary. 'This crocodile suddenly turned up and stole all their sausages.'

A man walks into a library and asks, 'Do you have a book on tides?' 'Sorry, sir,' says the librarian, 'that one's just gone out.'

SECOND-HAND GOODS

I just bought a pair of second-hand binoculars. They cost me £500. I reckon the bloke saw me coming a mile off.

Dick is trying to sell his car. It's not worth much. Its value triples every time he fills it with petrol.

SECRET AGENTS

When James Bond first got his job as a spy, it took them a while for them to process his 'Licence to Kill'. For a week or two he had to make do with a 'Licence to Wedgie'.

QUESTION MASTER: NAME AN OCCUPATION IN WHICH YOU DISGUISE YOUR APPEARANCE.
CONTESTANT: DOCTOR.

FAMILY FEUD

SECRETS

You can confide in me and your greatest most intimate secrets will be entirely safe . . . with me and my Facebook group.

A little boy discovers a clever trick at school. An older friend tells him that all grown-ups have a secret. If you pretend you know what it is, you can get them to give you anything you want. When he gets home, the little boy tells his mum, 'Mum, I know the whole truth!' His mum looks horrified. She gives him £20 and says, 'OK. But, whatever you do, don't tell your father!' Later the little boy tells his dad, 'I know the whole truth!' Dad gives him £40 and says, 'OK. But whatever you do, don't tell your mother!' The next morning, the little boy sees the milkman coming up the path and tries his trick again. 'I know the whole truth!' he tells the milkman. 'Do you?' says the milkman, and throws open his arms. 'Come on and give your daddy a hug then!'

SECURITY

I built an electric fence around my property last night. My neighbour's dead against it.

SELF-DENIAL

I've decided to give up the past tense for lend.

SELF-HELP

I've just published a self-help book about how to fall down the stairs. It's a step-by-step guide.

A man walks into a library and asks where the books on self-help are kept. The librarian says, 'If I told you, wouldn't that would be defeating the object?'

SERVANTS

Lady Muck gives her chambermaid a week's notice. The chambermaid is very cross and tells Lady Muck just what she thinks of her. 'You may be a fine lady but I'm better than you in almost every way!' she says. 'I'm a better housekeeper than you, I'm a better cook and, not only that, I am much more attractive.' 'I don't know who told you that!' says Lady Muck. 'It was your husband,' says the chambermaid. 'And that's not all. Apparently I'm better than you in bed.' 'Oh!' says Lady Muck. 'And I suppose you're going to say my husband told you that as well!' 'No,' says the chambermaid. 'It was the gardener.'

Lady Constance invites a new friend over for tea. The door is opened by a rather homely-looking gentleman who shows the friend into the parlour. 'Was that your husband?' enquires the friend. 'Of course it was,' says Lady Constance. 'If I had a butler that ugly, I'd fire him.'

Lord Muck comes home in a bad temper and tells Lady Muck, 'I'm giving my chauffeur the sack! That's twice he's nearly killed me.' 'Oh, don't do that, dear,' says Lady Muck. 'Why not let him have one last chance?'

Lady Fortnum has invited all her friends over for a magnificent party. She tells her butler, 'I want you to stand at the front door and call the guests' names as they come in.' 'Can I really?' says the butler. 'I've been wanting to do that for years.'

SEWAGE

George was awarded a long-service medal in recognition of his 40 years of service as the sewer-pipe repair man of Buckingham Palace. The medal was given to George personally by the Queen, who pinned it on him using a ten-foot pole.

SEX

Vera goes into the local hospital to complain that ever since her husband Harry went in for treatment, he has lost all interest in sex. 'I can't understand it,' says the hospital manager, 'he was a patient in the ophthalmology department. All we did was correct his eyesight.'

Brenda asks Tom, 'How many women have you ever slept with?' 'Only you,' says Tom. 'Aw!' says Brenda. 'Is that really true?' 'Yes,' says Tom, 'the others all kept me awake all night.'

A vigorous young couple move into a terraced house. Each night, their lovemaking is so intense and noticeable that afterwards the neighbours on both sides have to sit and have a cigarette.

Gary complains that his girlfriend keeps laughing during sex. It doesn't matter what she's reading.

Janet blames her lack of children on the sex education she got from her mother, who told her that the man goes on top and the woman goes underneath. And so, for all their married life, Janet and her husband have slept in a bunk bed.

Having sex is said to be a bit like riding a bike. Unfortunately, if that's true, I seem to own a unicycle.

If there was a tax on sex, I think I'd be due a fairly significant rebate.

An old man takes his wife to the doctor. The doctor checks her cardiovascular activity and tells her husband, 'Because of your wife's condition, she needs regular exercise and stimulation. The best thing would be for her to have sex three times a week.' 'Oh yes,' says the old man, 'which days?' 'Monday, Wednesday and Friday would be ideal,' says the doctor. 'OK,' says the old man, 'well, I can bring her on Monday and Wednesday but I can't do Fridays, so she'll have to get a taxi.'

According to a recent survey, 98 per cent of Scousers say they have had sex while they were in the shower. The other 2 per cent said they'd never been to prison.

Mary Whitehouse and her husband slept in separate bedrooms because, she said, their sleeping patterns were so very different. Mrs Whitehouse used to make hundreds of speeches each year. Most of them after walking into her husband's bedroom to check what he was doing after lights out.

A colonel and a major are in the officer's mess having a discussion about sex. The colonel argues that sex is 90 per cent work and only 10 per cent pleasure. The major disagrees and says that sex is 90 per cent pleasure and only 10 per cent work. As they can't agree, they try to find someone else to decide. In the end, the only other person available is a humble private who's cleaning the toilets. They ask him what he thinks and he tells them, 'Well, obviously it's 100 per cent pleasure. If there was any work involved, you lot would get me to do it for you!'

A polling company asked 1,000 people, 'Would you sleep with Boris Johnson'? In reply, 1 per cent said 'No', 2 per cent said 'Yes' and 97 per cent said 'Never again'.

A junior doctor goes to the hospital psychiatrist and says, 'You've got to help me. I keep going out with different nurses here and even though we have nothing in common we end up having meaningless sex, which leaves me feeling guilty and depressed in the morning.' 'I see,' says the psychiatrist. 'So you want me to help you overcome your addiction to casual sex and strengthen your resolve to resist these beautiful young women.' 'No!' says the junior doctor. 'I want you to help me stop feeling guilty and depressed!'

Gary gets a letter from his mother. She writes, 'Ever since you left home, your father has turned into an insatiable sex maniac. Please excuse the wobbly writing.'

> "THE DIFFERENCE BETWEEN SEX AND LOVE IS THAT SEX RELIEVES TENSION AND LOVE CAUSES IT."
>
> WOODY ALLEN

> "WITH ME, NOTHING GOES RIGHT. MY PSYCHIATRIST SAID MY WIFE AND I SHOULD HAVE SEX EVERY NIGHT. NOW WE'LL NEVER SEE EACH OTHER!"
>
> RODNEY DANGERFIELD

> **MY HUSBAND COMPLAINED TO ME. HE SAID, 'I CAN'T REMEMBER WHEN WE LAST HAD SEX.' AND I SAID, 'WELL, I CAN. AND THAT'S WHY WE AIN'T DOIN' IT.'**
>
> ROSEANNE BARR

Farmer Giles' son walks into the barn one day and finds his dad dressed in stockings and suspenders and dancing alluringly by the side of his Massey Ferguson. 'What the hell are you doing?' asks his son. 'Well,' says the farmer, 'your mother has been feeling very depressed about our love life recently. So we went to marriage guidance counselling, and they told me I needed to start doing something sexy to attract her.'

A woman goes to the doctor. He examines her and tells her she has a strained groin. 'How frequently do you have sex?' asks the doctor. 'Five times every week,' says the woman. 'On Monday, Tuesday, Wednesday, Friday and Sunday.' 'I would suggest,' says the doctor, 'that you cut that down a little and perhaps leave out the Tuesday session.' 'I can't do that,' says the woman, 'that's the only night my husband's home.'

Bill and Graham are talking. 'I'm worried about my wife,' says Bill. 'She just doesn't seem to enjoy sex at all. She just lies there. Clearly nothing I do gives her any pleasure.' 'Don't worry about it,' says Graham. 'She's exactly the same with me.'

Norman had a very embarrassing experience. His sex tape was leaked onto the internet and found its way on to YouTube, Facebook, Twitter and Reddit. But despite an enormous amount of effort, he still couldn't get anyone to watch it.

Tom and Brenda are in bed having sex. Tom notices that Brenda doesn't seem to be enjoying the experience. 'What's the matter?' he asks. 'Are you having trouble thinking of someone else as well?'

> **I REMEMBER THE FIRST TIME I HAD SEX – I KEPT THE RECEIPT.**
>
> GROUCHO MARX

A woman tells her husband, 'The doctor says I need to start having sex five times a week.' 'OK,' says the husband. 'Put me down for Monday and Friday.'

An audience gathers to hear an aged and esteemed world expert on physical relationships give a lecture on the subject of sex. The expert gets up, walks to his lectern and says, 'Ladies and gentlemen, it gives me great pleasure . . .' and then goes back to his seat again.

Ted tells Ken, 'I went to the doctor this morning and he says that if I don't stop having sex, I'm going to be dead in two weeks.' 'Why's that?' asks Ken. 'I've been having it with his wife,' says Ted.

According to a survey, the majority of men prefer casual sex. Mind you, that's because most of them think you don't have to wear a tie.

Bill is at Geoff's house when they see a couple of dogs mating in his front garden. 'My wife likes doing it like that,' says Bill. 'Really?' says Geoff. 'Mine would never do that.' 'OK,' says Bill, 'the trick is to give her a few glasses of whisky first. Then she'll be up for anything.' They meet a few days later and Bill asks if the trick worked. 'It did,' says Geoff, 'but I had to give her nearly the whole bottle before she'd let us do it in the front garden.'

A man gets into bed and asks his wife if she's in the mood. 'Not tonight,' says the wife, 'I've got a headache.' The next night the man gets into bed and asks if she's in the mood now. 'No,' says the wife, 'I've had a tiring day.' The next night the man gets into bed and asks once again. 'I can't believe this,' says the wife. 'Three nights in a row! Are you some kind of sex maniac?'

Tom managed to make love for an hour and two minutes yesterday. Then he found out it was the night they put the clocks forward.

Q: What's a man's idea of foreplay? **A:** Brushing his teeth.

Betty and Fred are in bed making love. Betty says, 'The price of milk is something terrible. I don't like that smell coming out of the downstairs lavatory. Did you hear the neighbours last night? What a racket . . .' Fred says, 'What on earth are you doing?' Betty says, 'Yesterday, you said you wanted me to moan a bit when we were doing it.'

Larry kisses Denise and says, 'From the first moment we met, I wanted to make love to you terribly. Denise says, 'Well, you can tick that box . . .'

Freddie buys a sex manual and tries to convince his wife to try out some of the moves. 'How about the wheelbarrow?' he asks. 'That's where you hold yourself up on your hands, I lift up your legs and away we go.' 'Well, OK,' says his wife. 'I'll try it, but only if you promise we won't go past my mum's house.'

Jack, a virile 80-year-old, goes to the doctor and complains that the last time he had sex with his wife he ended up freezing cold, but the time before that he'd felt very hot and sweaty. Puzzled, the doctor calls Janice, the man's wife, for an explanation. 'Nothing to worry about,' says Janice. 'The last time the old fool tried it on it was in the middle of winter; and the time before that was in the heatwave we had three years ago.'

Barry always thought sex was a pain in the neck. Then he discovered he'd been doing it wrong.

Neville manages to talk his new girlfriend into bed for some whoopee. When it's over, his girlfriend says, 'That has to be the worst sex I've ever had. It was absolutely terrible.' 'That's hardly fair,' says Neville. 'How can you form an opinion after only 30 seconds?'

Phil's love-life is now almost non-existent. It's got so bad he calls his waterbed the 'Dead Sea'.

Betty always closes her eyes when she has sex; she hates to see her husband having a good time.

Pete goes into the kitchen one morning and finds his wife standing at the stove. Suddenly she tears off her dressing gown and nightie and says, 'Ravish me now, Peter. Here on the table.' Never one to say no, Pete throws off his pyjamas, lays his wife on the table and gets on with it. 'This is a nice surprise,' he pants. 'What's the occasion?' 'There's no occasion,' says his wife. 'It's just that I'm trying to soft boil an egg and the timer is broken.'

What did the prostitute, the lawyer and the psychiatrist all say to each other after they'd had an hour-long threesome – 'That'll be $200.'

Gus tells his wife he had sex with her sister last week. 'You disgust me,' says his wife. 'No, honestly,' says Gus, 'we didn't mention you once.'

Nobby is watching *Match of the Day*. His wife turns to him and says, 'Do you fancy any nookie tonight, love?' 'Oh yes,' says Nobby. 'But let me just watch the rest of the football.' 'You know you can record it?' says his wife, 'Can I? Fantastic!' says Nobby. 'You get the camcorder set up and I'll be there as soon as the match has finished.'

Harry buys a book called *101 Mating Positions*. He's very disappointed when he gets it home and finds it's an introduction to playing chess.

My wife says she definitely thinks sex is better on holiday. I'm beginning to wish I'd gone with her now.

A couple are lying in bed after making love. 'Did you fake it this time?' asks the man. 'No,' says the woman, 'that time I really was asleep.'

One night, Norma surprises her husband, Nobby, in the bedroom. She dresses up in a sexy policewoman outfit and tells him, 'You're under arrest! I am charging you with being good in bed.' Five minutes later, she tells him, 'The charges are being dropped due to lack of evidence.'

Gwen says to her husband Dave, 'I'll tell you what. Let's each pick one person in the world that we are allowed to sleep with and the other one of us can't get mad about it. My one is Ryan Gosling. Who's yours?' 'The babysitter,' says Dave.

SEX AIDS

I bought my bulldog a sex toy for Christmas, it's a rubber human leg.

Marvin and Xanthe have been married for 20 years and every time they snuggle up in bed, Marvin insists on switching off the light and making love in the pitch dark. Xanthe has always thought this was a bit weird and one day, halfway through a night-time session, she decides to find out what's going on. She flicks on the bedside light and is horrified to see Marvin lying there holding a phallic sex toy. 'I don't get it!' says Xanthe. 'How could you have deceived me like this all these years? You'd better explain yourself.' 'OK, I'll explain the toy,' says Marvin. 'And then maybe you can explain our three children.'

SEXUALLY TRANSMITTED DISEASES

Q: How did Herpes walk out of the hospital? **A:** On crutches.

> " I WENT TO MY DOCTOR AND TOLD HIM 'MY PENIS IS BURNING.' HE SAID, 'THAT MEANS SOMEBODY IS TALKING ABOUT IT.' "
>
> GARRY SHANDLING

A man goes to the doctor and says, 'Doctor! You've got to help me. I think I've got Hermes.' 'You mean herpes,' says the doctor. 'No,' says the man, 'I think I might be a carrier.'

Terry and Janet are making love in the back seat of a Ford Transit when Janet whispers, 'Do you know what would be really sexy? I think I'd like to be whipped!' Terry looks around for something he can use. The seatbelts don't stretch far enough and he thinks jump leads will be potentially dangerous. Then he has a flash of inspiration. He unscrews the aerial from the top of the vehicle and use this to give Janet's backside a good spanking. Two days later they are at the local clinic where a doctor is examining the unpleasant marks that have developed all over her bottom. 'Did you get these having sex?' asks the doctor. Janet confesses the details of the kinky session that led to the problem. 'I thought so,' says the doctor. 'I'm afraid I have to tell you that you have got the worst case of van aerial disease I've ever seen.'

SHAKING HANDS

> THE IMPORTANT THING IS THAT HE SHOOK HANDS WITH US OVER THE PHONE.
> ALAN BALL

> I'M HONOURED TO SHAKE THE HAND OF A BRAVE IRAQI CITIZEN WHO HAD HIS HAND CUT OFF BY SADDAM HUSSEIN.
> GEORGE BUSH

SHAVING

A man goes to the barber and asks for a shave. However, the barber turns out to be cack-handed with the cut-throat razor and the man ends up with cuts and nicks all over his face and throat. Shaken by the experience, he gets up from the barber's chair and asks for a glass of water. 'Are you feeling all right?' asks the barber. 'I'm fine,' says the man, 'I just want to see if my face leaks.'

A man is having a shave at the hairdresser's. He notices a pretty girl sweeping the floor and asks if she fancies a drink afterwards. 'I can't,' says the girl. 'I've got a boyfriend.' 'Don't worry about that,' says the man. 'Just tell him you're going out somewhere with a girlfriend.' 'You can tell him yourself,' says the girl. 'He's the one shaving you.'

Q: Which man shaves ten times a day but still doesn't have a beard? **A:** The barber.

There are two possible reasons for using shaving cream. One is that it may soften the hair; the other is that it reminds you where you've got up to.

SHE WAS ONLY . . .

- She was only a doctor's daughter, but she definitely knew how to operate.

- She was only a drover's daughter, but she could certainly keep her calves together.

- She was only a fishmonger's daughter, but she'd jump on the slab and say, 'Fillet!'

- She was only a gravedigger's daughter, but she liked to lie under the sod.

- She was only a photographer's daughter, but she was extraordinarily well developed.

- She was only a weather forecaster's daughter, but she certainly had a warm front.

- She was only an optician's daughter, but she certainly made a spectacle of herself.

- She was only a florist's daughter, but everyone agreed she had the best tulips in town.

- She was only an insurance broker's daughter, but all the guys liked her policy.

- She was only a jockey's daughter, but all the horse manure.

- She was only a lighthouse keeper's daughter, but she never went out at night.

- She only a moonshiner's daughter, but I love her still.

- She was only a musician's daughter, but she was familiar with all the bars in town.

▶ She was only a teacher's daughter, but she taught all the boys a lesson.

▶ She was only a statistician's daughter, but she knew all the standard deviations.

▶ She was only a violinist's daughter, but when she took off her G-string, the boys all fiddled.

▶ She was only a quarryman's daughter, but all the guys took her for granite.

▶ She was only an electrician's daughter, but she could certainly spark your interest.

▶ She was only a policeman's daughter, but she wouldn't let the police dog handler.

▶ She was only a barman's daughter, but she certainly knew how to pull them.

▶ She was only a draughtsman's daughter, but she knew where to draw the line.

▶ She was only an editor's daughter, but she knew when to cut it out.

▶ She was only a flag-waver's daughter, but she never let her standards down.

SHEEP

Reginald developed an addiction to sheep – he had dozens of them in his garden, pictures of them on the walls, and fleeces covering all his furniture. It got so bad he had to join 'Gambollers Anonymous'.

> ANNE ROBINSON: WHICH LETTER OF THE ALPHABET SOUNDS EXACTLY THE SAME AS THE TERM FOR A FEMALE SHEEP?
> CONTESTANT: BAA.
>
> THE WEAKEST LINK

SHIPWRECKED

Tom and Dick are talking. 'If you were ever stranded on a desert island,' says Tom, 'who, in all the world, would you want to be stuck there with?' 'That's easy,' says Dick, 'it would definitely be my Uncle Bert.' 'Why him?' asks Tom. 'Well,' says Dick, 'he's got a boat.'

Three idiots are stranded on a desert island. They see a boat moored off the coast and decide to swim for it. The first gets halfway, but is too tired to go on and drowns. The second also gets halfway, but he too gets tired and vanishes under the waves. The third tries his luck. He swims for an hour and realises that he's only got halfway too. 'Wow,' he says. 'This is harder than it looks.' So he swims back to the island.

A man is stranded on a desert island with a dog and a pig. He has plenty of food and water and he has the animals for company but, nevertheless, after a few months he begins to feel lonely and the pig starts to look more and more attractive. However, every time he approaches the pig with amorous intent, the dog starts growling at him. Then, one day, the man sees a speck on the horizon. He swims out and finds a lifeboat with the most beautiful woman he has ever seen lying inside it, unconscious. He takes her back to his island and nurses her back to health. Finally, she recovers and says, 'I owe you my life. To show my gratitude, I will literally do anything you ask.' 'Wow!' says the man. 'OK. Would you mind taking my dog for a walk?'

Following the wreck of their cruise liner, an Englishman, an Irishman, an American and a Scotsman end up stranded on a desert island. They discover that the inhabitants of the island are friendly and after two months the Irishman has established a farm, the Scotsman has opened a shop and the American is helping them build a road. The Englishman, meanwhile, is still on the beach waiting for someone to introduce him.

A group of US Presidents are on a cruise. One night the ship hits a rock and starts to sink. George Bush senior says: 'What do we do?' Jimmy Carter says: 'Get to the lifeboats.' Obama says: 'Women and children first.' George W. Bush says: 'Screw the women.' Clinton says: 'Do we have time?'

SHOES

A man goes into a shoe shop and chooses a pair of shoes. He tries them on and the assistant asks if they are comfortable. 'They're a little bit tight,' says the man. 'OK,' says the assistant, 'try pulling the tongue out a little bit. Is that any better?' 'No,' says the man, 'they thtill feel jutht ath tight.'

Q: Why did my wife cross the road?
A: To go back to the same shoe shop we visited three flipping hours ago.

I bought some training shoes. To be honest, I didn't find them a suitable preparation for proper shoes.

Mary has two left feet. When she last went on holiday, she had to buy a pair of flip-flips.

I tried using a pair of earphones as shoelaces and it's great – now they tie themselves.

Harry is having a big argument with his doctor because he doesn't believe he needs a pair of orthopaedic shoes. The doctor finally persuades him to try them on. 'Is that any better?' asks the doctor. 'Yes,' says Harry. 'I stand corrected.'

SHOPLIFTING

Benjamin is caught trying to run out of a store carrying three weight-lifting sets. He confesses to the crime in court, and says he suffered a 'moment of weakness'.

Bill Smith is in court watching his wife being sentenced for shoplifting. 'Mrs Smith stole five apples, your honour,' says the court clerk. 'I see,' says the judge. 'Well, I think it would be fair to sentence her to a week for each one. That makes 35 days.' 'Not so fast!' shouts Bill. 'Ask her about the bunch of grapes . . .'

SHOPPING

> "MY WIFE WILL BUY ANYTHING MARKED DOWN. LAST YEAR SHE BOUGHT AN ESCALATOR."
>
> HENNY YOUNGMAN

When my wife and I go out shopping we always hold hands together. If I let go, she buys something.

Norman sent a suggestion to his local supermarket. He told them it would save him a lot of time and effort if they put everything he liked into a single aisle labelled 'unhealthy crap'.

A woman sends her husband to the shops. 'Get one pint of milk,' she tells him, 'and if they have any avocados, could you get six.' A few minutes later he's back carrying six pints of milk. 'Why did you get all those?' asks the wife. 'Because the shop had avocados,' says the man.

One day a farmer walks into town and goes to the hardware shop where he buys a bucket and a gallon of paint. Later, he visits the market where he picks up a couple of chickens and a goose. Just then, a little old lady asks if he would walk her home as it's beginning to get dark. 'OK,' says the farmer, 'but I'm having trouble carrying all these things I've bought.' 'Well,' says the little old lady, 'put the can of paint in the bucket, carry the bucket in one hand, put one chicken under each arm and carry the goose in your remaining free hand.' 'Thanks very much,' says the farmer, and proceeds to walk the old lady home. As they pass through a dark alleyway, the old lady turns and says, 'I hope you're not going to take advantage of me, hold me up against the wall and have your evil way with me?' 'How could I possibly do that?' says the farmer. 'I'm carrying a bucket, a gallon of paint, two chickens, and a goose.' 'Well,' says the little old lady, 'you could set the goose down, cover him with the bucket, put the paint on top of the bucket, and I'll hold the chickens!'

Ted and Marjorie are out at the shops. Marjorie realises she hasn't seen Ted for a little while so she gets out her mobile and calls to find out where he's got to. 'You remember that jewellery shop we saw just before your birthday last year? And they had that diamond necklace that you loved but which I didn't think we could afford,' says Ted. 'Yes,' says Marjorie excitedly. 'Well,' says Ted, 'I'm in the pub next door to that.'

My supermarket knows all about me. As a loyalty-card holder I will receive coupons based on what they know I keep buying. Each week I get a coupon for a five-pound bag of potatoes, every two weeks I get a coupon for a large pack of oven chips, and once a year I'll be sent a coupon for a single condom.

Dick goes into a greengrocer's and asks for six pounds of potatoes. 'Sorry, mate,' says the green grocer. 'We only sell kilos now.' 'OK,' says Dick. 'Give me six pounds of kilos instead.'

> BARGAIN BASEMENT ON TOP FLOOR.
>
> ADVERT IN A DEPARTMENT STORE WINDOW

Nigel has a house full of shopping trolleys. He can't resist a bargain, and they're only a pound each!

Sandra goes into a store, holds up a pair of pineapples and asks, 'How much are these?' 'Today's a special,' says the owner, 'three pounds the pair!' Sandra holds up one of the pineapples. 'How much for this one?' 'Two pounds,' says the owner. Sandra puts it down and picks up the second pineapple. 'OK, I'll have this one for the other pound.'

Barry was arrested by the security guards in the supermarket yesterday. Apparently when the checkout girl said, 'Strip down, facing me' she was actually referring to his Visa card.

A man calls the TV shopping channel. 'Can I help you?' asks a voice at the other end of the line. 'No thanks,' says the man, 'I'm just looking.'

> WAL-MART . . . DO THEY, LIKE, MAKE WALLS THERE?
>
> PARIS HILTON

SHORTBREAD

Have you heard, they're not making shortbread any longer?

SHOW-OFFS

An atheist, a vegan and a BMW owner walk into a bar. I only know because they told everyone within less than two minutes.

SICK LEAVE

An industrial tribunal is hearing the case of Jim Smith, who was seen taking part in a local cycling marathon while on sick leave from work. 'It's true that Mr Smith entered this race and came in fourth,' says his union rep. 'But if he hadn't been so ill, it would have been an easy win.'

SINGLE LIFE

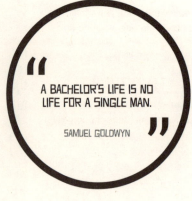

> A BACHELOR'S LIFE IS NO LIFE FOR A SINGLE MAN.
>
> SAMUEL GOLDWYN

> THE GREAT THING ABOUT BEING SINGLE IS THAT YOU CAN DO WHAT YOU WANT WHEN YOU WANT, AND THE BAD THING IS YOU'VE GOT NOTHING TO DO AND NO ONE TO DO IT WITH.
>
> JAMES O'LOGHLIN

Even though I've been married for years, I still live the single life. Terrible food and no sex.

SIZE

Jasper recently bought himself a tiny flat in London. It's so small he cleans the windows with contact lens fluid.

SKELETONS

Two skeletons are talking in the graveyard when one of them puts up an umbrella. 'Is it going to rain?' asks the first. 'Yes,' says the other. 'I can feel it in my bones.'

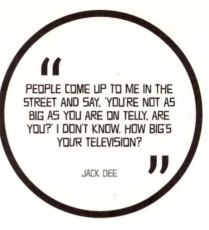

"PEOPLE COME UP TO ME IN THE STREET AND SAY, 'YOU'RE NOT AS BIG AS YOU ARE ON TELLY, ARE YOU?' I DON'T KNOW. HOW BIG'S YOUR TELEVISION?"

JACK DEE

SKIING AND WINTER SPORTS

Say what you like about the luge as a sport, but it's fast, thrilling and the only contest you can die halfway through and still win.

"SKIING COMBINES OUTDOOR FUN WITH KNOCKING DOWN TREES WITH YOUR FACE."

DAVE BARRY

SKIN CONDITIONS

Scientists have spent years researching the biggest cause of dry skin. They've just announced, it's towels.

SKUNKS

Billy used to have a pet skunk, but it died. It was short-sighted and it fell in love with a gas leak.

SLAVES

In the days of Ancient Rome, the captain of a galley tells the slaves below deck, 'I have good news and bad news. The good news is that our galley has been selected to take the Emperor to his new palace! The bad news is that he wants to go water skiing on the way.'

In the coliseum in ancient Rome, gladiators lead a slave out into the arena, tie him to the ground and then produce a massive gong. They then proceed to roll the gong up and down the slave's chest while singing, 'We're rolling a gong on the breast of a slave . . .'

SLEEP

I like sleeping. It's a bit like death, but without the commitment.

Taking regular naps helps stop you getting old. This works particularly well if you take them at the same time as driving.

Why do people use the expression 'I slept like a baby' to mean they had a good night's sleep. Babies wake up screaming every couple of hours!

Larry rings Bill at just gone midnight. 'Did I wake you?' asks Larry. 'No,' says Bill. 'Do you want to try ringing back later?'

James can't get to sleep. He's tried counting sheep, but by the time he's got past 100,000 his alarm usually goes off.

First thing this morning, there was a tap on my front door. My plumber has an odd sense of humour.

Norman fell asleep with his head under the pillow. In the morning he woke up, found all his teeth had gone and a pile of 50p pieces on the bedside table.

A woman goes to the doctor and asks for some sleeping pills for her husband. 'What's the matter with him?' asks the doctor. 'He keeps waking up,' says the woman.

Q: What's big, hairy and sticks out of a man's pyjamas? **A:** His head.

SLEEPOVERS

Bonnie visits her friend, who lives in a remote farmhouse. A taxi drops her off and she and her friend spend the day together. As night falls, a terrible storm starts up, and when they phone for a taxi to take Bonnie home they find the lines are down. Since it's late, the friend asks Bonnie to stay the night. Bonnie agrees, but soon after, she vanishes and the friend spends hours searching for her. Eventually, Bonnie stumbles in the door, soaked through and covered in mud. 'Where did you go?' asks the friend. 'I popped home to get my nightie,' replies Bonnie.

SMOOTH TALKING

Bob is an incredibly smooth talker. Once he even managed to make his wife feel sorry for the poor hitch-hiker who had lost her bra and pants in his car.

SNAILS

A snail is crawling up an apple tree. A blackbird says, 'What are you doing? It's February. There aren't any apples on that tree yet.' 'I know,' says the snail, 'but by the time I get up it, there will be.'

I tried taking the shell off my racing snail because I thought that would make him go a bit faster but it didn't work at all. If anything, it made him more sluggish.

SNAKES

Two snakes are talking. One asks, 'Do you know if we're poisonous?' 'Yes, we are,' says his mate. 'That's bad news!' says the first. 'I've just bitten my tongue!'

Basil goes to the pub with his pet snake. He orders two pints, one for himself and one for the snake. The barman watches the snake as it struggles to lift the heavy glass to its mouth. No matter what it does, it can't get a grip, and half the beer gets slopped over the table. Eventually the barman says, 'I'm sorry, sir. I'm going to have to ask you both to leave.' 'What's the matter?' says Basil. 'I'm not causing any trouble.' 'It's not you, sir,' says the barman. 'It's your snake. I'm afraid he just can't hold his drink.'

A man is selling his pet python on an internet auction site. A man sends him a message: 'How many feet?' 'None, you idiot,' replies the man, 'it's a flipping snake!'

SNORING

> QUESTION MASTER: A WAY TO PREVENT SNORING? CONTESTANT: PUT A PILLOW OVER HIS FACE.
>
> FAMILY FORTUNES

A man goes to his doctor and says, 'Doctor, you've got to help me. I'm exhausted. I can't get to sleep because the sound of my own snoring keeps waking me up.' 'OK,' says the doctor. 'So have you tried sleeping in a different room?'

Nobby snores so loudly it scares the rest of his family. Particularly when he's driving them somewhere.

SOCIAL MEDIA

Q: What's black and receives constant abuse on the internet? **A:** Punctuation.

We can get a good idea of what it was like living in ancient Egypt from Facebook. Everyone spends all their time writing messages on walls and worshipping cats.

SOCIAL WORKERS

Q: How many counsellors does it take to change a light bulb?
A: None, but it takes nine of them to collaborate on a paper called 'Coping with Darkness'.

A pair of psychiatrists meet in the corridor of a hospital. 'Do you know where the toilets are?' asks one. 'I'm afraid I don't,' says the other. 'Well, never mind,' says the first. 'At least we got to talk about it.'

There's one big difference between a social worker and a Rottweiler. If a Rottweiler grabs your baby, you have some chance of getting it back.

SOLAR POWER

If scientists are supposed to be so clever, why have none of them come up with a solar-powered air conditioner?

> SOLAR ENERGY IS NOT SOMETHING THAT IS GOING TO COME IN OVERNIGHT.
>
> GERALD FORD

SPACE TRAVEL

A robot rover has landed on the red planet, but has failed to find any evidence of beer, football or porn. NASA scientists say this has finally disproved the widely held belief that men are from Mars.

Did you hear about the idiots' mission to Mars? They couldn't get their rocket to lift off because no one had a big-enough milk bottle.

Brenda was disappointed by the space programme. She figured that if they'd managed to stick one man on the moon, what was stopping them from sending them all there?

SPAIN

Tom is going to Spain for a holiday to watch the annual 'Running of the Bulls', which is followed by the annual 'Burying of the Idiots'.

SPECIMENS

Dick isn't sure what's meant by the word 'specimen'. He thinks it refers to an Italian astronaut.

SPEECH IMPEDIMENTS

Norman goes to the doctor as he can't stop angrily shouting 'ay, ee, I, oh, you' at everyone he meets. The doctor diagnoses him with irritable vowel syndrome.

SPEED

Q: Which is faster – hot or cold?
A: Hot, because it's possible to catch a cold.

SPEEDING

A policeman pulls over a speeding motorist. 'You were doing 50 miles per hour according to my radar,' says the policeman. 'Rubbish,' says the driver. 'It was well under 40. In fact, it was more like 35.' 'The radar is very accurate, sir,' says the policeman. 'Come off it,' replies the driver. 'Come to think of it, I was barely touching 30. And I'll sue anyone who says otherwise.' The driver's wife leans over from the passenger seat. 'Please excuse my husband, officer. He tends to get a little rowdy after a few drinks.'

SPELLING MISTAKES

Apparently a simple spelling mistake has led a late-night adult TV channel to commission a 12-part documentary on the history of barges and long boats. The series is called 'Canal Knowledge'.

SPIDERS

Harry decides to get himself a tarantula and goes along to his local exotic pet shop. The pet shop owner shows him the range of gigantic spiders they have in stock and tells him prices start at £100. 'Blimey! That's expensive for a spider,' says Harry. 'Do you think it would be cheaper if I got one off the web?'

SPONSORSHIP

Why does 'Robinson's Juice' sponsor the tennis at Wimbledon each year? Has it never occurred to them to sponsor a squash tournament?

THIS PORTION OF 'WOMAN ON THE RUN' IS BROUGHT TO YOU BY PHILLIPS' MILK OF MAGNESIA.

AMERICAN RADIO ANNOUNCEMENT

SPORT

> THE 'WASHINGTON BULLETS' ARE CHANGING THEIR NAME. THEY DON'T WANT THEIR TEAM TO BE ASSOCIATED WITH CRIME. FROM NOW ON, THEY'LL JUST BE KNOWN AS THE 'BULLETS'.
>
> JAY LENO

> LIKE ALL MEN, I LIKE TO WATCH SPORTS, BUT I'M STILL TRYING TO FIGURE OUT BOXING. THAT'S A BIG TOUGH MAN'S MASCULINE SPORT. BUT, YOU KNOW WHAT THE PRIZE MONEY IS CALLED IN A HEAVYWEIGHT BOXING MATCH? A PURSE. THE TWO BIGGEST, BADDEST MEN IN THE WORLD FIGHTING FOR A PURSE. A PURSE AND A BELT.
>
> MIKE DUGAN

Neville went to see the gold medal his neighbour had won at the Olympics. It turned out he was so proud of it, he'd had it bronzed.

During the 100 metres at the World Athletics Championship, an African, an Asian, an American and a European all ended up getting shot by the starting pistol. The authorities have confirmed that the incident was race-related.

It has been reported from the Paralympics that three athletes in wheelchairs have been banned from taking part after they tested positive for WD40.

Larry had a very successful career as a repairman before he went to jail; he could fix anything – football matches, darts tournaments, dog races . . .

SPYING

Ever since we split, my ex-girlfriend has been obsessed with checking up on what I'm doing and Googling my name. I could see her doing it quite clearly through her dining room window last night.

STAINS

Yesterday I spilled stain remover all over my best trousers. I've no idea how to get it out.

STALKING

My girlfriend has accused me of being a stalker. OK, she's not really my girlfriend at the moment.

STAR WARS

The next *Star Wars* film is going to be set in the Cayman Islands, where a financially dodgy cab company has been set up by Darth Vader's brother. His name is Taxi Vader.

My wife told me she was leaving me because I keep making stupid *Star Wars* puns. I said, 'Divorce is strong with this one.'

STATISTICS

Uncle Nigel is a statistician. He wanted to be an accountant, but they said he lacked the personality.

Apparently, a study has revealed that 99 per cent of people are stupid. Luckily I'm in the other 4 per cent.

According to a recent research study, five out of six scientists say Russian roulette is completely safe.

It is a statistical fact that if you have a 50/50 chance of something going right, nine times out of ten it will go wrong.

A survey released today shows shocking results. Apparently just three out of four people make up as much as 75 per cent of the population.

According to studies, 90 per cent of the people in any group think they're in the top 10 per cent.

Statistically, the likelihood of bumping into someone you know increases significantly every time you go out with someone you don't want anyone to see you with.

If you look at a graph of average life expectancy and IQ, you'll see that the lines crossed quite recently – going in opposite directions.

STEAM ROLLERS

It took me some time to get over my wife. I accidentally ran over her while driving a steamroller.

> MR AZRUNI'S UNCLE LIVES IN ISTANBUL AND IS A ROAD ENGINEER. HE WAS RUN OVER BY A STEAM ROLLER ABOUT FIVE MONTHS AGO AND IS STILL IN THE HOSPITAL IN ROOM 21 TO 27.
>
> VICTOR BORGE

'Mrs Smith, I think your son is spoilt.' 'He is not, Mrs Jones, and what's more, I don't think it's any of your business.' 'Suit yourself, but wait until you see what the steamroller's done to him.'

STOCKBROKERS

Recent reports indicate a significant downturn in London stockbrokers' enthusiasm for fooling around under the table with each other. This had led to a massive drop in the Footsy Index.

STOWAWAYS

A ship's captain catches a tramp trying to sneak aboard a liner that's about to set off on a five-day cruise. 'But why can't I come with you just this once?' says the tramp. 'Sorry,' says the captain, 'but beggars can't be cruisers.'

STUDENTS

Two students are talking. 'I've just had a complete disaster,' says one, 'I wrote to my mum and dad saying I needed some money to get a new laptop.' 'What happened?' asks his friend. 'The worst possible thing,' says the first, 'they sent me a new laptop.'

One night, three students go out partying and the next morning are late arriving for college. They tell their teacher that the delay was, in fact, due to a flat tyre. 'OK,' says the teacher, 'in that case we will start today with a simple test which will only take 30 seconds. You will all sit separately and write down the answer to the following question: Which tyre?'

SUBMARINES

Ken invented the world's first submarine to be entirely made from polystyrene. Unfortunately, it didn't go down very well.

I haven't had much luck with my latest invention. The world's first soft-top convertible submarine.

SUCCESS

If you try but don't succeed, then the best thing to do is cheat. And then if you still don't succeed, keep repeating the process until you get caught. And then say it was someone else who did it.

Dick's ambition in life is to become so important and renowned that if anyone ever killed him, it would be classified as assassination rather than murder.

> AFTER HIS DEATH, SOCRATES' CAREER SUFFERED A DRAMATIC DECLINE.
>
> SCHOOLBOY HOMEWORK ANSWER

Once I thought I'd found the key to success. Unfortunately, a couple of days later, somebody changed the lock.

It matters not whether you win or lose. On the other hand, whether I win or lose is a matter of the utmost concern.

> I WOULD ASK ANYONE TO TRY TO UNDERSTAND THE WORLD HE LIVES IN. WE ALL HAVE TO ACCEPT THAT HE IS MARRIED TO 'SPICE GIRL' VICTORIA ADAMS. AND I THINK HE COPES VERY WELL WITH IT.
>
> KEVIN KEEGAN

> " A MAN OWES HIS SUCCESS TO HIS FIRST WIFE AND HIS SECOND WIFE TO HIS SUCCESS. "
>
> JIM BACKUS

> MY SECOND HIT WAS A FLOP.
>
> SHAKIN' STEVENS

Norman built a cabinet to house all his awards, but one day it collapsed and killed him. The investigators said he'd been a victim of his own success.

I beat a new record every day – the number of days I've managed to stay alive.

> " BEHIND EVERY SUCCESSFUL MAN IS A SURPRISED WOMAN. "
>
> MARYON PEARSON

> IT'S NEVER JUST A GAME WHEN YOU'RE WINNING.
>
> GEORGE CARLIN

SUICIDE

Jack is in prison. The warder passes his cell, looks in and sees Jack hanging from the ceiling by his feet. 'What the hell do you think you're doing?' asks the warder. 'What does it look like?' says Jack. 'I'm hanging myself.' 'You idiot,' says the warder. 'You're supposed to put the rope round your neck.' 'I tried that,' says Jack. 'But it was no good at all. I just couldn't breathe.'

"SUICIDE IS MAN'S WAY OF TELLING GOD, 'YOU CAN'T FIRE ME – I QUIT!'"

BILL MAHER

Barry lost his job with the Samaritans. Apparently if someone calls and says, 'I'm depressed, so I've gone out and I'm lying down on the railway track', it is not appropriate to tell them to 'remain calm and stay on the line'.

HOST: WHAT 'K' IS A SUICIDE MISSION FOR A PILOT?
CONTESTANT: KAMA SUTRA?

BLOCKBUSTERS

An ageing millionaire is being driven along the coast road. He leans forward and tells his chauffeur, 'James, I'm afraid I've had some rather bad news from the doctor, and I can't face being ill so I've decided I am going to commit suicide.' 'Oh dear,' says the chauffeur, 'is there anything you'd like me to do?' 'Yes please,' says the old man, 'could you just drive me over that cliff over there!'

Did you hear about the cannibal who attempted suicide? Apparently he got himself into a right stew.

Bert is arrested for the murder of his wife in Switzerland. He tells the police, 'I thought assisted suicide was legal in this country.' 'It is,' says the police officer, 'but that's if you go to a specially licensed clinic. You can't just do it yourself the moment your plane touches down at Zurich airport.'

SUPERHEROES

Two little boys are talking. 'In my family we call my granddad "Spider Man".' 'Wow!' says his friend. 'Does he have superpowers?' 'No,' says the first, 'he's just never able to get back out of the bath tub.'

Dick believes he has developed an amazing superhero ability. He's capable of using his amazing psychic power to melt ice cubes if he stares at them for long enough. It usually takes about two hours, even less if it's a warm day.

SUPERMODELS

Two supermodels are talking. One says, 'I had to insure my face for a million pounds?' 'Really?' says the other. 'So when you got the payout, what did you spend it on?'

A supermodel is late for a photoshoot because her taxi doesn't turn up. She decides to get a bus instead but, when it arrives, she finds that her skirt is so tight that she can't get up the step and climb aboard. So, to loosen it, she reaches behind her, lowers her zip and tries again. Still her skirt is too tight. So again she reaches behind, lowers the zip some more and once again tries to climb up. Still her skirt is too tight. The bus driver is now shouting at her to get on, so she reaches behind to lower the zip yet again. Suddenly, she feels two manly hands on her backside push her up on to the bus. She turns and angrily tells the man behind her, 'How dare you! I don't know you well enough for you to take hold of my buttocks like that.' 'No,' says the man, 'and I don't know you well enough for you to unzip my trousers three times either!'

SUPERSTITION

I'm suffering from Déjà Voodoo. The feeling that someone far away is sticking pins in you again.

I think I've been possessed by a haunted yogurt. I should never have eaten that 'Paranormal Activia'.

Hundreds of years ago men would curse and beat the ground with sticks. Then it was called witchcraft. Today, we know it as golf.

Superstitions are a load of rubbish. I've walked under ladders and broken mirrors loads of times and nothing has ever happened to me. Touch wood.

SUPPOSITORIES

I had to get a suppository from IKEA. The instructions said I had to put it up myself.

SURGERY

I always wanted to be a surgeon when I was a little boy. Sadly though, very few people were willing to be operated on by a seven-year-old.

A man has just had an operation in hospital. A nurse asks him how it went. 'OK,' says the man, 'but, in the middle of the procedure, I heard the doctor use a four-letter word which I didn't like.' 'Oh no,' says the nurse. 'What was the four-letter word?' 'Oops!' says the man.

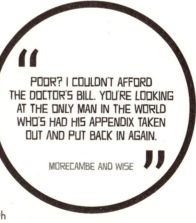

> POOR? I COULDN'T AFFORD THE DOCTOR'S BILL. YOU'RE LOOKING AT THE ONLY MAN IN THE WORLD WHO'S HAD HIS APPENDIX TAKEN OUT AND PUT BACK IN AGAIN.
>
> MORECAMBE AND WISE

My dad used to wear his heart on his sleeve. It was the result of an unfortunate medical blunder at Papworth Hospital.

The inventor of the clockwork radio has now applied his mind to the world of advanced transplant surgery. And that's why my granddad has become the recipient of the world's first clockwork pancreas.

A patient is in hospital for an operation. He tells the doctor, 'I'm quite concerned about this. Apparently this operation is only successful on one out of a hundred occasions.' 'Well,' says the doctor, 'this is your lucky day! The last 99 patients I operated on all died!'

A man goes into hospital to have his appendix removed. The next morning, he comes round but cannot understand why he has woken up with such a terrible sore throat. 'I'm sorry,' says a nurse, 'but there were a lot of medical students watching when the doctor did your operation. When he finished, they were so impressed, he took your tonsils out for an encore.'

A nurse asks a doctor why he looks so upset. 'It's the patient I was operating on this afternoon,' says the doctor, 'I'm afraid he died.' 'But, doctor,' says the nurse, 'you weren't performing an operation this afternoon. You were conducting a postmortem.' 'Really?' says the doctor. 'So who was the guy I did a postmortem on this morning?'

A man is brought into an operating theatre and prepared for surgery. He asks the doctor, 'How long do you think I'll be in hospital?' 'If all goes well,' says the doctor, 'you'll be out of here in about a week.' 'What about if things don't go well,' asks the man. 'Then,' says the doctor, 'it'll be much quicker.'

Larry has got breasts on the brain. He regrets having that cosmetic surgery now.

THINGS YOU DON'T WANT TO HEAR DURING SURGERY

- 'Sterile, schmerile. That floor's been mopped this morning hasn't it?'

- 'Is that the fire alarm! Oh no! We've all got to get out now!'

- 'Hey, look what I can do if I stick my finger in here! Who else wants to make his leg twitch?!'

- 'Could you move that TV slightly so I can see it properly. The football's about to start.'

- 'Oops! OK. There is a way to fix this. But it will involve giving the patient a sex change . . .'

- 'I know I shouldn't really have done that, but the voices in my head were overpowering.'

- 'Woah! Is that the time! I've got to pop out for a few minutes to put some more money in the parking meter!'

- 'Oops! Never mind! He won't know. He's out cold.'

- 'There! Not bad for someone who isn't even properly qualified.'

- 'This is quite difficult to do when you've got a hangover.'

- 'Did anyone count the number of clamps we started with?'

- 'Hang on. I think I recognise this patient. He's the guy my wife had an affair with a few years ago. I've been waiting to get my hands on him . . .'

SUSPICION

Sandra is very suspicious. If her husband comes home early, she thinks he's after something; if he comes home late, she thinks he's just had it.

SWANS

Eddie and Cynthia are walking in the local park. 'Aw!' says Cynthia. 'Look at the swans on the lake. Did you know, they mate for life.' 'Yes, I did,' says Eddie. 'And look how bad-tempered they are.'

SWEET NOTHINGS

Brenda turns to Tom in bed and says, 'Darling, I want you to whisper something soft and gooey into my ear.' 'OK,' says Tom, and he leans over and gently whispers, 'Sticky toffee pudding.'

SWIMMING

Hector the Head was born without a body, but, despite this disadvantage, he's fiercely competitive. One day he invites three of his friends to an organised contest at the local swimming pool. The friends aren't too sure about this, but they know that Hector has been practising and seems confident of winning, so they agree to give it a go – the first to complete a length will win. The four friends stand at the end of the pool, and when the whistle blows they all dive in. Sadly, Hector sinks to the bottom in a trail of bubbles and has to be hauled out in a net. 'What happened?' says one of his friends. 'You seemed so sure you had a chance. 'I'll tell you what happened,' fumes Hector. 'For five years I've been learning to swim with my ears, and just before the race starts, someone sticks a flipping swimming cap on my head.'

SWITZERLAND

I'm not sure what the best thing is about Switzerland, but the flag's obviously a big plus.

TAKEAWAYS

Fred opens the door to the pizza delivery boy. 'Don't expect a tip,' says Fred. 'I never give one.' 'That's OK,' says the boy. 'I wasn't expecting anything. The guys at the store said you wouldn't give me one. They figure you must be pretty hard up.' 'Do they?' exclaims Fred. He pulls out an extra £10 and hands it to the boy. 'Then tell the guys about that, why don't you?' 'I will,' says the boy. 'And I'll put this money towards my college fund.' 'Oh yes,' says Fred. 'So what are you studying?' 'Psychology,' says the boy.

Jane used to be married to Sam, the owner of a fried fish shop, but he died and she married Vernon, a poet. You could say she went from batter to verse.

Tom phones his local takeaway and asks, 'Do you deliver?' 'No, mate,' says a voice, 'but we do lamb, chicken and beef.'

I went to my local Chinese restaurant and ordered a number 13, a 27, a 35, and a 41. I had to send them back. They tasted a little odd.

Norman is buying a portion of chips. 'Is the salt and vinegar free here?' asks Norman. 'Of course it is,' says the chip-shop man. 'Oh good,' says Norman. 'In that case, I'll have three kilos of salt and a couple of bottles of vinegar.'

TATTOOS

There's nothing like getting a tattoo on your neck to let everyone know just how uninterested you are in being employed.

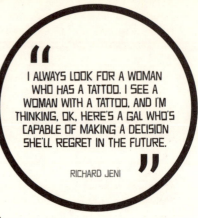

> I ALWAYS LOOK FOR A WOMAN WHO HAS A TATTOO. I SEE A WOMAN WITH A TATTOO, AND I'M THINKING, OK, HERE'S A GAL WHO'S CAPABLE OF MAKING A DECISION SHE'LL REGRET IN THE FUTURE.
>
> RICHARD JENI

Nobby goes to the tattoo shop and asks for a picture of an Indian on his back. After a few minutes he says, 'Don't forget. Give him a great big tomahawk in one hand.' 'I'll do that in a minute,' says the tattooist, 'I'll just finish his turban first.'

TAX

Kevin is trying to fill in his taxes, but he's unsure whether to screw them up himself or hire an accountant to do it for him.

One crotchety old man says to another, 'There should be a tax on people having sex.' 'There is,' says the other, 'it's called children.'

A tax official goes to Father O'Callaghan to ask about one of his congregation. 'We have records of a Seamus Murphy who claims to have made a charitable donation of £30,000 to your church,' says the official. 'Would you mind checking your records to see if is in fact the case.' 'Oh, there's no need for that,' says the Father O'Callaghan. 'If he's not made the donation already, he certainly will have by tomorrow.'

TAXIS

Nigel catches a cab to the train station. He remembers that he needs to take a detour to the office and leans forward to tap the cabby on the shoulder. The cabby screams and jumps in his seat, then pulls to a halt at the side of the road as he gasps for breath. 'I'm sorry,' he wheezes. 'I forget sometimes . . . For the last 30 years I drove a hearse.'

Have you heard about the former President of France who's now a taxi driver? He's called Francois Meter-on.

Bernice is taking a cab home when she realises she has no cash in her purse. 'Don't worry,' says the driver. 'We'll come to an arrangement. You take off your bra and I'll forget about the ten pounds you owe me.' 'Are you kidding?' says Bernice. 'My bra's worth at least £30. For that kind of money you're going to have to drive me to the airport and back.'

The Rolls-Royce of Lord Jinks-Howitzer breaks down on the way to his country house. The chauffeur stays with the car while His Lordship has to take a mini-cab home. 'Where to, guvnor?' asks the driver. 'Good grief, man,' says the peer. 'Do you think I'd give my address out to the likes of you?'

TEA

Q: What's the difference between the PG Tips monkey and the Aston Villa team?
A: Some people can remember seeing the PG Tips monkey holding a cup.

TECHNOLOGY

As a rule of thumb, never buy an item of electrical equipment that weighs less than the manual needed to understand how to work it.

> THE 19TH CENTURY WAS A TIME OF A GREAT MANY THOUGHTS AND INVENTIONS. PEOPLE STOPPED REPRODUCING BY HAND AND STARTED REPRODUCING BY MACHINE.
>
> SCHOOLBOY HOMEWORK ANSWER

You should always be careful to avoid letting technological devices know that you are in a hurry.

When CDs first appeared, we were forever being told you could mess them up however you liked and they'd still play. So, as an experiment, I set fire to a Dire Straits CD, trampled it in gravel and dunked it in boiling porridge. Unluckily, the flippin' thing still played perfectly.

I can't think what my mum and dad found to do before the internet. I've asked my 13 brothers and sisters, and they can't think either.

Tom has had a remote control garage door fitted and is standing in his living room demonstrating it to Harry. 'Look,' he says, 'I press this button and the garage door automatically opens.' Harry listens and hears the whirr of the door opening outside. 'And I press this button,' says Tom, 'and the garage door automatically closes again.' Harry listens and hears a loud crash. 'What was that?' he asks. Tom looks out of the window and says, 'That was my wife choosing the wrong moment to drive to the shops.'

A bar installs a robot bartender that can change its conversation according to a customer's IQ. If the customer has an IQ over 150, the robot talks about quantum physics, economic theory and classical literature. If the customer has an IQ over 100, the robot talks about current affairs, television and sports. Between 50 and a 100, the robot talks about the weather, soap operas and bingo. Anything less than that, it's the Kardashians, lottery numbers and the political wisdom of Donald Trump.

And lo, God came forth and verily widescreen television did appear before the tribes of Israel. Sony 16:9.

TEENAGERS

Babies and small children are cute, but teenagers appear to be God's delayed punishment for having sex.

TELEVISION

Dick doesn't know why they put the brightness control on his TV. He keeps turning it up, but it doesn't seem to make the programmes any less stupid.

A little boy is watching the television in his room when he comes out and asks, 'Dad! What does love juice mean?' Dad is horrified to think what the little boy has been watching but nevertheless decides to give a full, frank and detailed explanation about the birds, the bees and the whole business of sexual reproduction. At the end, the little boy is sitting there with his mouth wide open. 'By the way,' says dad, 'what were you watching when they started talking about love juice?' 'The tennis,' says the little boy.

> FOR THOSE OF YOU WATCHING IN BLACK AND WHITE, THE GREEN BALL'S THE ONE BEHIND THE BLUE.
>
> TED LOWE

Phil has found a way to get out of buying a television licence. He just photocopies his old one and watches repeats.

In the six o'clock news each day, the presenter begins by saying 'Good evening' and then spends the next half-hour telling you why it isn't.

It's been announced that ITV is launching a new reality game show. It's called *Help! I'm an Ex-Celebrity! Get Me Back on Television!*

I like that TV reality show where a team comes and rips everything out of a couple's house ready to start up all over again from nothing. I think it's called *Changing Bailiffs*.

Harry says he knows what it feels like to be a competitor on *The Voice*. He farted on the bus this morning and four people turned round to look at him.

Q: How many 'X Factor' stars does it take to change a light bulb.
A: Five. One to put the light bulb in a little bit like Christina Aguilera or Justin Timberlake would have done it, and four to tell them it was either the worst or the most incredible light bulb replacement they have ever seen in their life.

The man who used to fix our television has switched professions and established his own unique self-help programme. If you're having some sort of emotional problem he'll come round to your house, hit you and swear at you until you feel better.

TEMPTATION

Barry went on a stag-do to London and ended up having sex with a model. A spokesman for Madame Tussauds has said that he is now banned for life.

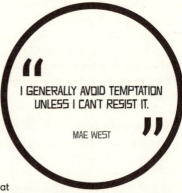

" I GENERALLY AVOID TEMPTATION UNLESS I CAN'T RESIST IT.

MAE WEST "

TENNIS

There has been uproar among animal lovers at the news from the Wimbledon tennis championships. Apparently, it's not the tennis players who keep grunting during the matches; it's the specially bred, small, round, luminous yellow hamsters which they use as balls.

I found a place online selling tennis balls at a bargain price but the site kept crashing. I think they were having problems with their server.

TESTICLES

A little boy is sitting in the bath examining himself. 'Mummy,' he says, 'what are these balls between my legs? Are they my brains?' 'No,' says his mum. 'At least, not yet.'

Neville goes back to work after suffering a serious groin injury. A friend asks if everything is OK. 'Not so great,' says Neville. 'They managed to save my testicles.' 'Surely that's good news, isn't it?' says the friend. 'Not really,' says Neville. 'They've gave them to me floating in a jar.'

TEXTING

When Harry's kids text him for money they always use the word 'plz'. Harry asks them what that means and they explain it is shorter than saying please. So he responds to their request 'no', which he tells them is shorter than saying 'yes'.

Texts from my gran have become so much more entertaining since I told her that WTF stands for 'Wow, that's fantastic!'

Gary starts receiving anonymous messages telling him to have a bath, to get his hair cut and combed tidily, and to keep his teeth clean. He asks a friend if he knows what this means. 'Oh no!' says the friend. 'I think someone's trying to groom you.'

Tom texts his wife, 'I won't be home till late. Please wash all my clothes ready for tomorrow and have a hot meal ready when I get in.' A few minutes later he texts again and says, 'I forgot to say, I got a promotion today, so I've gone out and bought you a new sports car.' His wife instantly texts back and says, 'Oh my God! Really?' Tom texts back, 'No. Not really. I just wanted to check you got my first message.'

Harry received an anonymous text yesterday. It read, 'B' 'A' 'G' 'N'. He thought it was bang out of order.

THERAPY

Norman goes to see his psychotherapist. 'My analysis,' says the therapist, 'is that you have an overwhelming preoccupation with vengeance.' 'Oh yeah?' says Norman. 'Well, we'll see about that, won't we?'

My analyst says I suffer from a narcissistic attitude that often leads to me misinterpreting the attitudes of others in social situations. Really, though, I think she just fancies me.

If you want to work to improve your psychological balance, first you need to become aware of all your character defects. Once you've done that, you can proceed to the next stage in the healing process – blaming your parents for them.

Jerry developed a paranoid fear that people were always taking advantage of him. It got so bad that he booked himself into a residential clinic. Last week he finished repairing their roof and now they've got him redecorating the staff lounge.

Q: How many sex therapists does it take to change a light bulb?
A: Two. One to screw it in, and another to suggest changing his technique.

Larry is a psychiatrist. He walks into the waiting room of his office and finds two men sitting there. One is dressed like Napoleon, the other is wearing a robe and sandals. Larry turns to the man in the uniform and says, 'Let me guess. You think you're Napoleon Bonaparte.' 'Of course I am,' says the man. 'Can't you tell?' 'I can see you're dressed like him,' says Larry. 'But why do you think you're him?' Napoleon says, 'Because Jesus Christ told me.' The man in the sandals throws down his magazine, 'For the last time! I did no such thing!'

Barry had to send his son to a child psychologist. He would have preferred to send him to a grown-up one, but they all worked out to be a lot more expensive. It went very badly when I visited a psychiatrist to discuss my innate fear of lying on couches.

Q: What does a psychologist have at the side of his bed? **A:** Freudian slippers.

THIEVES

Two idiot thieves stole a calendar. Each of them got six months.

THINNESS

Don is a very weedy, thin man. When he goes to the doctor's, they don't need to use the X-ray machine to examine him; they just hold him up against a sunny window.

Last night I had a dream that I weighed less than 1,000th of a gram. I was just like – 0mg!

Mabel was such a thin girl. One day she swallowed an olive and four guys left town.

THREESOMES

Last night Josh almost had a threesome. All he needed was for two other people to come round and join him.

A young man picks up an older woman at a bar. When they get to her house, she suddenly asks, 'How would you feel about a mother and daughter threesome?' The young man is delighted by the idea. The woman is in her fifties, but is very attractive and the man reckons her daughter must be a stunner. 'Yes, please,' he says. 'Great!' she says, then calls up the stairs, 'Mum! Get your teeth in! He's up for it!'

Gary is in trouble with his girlfriend. Last night, she asked him which of her friends he fancied having a threesome with. He realised too late he should only have said one name.

TIME

Time, they say, is the best teacher. But it's not that good, because all its students die when they graduate.

I haven't owned a watch for I don't know how long.

TIME MACHINES

Barry is going to have to rethink the business model for his time-machine rental company. Too many of his customers keep bringing them back for a refund the day before they rented them.

TIME WASTING

Tom's boss sends him on a training course about time wasting. It goes on for three weeks.

TIPPING

A man runs into a bar, orders a beer, and drinks it in one gulp. He puts down a £5 note then runs out again. The barman sees an opportunity for some pilfering and tucks the money into his top pocket. The voice of his boss booms across the room. 'Hey! What are you doing? I saw you steal that note!' The barman gulps and says, 'You've got it all wrong, boss. That guy drank a beer, gave me a tip, then ran off without paying.'

TOILET PAPER

How many guys does it take to replace an empty roll of toilet paper? No one knows. Call me when it happens.

What's the definition of success for a sheet of toilet paper — being used to wipe someone's nose.

Life is like being a piece of toilet paper. One day you're on a roll, the next, you're taking crap from some bum.

TOILETS

An American tourist is in London seeing the sights and visiting many pubs. He then finds himself in a high-class neighbourhood of stately residences. Unfortunately, after all his drinking, he is now desperate for a wee. He finds a side street and is about to relieve himself when he is apprehended by a policeman. 'I'm sorry, officer,' says the American, 'but I have to go and I can't find a public toilet.' 'Follow me,' says the policeman, and leads him through an alley to a gate. 'You can go in there,' says the policeman. 'Whiz away wherever you want.' The tourist enters and finds himself in a beautiful garden of manicured lawns and sculpted hedges. Since he has the policeman's blessing, he unburdens himself and is greatly relieved. As he goes back through the gate, he says, 'Thank you so much. Is that what you call "English hospitality"?' 'No, sir,' says the policeman, 'that's what we call "the French Embassy".'

> **TOILETS WERE INVENTED BY THE ROMANS IN THE SECOND CENTURY. THE VERY NEXT DAY, 'OUT OF ORDER' SIGNS WERE INVENTED.**
>
> ERMA BOMBECK

They've had to start making toilet rolls specially designed for idiots. There are instructions printed on each sheet.

A man is using a public toilet when a pound coin falls out of his pocket into the toilet bowl. He can't bring himself to stick his hand into the filthy water just to get one pound back. So he throws a ten-pound note in as well. 'Now it's worth it!' he says, and rolls up his sleeve.

TOILET OUT OF ORDER. PLEASE USE FLOOR BELOW.

SIGN ON DOOR OF TOILET IN OFFICE BLOCK

Bennie works as a toilet cleaner, but his employer discovers he's illiterate and fires him. A new job is hard to come by, so he starts his own business. Years pass and Bennie eventually becomes the head of a multimillion-pound corporation. He's interviewed by a business magazine and the reporter is fascinated by his humble origins. 'So you were fired for being illiterate. Wow! Just think what you'd be doing now if you could read and write.' 'I know exactly what I'd be doing now,' says Bennie. 'I'd be cleaning toilets.'

If you see a sign on the door of the gents' toilet saying 'wet floor', please remember – it's not meant as a request.

Did you hear about the idiot who got locked in a public toilet? He was trapped in there so long he ended up peeing his pants.

TOLERANCE

My people skills are excellent. Unfortunately, the same cannot be said of my tolerance to idiots.

TORTILLAS

Barry has written a song about a tortilla. Actually, it's not so much a song as a wrap.

TOURIST ATTRACTIONS

Barry has bought a framed painting of the Leaning Tower of Pisa to put over the mantelpiece in his living room. He has spent the past three days trying to hang it so it looks right.

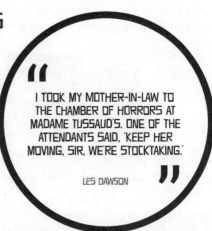

" I TOOK MY MOTHER-IN-LAW TO THE CHAMBER OF HORRORS AT MADAME TUSSAUD'S. ONE OF THE ATTENDANTS SAID, 'KEEP HER MOVING, SIR, WE'RE STOCKTAKING.' "

LES DAWSON

TOYS

INSTRUCTIONS PRINTED ON A PACKET OF SILLY PUTTY

We had to cut down on Christmas presents this year. I gave my son an empty box and told him it was the 'Action Man Deserter Kit'.

A man goes to the doctor with his son and confesses that he has managed to get four plastic toy horses stuck up his nose. The doctor examines him and says, 'Don't worry. His condition is stable.'

TRAFFIC

If someone cuts you up in traffic, just turn the other cheek. Nothing gets the message across like a good mooning.

What do you get if you cross a motorway with a blindfold? Splattered all over the fast lane.

The traffic is terrible round here. Last week my son had to abandon his vehicle and complete his driving test on foot.

> ANOTHER MOTORING FLASH. ON THE A30 THIS AFTERNOON A TANKER-LOAD OF BLEACH ON ITS WAY TO THE WEST COUNTRY OVERTURNED ON A NOTORIOUS ACCIDENT BLACK SPOT, TURNING IT IMMEDIATELY INTO A NOTORIOUS ACCIDENT WHITE SPOT.
>
> THE TWO RONNIES

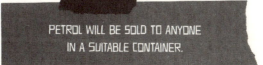

SIGN AT A PETROL STATION

TRAGEDY AND COMEDY

Donald Trump is on a campaign trip and visits a nursery school where the children are having an English class. The teacher says, 'Who can give me a sentence with the with the word "accident" in it?'. None of the children stick their hands up. 'OK,' says the teacher. 'How about "loss"? Can anyone think how to use that word?' Again, the children say nothing. 'Very well,' says the teacher. 'How about the word "tragedy"? Any ideas?' The children give her blank looks. 'I think you need an incentive,' says Trump. 'Tell you what. I'll give $50 to the first student who can use all three words in the same sentence.' Immediately, little Johnny sticks his hand up. 'Very good,' says Trump. 'Let's hear it.' Little Johnny says, 'If you were run off the road in your car and killed, it would be a terrible tragedy, but it would not be a great loss, and probably not a goddamn accident either.'

> "TRAGEDY IS WHEN I CUT MY FINGER – COMEDY IS IF YOU FALL INTO A SEWER AND DIE."
>
> MEL BROOKS

THE EIGHTH-GRADERS WILL BE PRESENTING SHAKESPEARE'S *HAMLET* IN THE CHURCH BASEMENT FRIDAY AT 7PM. THE CONGREGATION IS INVITED TO ATTEND THIS TRAGEDY.

PARISH NOTICES

TRAINS

Bill is really pleased when his wife gets him an expensive gift experience package that will enable him to fulfil a lifetime's ambition to drive a full-size train. Apparently it's a special offer from the rail company to help them cover the next drivers' strike. And it still works out ten pounds cheaper than an off-peak return.

> "I WAS ON THE SUBWAY, SITTING ON A NEWSPAPER, AND A GUY COMES OVER AND ASKS, 'ARE YOU READING THAT?' I DIDN'T KNOW WHAT TO SAY. SO I SAID YES. I STOOD UP, TURNED THE PAGE, AND SAT DOWN AGAIN."
>
> DAVID BRENNER

A man is on a busy commuter train. He calls his wife on his mobile phone and says, 'Darling, it's Matthew. I'm on my way home. I got held up in the office. No, honestly, it's true. I've been in a meeting at work. No, I swear to you, my darling. I haven't been anywhere else or been to see anyone else.' Finally, a girl sitting opposite can't resist any longer. 'Hey, Matthew!' she shouts. 'Will you get off that phone and get back into bed!'

A man is complaining at the ticket office of a railway station. 'What's the point of having a timetable,' says the man, 'when the trains are always late?' 'Ah! But look at it this way,' says the man in the office, 'if we didn't have a timetable, how would you know they were late?'

Beryl complains to her friend that she felt sick when she was riding on the train. 'I was travelling with my back to the engine,' she says. 'I hate that.' 'You should have asked the person in the opposite seat to swap with you,' says the friend. 'I couldn't have done that,' says Beryl. 'There was no one there.'

A train breaks down in the middle of its journey. The conductor gets on the intercom and says, 'One of our engines has broken down. But, let's look on the bright side, the secondary engine is still working fine, so we'll be able to continue our journey at only a slightly lower speed.' Half an hour later, the second engine packs up. The conductor gets on the intercom again. 'Ladies and gentlemen,' he says, 'both our engines are out and we have no power. But, look on the bright side. At least you're not on a plane.'

An ancient locomotive is chugging along the line. It's very slow and one of the passengers calls over the conductor to complain. 'Good Lord, man,' he says. 'Can't you go any faster than this?' 'I can,' says the conductor. 'But sadly I'm not allowed to leave the train.'

> "I KNEW I WAS GOING TO TAKE THE WRONG TRAIN, SO I LEFT EARLY."
>
> YOGI BERRA

Do you know why steam trains can't sit down? They usually have a tender behind.

Two men are talking at the train station about how busy it is on the morning commute. 'I say a prayer to St Christopher, the patron saint of travellers,' says one man, 'and I usually find a seat even if the train is crowded.' 'That's nothing,' says the second man. 'I find that if I pray to Allah loudly enough, I can usually get a whole carriage to myself!'

> WE APOLOGISE FOR THE LATE RUNNING OF THIS TRAIN. THIS IS DUE TO US FOLLOWING A TRAIN THAT IS IN FRONT OF US.
>
> BRITISH RAIL EMPLOYEE

TRAMPS

Nobby isn't very good with words. He thought that 'trampoline' was the name of a cleaning liquid you could use on vagrants.

A tramp asks a student for some change. 'No,' says the student. 'You'll only spend it on drink and drugs.' 'Yeah?' says the tramp. 'So what are you going to spend it on?'

TRANSVESTITES

Ron's wife told him to his face that she suspected him of being a transvestite. He took his suitcase, packed her things and left.

TRAVEL

> QUESTION MASTER: WHAT IS THE ITALIAN WORD FOR 'MOTORWAY'?
> CONTESTANT: EXPRESSO.
>
> STEVE WRIGHT SHOW

TREES

Barry woke up this morning and discovered that the tree outside his house had completely disappeared. He ended up taping 'missing tree' posters to the local cats to see if anyone knew where it had got to.

Q: What do you get hanging from cherry trees? **A:** Sore arms.

If a tree falls in the forest, do all the other trees laugh at it?

TUG OF WAR

The Anglo-French tug-of-war championship had to be called off yesterday – they couldn't find a piece of rope 30 miles long.

TURKEYS

Q: Why did the turkey cross the road? **A:** To show he wasn't chicken.

TURTLES

In the middle of a deep forest, a little baby turtle starts climbing a tall tree. He climbs and climbs until eventually he reaches the top branch, where he jumps off, frantically waving his little legs until he crashes into the ground below. A couple of birds are sitting watching. One says to the other, 'I really think we'd better tell him he's adopted.'

TWINS

Apparently, when they were born, the Chuckle Brothers were a pair of conjoined twins. They had to be separated in an eight-hour operation known as a Tometoyoutomy.

Nobby was appalled when his wife gave birth to twin boys. Despite all his pleading, she refused to name the father of the second child.

I'm never keen on twins. It's rare I even like one of a person.

TYPES OF PEOPLE

There are two types of people in this world. People who love closure and . . .

There are two types of people in the world. Those who can extrapolate from incomplete data.

There are ten sorts of people in the world. Those who understand binary and those who have regular sex.

UGLINESS

Don't ever risk getting into a punch-up with an ugly person. They have nothing to lose.

Harry tells his wife, 'You look like a million dollars.' 'Aw! Thanks, love,' says his wife. '. . . after taxes,' continues Harry.

Nigel was not what you'd call handsome, in fact his first job was posing for the 'before' picture in advertisements for spot cream.

Glenda gets talking to another woman at a cocktail party. 'Don't look now,' she says. 'But the man standing by the window has to be the ugliest guy I saw in my life. His face could stop a clock.' 'That man happens to be my husband,' says the woman. 'I'm so sorry,' says Glenda. '*You're* sorry . . .!?' replies the woman.

My husband is so ugly. Last week he was captured by cannibals, but after they got a good look at him, they ordered a salad.

Ken is beginning to think he might be ugly. Last week, he was fired from a job on a building site because of his appearance.

After a night of drink, drugs and wild sex Dave woke up to find himself next to a really ugly woman. That's when he realised he'd made it home safely.

UGLINESS - INSULTS

- Everybody has the right to be ugly. Unfortunately, you seem to have abused that privilege!

- Not only must you have fallen out of the ugly tree, you must have hit every branch on the way down.

- If I had a dog that looked like you, I'd get the vet to shave its backside and walk it everywhere backwards.

- You have a very unusual face. If I had one like that, I'd consider taking my parents to court!

- Aren't you supposed to have a licence to be that ugly?

- If you look at my face, you'll see I don't care. And if you look at your own face, you'll see that God didn't care much either.

UNDERSTANDING

A man goes the doctor and says, 'Doctor, I feel that nobody understands me.' 'Sorry,' says the doctor, 'I've no idea what you're talking about.'

UNEMPLOYMENT

Barry owned the world's laziest goat. He called it Billy Idol.

UNIDENTIFIED FLYING OBJECTS

A Scottish man phones the emergency services to say that he can see an enormous, glowing UFO hovering over his house. The emergency services put him onto the Met Office who confirm that what he can see is, in fact, the sun.

USED CARS

Brian's second-hand car company has fallen foul of the rules on clear and truthful advertising. Now he has to have a sign in the showroom window saying: 'Used Cars: Why go elsewhere to be cheated? Come here first!'

I was out with my wife yesterday, we were driving our old car when the brakes failed. We were on top of a slope, going downhill fast with nothing to stop us. I panicked and shouted, 'My God! What am I going to do?' My wife shouted back, 'Brace yourself! And try and crash into something inexpensive!'

A man storms into his local garage. 'When I bought that second-hand truck from you yesterday, you said it was rust-free.' 'Yes,' says the mechanic. 'That we did.' The man says, 'But when I got it home and looked under the chassis, I found it was covered in rust.' 'So?' says the mechanic. 'Did we charge you for it?'

Bert's car used to make a banging noise every time it turned a corner. The mechanics eventually got to the bottom of it – they took his bowling ball out of the boot.

I went to see a second-hand car advertised in the local paper. When I got there I found it was covered in dents and scratches. 'What's this?' I said. 'Your ad said it had one careful owner.' 'That's right,' said the seller. 'It did have one careful owner. But the rest of them were maniacs.'

USEFULNESS

YOU'RE ABOUT AS MUCH USE AS A . . .

▶ . . . a Braille speedometer.

▶ . . . a fire-proof match.

▶ . . . a glass hammer.

YOU'RE ABOUT AS MUCH USE AS A . . .

▶ . . . a helicopter ejector seat.

▶ . . . an inflatable dartboard.

▶ . . . a silent alarm clock.

▶ . . . a solar-powered torch.

▶ . . . a flammable fire extinguisher.

▶ . . . a concrete trampoline.

▶ . . . a soluble lifeboat.

▶ . . . a black highlighter pen.

▶ . . . a waterproof sponge.

▶ . . . a waterproof teabag.

▶ . . . a lead parachute.

▶ . . . a concrete life-vest.

▶ . . . a condom vending machine in the Vatican.

▶ . . . a one-legged man at an arse-kicking contest.

▶ . . . an ashtray on a motorcycle.

▶ . . . dental floss at a Willie Nelson concert.

VACUUM CLEANERS

I sat on a vacuum cleaner attachment the other day and had to go to A&E. They couldn't get it out, but on the bright side, they say I'm picking up nicely.

Nobby ended up in hospital with a terrible injury. He is now writing a letter of complaint to let the manufacturers know that the 'Dyson Ball Cleaner' has a potentially misleading name.

Have you heard the joke about the vacuum cleaner? It sucks.

VAGUENESS

The best thing about being vague is . . . lots of stuff.

VALENTINE'S DAY

Nobby comes home with a floral arrangement for his wife. 'Happy Valentine's Day!' he says, but Norma is unimpressed. 'Were they selling these off cheap in the flower shop?' she asks. 'No,' says Nobby. 'Oh really?' she says. 'So why do the flowers spell "RIP Granddad"?'

I always thought it would be a thrill to get an anonymous Valentine's Day card slipped under my door with a message from a mysterious admirer. It turns out not to be so thrilling and romantic when it happens on your first night in prison.

VAMPIRES

Dracula finally died yesterday afternoon. He had to get up to go to the toilet, but forgot he hadn't closed the curtains on the landing.

Vampires aren't supposed to cast a reflection in a mirror. But if that's true, how do they always manage to keep their hair so neat?

VASECTOMY

Reggie asked his family if he should have a vasectomy. They took a vote and the motion was carried by twelve votes to two.

> **"** I TOLD MY DOCTOR I WANTED A VASECTOMY. HE SAID, WITH A FACE LIKE MINE, I DON'T NEED ONE. **"**
>
> RODNEY DANGERFIELD

VEGETARIANS AND VEGANS

A new study has shown that there is a significant risk that vegans will go blind. Apparently it's from having to squint at the small print on all those ingredient labels.

Q: What does a vegetarian cannibal eat? **A:** Swedes.

Q: How many vegetarians does it take to eat a bacon sandwich? **A:** One, if nobody's looking.

> **"** I'M NOT A VEGETARIAN, BUT I EAT ANIMALS WHO ARE. **"**
>
> GROUCHO MARX

VEHICLE THEFT

A police van has been stolen. Unfortunately, the police can't tell anyone the vehicle registration or give a description because it belonged to the Special Branch and they don't want anyone to know what it looks like.

VENGEANCE

A man walks into a crowded bar carrying a gun. 'OK,' he shouts, 'somebody here has been messing around with my girlfriend and I'm going to deal with them.' 'You won't have enough bullets!' says a voice from the back of the room.

VENICE

Harry's uncle was run over by a boat in Venice. Everyone sends him their gondolences.

VENTRILOQUISM

A ventriloquist is touring the country, and one night has to take lodgings with a farmer. Before the farmer takes him to his room, he shows him round the farm. First, the farmer shows the ventriloquist his donkey. The ventriloquist says, 'Hello, Mr Donkey. Do you like it here on the farm?' The ventriloquist then throws his voice to make the donkey reply, 'Oh yes. The farmer is very kind to me and gives me lots of carrots.' 'My goodness,' says the farmer, 'I've had that animal 20 years and he's never said a word to me!' Next, the farmer takes the ventriloquist to see his cow. The ventriloquist again asks, 'Hello, Mrs Cow. Do you like it here on the farm?' And again he makes the animal reply, 'Oh yes. The farmer is very kind to me. He milks me every morning and his hands are always lovely and warm.' The farmer is again astounded and he is about to take the ventriloquist to see his field of sheep but suddenly stops and says, 'Actually, it's probably best not to ask the sheep anything. I know a few of them tell some awful lies about me!'

Britain's most famous ventriloquist has been found dead. It's believed he committed suicide as his body was found next to a kacket of kills and a gottle of geer.

A ventriloquist walks into a bar and a voice from the other side of the room says, 'Ouch.'

My uncle was a well-known ventriloquist. Last week I went to his funeral. At the end of the service we all sang, 'All Things Gright and Geautiful!'

An unsuccessful ventriloquist decides to switch careers and advertises himself as a psychic. If you want to speak to your dearly departed, he charges £50 for 15 minutes. If you want to speak to your dearly departed while he drinks a glass of water, it's £75.

VETS

Tom went to the vet's and noticed they had a 'Two for the Price of One' offer. He couldn't resist, but he got into trouble at home. Only one of their cats had really needed to be put down.

Rather than treat animals with drugs, our vet prefers to use holistic, natural methods. It's quite controversial though. Last week he put my dog down by wrestling with it for ten minutes.

Terry asks Dick, 'Tell me – what's your pet hate?' 'Having injections at the vets,' says Dick.

VIAGRA

Never take iron tablets and Viagra at the same time – you'll end up with a willy that always points due north.

Old Norman comes home with a supply of Viagra from the chemist's. 'I can't believe the price of these things,' says Norman. 'Ten quid a tablet!' 'Never mind. Look on the bright side,' says his wife. 'That's only £20 a year.'

An old man goes to the doctor because he's having problems with his sexual performance. 'Oh, we can easily sort that out!' says the doctor, and writes him a prescription for a bottle of Viagra. A few weeks later, the doctor sees him again and the old man thanks him profusely. 'It's a miracle,' he says, 'it's given me a whole new lease of life.' 'Excellent,' says the doctor, 'so what does your wife think about it?' 'I'm not sure,' says the old man. 'I haven't been home yet.'

Ken puts a bit of powdered Viagra in his tea each morning. It's not to help his sexual performance. It's just to stop his biscuit going soft when he dunks it.

Gladys accidentally overdoses her husband with Viagra and he dies of a heart attack. She goes into a chemist's and asks if they have something to cure him. 'I don't understand,' says the chemist. 'I thought you said he was dead?' 'He is dead,' says Gladys. 'Now I'm trying to find a way to close the coffin.'

A man goes to the chemist's to get some Viagra, but they gave him Tippex by mistake. He ended up with a massive correction.

Never take more Viagra than it says on the instructions or it will end badly. Trust me, I found out the hard way.

VIKINGS

Sven was the worst Viking in Norway because he always burned first and pillaged second.

VIOLENCE

A man has been attacked outside a public house. The policeman asks him, 'Are you able to describe the person who hit you?' 'Yes,' says the victim. 'In fact, that's exactly what I was doing when he got cross and started walloping me.'

> "I said, 'How did you get those two black eyes?' She answered, 'The lodger gave them to me.' I went straight up to that lodger: 'Did you give my wife two black eyes?' 'Yes,' he said, 'she's been unfaithful to us.'"
>
> MAX MILLER

Freddie is offered a job in Chicago, but he's worried that the city has a reputation for violent crime. His neighbour grew up in Chicago so he goes to ask what the place is really like. 'You can't beat Chicago,' says the neighbour. 'The best people in the world live in Chicago.' 'How about crime?' asks Freddie. 'I never had no trouble myself,' says the neighbour. 'In ten years I never got robbed or mugged once.' 'It doesn't sound too bad at all,' says Freddie. 'By the way, what kind of work did you do over there?' 'I was the rear-gunner on an ambulance,' says the neighbour.

VIRGINITY

Barry has noticed a woman who always comes into the pub on her own. He goes over and tries chatting her up. 'Sorry,' she tells him. 'I'm not interested. I know it sounds rather old-fashioned, but I've decided to keep myself pure until I meet the man I love.' 'Oh,' says Barry. 'That must be difficult for you.' 'Not really,' says the woman, 'although my husband's not mad about the idea.'

VITAMINS

Bill gets knocked down when someone throws a large bottle of Omega-3 tablets at him. When he comes round, he asks the doctor if he's going to be OK. 'Yes,' says the doctor, 'luckily you've only suffered super-fish-oil injuries.'

VOLUNTARY WORK

Gary goes to the Job Centre. 'Have you ever thought about voluntary work?' asks the assistant. 'No chance,' says Gary. 'I wouldn't do that if you paid me!'

VOYEURISM

The old man who lived in the flat above me died recently, and the landlord discovered that he'd drilled holes in his floors so he could spy on the people in the rooms below him. But even if he was an old pervert, I still like to think he's up there somewhere, looking down on us.

WAKING UP

There's just one thing that will wake you up quicker than a hot cup of coffee — a hot cup of spilled coffee.

WALES

Harry and Vera are on holiday touring round Wales. One day they arrive on the coast near Anglesey and see a sign saying 'Welcome to Llanfairpwllgwyngyllgogerychwyrndrobwllllantysiliogogogoch.' Harry tries to pronounce the name, causing Vera to collapse in fits of giggles. Harry gets cross with his wife's mockery and the pair begin to argue about the pronunciation of the name. In the end, they go into a nearby restaurant and march up to the cashier. Vera says, 'I wonder if you could settle an argument please. Could you tell my husband exactly how the name of the place we're currently in should be pronounced.' The cashier leans over to Harry and says very slowly and clearly, 'Mc-Don-alds.'

Q: How should you grate cheese in Wales? **A:** Caerphilly.

WARNING SIGNS

DO NOT ACTIVATE WITH WET HANDS.

WARNING NOTICE ON A HAND-DRYER IN A GERMAN PUBLIC TOILET

I had to take the batteries out of my carbon monoxide detector. The constant beeping noise was making me feel nauseous.

WASTE DISPOSAL

Did you hear the joke about the waste tip? It was total rubbish.

Gary's dad was a binman, so he used to hate it when his dad was supposed to come and collect him from school. It wasn't the fact that he was a binman, or that he turned up in the bin lorry. It was just that he never knew which day he was going to turn up.

> " SHE RAN AFTER THE GARBAGE TRUCK, YELLING, 'AM I TOO LATE FOR THE GARBAGE?' 'NO, JUMP IN!' "
>
> HENNY YOUNGMAN

Q: Where does the Lone Ranger take his recycling?
A: To the dump, to the dump, to the dump, dump, dump, to the dump, to the dump, to the dump, dump, dump . . .

'Mummy, Mummy. What's a waste disposal unit?' 'Shut up child and just keep chewing.'

WATER

During the drought last year the local swimming pool had to save water. So they announced they were closing lanes seven and eight.

> THE SERVICE WILL CLOSE WITH 'LITTLE DROPS OF WATER'. ONE OF THE LADIES WILL START (QUIETLY) AND THE REST OF THE CONGREGATION WILL JOIN IN.

PARISH NOTICES

WEALTH

People are always saying, 'Early to bed and early to rise, makes you healthy, wealthy and wise.' But how many healthy, wealthy and wise chickens do you know?

A man is slouched over a bar, drinking himself senseless. 'Do you know what?' he tells the barman. 'My wife made me a millionaire.' 'That's good,' says the barman. 'So what were you before you met her?' 'A billionaire,' says the man.

> "MONEY DOESN'T MAKE YOU HAPPY. I HAVE $50 MILLION, BUT I WAS JUST AS HAPPY WHEN I HAD $48 MILLION."
>
> ARNOLD SCHWARZENEGGER

Algernon was a very, very wealthy man. He was so rich that he had a doorman for every door in his house. And that included each of the kitchen cupboards.

A man and woman are preparing to go out for a meal, but the woman can't decide what to wear. 'Which looks better?' she asks her husband. 'My Chanel dress or Armani suit? Diamonds or pearls? The Rolex or Cartier watch?' 'I really don't care,' says the man, 'but if you don't hurry up, we're going to miss the early-bird half-price special offer.'

The secret to great wealth is thrift. For example, that must be how Bill Gates became so rich. Clearly that man has never spent more than five dollars on a haircut.

Brian tells his friend Joe, 'Y'know, if I was given all the money that David Beckham has, I'd actually be richer than he is.' 'How do you work that out?' asks Joe. 'Would you invest it better than he does?' 'No,' says Brian. 'But I'd still be doing a bit of mini-cabbing on the side.'

Terry hears about the death of a local millionaire and breaks down in tears. His friend comes over to see what's the matter. 'Hey. This guy wasn't a relative of yours, was he?' 'No,' sniffs Terry. 'That's what's so sad.'

WEATHER

I love summer in Britain. I think it might be my favourite day of the year.

A Native American chief believes a bad winter is coming, so he sends out all the braves to collect firewood. Nevertheless, the chief still thinks he'd better not just rely on his instinct, so he decides to check the local weather forecast. He calls up the local weather station and asks if they think a bad winter is coming. 'Yes, we do,' says the weatherman. On hearing this, the chief tells his braves they must go back into the forest and find even more wood. Again though, the chief has his doubts and calls the weather station to ask, 'Are you absolutely sure it is going to be a bad winter?' 'Yes,' says the weatherman, 'in fact it's not just going to be bad, it's going to be severe.' On hearing this, the chief tells his braves they must go back out yet again and find even more wood. Again, the chief checks back with the weather station and asks them, 'Look! Are you really sure this winter is going to be severe? 'Are you kidding?' says the weatherman. 'It's going to be the worst on record. Apparently the Injuns are all gathering wood like crazy!'

Ever since it started raining, my wife has just been standing looking sadly through the window. If the weather gets any worse, I think I'm going to have to let her in.

It rains constantly where I live. It's so bad, the local trains don't have brakes, they have anchors.

Dick hears a severe weather warning. Anyone travelling in the current wintry conditions is advised to take emergency equipment with them including a shovel, a sleeping bag, food and drink, de-icer, rock salt, a first-aid kit and a pair of jump leads. Half an hour later, he's sitting on the bus wondering why everyone is staring at him.

Vera calls up the stairs, 'Sun's just come out.' Harry grabs his sun cream, puts on his T-shirt and runs down the stairs, only to find their son hand-in-hand with his best friend Lionel.

Dick and Norman are out for a walk when the skies open and it starts pouring down. Dick is carrying an umbrella, but when he opens it and puts it up, Norman sees that it's torn to shreds. 'Why did you bring that piece of rubbish with you?' asks Norman. 'Well,' says Dick, 'I didn't think it would rain.'

In Mississippi they call a divorce a 'Kansas Tornado'. In either event, someone loses a trailer.

WEDDINGS

Barry calls a friend and says, 'Guess what! I've just arrived in Australia and it's going to be an incredible surprise for my fiancée.' 'It certainly is,' says his friend, 'she's still over here and your wedding's this afternoon.'

At a wedding reception, the photographer is lining up his next picture. He calls out, 'I want all the married men here to stand next to the person who has made your life worth living.' The man standing behind the bar is almost crushed to death.

A little boy is at a wedding with his daddy. During the service he asks, 'Why are the man and lady holding hands like that?' 'It's a formality, son,' says the dad, 'it's a bit like two boxers shaking hands before they start a fight.'

Brenda goes to a wedding. It is a very emotional affair. Even the cake was in tiers.

A couple get married and, by the time of the reception, the bride is a little tipsy. This makes it difficult for her when she tries to make her speech thanking the guests for all their wedding gifts. She stumbles through and finally points unsteadily at an electric coffee percolator, saying, 'And, last of all, I'd like to thank my new mother-in-law for this wonderful electrical device that will be such a help and bring such pleasure in our new home – this lovely perky copulator!'

A young couple appear at the vicar's door and demand to be married right there and then. 'I can't do that,' says the vicar. 'You'll have to book the church properly for next week.' 'Damn it!' says the boy. 'In that case, could you just say a few words to tide us over the weekend?'

Sally is on her wedding night. She comes out of the bathroom and stubs her toe. 'Careful, my precious angel,' says her husband. 'Come to bed so I can kiss it better.' After they've made love, Sally goes back to the bathroom and stubs her toe again. Her husband says, 'Watch what you're doing, you clumsy mare. I'm trying to get some sleep here.'

Sandra goes to a church wedding and the usher asks her if she's a friend of the groom. 'Certainly not,' says Sandra. 'I'm the bride's mother.'

Simon and Julie left the wedding a bit late. At the ceremony they exchanged an engagement ring, a wedding ring and a teething ring.

Q: How do you know you're at a redneck wedding?
A: Everyone is sitting on the same side of the church.

Fred's son is about to get married. Fred tells him, 'Son, remember this moment. You'll look back on this as the happiest day of your life.' 'But,' says the son, 'I'm not getting married until tomorrow!' 'Precisely!' says Fred.

I've heard that these days lots of people meet their future partners at weddings. I hope that turns out to be true, because I'm not that keen on the woman I'm getting married to next Saturday.

WEIGHT AND WEIGHT LOSS

Enid has lost pounds by following a simple weight-loss regime. To stop her snacking in the evenings, she gets her husband to hide her teeth after the six o'clock news.

Your waist is bound to expand when you reach middle age. That's why the Roman numeral for 40 is 'XL'.

Ken tells Norman, 'I had to give my wife some bad news last night. The doctor says unless I can lose ten stone, I've only got six months to live.' 'Oh no,' says Norman. 'How did your missus take it?' 'She was so upset,' says Ken, 'that she immediately went and started making me my favourite five-course dinner.'

SIGN AT A VILLAGE HALL

A pair of yokels are discussing a problem. One of the yokels wants to sell a pig and has been asked how much it weighs. However, the scales he normally uses are broken. 'There's an easy way round that,' says the other yokel. 'You need to do three things. First, make yourselves a balance from a pole and a pair of baskets. Next, put the pig in one basket and load the other basket with mud till they even out.' 'What's the third thing I do?' asks the first yokel. 'Then,' says the friend, 'you guess the weight of the mud.'

I believe that to get an accurate idea of how much you weigh, you have to strip naked before getting on the scales. And that's why I am now banned from Boots.

WHALES

Two whales walk into a bar. The first whale says, 'Weeeeeoooooouuuhhhh!' The other whale tells him, 'Do shut up, Kevin. You're drunk again.'

WIDOWHOOD

An old couple are talking about the future and what each of them will do if the other dies and they're left alone. 'Don't worry about me,' says the old lady. 'If you go first, I think I'll find two or three other ladies, perhaps a few years younger than I am, and get them to move in with me. What about if I go first?' 'I'd probably do the same,' says the old man.

A woman hears a knock at the door and finds a man with a large box on her doorstep. 'Are you Widow Smith?' asks the man. 'How dare you?' says the woman. 'I'm not Widow Smith. I'm Mrs Smith.' 'I wouldn't be so quick there,' says the man, 'you haven't seen what's in this box yet.'

June has been widowed three times. Her first two husbands died as a result of eating poisonous mushrooms. The last one was stabbed. He said he didn't like mushrooms.

Knowing he didn't have long to live, Norman gave his wife £20,000 to buy a funeral plot and a nice stone. So she had him cremated and bought a diamond ring.

WIGS

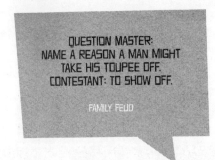

QUESTION MASTER:
NAME A REASON A MAN MIGHT
TAKE HIS TOUPEE OFF.
CONTESTANT: TO SHOW OFF.

FAMILY FEUD

WILL POWER

I don't have a problem with will power. It's my won't power that is sadly lacking.

WINDOWS

A man arrives at work one winter's morning and immediately gets a text from his wife that reads, 'Windows frozen'. He texts back, 'Boil the kettle and pour some hot water over them'. A few minutes later, he gets another text from his wife saying: 'The computer's stopped working completely now'.

Larry goes round to his neighbour's and finds him carefully taking the panes of glass out of his windows and loading them into the back of his truck. 'What are you doing?' says Larry. 'Going to the car-wash,' says the neighbour. 'With all that glass in the back?' says Larry. 'Yeah,' sighs the neighbour. 'We still haven't found a decent window cleaner.'

> "IF YOU FALL OUT OF THAT WINDOW AND BREAK BOTH YOUR LEGS, DON'T COME RUNNING TO ME."
>
> GROUCHO MARX

WINE

A Frenchman goes on holiday to America. He walks into a McDonald's in New York, gets to the counter and asks for a glass of wine. A New York native in the queue behind him laughs, 'You stupid Frenchman! This is McDonald's! You can't order a glass of wine in here!' 'I'm sorry!' says the Frenchman. 'You've come in here just for the food – and you're calling *me* stupid?!'

> "FRENCH WINE GROWERS FEAR THAT THIS YEAR'S VINTAGE MAY BE ENTIRELY SPOILED DUE TO THE GRAPE-TREADERS' SIT-IN."
>
> THE TWO RONNIES

WITCHES

People have said many bad things about the Salem Witch Trials, but have you noticed that since then we've had very little trouble with witch attacks?

WITNESSES

The main occasions that require witnesses are: 1. A crime; 2. An accident; 3. A wedding. That seems to tell you everything you need to know.

WORK

Dick doesn't mind going to work in the morning. He just really hates the eight-hour wait to come back home again.

Ken is his own boss. He doesn't find it very satisfying though. There's no fun in stealing office supplies from your own cupboard.

Calling into work sick is much more fun when you call a company you don't actually work for.

I have one of those jobs where nobody notices what I do, until I stop doing it.

My boss described me as a miracle worker. He thinks it's a miracle if I do any work.

Don't forget, you should avoid drinking tea or coffee when you're at work. The caffeine might keep you awake all day.

It can be very stressful if your boss is neurotic. It's even worse if you're the reason he's neurotic.

Larry thought he would request that a suggestion box was installed at his workplace. Unfortunately, he couldn't find any way of putting the idea across.

"WELL, WE CAN'T STAND AROUND HERE DOING NOTHING, PEOPLE WILL THINK WE'RE WORKMEN."

SPIKE MILLIGAN

> **AFTER TEA-BREAK, COULD STAFF PLEASE EMPTY TEAPOT AND STAND UPSIDE DOWN ON DRAINING BOARD.**
>
> SIGN IN OFFICE KITCHEN

Tom's boss organised a paintballing weekend in the New Forest as a team-building exercise with the members of the visiting New York office. Tom quite enjoyed it, till the Yanks flew over in a B52 and drenched him with a quarter of a million gallons of Dulux.

Barry has always dreamed of being able to work from home. And finally his dream has come true . . . His wife has thrown him out, and he's having to sleep in his office.

This story is about four people whose names were Everybody, Somebody, Anybody, and Nobody. An important job needed doing and Everybody was sure that Somebody would do it. Anybody could have done it, but Nobody did it, which made Somebody angry because it was Everybody's job. But Everybody thought Anybody could do it while Nobody realised that Everybody wouldn't do it. So in the end Everybody blamed Somebody when Nobody did what Anybody could have done.

> " ALL I'VE EVER WANTED WAS AN HONEST WEEK'S PAY FOR AN HONEST DAY'S WORK. "
>
> STEVE MARTIN

Sandra goes up to the company CEO at the annual works picnic. 'You must be the boss,' she says. 'I am,' he says. 'But we've never met before. How did you recognise me?' Sandra says, 'My husband's impressions.'

Billy-Bob applies for a job as a cowboy and insists on getting $500 a week. 'That's too much,' says the ranch foreman. 'You've no experience. The most I can pay is $250.' 'But I'm worth it,' says Billy-Bob. 'I'll have no idea what I'm doing; that means I'll have to work twice as hard.'

What do large organisations have in common with mating elephants? All the decisions are made at a high level, there's a lot of trumpeting and screeching involved, and it takes two years to see the results.

Working in a paperless office might sound like a good idea, but what do you do when you have to go to the toilet?

Sam takes on a new job as the manager of a packing plant. He wants to shake things up a bit so he goes out on the shop floor to find someone who he can make an example of. He soon comes across a young man sitting on a crate and calls him over. 'You're finished here,' says Sam. 'We've got no time for slackers in this organisation. Here's £50. Now get out and don't come back!' The young man takes the money and leaves. Sam calls over one of the workers. 'I just fired that guy. We'll need a replacement. What did he do round here?' 'Nothing,' says the worker. 'He was delivering a pizza.'

> **"ALWAYS SAY THAT IF A JOB'S WORTH DOING, IT'S TOO HARD."**
>
> SCOTT ADAMS

My boss says I do the work of two men: Laurel and Hardy.

Gary says he worked extremely hard to get to where he is today. He's an unemployed arts graduate.

Dick phones his boss at five o'clock in the morning and tells him, 'I've caught the train out of London and I'm heading to the south coast.' 'Why are you calling me this early?' asks the boss. 'And where the hell are you going?' 'Don't be like that,' says Dick, 'you're the one who told me to be in Brighton early this morning.'

I tried setting up a business as a shepherd, but I just couldn't get the staff.

Yesterday my boss told me that he questioned my enthusiasm. I said I couldn't believe he'd woken me up just for that.

WORLD AFFAIRS

Nobby is reading Harry a story from the newspaper. 'It says here that 15 Brazilian monkeys were killed in a plane crash yesterday.' 'That's terrible,' says Harry. 'Just terrible. But remind me, how many is in a brazillion?'

WORMS

Two silk worms challenged each other to a race. It ended in a tie.

WRONG NUMBERS

Betty answers the phone and starts chatting. Her husband looks at his watch and sees she's been talking for ten minutes. He looks again a little later and finds that another ten minutes have passed. He looks again after another ten minutes have passed, but a few minutes after that she puts down the phone. 'Blimey,' her husband says. 'Only 34 minutes. That's short for you.' 'Yes, says Betty. 'It was a wrong number.'

X-RAY VISION

If Superman has X-ray vision that enables him to see through anything, why doesn't he see through everything and therefore see nothing at all?

YOGA

Barry has been practising yoga to make himself more supple. He's doing pretty well. He's now able to get his left buttock into his mouth.

I was in the middle of my yoga lesson when my instructor blurted out that he found me very attractive, then ran out of the room. It was a nice compliment, but he'd left me in an extremely awkward position.

YORKSHIRE

Tom goes on holiday to Yorkshire. He goes into a shop and asks for towels and they give him directions to the local bird sanctuary.

YOUTH

Youth gangs today have no class. All they ever do is drive past and stop and shoot each other. Why can't it be like it used to be like the good old days as depicted in *West Side Story*? In those days, they used to have a little dance with each other first.

Youth is the time when you know that all the problems you face are your mum and dad's fault. Maturity is the time when you realise that all your problems are your kids' fault.

When he was a young man, Norman went off the rails for a while. And that's why he lost his job as a train driver.

ZIP FASTENERS

Jill is teaching her little boy how to zip up his new winter coat. She tells him that the secret is to match up the two sides properly before you pull the tab. The little boy asks, 'Why the hell did they make that a secret?'

> THE MAN WHO INVENTED THE ZIP FASTENER WAS TODAY HONOURED WITH A LIFETIME PEERAGE. HE'LL NOW BE KNOWN AS THE LORD OF THE FLIES.
>
> THE TWO RONNIES

ZODIAC SIGNS

It's been reported that the world's Capricorns have voted for industrial action and are going out on strike, demanding to be given better horoscopes.

Harry goes into a pet shop and says he would like to buy a tropical fish. 'Do you want an aquarium?' asks the pet shop man. 'I don't care what star sign it is,' says Harry.

> WHEN I WAS A BOY, I SAID, 'DADDY, TAKE ME TO THE ZOO.' MY FATHER SAID, 'SON, WHEN THE ZOO WANTS YOU, THEY'LL COME AND GET YOU.'
>
> FRED ALLEN

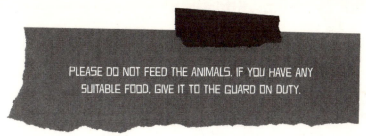

PLEASE DO NOT FEED THE ANIMALS. IF YOU HAVE ANY SUITABLE FOOD, GIVE IT TO THE GUARD ON DUTY.

SIGN DISPLAYED AT A ZOO IN HUNGARY

ZOOS

Norman goes to the zoo with his young grandson, but is very embarrassed when the boy points at one of the animals and says in a loud voice in front of all the other visitors, 'Look, Granddad! A frickin' elephant!' Norman takes the boy aside and says, 'Don't talk like that. It's not nice.' 'But that's what it says there,' says the little boy pointing at the sign on the enclosure, 'A F R I C A N elephant.'

Bernie gets a job at the local zoo, but it all goes pear-shaped when he accidentally kills a tank of rare fish. He hides the accident by tipping the fish into the food bowl of Lenny the lion. A few hours later, he manages to kill a chimpanzee by accidentally decapitating it with a hedge trimmer. Horrified, he again dumps the evidence in Lenny's food bowl. Next, he's driving a truck behind the Insect House and manages to run over one of the beehives. He shovels up the mess and chucks it into Lenny's enclosure, then he quits and is never seen again. The next day a new lion is delivered to the zoo. The new lion goes up to Lenny and says, 'What's the food like here?' 'Pretty boring most days,' says Lenny, 'but yesterday was great. We had fish and chimps with mushy bees.'

Tommy's dad brings him home after a day out. He tells Mum that Tommy got kicked out of the zoo because he was feeding the ducks. 'What's the matter with that?' asks Mum. 'To the alligators!' says Dad.

ZEEE LAST JOKE

Have I told you this déjà vu joke before?

INDEX OF JOKE CATEGORIES

A

Abstinence 4, Accidents 4, Acrobatics 6, Actors and Acting 7, Adam and Eve 7, Addiction 8, Adoption 8, Advertising 8, Advice 9, Affairs and Adultery 9, Afterlife 12, Ageing 14, Agreement 15, Air Guitar 16, Air Travel 16, Alcohol 17, Allergies 20, Alligators 20, Amputation 20, Ancestry 21, Ancient Rome 21, Anger Management 22, Animal Husbandry 22, Animal Rights 23, Animal Testing 23, Anniversaries 23, Antiques 24, Apathy 24, Aphrodisiacs 24, Apologies 25, Applause 25, Apple Electronics 25, Apples 26, Archaeology 26, Architecture 26, Arguments 26, Armed Forces 27, Art 31, Arthritis 32, Aspiration 32, Assertiveness 32, Attention 32, Attractiveness 33, Auctions 34, Auditors 34, Autobiography 34, Autocorrect 34, Awards 35

B

Babies 36, Back Problems 36, Backsides 37, Bad Language 37, Bagpipes 38, Baking and Bakery Products 39, Ballooning 40, Banks and Banking 40, Baptism 41, Barbecues 41, Barriers 42, Bathrooms and Bathroom Products 42, Batteries 43, Bears 44, Beauty and Beauty Treatment 45, Beds 45, Big Questions 46, Bikes 47, Bills 47, Bingo 47, Biology 48, Birds 48, Birthdays and Birthday Presents 49, Bisexuality 51, Blacksmiths 51, Blame 51, Blindness 51, Boats 52, Bombs 52, Bones 53, Boomerangs 53, Borrowing 53, Boxing 54, Boy Scouts 54, Brass Bands 54, Break-ups 54, Breakfast 56, Breatfeeding 56, Breasts 56, Bubble-wrap 57, Bullying 57, Bureaucrats 58, Buses 58, Business 59, Busy 60, Butchers 60, Butter 60

C

Cage Fighting 61, Calamity 61, Call Centres 61, Camels 62, Camouflage 62, Canals 62, Candles 62, Cannibalism 63, Capital Punishment 64, Car Accidents and Breakdown 64, Carpets 66, Cars 66, Cartoon Characters 68, Castles 68, Catalogue Shopping 68, Cats 69, Cattle 70, Caught Short 71, Celebrities 71, Chain Letters 72, Challenges 72, Charisma 72, Charity 72, Chastity Belts 75, Chat-ups 75, Cheese 77, Chemists 77, Cheques 78, Chickens 78, Childbirth 79, Children 81, Children's Television 83, Chinese 84, Chinese Whispers 84, Chocolate 84, Choking 84, Christmas 84, Church 86, Cigarettes 88, Cinema 89, Circulation 90, Circumcision 90, Circus 90, Claustrophobia 92, Cleaning Ladies 92, Clergy 92, Clocks and Timepieces 93, Cloning 94, Clothes 94, Coffee 97, Colour Blindness 97, Colourful Yet Mysterious Objects 98, Common Sense 99, Communication 100, Competition 100, Complaining 100, Compost 100, Computers 101, Concision 101, Concrete 101, Conferences 101, Confession 102, Congestion 103, Conscience 103, Constipation 103, Construction 104, Consultants 104, Contraception 105, Conversation 106, Cooking 107, Corrosion 107, Corruption 108, Cosmetic Surgery 108, Country and Western Song Titles 109, Court 110, Cowboys 111, Creation 112, Creative Writing 113, Cremation 113, Cricket 113, Crime 114, Crimes of Passion 117, Crisps 117, Crocodiles 117, Crosswords 118, Crowds 119, Cruises 119, Culture 119, Currency 120, Customs 120

D

Dancing 121, Darkness 121, Darts 121, Dating 122, Dead Sea 127, Deafness 127, Death 128, Decisions 130, Decor 130, Decorating 130, Déjà Vu 131, Dentists 132, Describing Things 133, Deserts 134, Detective Work 134, Diarrhoea 135, Dictionaries 136, Diet 136, Different Perspectives 137, Dinosaurs 137, Diplomats 138, Disabilities 138, Disasters 140, Disease 140, Dislikes 141, Diving 141, Divorce 141, DIY 143, DNA 144, Dogs 144, Dog Food 150, Doors 150, Doughnuts 151, Drink Driving 151, Driving 152, Driving Offences 153, Driving Test 154, Drugs 154, Drunkenness 156, Ducks 160, Dyslexia 161

E

Easter 162, Economics and Economists 162, Education 164, Efficiency 166, Electrical Goods 166, Electricity 166, Elephants 167, Email 168, Emergencies 168, Emergency

THE SEVENTH COMMANDMENT IS THOU SHALL NOT ADMIT ADULTERY.

SCHOOLBOY HOMEWORK ANSWER

Services 169, Emissions Test 169, Encouragement 169, End of the World 169, Enemies 170, Energy Efficiency 170, Engagement 170, Entertainment 171, Epilepsy 172, Equality 172, Escalators 173, Escape 173, Eskimos 173, Eternal Life 173, Eurovision Song Contest 174, Exaggeration 174, Examination 174, Exercise 174, Experience 176, Expertise 177, Explorers 177, Eyesight 178

F

Facts of Life 179, Failure 180, Fairy Tales 180, Faith Healing 180, Families 180, Family Planning 181, Fancy Dress 181, Farewell 181, Farming 182, Father's Day 183, Fear 183, Female Impersonation 183, Fertility Treatment 183, Fighting 184, Filing 184, Fire and Fire Services 184, Firing Squad 185, Fish and Fishing 186, Flamingos 187, Flatulence 187, Flirting 187, Food 188, Fools 191, Football 191, Foreign Languages 194, Foreign Travel 194, Forestry 197, Forgery 197, Fred Astaire and Ginger Rogers 197, Freedom 197, Freedom of Speech 198, Fridges 198, Frisbee 198, Frugality 198, Fruit 200, Fuel 200, Funerals 201, Fur Coats 202, Furniture 203, Future 203

G

Gambling 204, Game Shows 206, Games 207, Gangsters 207, Gardening 207, Genealogy 209, Geography 210, George Best 211, Ghosts 211, Golf 212, Good Deeds 214, Gorillas 214, Grandparents 214, Graveyards 215, Green Energy 215, Greetings Cards 216, Gullibility 216, Guns 216, Gymnastics 217, Gynaecology 217

H

Habits 218, Hair 218, Halloween 219, Handwriting 219, Handymen 219, Hardware 220, Head Lice 220, Headaches 220, Health 221, Health Food 222,

Hearts and Heart Conditions 222, Heroism 223, Hide and Seek 223, Hippos 224, Hipsters 224, History 224, Hitchhikers 226, Hoaxes 226, Hold-ups 227, Holes 227, Holidays 228, Home 229, Home Entertainment 229, Homelessness 229, Homesickness 229, Honesty 230, Honeymooners 230, Horror Movies 230, Horse Racing 230, Horses 231, Hospitality 232, Hospitals 232, Hostages 234, Hotels 235, House Hunting 237, Household Products and Appliances 237, Housework 238, Humility 240, Humour 240, Hunting 240, Hygiene 241, Hypnotism 241, Hypochondria 241, Hypocrisy 241

I

Ice Cream 242, Identity Theft 242, Illness 242, Imagination 244, Immaturity 244, Immigration 244, Imports 244, Impossibility 245, Inbreeding 245, Incontinence 245, India 245, Inflation 246, Ingratitude 246, Inheritance 246, Injections 248, Insects 248, Insecurity 249, Insomnia 249, Insults of a General Nature 250, Insurance 251, Intelligence and the Lack of It 252, Internet 255, Interrogation 256, Intolerance 256, Intruders 256, Inventions 256, Invisibility 257, Invitations 257, IT Workers 257

J

Jack-in-the-Box 258, Jehovah's Witnesses 258, Jewellery 258, Job Applications 259, Jobs 261, Journalism 262, Jumble Sales 262, Jungle 262

K

Key Rings 263, Kidnapping 263, Kleptomania 263, Knock Knock! Who's There? ... 264

L

Ladders 266, Landmines 266, Language and Grammar 266, Lap Dancing 267, Late Home 267,

> **MY FATHER GAVE ME A SMALL LOAN OF A MILLION DOLLARS.**
>
> DONALD TRUMP

Laundry 267, Law and Lawyers 269, Laziness 272, Lessons in Life 273, Libraries 277, Life 277, Life-Saving 278, Lifts 278, Lingerie 278, Lions 279, Listening 279, Literacy 279, Literature 280, Loans 282, Lobsters 283, Logic 283, Longevity 283, Loquaciousness 283, Lost 284, Lottery 284, Love 286, Lowpoints in Life 287, Lozenges 288, Luck 288, Luggage 288, Lying 289

M

Magic 290, Magnets 291, Make-up 291, Manners 291, Manure 293, Margaret Thatcher 293, Marine Life 293, Marriage 294, Marriage Guidance 300, Martial Arts 300, Massage 300, Maths 300, Mechanics 301, Medals 302, Medicine 303, Mementoes 304, Memorabilia 304, Memory 304, Men and Women 305, Mental Problems 307, Metric System 309, Mexicans 309, Middle East 310, Milk 310, Mimes 310, Miracles 310, Mirages 311, Mirrors 312, Misheard 312, Missing Persons 312, Missing the Point 313, Mistakes 313, Mistresses 313, Mobile Phones 314, Mobility 315, Money 315, Monsters 317, Mormonism 318, Mothers 318, Mothers-in-Law 318, Motor Racing 319, Motoring Offences 319, Mountains 320, Mud-wrestling 321, Music and Musicians 321, Mysteries 327, Mysterious Flying Objects 328

N

Nailbiting 329, Names 329, Napkins 331, Narcissism 332, Native Americans 332, Neighbourhood Watch 332, Neighbours 332, Newspapers 333, Noah 334,

Noise 334, Non-conformity 334, North Korea 334, North Pole 335, Northern Ireland 335, Noses 335, Nostalgia 335, Nudity 335, Nuisance Phone Calls 336, Nursing Homes 336

O

Obesity 339, Obviousness 342, Ocelots 342, Octopi 342, Ointment 342, Omniscience 342, Online Security 343, Online Shopping 343, Open-mindedness 344, Optimism and Pessimism 344, Organ Donation 345, Organs 345, Orgies 346, Origami 346, Origins 346

P

Pain 345, Paint 345, Pandas 345, Panto 345, Parachutes and Skydiving 346, Parenting 346, Parrots 347, Parties 348, Past, Present and Future 349, Peace 349, Pedantry 349, Penguins 350, Penises 350, Pens and Pencils 351, People 351, Perfume 351, Personal Smells 352, Perversion 352, Pets 353, Philosophy 354, Phones 355, Photography 356, Physique 356, Piano Tuning 356, Pigeons 357, Piles 357, Pirates 358, Plagiarism 359, Platonic Relationships 359, Plumbers 359, Poaching 359, Poisoning 360, Polar Exploration 360, Police Investigations 360, Politics 361, Pollution 362, Popularity 362, Pornography 362, Post 363, Posture 364, Potatoes 364, Poverty 364, Power Cuts 365, Prayers 365, Predictive Text 365, Pregnancy 366, Prejudice 366, Presents 367, Prison 367, Privilege 368, Prizes 368, Proof-reading 369, Property 369, Proposals 369, Prostitutes 369, Prozac 370, Psychics 370, Psychology 372, Public Speaking 372, Punctuality 372, Punctuation 373, Pushed Around 373

Q/R

Queues 374 Rabies 375, Radio 375, Radioactivity 375, Raffles 376, Ramblers 376, Recycling 376, Redheads 377, Rednecks 377, Referees 378, Reincarnation 379, Relations 379, Relationships 380, Religion 380, Remote Controls 382, Repairs 383, Repetition 383, Rescue 383, Respect 383, Responsibility 384, Restaurants 384, Retail 388, Retirement 388, Rhubarb 388, Riddles 389, Rioting 390, Roads 390, Robin Hood 390, Routine 391, Rowing 391, Royalty 391, Russia 391

S

Sacked 392, Sacrifices 392, Safety 392, Samaritans 393, Sandwiches 393, Scallies 393, Scars 393, Schizophrenia 394, Science 394, Scottish Dress 395, Scrabble 396, Sean Connery 396, Seaside 396, Second-hand Goods 397, Secret Agents 397, Secrets 398, Security 398, Self-denial 398, Self-help 398, Servants 399, Sewage 399, Sex 400, Sex Aids 406, Sexually Transmitted Diseases 406, Shaking Hands 407, Shaving 407, She Was Only 408, Sheep 409, Shipwrecked 410, Shoes 411, Shoplifting 411, Shopping 412, Shortbread 414, Show-offs 414, Sick Leave 414, Single Life 414, Size 415, Skeletons 415, Skiing and Winter Sports 415, Skin Conditions 415, Skunks 416, Slaves 416, Sleep 416, Sleep-overs 417, Smooth Talking 417, Snails 417, Snakes 418, Snoring 418, Social Media 418, Social Workers 419, Solar Power 419, Space Travel 419, Spain 420, Specimens 420, Speech Impediments 420, Speed 420, Speeding 420, Spelling Mistakes 421, Spiders 421, Sponsorship 421, Sport 422, Spying 422, Stains 423, Stalking 423, Star Wars 423, Statistics 423, Steam Rollers 424, Stockbrokers 424, Stowaways 424, Students 425, Submarines 425, Success 425, Suicide 427, Superheroes 428, Supermodels 428, Superstition 429, Suppositories 429, Surgery 429, Suspicion 432, Swans 432, Sweet Nothings 432, Swimming 432, Switzerland 432

T

Takeaways 433, Tattoos 434, Tax 434, Taxis 434, Tea 435, Technology 435, Teenagers 436, Television 437, Temptation 438, Tennis 438, Testicles 439, Texting 439, Therapy 440, Thieves 441, Thinness 441, Threesomes 441, Time 441, Time Machines 442, Time Wasting 442, Tipping 442, Toilet Paper 442, Toilets 443, Tolerance 444, Tortillas 444, Tourist Attractions 444, Toys 445, Traffic 445, Tragedy and Comedy 446, Trains 447, Tramps 448, Transvestites 449, Travel 449, Trees 449, Tug of War 449, Turkeys 450, Turtles 450, Twins 450, Types of People 450

U/V

Ugliness 451, Understanding 452, Unemployment 452, Unidentified Flying Objects 452, Used Cars 453, Usefulness 453, Vacuum Cleaners 455, Vagueness 455, Valentine's Day 455, Vampires 456, Vasectomy 456, Vegetarians and Vegans 456, Vehicle Theft 457, Vengeance 457, Venice 457, Ventriloquism 457, Vets 458, Viagra 458, Vikings 459, Violence 459, Virginity 460, Vitamins 460, Voluntary Work 460, Voyeurism 460

W

Waking Up 461, Wales 461, Warning Signs 462, Waste Disposal 462, Water 463, Wealth 463, Weather 464, Weddings 465, Weight and Weight Loss 467, Whales 468, Widowhood 468, Wigs 468, Will Power 469, Windows 469, Wine 469, Witches 470, Witnesses 470, Work 470, World Affairs 473, Worms 473, Wrong Numbers 473

X/Y/Z

X-ray Vision 474, Yoga 475, Yorkshire 475, Youth 475, Zip Fasteners 476, Zodiac Signs 476, Zoos 477, Zeee Last Joke 477